D1277588

03-87 5134

LB 2343.4 .K73 2003
Kramer, Gary L., 1945-
Student academic services

GLOUCESTER COUNTY COLLEGE
LIBRARY
1400 TANYARD ROAD
SEWELL, NJ 08080

WITHDRAWN FROM
RCSJLIBRARY

STUDENT ACADEMIC SERVICES

STUDENT ACADEMIC SERVICES

An Integrated Approach

Gary L. Kramer and Associates

o

JOSSEY-BASS
A Wiley Imprint
www.josseybass.com

Copyright © 2003 by John Wiley & Sons, Inc. All rights reserved.

Published by Jossey-Bass
A Wiley Imprint
989 Market Street, San Francisco, CA 94103-1741   www.josseybass.com

No part of this publication may be reproduced, stored in a retrieval system, or transmitted in any form or by any means, electronic, mechanical, photocopying, recording, scanning, or otherwise, except as permitted under Section 107 or 108 of the 1976 United States Copyright Act, without either the prior written permission of the Publisher, or authorization through payment of the appropriate per-copy fee to the Copyright Clearance Center, Inc., 222 Rosewood Drive, Danvers, MA 01923, 978-750-8400, fax 978-646-8700, or on the web at www.copyright.com. Requests to the Publisher for permission should be addressed to the Permissions Department, John Wiley & Sons, Inc., 111 River Street, Hoboken, NJ 07030, (201) 748-6011, fax (201) 748-6008, e-mail: permcoordinator@wiley.com.

Jossey-Bass books and products are available through most bookstores. To contact Jossey-Bass directly call our Customer Care Department within the U.S. at 800-956-7739, outside the U.S. at 317-572-3986 or fax 317-572-4002.

Jossey-Bass also publishes its books in a variety of electronic formats. Some content that appears in print may not be available in electronic books.

Library of Congress Cataloging-in-Publication Data

Kramer, Gary L., 1945-
  Student academic services : an integrated approach / Gary L. Kramer and associates.—1st ed.
    p. cm. — (The Jossey-Bass higher and adult education series)
  Includes bibliographical references and index.
  ISBN 0-7879-6102-7 (alk. paper)
  1. College student development programs—United States. 2. Education, Higher—Aims and objectives—United States. 3. Student affairs services—United States. I. Title. II. Series.
  LB2343.4.K73 2003
  378.1'94—dc21
                                        2003007928
Printed in the United States of America
FIRST EDITION
HB Printing   10 9 8 7 6 5 4 3 2 1

The Jossey-Bass
Higher and Adult Education Series

CONTENTS

PART THREE

New Directions for Practice

PREFACE

STUDENT ACADEMIC SERVICES: *An Integrated Approach* systematically presents critical student academic services that are central to the mission of institutions of higher education, and it shows how, under effective management and leadership, these can come together as an interconnected, collaborative system of services that support student development and success. In particular, this book examines student academic services as they have evolved in higher education, and it emphasizes these services within the context of a learning organization. This is manifested, for example, in chapters that focus on student and organizational learning issues in association with student development, continuous improvement, student readiness and assessment, enabling, encouraging, and empowering the staff to help students take charge of educational planning and opportunities, and managing student academic services to ensure a supported and collaborative enterprise.

Student academic services are defined and described herein as a set of services directly connected to the academic purposes of the institution. Thus, the services discussed in this book are about identifying, selecting, orienting, matriculating, registering, advising, documenting the records of, awarding funds to, and graduating students. Typically, these student services are found in the offices of recruitment or school and college relations, enrollment management, orientation, advising and counseling, records, registration, credit evaluation, financial aid, and graduation. Although these offices are routinely found in the traditional and vertical organization of most institutions, the emphasis in this book is on a system of services that are connected, collaborative, comprehensive, and horizontally organized, using the student-centric view. Several chapters address quality practices that link and collaboratively deliver vital student academic services—from point of contact to enrollment to graduation.

Student academic services have a long, eventful history and a purposeful role in higher education. With the expansion in size and complexity of institutions, faculty members, who were once charged as the sole providers of student development and advising, have shifted to primarily academic concerns, and institutions have hired professionals to select, admit, and register students, record academic transactions, and so on.

Only in recent years have longtime independent services—such as student records maintenance, registration, orientation, advisement, and admissions—begun to be organized as a system of services with a focus on student needs.

Yet on most campuses today, students are tossed from one organization to another. In some cases, campus services are divided into separate camps of student life and academic affairs organizations. For example, it is common to find advising and orientation services separated by organizational lines. Thus, students are left to unscramble the services they need from the institution's vertical or departmental organizations. Furthermore, recent trends demonstrate either a pronounced shift away from academic organizations or the further splintering of student academic services. Darlene Burnett (2002), one of the authors in this book, has summarized the traditional student services model in the following figure.

What is the impact of these vertical shifts? What barriers do they set up for students? Faculty members? Administrators? What is the best way to organize and deliver a system of effective, timely, and accurate services to students at the two-year college?—or small college?—or large university? In addition, information technology has recently revolutionized the way colleges and universities offer services to an ever-growing and diverse student population. How effective is the use of technology in augmenting the human-technology nexus, in collapsing organizational (vertical) walls, and in delivering self-help academic services to such students as distance learners and students with disabilities. More important, how can technology help integrate academic student services, accommodate the student-centric view, and blend student academic services with career and financial planning?

The new emphasis on customer service and student learning and the increased heterogeneity of students, including older and distance learners, have instigated a growing demand for personalized services. Also, the expansion—as well as complexity—of services in recent decades has made necessary an enormous growth of service centers and related organizational models. *Student Academic Services: An Integrated Approach* is meant to be a practical, helpful guide to assist providers of student academic services at every level and position as they respond to these trends.

As campus and student demographics have changed, several models for the organization and delivery of student academic services have also changed. Changing demographics, student diversity, the incorporation of information technology in every sector of the campus, and higher education globalization trends have significantly affected, changed, and challenged the traditional organizational model of student services.

Figure 1. Lessons Learned

In the traditional student services model, each office is focused on an area of responsibility

- Major processes are segregated
- Systems are not integrated
- Reporting structures vary
- Communications and interactions are limited
- Administrative and academic functions are not linked

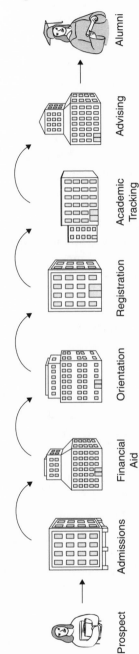

Prospect | Admissions | Financial Aid | Orientation | Registration | Academic Tracking | Advising | Alumni

The Purpose of This Book

In addition to discussions on practical delivery and management approaches, this book provides insight into the research literature on student development and learning, as well as on student readiness, assessment, and critical success factors for programs. In particular, this book addresses how students can become vulnerable to failure at various points in their undergraduate career, and it describes the important, supportive role student academic services play in student retention and success. Thus, several chapters in this book describe highly integrated student academic services practices from several institutions—campuses that reflect the student-centered perspective and a holistic, interdependent approach to assessing and addressing student needs. These frameworks are results-oriented and place strong emphasis on student learning and achievement.

Managing and leading student academic services to ensure a collaborative enterprise receives important attention throughout the book, particularly in the last section. Management tools associated with assessment—such as evaluation and continuous improvement—are specifically discussed. For example, leaders of student academic services who want to make a qualitative difference in the institution must effectively respond to these five systemic questions raised by Peter Drucker (1993): (1) Who do we serve? (2) What services do we offer? (3) How do we know we are doing a good job? (4) What is the best way to provide the desired services? and (5) What is the best way to organize?

Drucker's five most important questions (1993) are valuable for any organization that is serious about program and service enhancements or change. But to improve student services, an organization must ask other questions as well, such as the following:

1. How prepared are students for learning, and what academic support and services do they need?

2. How should students' readiness needs be addressed within the institutional environment?

3. At what point are students vulnerable to failure, and how should student academic services rally to support student development, growth, retention, and achievement?

4. What is meant by the student-centric view (versus the department-centric view), and how can being student-centered lead to the creation of a seamless, integrated, horizontal, and collaborative student academic services environment?

5. How do we know that students are engaged in the learning process, are receiving the support they need, and are making progress?

6. What delivery model(s) work best for a given institution or mission? Where are the successful programs, and what critical success factors drive these best practices? What metrics do they employ?

7. What is meant by managing and ensuring a collaborative student academic services enterprise?

8. Are standards for student services clearly defined? Who sets them, what should they be, and do they map to the campus culture?

9. How should existing and natural connections be managed among the various student academic services to ensure a maximally, personally, and coherently responsive system to address student needs, learning, and satisfaction?

10. What are the training issues involved in motivating and coordinating the work of service providers as they seek to deliver timely, comprehensive, and accurate academic services to students?

These questions are at the heart of this book and serve as a guide to the discussions herein. So, too, is the belief that high-functioning student academic services and an institutional emphasis on and commitment to quality academic programs result in retention, timely graduation, personal growth, and a satisfying college experience for students. This book not only advances concepts related to the delivery of student academic services but also advocates, on behalf of students, a future, institutionally systemic, and organizationally interconnected model of coherent, collaborative, and comprehensive services.

Intended Audience

The book is targeted at campus managers and practitioners who are responsible for the support, direction, and coordination of student academic services on the campus, or any other institutional leader who is concerned with (1) supporting student development and achievement and increasing retention through a collaborative and integrated model of student academic services, (2) working together with other campus leaders to promote success for all students in college, and (3) achieving the student-centered approach through seamlessly interconnecting undergraduate academic services. In short, this book will assist practitioners in articulating what they are trying to do and how their efforts are consistent with institutional trends and best practices. It is founded on promoting success for all students in college through an improved collaborative delivery of services.

In addition, faculty members and students in graduate higher education degree programs may find this volume useful in their program of study on student academic services, particularly as it relates to (1) strategic approaches to student development, (2) profiles of student academic services, and (3) new directions for practice. Furthermore, practitioners can use this book to help examine their daily work—particularly methods, models, standards, and practices that focus on improving the delivery of an integrated and collaborative program of student-centered academic services.

The Organization of This Book

This book is divided into three parts and twenty chapters. Part One, "Taking a Strategic Approach to Student Development," examines and defines student academic services as they have evolved in higher education. The three chapters in this section emphasize through models, current practices, and trends that student progress occurs when clear and consistent interrelationships and collaboration among campus student academic services are present.

In Chapter One, "Stimulating and Supporting Student Learning," Roger Winston Jr. sets the book's foundation by tracing the evolution, changes, and definition of student academic services to build a case, on behalf of students' progress and development, for a more comprehensive and coordinated perspective of student academic services. The research literature on student development is presented to document when and how students are vulnerable to failure at various points in their undergraduate years and to demonstrate the importance of academic support services to student retention, growth, and achievement.

Chapter Two, "Student Academic Services: Models, Current Practices, and Trends," by Darlene Burnett and Diana Oblinger, provides an overview of current practices and trends in student academic services. As campuses and students have diversified, several models for the organization and delivery of student academic services have evolved. This chapter presents different models of interaction that reflect the student-centered perspective. Also, through different frameworks, the chapter presents to readers the larger objectives of student learning and success that underlie integrating student academic services. Appropriately, this chapter sets the stage for the next section, which focuses on specific services.

In Chapter Three, "The Interrelationship of Student Academic Services," John Schuh defines how academic services intersect with one another and explains how they can work together to provide more coherent, student-centered support. The chapter's overall emphasis is on the potentially collaborative and supportive nature of these areas rather than on their separate places and functional roles within the academic enterprise. Student academic services are challenged in offering timely, connected, courteous, and accurate services to students. But the exchange and connecting of services can be equally challenging. Thus, this chapter interweaves the student-centric view in offering services. It presents the importance of collegiality, collaboration, and connection of academic services as being just as central to successful student matriculation as it is to graduation from the institution.

Chapters Four through Twelve, in Part Two, "Profiles of Student Academic Services," describe individual functional units, from admissions to graduation. Each chapter in this section cultivates a systems perspective that allows readers to evaluate and align their work with the goals of the students and the institution.

Beginning with Chapter Four, "Enrollment Management and Conceptual Underpinnings," author Jim Black discusses the formal introduction of the student to the institution. Enrollment management on most campuses involves not only attracting students to apply for admission to an institution but also retaining them to graduation. This chapter concentrates on these aspects of enrollment management and its interrelationship with other student academic services.

In Chapter Five, "The Assessment of Readiness for Student Learning in College," Gary Peterson, Janet Lenz, and James Sampson Jr. discuss how colleges and universities often think of academic preparation primarily in terms of scores earned on academic aptitude or placement tests. The authors advance a concept for "the state of readiness for student learning" that entails a broad spectrum of skills, attitudes, and knowledge that undergird academic performance. They propose that students should have immediate and easy access to a comprehensive, structured readiness assessment experience upon entry into college. The outcome of this experience is a diagnosis of individual "readiness needs" and a plan for how these needs can be met within the institutional environment. Thus, students are not left to "self-diagnose" their readiness needs and search for appropriate services for assistance. Furthermore, an examination of the availability, accessibility, and effectiveness of campus student services can be conducted through the application of the readiness model.

As Bonita Jacobs points out in Chapter Six, "New Student Orientation in the Twenty-First Century: Individualized, Dynamic, and Diverse," new student orientation is a relatively new student services function. It was originally created as an early registration period for incoming freshmen, but the orientation has evolved into a comprehensive colloquy designed to deliver—in addition to advising and registration—sessions on academic success, career and life goals, campus adjustment, housing, financial aid, and campus life. No longer does orientation operate as a single function designed to matriculate students into the college system. Rather, it is a dynamic series of events and activities planned and implemented by a wide range of students, administrators, and faculty and staff members. Because new student orientation can be delivered in multiple ways, this chapter not only discusses the traditional orientation offered on most campuses but also takes a look at a variety of new student orientation delivery methods within the context of an interconnected array of student academic services.

In "Course Planning and Registration," Chapter Seven, Louise Lonabocker and J. James Wager describe academic scheduling and registration—the often unsung and invisible (unless there is a problem) heroes of student academic services. This chapter's emphasis is on the connections of these services to other student academic services, particularly those described in the following chapter. In particular, a primary focus of this chapter will be the use of advances in information technology to make services available 24/7 to both students and the campus community.

Robert Reardon and Jill Lumsden, in Chapter Eight, "Career Interventions: Facilitating Strategic Academic and Career Planning," connect career planning services with career placement, academic internships, academic advising, and counseling. This chapter explores the practical implications of these different administrative arrangements and offers a theory-based model for a comprehensive and integrated career services unit. It focuses on a career portfolio program that is student-centered and uses the Internet and campus-based information systems. This program enables students to conceptualize university experiences as strategic learning events that, over time, will help prepare them for varied life and career roles. Implications of this career portfolio program for career planning services in higher education are also explored.

In Chapter Nine, "Supporting Student Planning," Virginia Gordon and Gary Kramer focus on campus venues of academic, career, and financial aid to support student planning. Many students equate the choice of academic major with a career choice. But institutions, often separate resources that assist students with their educational decisions from those that help them with their career decision making—in particular, the ever-important funding sources in the financial aid and scholarship office, which are required for students to complete a program of study. This chapter emphasizes the importance of students achieving success with their college experience, particularly in their planning toward graduation, as it applies to connecting them to and integrating key academic, career, and financial services.

Chapter Ten, "Applying Quality Educational Principles to Academic Advising," by Elizabeth and Don Creamer and Kimberly Brown, focuses on a unified flow of academic advising services—from preenrollment or entry to graduation. Academic advising is a service in which faculty members, academic departments, and professional advisers come together to ensure quality student experiences, progress, and timely graduation. Considerable collaboration and organization are required to successfully deliver quality and comprehensive student academic advising. Thus, this chapter emphasizes a systemic and strategic view of academic advising as an interconnected student academic service, and it considers the perspective and needs of students as well as the adviser's role in conveying pathways for students to satisfy program requirements, including timely graduation.

In Chapter Eleven, "The Essential Academic Record," W. W. (Tim) Washburn and Gene Priday describe the student academic record with its accompanying processes and its interrelationship with other student academic services. In most higher education settings, an overwhelming amount of changing information exists regarding academic policies, major and general education program requirements, graduation policies, grade processing, transfer-credit evaluation, graduation certification, class scheduling, and so on. This chapter discusses these critical academic record functions and other related matters essential to the faculty members', departments', and students' needs for accurate, secure, and accessible academic records. Vital to this chapter is the academic credit record, including transfer credit, institutional degree posting, and the awarding of a diploma.

Essential to the provision of student academic services is the obligation of all support staff and faculty members to provide accurate and timely information to students. In addition, they are to abide by ethical standards and principles regarding student access to and the delivery of academic information. This chapter identifies these ethical principles and their application to statutory law, such as providing accurate information, privacy concerns, the disability act, and ethnic or racial discrimination.

Chapter Twelve, "Student Financial Services," authored by Rita Owens and Bernard Pekala, reviews financial aid and scholarship services. This field of services has grown at a tremendous rate over the past four decades.

In some respects, this growth parallels the rise of the financial aid domain as a specialty profession within the student academic services field. This chapter describes the "gold standard" philosophy of providing maximum support for students, and it concentrates on the emerging need for financial counseling and academic planning as well as the ever-growing importance of connecting academic plans with financial resources.

Part Three, "New Directions for Practice," reasserts the central theme of this book, which is to take readers systematically through key student academic services and then show how these can come together under effective management and leadership as interconnected services that are supportive of student development and success. Part Three—Chapters Thirteen through Twenty—applies the managing theme to the promotion of student success. Finally, this section emphasizes why managers of student academic services must work together with other campus leaders to unify and develop the staff to ensure a collaborative approach in the delivery of services to a diverse student body.

Chapter Thirteen, "Comprehensive Academic Support for the Students During the First Year of College," by Joseph Cuseo, argues that marshaling the university community's resources is perhaps never more important than in the student's first year of college. Simply put, new students face many challenges that make them likely candidates for attrition. A successful first-year experience on campus is contingent upon several factors. For example, timely, customized, and purposeful assistance for new entering students can not only ease their transition to college but can also clarify and align institutional and student expectations and opportunities. This chapter also emphasizes the connection between and importance of first-year and graduation planning.

In Chapter Fourteen, "Responding to Students' Needs," Carmy Carranza and Steven Ender focus on student academic readiness for the college curriculum across the higher educational spectrum. And they discuss the services, programs, and strategies that can be implemented by the academy to address an array of academic deficiencies or enhance classroom learning for those students who seek additional assistance to further their learning experience. The chapter highlights the relationship between these services and traditional academic services offices, such as the registrar, admissions, orientation, advising, and the freshman year experience.

In Chapter Fifteen, "Student Diversity and Academic Services: Balancing the Needs of All Students," Vasti Torres tackles student diversity in academic services. Offering the right amount of help and the right student services at the right time to an increasingly diverse and demanding student population is at once important and complex. To be effective, student academic services providers must collaborate with one another to meaningfully serve international students, distance learners, students with disabilities, and multicultural students with the same consistency, accuracy, and personalization they would use in serving any other student on the campus. This chapter discusses the challenges and opportunities of student academic services in helping a diverse body of students achieve success in their educational journey.

In "Putting Academic Services On-Line," Chapter Sixteen, Sally Johnstone and Patricia Shea present information technology as being pivotal in the systematic, consistent, and accurate delivery of planning information to students, particularly for the distance learner. On-line student academic services, effectively integrated, are fundamental to a comprehensive on-line student information system. Moreover, a clear and functioning alliance between electronic student information systems and service providers is tantamount to providing students with accessible, reliable, consistent, and timely information. Perhaps in no other way is it more possible to truly bring about a horizontal organization than in information technology. Issues associated with the development of Web portals and the "e" factor in general are discussed, particularly the potential of information technology to flatten organizational barriers while empowering students and providers to access academic services and perform key functions. Self-service, twenty-four-hour access, and the human-technology nexus are other important topics of discussion in this chapter.

In Chapter Seventeen, "Promoting and Sustaining Change," Earl Potter concentrates on managing the change that inevitably occurs in the organization, particularly in student academic services. By setting the stage for change and building a culture of evidence, this chapter's focus is continuous improvement through quantitative and qualitative program assessment and evaluation. In this context, the chapter focuses on planning for change and using appropriate management tools and methods to arrive at sustainable change.

In "Student-Centered Academic Services," Chapter Eighteen, George Kuh, Anthony English, and Sara Hinkle center their attention on future trends and the importance of ensuring a collaborative enterprise for students to negotiate academic support services. This chapter forecasts student academic services' viability and role in higher education's future. Moreover, it presents an effectiveness model based on adaptation to change, understanding student need and development, and institutional direction. This chapter claims that student academic services are most effective when campus leaders, who take the student-centric or developmental view, collaborate to seamlessly interconnect undergraduate academic services.

Chapter Nineteen, "Developing Providers," by Diane Foucar-Szocki, Rick Larson, and Randy Mitchell, focuses on motivating and coordinating the work of student services providers in delivering high-quality, timely, comprehensive, and accurate academic services to students. It emphasizes developing staffs and addressing staff empowerment in a collaborative way. The chapter addresses a customer support system that is interlinked and consistent with information technology, providing timely, accurate, and thorough services through teamwork and a balanced distribution of technology, generalists, and specialists. Overall, this chapter emphasizes that student academic services should be a learning organization that focuses on the individual and encourages continuous improvement by enabling and empowering students to take charge of their educational planning and opportunities.

Finally, Gary Kramer, in Chapter Twenty, "Leading Student Academic Services in the Twenty-First Century," based on the questions posed at the beginning of this preface, summarizes best practices and offers a series of recommendations to transform and lead student academic services in the future.

Acknowledgments

I would like to thank my author-colleagues, who have shared their experience, perspectives, and scholarship in the area of student academic services. Obviously, without them, there would be no book. I also owe much to Peter Gardner and Shannon Openshaw of Brigham Young University (BYU) for their assistance in editing the manuscript and in organizing all the detail associated with this book project. Many, many thanks to them for providing editorial feedback and for the long hours in final manuscript preparation.

And, finally, my colleagues at BYU and my family, especially my wife, Lauri, deserve special recognition. I am grateful for their adjustments of need and expectation, at moments inconvenient, allowing me the time and energy to complete this work. I thank them for their support, patience, and understanding.

August 2003   GARY L. KRAMER
                                              Brigham Young University
                                                      Provo, Utah

REFERENCES

Burnett, D. "IBM Best Practices: Introduction and Update." Paper presented at the seventh annual Innovation in Student Services Forum: Integration for the Future, University of California, Berkeley, July 24–26, 2002.

Drucker, P. F. *The Five Most Important Questions.* San Francisco: Jossey-Bass, 1993.

ABOUT THE AUTHORS

Jim Black is the associate provost for Enrollment Services at the University of North Carolina at Greensboro. His areas of responsibility include admissions, financial aid, the registrar's office, student academic services (primarily responsible for advising and retention initiatives), the Student Success Center, the evening university, satellite campuses, and the student information system (SCT Banner). He is founder of the National Conference on Student Retention in Small Colleges and is cofounder of the National Small College Admissions Conference and the National Small College Enrollment Conference. He currently serves as director of the Strategic Enrollment Management Conference of the American Association of Collegiate Registrars and Admissions Officers. Black has delivered keynote addresses and conducted training workshops for business leaders and educators worldwide. He has published numerous articles and book chapters on student academic services. In 1999, 2000, 2001, and 2002, Jim Black was selected as an IBM Best Practices Partner, one of only twenty-three in the world.

Kimberly S. Brown has served as an administrator in the field of academic advising for five years and is currently the director of the University Academic Advising Center (UAAC) at Virginia Tech. The UAAC administers the University Studies program for new undergraduate students who want to explore a variety of degree programs before they commit themselves to one particular major. In addition, the center serves students who are in transition between academic programs. Prior to her administrative role at Virginia Tech, Brown was promoted to the position of interim director of academic advisement at Weber State University in Ogden, Utah. Brown is also a Ph.D. candidate in the educational leadership and policy studies program at Virginia Tech, focusing on higher education administration. She is an active member of the National Academic Advising Association, presenting at both regional and national conferences.

Darlene Burnett is a consultant who helps institutions create student-centered experiences and environments that enable the delivery of high-tech and high-touch services. She has spent the last thirteen years working with institutions on a range of issues. During her last ten years with IBM, she helped colleges and universities address student services challenges and develop solutions based on best practice models. Seven years ago, Darlene began research on student-centered services with the goal of identifying best practices. This resulted in the development of an IBM consulting strategy and model for best practices in student services. Burnett has incorporated the best practice model into the design and development of Internet-enabled student services and one-stop service centers, coupled with the infrastructure and support needed to sustain high levels of student satisfaction. Burnett managed the Best Practices Forum, has written numerous publications, and coedited *Planning for Student Services: Best Practices for the 21st Century* (1999). She presents frequently at conferences and campus events and continues to serve as an IBM consultant for best practices in student services. Before joining IBM, Burnett worked for Pittsburg State University, developing administrative applications. At the University of Kansas she developed academic computing support.

Carmy Carranza, professor and director/chair of the Learning Center and Act 101 at the Indiana University of Pennsylvania, holds a B.S. in secondary mathematics education, an M.A. in rhetoric and composition, and a doctorate in education, with a concentration in developmental education. She has thirty-eight years of teaching experience. Her research on developmental students' perceptions of the factors that influence success was granted an Outstanding Research Award by the National Association of Developmental Education. Her recent publications include a column for *Research and Teaching in Developmental Education* and a textbook, *Listen to What Students Say: A College Success Guide* (2000). Carranza does consulting in the areas of academic support, retention, developmental education, and paraprofessional tutor training.

Don G. Creamer is professor and coordinator of higher education and student affairs at Virginia Tech, where he also serves as codirector of the Educational Policy Institute of Virginia Tech. He is president of the Council for the Advancement of Standards in Higher Education and is vice president of the Educational Leadership Foundation of the American College Personnel Association. Creamer's research and consulting interests have frequently focused on academic advising, and he is author of several articles and book chapters on the subject. He is also author or coauthor of five books, including *Improving Staffing Practices in Student Affairs* (1997) and *The Professional Student Affairs Administrator: Educator, Leader, and Manager* (2001).

Elizabeth G. Creamer is associate professor in women's studies and in higher education and student affairs at Virginia Tech. Creamer spent the first fifteen years of her career as a full-time administrator, working first in leadership positions in financial aid and later in academic advising. Between 1988 and 1998, she was active in various leadership positions in the National Academic Advising Association. She served a term as the newsletter editor, as the regional representative from the mid-Atlantic region, as a national cochair (1996), and as the vice president for development. Since 1995, she has moved to a faculty position and now combines teaching, research, and administrative duties. Creamer's research interests are in topics related to faculty matters, including faculty research productivity and collaboration. She is the author of more than thirty-five articles and book chapters, as well as the books *Assessing Faculty Publishing Productivity Issues of Equity* (1998) and *Working Equal: Collaboration Among Academic Couples* (2001).

Joseph B. Cuseo holds an M.S. in experimental psychology and a Ph.D. in educational psychology and assessment from the University of Iowa. Currently, he is professor of psychology at Marymount College in Palos Verdes, California, where he directs the new student seminar—a required course for all new students—and he assists with faculty development and student retention activities. Cuseo is a member of the advisory board for the National Resource Center for The First-Year Experience and Students in Transition and has received the center's Outstanding First-Year Advocate Award. He is also the ten-time recipient of the Faculty Member of the Year Award (by student vote) on his campus.

Steven C. Ender is executive assistant to the president for university planning and is professor at Indiana University of Pennsylvania (IUP). He received his doctorate in counseling and human development services from the University of Georgia in 1981. Ender's career has included teaching at both the undergraduate and the graduate level. He has developed university-wide programs in learning assistance, peer education, academic advising, and educational enhancement for high school students who are at risk academically. He has served as vice president for student affairs at IUP and as director of social equity for the Pennsylvania State System of Higher Education. Ender has been appointed to various editorial boards and has written and edited numerous books, book chapters, and articles in the professional literature.

Anthony M. English is an Ed.D. student in higher education at Indiana University Bloomington (IUB). He serves as the lifelong learning program coordinator in IUB's Division of Continuing Studies. Prior to pursuing his doctorate, English worked as a financial analyst at Hewlett-Packard in California. He earned both his M.A. in history and his B.S. in business administration (accounting) from San Diego State University. His scholarly interests focus on the administration of continuing studies and student affairs units.

Diane Foucar-Szocki is associate professor and coordinator of the Adult Education/Human Resource Development program at James Madison University and is director of Virginia's Workforce Improvement Network (WIN). She consults with education, government, and industry on issues of professional development, including workforce development and literacy, performance analysis, performance improvement, action learning, and evaluation. Foucar-Szocki is author of several articles and reports on group learning, staff development, and adult literacy and is a member of the Harrisonburg City School Board.

Virginia N. Gordon is assistant dean emeritus and adjunct associate professor at Ohio State University. She has extensive experience in teaching, administration, advising, and counseling in higher education settings. Her bibliography includes more than forty books, monographs, book chapters, and articles on the administration of advising, career advising, working with undecided students, and adviser training. She is a past president of the National ACademic ADvising Association (NACADA) and founder and first director of the National Clearinghouse on Academic Advising. Gordon has received national acclaim and numerous awards for her contributions to the field. And the NACADA has most fittingly named its award for outstanding contributions to the field of academic advising the Virginia N. Gordon Award.

Sara E. Hinkle is a Ph.D. student in higher education at Indiana University Bloomington (IUB). She currently works as a project associate for the NSSE Institute and is a judicial officer in the Office of Student Ethics at IUB. Hinkle received her B.A. in psychology from Gettysburg College and her M.S. in counseling from Georgia State University. She has worked as a student affairs administrator at Oglethorpe University and Brenau University, both in metro Atlanta, and has also worked with the Semester at Sea program before beginning her doctoral studies at IUB.

Bonita C. Jacobs is vice president for student development and associate professor of higher education at the University of North Texas. Previously employed in orientation at Western Carolina University and at Stephen F.

Austin State University, Jacobs's primary research interest is in new student orientation and transition. She was the editor of the *Journal of College Orientation and Transition* from 1997 to 2000 and received the 1999 NODA President's Award and the 2000 NODA Award for Outstanding Scholarly Contributions to the Orientation Profession. She also served on the NODA board of directors, budget committee, publications committee, and bylaws committee, as well as chairing the editorial board, the special projects committee, and the awards selection committee. She was the program chair for NODAC '93, the preconference program chair for NODAC '87, and the program chair for SROW '95 and SROW '91, and she is a former chair of ACPA Commission II (admissions and orientation). She has published extensively on orientation issues and is a noted speaker and consultant on new student transition.

Sally M. Johnstone is the founding director of WCET, the cooperative advancing the effective use of technology in higher education. Johnstone's areas of expertise include the effects of the integration of technology on higher education institutions and system organizations, collaborations, quality assurance issues, project development and evaluation, and international projects, and she generally supports WCET members in the planning for and implementation of eLearning. Johnstone writes a monthly column for *Syllabus* magazine on distance learning and a semiannual column for *Change* magazine, for which she also serves as a consulting editor. She has served on the boards of the American Association for Higher Education and the U.S. Open University. She has authored about twenty articles, four book chapters, and five books or major reports on distance and distributed learning. She also leads workshops and gives about a dozen invited addresses each year to higher education organizations. She earned her Ph.D. in experimental psychology from the University of North Carolina at Chapel Hill.

Gary L. Kramer, a former dean and director of student services at two campuses, is the associate dean of student academic and advisement services and is professor in the counseling psychology department at Brigham Young University. He received his Ph.D. from Oregon State University. He has published seventy refereed journal articles, book chapters, book reviews, monographs, grant proposals, and institutional reports. He is also the editor of two books, four monographs, and the author of six monograph chapters and chapters in books. Kramer has delivered more than a hundred professional papers, including keynote addresses for twelve professional organizations. In addition to having served as the National

ACademic ADvising Association president, Kramer has received the association's awards for researcher of the year, distinguished service, and excellence in the field.

George D. Kuh is chancellor's professor of higher education at Indiana University Bloomington. He directs the College Student Experiences Questionnaire Research Program and the National Survey of Student Engagement, funded by the Lumina Foundation for Education and The Pew Charitable Trusts and cosponsored by The Carnegie Foundation for the Advancement of Teaching. Kuh's contributions in the areas of student engagement, assessment, institutional improvement, and college and university cultures have been recognized with awards from the American College Personnel Association, the Association of Institutional Research, the Association for the Study of Higher Education, the Council of Independent Colleges, and the National Association of Student Personnel Administrators.

Rick Larson is the associate vice president for student life at James Madison University (JMU) and has responsibilities for residence life, multicultural/international student services, university centers, recreation, and judicial affairs. He previously worked as a general manager, organization development facilitator, and Total Quality Management trainer for Marriott Corporation. From JMU he earned his bachelor's degree in individualized study in human resource development and is currently pursuing a master's degree in adult education/human resource development. Larson's twenty-two-year career has included programming, construction, training, management, and leadership.

Janet G. Lenz is associate director for career advising, counseling, and programming at the Career Center at Florida State University (FSU) and is a senior research associate in the FSU Center for the Study of Technology in Counseling and Career Development. She received her bachelor's degree in sociology from Virginia Commonwealth University and both her master's degree in student personnel administration and her Ph.D. in counseling and human systems from FSU. Lenz has also worked as an arts and sciences placement coordinator and career counselor at the Career Center at the University of Texas at Austin and as the assistant director at the Career Planning and Placement Center at the University of North Carolina at Greensboro.

Louise Lonabocker is director of student services at Boston College. She earned her Ph.D. in higher education administration at Boston College in 1981 and has been employed there since 1970. Lonabocker is a past president of the American Association of Collegiate Registrars and Admissions Officers (AACRAO). She has previously served on the AACRAO board of directors and has chaired or served on several AACRAO committees. Lonabocker has also been a frequent conference panelist or presenter at the AACRAO, the New England Association of Collegiate Registrars and Admissions Officers, the College and University Computer Users Association (known as CUMREC), and EDUCAUSE, has been a contributor to *College & University*, and is an editor and contributor for the AACRAO publication *Breakthrough Systems: Student Access and Registration*. As director of student services, Lonabocker oversees academic, financial, and auxiliary services. Formerly the university registrar, she has been involved in a number of student services projects at Boston College, including the development of the U-VIEW system for student access to information on ATM machines, U-DIAL—the interactive voice response system used for registration, Agora—the Web-based student access system, and Project Delta—a university-wide effort to improve customer service, increase productivity, and reduce costs.

Jill A. Lumsden is currently career development coordinator at the Career Center at Florida State University (FSU), where she coordinates the FSU on-line Career Portfolio Project. She received her master's and specialist in education degrees in counseling and human systems, with a specialization in career counseling, from FSU in 1999. Her previous position at the Career Center was assistant director for career advising, counseling, and programming. Before earning her graduate degrees, she worked as a job placement counselor in Tacoma, Washington, where she assisted veterans transitioning out of the military. She is a national certified counselor.

Randy Mitchell is associate vice president for student success programs at James Madison University and is responsible for admissions, academic and career advising, leadership, disability services, and orientation. He has coordinated numerous renovation and innovation projects and serves as an assistant professor of psychology. Randy has published and presented extensively in the student services arena and has written three books: *Metaphors, Semaphores and Two by Fours* (1997), *Fables, Labels and Folding Tables* (1999), and *Listen Very Loud* (2001).

Diana Oblinger is a consultant who focuses on higher education issues—in particular, distributed learning. She is also a senior fellow with the EDUCAUSE Center for Applied Research and serves as an adjunct professor of adult and community college education at North Carolina State University. Previously, Oblinger was the vice president for information resources and the chief information officer for the sixteen-campus University of North Carolina system. At IBM she was the academic programs and strategy executive and director of the Institute for Academic Technology. Before joining IBM, Oblinger was a faculty member at Michigan State University and the University of Missouri-Columbia, where she also served as an academic dean.

Rita R. Owens has worked in higher education administration for more than twenty-five years. She gained her expertise in various enrollment management positions at Virginia Polytechnic Institute and State University, Babson College, and Boston College and as customer services manager for Diversified Management International. Rita became associate vice president for student information services at Boston College in March 2001. In that role, she provides strategic direction for all student systems as well as overseeing the Office of Student Services and Academic Technology Services. From 1996 to 2000, she was the project leader for service strategies at Boston College. In that role, she led the transformation of Boston College's student services by creating the Office of Student Services. Rita is a frequent presenter at the American Association of Collegiate Registrars and Admissions Officers, EDUCAUSE, and the IBM Forum on Student Services, she and is the Boston College representative for the IBM Best Practice Partners in Student Services. She has published several articles on her work. Owens received a B.A. from Westfield State College and an M.A. from Virginia Polytechnic Institute and State University.

Bernard A. (Bernie) Pekala is director of student financial strategies at Boston College. He is the university's chief strategist in the area of student financial aid, student employment, campus-based loans, accounts, collections, receivables, reconciliations, and payments. He is responsible for monitoring student financial initiatives, determines critical need analysis policies and funding strategies, reviews research, analyzes data and prepares financial models, and incorporates the strategic importance of new technology in the delivery of student financial services. He has developed his knowledge and management skills in various financial roles at Tufts University, Emerson College, and Boston College. His undergraduate studies in political science and graduate studies in education were completed at Tufts University.

Gary W. Peterson earned his Ph.D. in counseling from Duke University in 1970 and is now professor and training director for the academic program Psychological Services in Education, in the College of Education at Florida State University. He is also senior research associate at the Center for the Study of Technology in Counseling and Career Development, which is part of the University Career Center. He teaches courses in personality assessment, research methods, and consultation and organizational development. He also serves as chair of the university admissions committee. Peterson's research interests include career problem solving and decision making, career assessment, and test construction.

Earl H. Potter III is dean of the College of Business at Eastern Michigan University and is former director of organizational development and employment services at Cornell University. Potter received his Ph.D. in organizational psychology from the University of Washington in 1978 and has been a Mellon faculty fellow at Yale University as well as a National Institute of Mental Health fellow at the University of Chicago. He is a member of the board of examiners for the Malcolm Baldrige National Quality Award, a senior examiner for the Michigan Quality Program, and a former fellow of the American Council on Education.

Gene F. Priday earned his master of public administration degree from Brigham Young University (BYU) in 1973. He has been actively involved in the Association of Records Managers and Administrators (Utah-Salt Lake Chapter), the Utah Association of Collegiate Registrars and Admissions Officers, and the Pacific Association of Collegiate Registrars and Admissions Officers, serving as president of each of these organizations. He has also been actively involved in the American Association of Collegiate Registrars and Admissions Officers, serving as local arrangements cochair for the 1997 annual conference. Priday has also presented at numerous state, regional, and national conferences and has been a contributing author in *College and University.* He began his career in higher education in 1972 and has held numerous leadership positions at BYU during this period. He has been actively involved in many computer development projects at the university, including the development of the Web registration system, computerized transcript, and document management (imaging) system. He was appointed University Registrar at BYU in 1987.

Robert C. Reardon has held full-time counseling and teaching positions at Florida State University (FSU) since 1966, when he was first employed as a counselor at FSU's Counseling Center. Today, he is a faculty member in the division of student affairs, and his current position is director of instruction, research, and evaluation at the Career Center. He is also professor in the Department of Educational Psychology and Learning Systems as well as (with Jim Sampson) serving as codirector of the Center for the Study of Technology in Counseling and Career Development.

James P. Sampson Jr. is currently a professor in the Department of Human Services and Studies at Florida State University (FSU), where he has taught courses in career development and computer applications in counseling since 1982. Since 1986, he has served as codirector of the Center for the Study of Technology in Counseling and Career Development, a research center established at FSU to improve the design and use of computer applications in counseling and guidance. He is also a National Certified Counselor and a National Certified Career Counselor. He received his Ph.D. in counselor education from the University of Florida in 1977.

John H. Schuh is professor of educational leadership at Iowa State University, where he is also department chair. Previously, he held administrative and faculty assignments at Wichita State University, Indiana University Bloomington, and Arizona State University. Schuh is the author, coauthor, or editor of more than 180 publications, including seventeen books and monographs, more than forty-five book chapters, and ninety articles. He is currently editor-in-chief of the *New Directions for Student Services* sourcebook series and is associate editor of the *Journal of College Student Development*. In 1994, Schuh received a Fulbright Award to study higher education in Germany.

Patricia A. Shea is assistant director at WCET. In that capacity, she is responsible for managing the annual conference and overseeing the membership program. In addition, she directs the Western Cooperative's Learning Anytime Anywhere Partnership project, funded by the U.S. Department of Education. In this project—Beyond the Administrative Core: Creating Web-Based Student Services for Online Learners, three partner institutions and a corporation collaborate in the development of Web-based student services. Prior to joining the WCET staff in 1996, Pat worked in the technology programs division of the National School Boards Association. She holds an M.A. in educational administration and supervision from George Mason University in Fairfax, Virginia, and is a former Fulbright scholar.

Vasti Torres is assistant professor of higher education administration at George Washington University's Graduate School of Education and Human Development in Washington, D.C. She teaches courses in student affairs administration and related topics. Prior to joining the faculty, she had sixteen years of experience in administrative positions, most recently serving as associate vice provost and dean for enrollment and student services at Portland State University in Portland, Oregon. Torres's most recent research focuses on how the ethnic identity of Latino students influences their college experience. She has written numerous articles on Latino/Hispanic students, survey development and use, and other diversity issues. She is the principal investigator for a grant investigating Latinos' choice to stay in college. She is active in several student affairs and higher education associations and is a program associate for the National Center for Policy in Higher Education. She has been honored as an emerging scholar by the American College Personnel Association. Torres holds a Ph.D. in counseling and student affairs administration from the University of Georgia.

J. James Wager currently serves as assistant vice provost for enrollment management and university registrar at the Pennsylvania State University. He is a member of the university faculty senate and serves on the W. K. Kellogg Leadership for Institutional Change in Higher Education initiative. Wager also spends time in the classroom teaching management courses and is a member of the university's Leadership Academy and Management Institute. As university registrar, Wager provides oversight for all academic records and associated activities for all the university's 80,000-plus students enrolled at twenty-four campuses across the Commonwealth of Pennsylvania. For the American Association of Collegiate Registrars, he has presented on numerous topics at annual and regional meetings, and he has also served on various committees. Wager serves as a board chair of the Association of American Universities Registrars and is the program coordinator of the Registrars' Summer Institute at Aspen. He has been an advocate for the delivery of student services using secure Web technology. Wager holds a B.S. in management with a minor in information systems and an M.P.A in public administration.

W. W. (Tim) Washburn has served as executive director of admissions and records at the University of Washington since 1975. Before that, from 1969 to 1975, he was university registrar. During his tenure, he has served as president of the Pacific Association of Collegiate Registrars and Admissions Officers, chair of the computing committee of the American Association of Collegiate Registrars and Admissions Officers, and vice chair of the College Board Council on Entrance Services. He currently serves on the University of Washington faculty council on academic standards and is a member of the president's advisory committee on diversity.

Roger B. Winston Jr. is professor emeritus of college student affairs administration at the University of Georgia, where he taught for more than twenty-five years. He is the author or editor of thirteen books on student affairs. His most recent books include *Learning Through Supervised*

Practice in Student Affairs (with Diane L. Cooper, Sue A. Saunders, Joan B. Hirt, Don G. Creamer, and Steven M. Janosik, 2002), *The Professional Student Affairs Administrator: Educator, Leader, and Manager* (with Don G. Creamer and Theodore K. Miller, 2001), and *Improving Staffing Practices in Students Affairs* (with Don G. Creamer, 1997).

PART ONE

TAKING A STRATEGIC APPROACH TO STUDENT DEVELOPMENT

THE GOALS OF HIGHER EDUCATION are firmly fixed on educating the whole person and on student learning. Furthermore, asserts the American Association for Higher Education, the American College Personnel Association, and the National Association of Student Personnel Administrators (1998), "learning is developmental, a cumulative process involving the whole person, relating past and present, integrating the new with the old, starting from but transcending personal concerns and interests" (p. 8). In this context, Roger Winston Jr., in Chapter One, raises a number of questions regarding life cycle development, and, in particular, he asks, how does an institution go about the plethora of higher education goals to deliver a well-conceptualized, student-centered, and integrated academic services system? Furthermore, we contend in Part One that institutions can only address these questions if they are committed to (1) realizing a student-centric institution and (2) creating a seamless educational experience for their students.

To further set the book's context and foundation, in this first part (Chapters One through Three), we examine the interrelationship of student development, success, and progress within an enriched and integrated student learning and educational experience. Specifically, in Chapter One, Roger Winston Jr. traces the evolution, changes, and definition of student academic services within the historical, theoretical, and philosophical foundations of higher education—all to build a case on behalf of students' progress and development and to speak for a more comprehensive and coordinated perspective on student academic services. Then, in Chapter Two, Darlene Burnett and Diana Oblinger present how institutions have gone about conceptualizing and delivering student-centered and integrated academic services. They provide an overview of current practices, trends, and models. Just as important, this chapter presents the larger objectives of student learning and success behind integrating student academic services. Quality student services, the authors in this book advocate, can serve as a differentiator in attracting and retaining students, as well as being a means of enriching a student's educational experience and the institution's relationship with the student. In short, as John Schuh points out in Chapter Three, qualitative student academic services can play an integral role in helping students connect with their institution. He further expands in this chapter the notions of facilitating student growth and learning, and he discusses how the interrelationship of student academic services adds to an institution's vitality. Schuh defines how academic services intersect with one another and explains how they can work together to provide more coherent, student-centered support. He presents the importance of collegiality, partnerships, and collaboration, as well as the connection of academic services, asserting that they are as central to successful student matriculation as they are to students' graduation from the institution.

REFERENCE

American Association for Higher Education, American College Personnel Association, and National Association of Student Personnel Administrators. "Powerful Partnerships: A Shared Responsibility for Learning." 1998. [http//:www.aahe.org.teaching/tsk_frce.htm].

STIMULATING AND SUPPORTING STUDENT LEARNING

Roger B. Winston Jr.

A TRUISM IN AMERICAN HIGHER EDUCATION is that colleges and universities exist to promote student learning and to advance or create knowledge. American higher education institutions are generally thought to have three crucial functions: teaching, research, and public service. Different types of institutions place varying degrees of emphasis on these three primary functions. Howard Bowen (1977) asserts that institutions can be categorized largely on the basis of their relative emphasis on these three functions. Community colleges focus principally on transmitting existing knowledge through instruction. Research-focused universities fundamentally emphasize the creation of new knowledge and its transmission to students, professionals, and the public. Other institutions, such as liberal arts colleges and comprehensive colleges and universities, fall somewhere between the other two in terms of relative emphasis. Most institutions of all types engage in all three functions but to widely varying degrees.

The principal goal of this chapter is to explore the concept of academic services and to identify the means of creating and delivering student services that will stimulate and support student learning. But first the chapter addresses the purposes of higher education, which are summarized here using Bowen's taxonomy of goals (1977) that can lead to the education of the whole person. These goals are then viewed within the context of a student-centric institution. A model of academic services is explored using examples of applications and considering possible ways it could be used to create new academic services or evaluate existing services. Finally, some of the obstacles to creating student-centric institutions are identified.

Purposes of Higher Education

Before addressing the question of academic services, it is essential that we consider the purposes of higher education. Bowen (1977) characterizes the purposes of higher education by describing the desirable student outcomes that can be influenced or produced as a result of attendance at a college or university. He asserts that the "goals of higher education are concerned with the development of the full potentialities of human beings and of society" (p. 54). Bowen identifies goals for individual students in the areas of cognitive learning, emotional and moral development, and practical competence.

In the area of cognitive learning (Bowen, 1977, pp. 55–56), outcomes include development of

- ○ Verbal skills (the ability to speak and write clearly, correctly, and gracefully; may include the acquisition of a second language)

- ○ Quantitative skills (the ability to understand basic concepts of mathematics and perform elementary statistical analyses; may include understanding the rudiments of accounting)

- ○ Substantive knowledge (acquaintance with the cultural heritage of the West and knowledge of other cultures and traditions; "command of vocabulary, facts, and principles in one or more selected fields of knowledge")

- ○ Intellectual tolerance (openness to new ideas, willingness to challenge orthodoxy, intellectual curiosity, the ability to deal with ambiguity and complexity, and understanding of the limitations of knowledge and thought)

- ○ Aesthetic sensibility ("knowledge of, interest in, and responsiveness to literature, the fine arts, and natural beauty")

- ○ Creativeness ("imagination and originality in formulating new hypotheses and ideas and in producing new works of art")

- ○ Intellectual integrity (ability to understand "truth" and its contingent nature; conscientiousness of inquiry and accuracy in reporting findings)

- ○ Wisdom ("balanced perspective, judgment, and prudence")

- ○ Lifelong learning ("love of learning; sustained intellectual interests; learning how to learn")

Under the category of emotional and moral development, Bowen's goals (1977, pp. 56–57) include

○ Personal self-discovery ("knowledge of one's talents, interests, values, aspirations, and weaknesses"; discovery of one's uniqueness and personal identity)

○ Psychological well-being ("sensitivity to deeper feelings and emotions combined with emotional stability; ability to express emotions constructively; appropriate self-assertiveness, sense of security, self-confidence, decisiveness, spontaneity; acceptance of self and others")

○ Human understanding ("capacity for empathy, thoughtfulness, compassion, respect, tolerance, and cooperation toward others, including persons of different backgrounds; . . . skill in communication with others")

○ Values and morals ("a valid and internalized but not dogmatic set of values and moral principles . . . ; sense of social consciousness and social responsibility")

○ Religious interests ("serious and thoughtful exploration of purpose, values, and meaning")

Bowen (1977) calls the third category of student goals "practical competence." He asserts that "virtually all of the goals included under cognitive learning and emotional and moral development apply to practical affairs" (p. 37). Following are traits (pp. 57–58) that are more specific to the practical concerns of life:

○ Need for achievement ("motivation toward accomplishment; initiative . . . , persistence, self-discipline")

○ Future orientation (ability to plan carefully, be a prudent risk taker, and have a realistic outlook toward the future)

○ Adaptability (openness to change, tolerance of new ideas, versatility and resourcefulness, and capacity to learn from experience)

○ Leadership ("capacity to win the confidence of others; willingness to assume responsibility; organizational ability")

○ Citizenship ("understanding of and commitment to democracy; knowledge of government institutions and procedures; awareness of major social issues . . . ; disposition and ability to participate actively in civic, political, economic, professional, educational, and other voluntary organizations; orientation toward international understanding . . . ; disposition toward law observance")

○ Economic productivity ("knowledge and skills needed for first job and for growth in productivity; . . . adaptability and mobility; sound career decisions; capability to bring humanistic values to the workplace and to derive meaning from work")

○ Sound family life ("personal qualities making for stable families" and long-term relationships)

○ Consumer efficiency (ability to manage personal finances; "ability to recognize deceptive sales practices and to withstand high-pressure sales tactics")

○ Fruitful leisure ("wisdom in allocation of time among work, leisure, and other pursuits . . . ; lifelong education, formal and informal, as a productive use of leisure; resourcefulness in overcoming boredom, finding renewal, and discovering satisfying and rewarding use of leisure time") and

○ Health ("understanding of the basic principles for cultivating physical and mental health; knowledge of how and when to use the professional health care system")

In a similar but less detailed fashion, Baxter Magolda (1999b) specifies four dimensions of student learning: (1) cognitive competence, which includes "critical thinking, complex meaning-making, intellectual flexibility, reflective judgment, and the ability to apply knowledge," (2) intrapersonal competence, which encompasses "a coherent sense of identity; a self-authored belief system to organize one's values, ethics, spirituality and moral development; a capacity for self-awareness and reflection; and integrity," (3) interpersonal competence, which includes "the capacity for interdependence and collaboration; appreciation of diversity; communication, problem solving and conflict-management skills, humanitarianism and concern for the community," and (4) practical competence, which includes "managing one's daily life and tasks and career and personal decision making" (p. 39).

Educating the Whole Person

Bowen's and Baxter Magolda's taxonomies of goals (Baxter, 1977; Baxter Magolda, 1999b) are firmly based in a belief that higher education should address the education of the whole person, not just his or her intellect. Education involves much more than the acquisition of academic knowledge.

Students are complex beings. Certainly they are not, nor have they ever been, disembodied intellects presented to institutions of high learning for molding. For students, learning does not take place in an environment divorced from societal (and often parental) pressure, expectations, and influences, or from internal uncertainties about academic competence, future lives and careers, and interpersonal relationships. Traditional-aged college students are experiencing a period of their life cycle development that requires them to make many significant and far-reaching decisions that have major consequences for the remainder of their lives. For example, they must ask themselves such questions as Who am I?—as a man or woman, as a member of an ethnic, racial, or cultural group, as having a particular sexual orientation, as a worker or practitioner of a profession, and as an actual or potential husband, wife, or partner—to name only a few. What will I do with the remainder of my life? Who will I share my life with? How do I make meaning of what I hear in class, read, and observe? How do I reconcile conflicting information, methods of inquiry, value systems, religious teachings, political positions, and expert opinions?

Older students are frequently experiencing major life transitions, which may include stresses within the family and personal uncertainty about abilities and academic competence. They also often have many competing demands for their time and attention, including full-time work and familial obligations.

Few would argue that what happens to students in the classroom and laboratory is unaffected by what happens to them outside those settings. For example, if a college student is experiencing a health problem (whether a head cold or life-threatening disease), an emotion-laden breakup with a significant other, or indecision about career plans or class performance demands requiring background knowledge and skills that the student has not mastered, he or she is not likely to perform well in classes or be able to integrate or use the ideas and factual information presented in classes. As the *Powerful Partnerships* (American Association for Higher Education, American College Personnel Association, and National Association of Student Personnel Administrators, 1998) document asserts, "learning is *developmental*, a cumulative process involving the whole person, relating past and present, integrating the new with the old, starting from but transcending personal concerns and interests" (p. 8).

Central to the notion of educating the whole person are three essential postulates. First, students are unique individuals who respond to higher education and make meaning of their experiences in individualistic ways.

Effective educational practices must recognize and respect individual differences among students and make accommodations in instructional methods, institutional organization structures, and cocurricular initiatives. Second, "learning is done by individuals who are intrinsically tied to others as social beings, interacting as competitors or collaborators, constraining or supporting the learning process, and able to enhance learning through cooperation and sharing" (American Association for Higher Education, American College Personnel Association, and National Association of Student Personnel Administrators, 1998, p. 9). Third, the social and physical environments of an institution have significant influences on students' behavior and learning. Their in-class and out-of-class interactions with faculty and, staff members, as well as with student peers, contribute to or detract from learning.

Pascarella and Terenzini (1991) found in their analysis and synthesis of research on college outcomes that students learn more, are more likely to persist through graduation, and report greater satisfaction with their college experiences when they are involved in activities and experiences directly related to academic subjects and when the curricular and cocurricular experiences are meaningful and complementary. They also report that alumni who had substantial extracurricular involvement, especially through leadership experiences, reported "significantly enhanced interpersonal and leadership skills important to job success" (p. 624).

If one accepts the assertion that higher education has a responsibility to educate the whole person, then how an institution goes about addressing the plethora of goals must rest on a system of well-conceptualized, energetically delivered, and integrated academic services. Such an institution could be appropriately labeled a student-centric college or university.

Student-Centric Higher Education

Even though higher education generally asserts that the education of students is its raison d'être, most institutions are organized and administered to address the interests of many constituencies, such as faculty members, governing boards, legislatures, alumni, grant givers, commercial enterprises, accreditation bodies, and administrative leaders. Almost inevitably, these constituencies develop different, often conflicting, interests. Because of limited resources or myopic vision, institutional leaders are frequently forced to favor the interests of some groups over others. Ironically, undergraduate students' interests often come in near the bottom at many institutions, especially large universities.

If one defines the purposes of higher education as focused exclusively on the transmission of known facts, theories, and methods of inquiry, as well as the creation of new knowledge through research or creative and critical analysis, then academic services would tend to support faculty members as they perform these functions and relieve them from the burden of organizational maintenance activities. But if one defines the purposes of higher education more broadly—as being concerned with the development of the full potential of the participants (students, faculty members, and administrators) in the higher education undertaking, then academic services can become quite comprehensive and complex.

A student-centric institution is one where the most important constituents are the students and the ultimate criterion for success is the promotion of their learning. Because of their experiences at the institution, students should arrive at functioning at higher levels of intellectual, interpersonal, and practical competence than when they initially enrolled. As Sandel and Sydow (1997) note, students should not be viewed as dependent on the faculty and staff; rather, the faculty and staff depend on students' presence for their existence. "We are not doing them [the students] a favor by serving them. They are doing us a favor by giving us the opportunity to do so" (p. 1). Within a student-centric institution, then, how should academic services be conceptualized?

What Are Academic Services?

Providing a concise definition of academic services is more complicated than it appears on the surface. For many, what first comes to mind when this term is used are programs and services that provide students with opportunities to practice or develop skills, such as tutoring, remedial courses in basic subjects, such as English or mathematics, or writing or language laboratories. Others may think of those functions that create and maintain an institution's academic infrastructure, such as administering financial aid programs, structuring class registration, maintaining academic transcripts, and soliciting and processing applications for admission. Yet another way to think of academic services (which are often referred to as student affairs programs) includes, for example, opportunities for students to receive leadership training, participate in service learning projects, receive psychotherapy to deal with anxiety or interpersonal conflicts, attend African American art exhibits, or serve on student judiciary panels. Traditionally, these conceptualizations of academic services have been associated with faculty members and student affairs professionals. The first conceptualization is closely tied to formal instruction in traditional academic disciplines; the second is often viewed as necessary but, similar to parking services, educationally irrelevant; the third is associated primarily with out-of-class learning through the cocurriculum. *All* these "services" are crucial to the effective functioning of student-centric colleges and universities and have a direct effect on the quality and scope of students' educational experience.

A Model for Conceptualizing Academic Services

If one accepts Bowen's conceptualization of the purposes of higher education (1977), then all of these programs, services, and learning opportunities are academic services because they promote the achievement of the goals of higher education. Academic services are conceptualized by the model depicted in Figure 1.1—inspired by models developed by Morrill, Hurst, and Oetting (1980) and Hurst and Jacobson (1985).

Figure 1.1. Conceptual Model of Academic Services

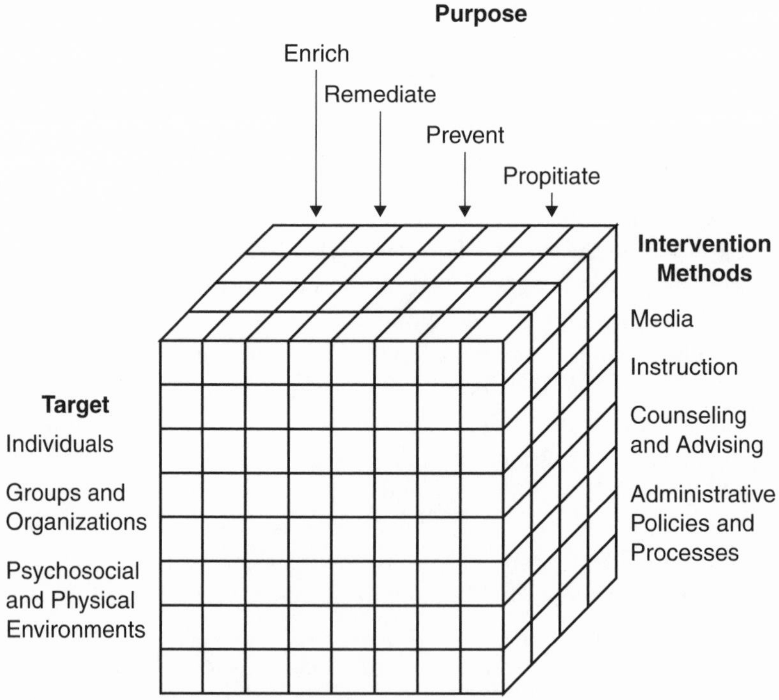

Note: *Based on and adapted from Morrill, Hurst, and Oetting (1980) and Hurst and Jacobson (1985). Reproduced by permission.*

Purpose

From the perspective of the student, academic services are institutional programs, services, learning opportunities, and interventions that (1) enrich or supplement learning and personal development, (2) correct or ameliorate academic or personal knowledge shortfalls, skill deficiencies, or maladaptive attitudes, (3) prevent the occurrence of foreseeable personal or academic difficulties, or (4) make collegiate life more convenient or pleasant.

Probably the most important purpose of academic services is to enrich the educational experiences and learning of all students. This includes encouraging students to pursue advanced topics in a discipline, relate classroom experiences and knowledge to their life, and integrate knowledge, methods of inquiry, and means of sharing findings or discoveries. Enrichment also relates to personal development, which may range from self-exploration (for example, through community service, leadership experience, or personal counseling) to career decision making (for example, through a counseling group, internship experience, or part-time work in areas of potential interests).

A second purpose of academic services is to assist students who need help in overcoming identified deficiencies or behaviors that hamper their success in the academic arena. This can range from instruction at a pre-college level in areas such as English, mathematics, and reading (areas traditionally associated with "developmental education programs") to dealing with individually identified problems, such as chronic test or public speaking anxiety or poorly developed study or time management skills. Remediation addresses the impediments to students' collegiate and life success that, in most cases, existed prior to the students' enrollment in higher education.

The third purpose of academic services is to prevent foreseeable problems from causing students to experience academic or personal difficulties. For example, students who graduate from high schools that failed to provide a demanding curriculum might be expected to experience difficulties in meeting the academic demands of a large state university. For instance, first-year programs (such as freshman year experience courses or freshmen interest groups) can be designed to address issues and provide support to students who we can predict are likely to experience difficulties. Prevention proactively addresses areas of student life with the aim to anticipate and prevent or lessen anticipated problems.

The fourth purpose of academic services (especially, services that form the infrastructure of the institution) is to propitiate or cause students to be favorably inclined toward the institution and the educational experiences and opportunities offered. In a loose sense, this may be likened to customer satisfaction. Virtually all colleges and universities experience a certain amount of attrition due solely to students' adverse reactions to the physical appearance of the campus, the attitudes of staff and service employees, the lack of amenities (such as private rooms in residence halls or convenient and safe parking), or annoyances (such as difficulty in registering for classes or the low quality or variety of foods served in dining facilities). Even though none of these issues directly affect the quality of the education offered, these kinds of concerns are important to students and may cause them to abandon an institution, even when their classroom experience is satisfactory. This should not be taken to mean, however, that an institution should structure its programs, services, and curriculum based exclusively on "student satisfaction." But because convenience, speed, and accuracy of services are qualities that affect students' evaluation of an institution and possibly their decision to persist, these services deserve serious attention.

Target

Delivery of academic services may focus on different facets of the student population or the institution. Targets include (1) individuals, (2) groups and organizations, and (3) psychosocial and physical environments.

INDIVIDUALS. Traditionally, much of what is done in higher education focuses on educating individuals. Even when dealing with collections (as in classes) of students, frequently the intention is to stimulate behavior change in individuals. Classes have been the traditional means of organizing education in the United States. In classes, collections of individual students are brought together to address a delineated topic for a specified period of time. Even so, individuals are the primary targets of the academic services.

GROUPS AND ORGANIZATIONS. Potentially potent influences in students' lives are their assigned and associational groups. Groups of students are generally informally structured and are formed by students based on similarity or shared interests, attributes, or goals. Social attraction or physical proximity often serve as the primary motivators for groups' formation. Frequently, these groups are identified and based on friendships.

Voluntary associational groups of students may be formalized as organizations such as social fraternities and sororities, academic honoraries, and clubs based in academic disciplines or in personal interests such as sailing, playing chess, or taking part in religious activities. It is through such avenues that students are socialized into various fields, given opportunities to explore possible careers and to have contact with practitioners and scholars, and form personal relationships and friendships with others who share common interests, beliefs, or values.

Student organizations can give many students opportunities to acquire or sharpen leadership skills and develop meaningful organizational competencies. Even though student organizations are ubiquitous on many campuses, perhaps approaching oversaturation on some, they hold great potential for contributing to accomplishing the goals of higher education, especially when the institutional representatives who work with them focus students' attentions on accomplishing educational objectives and developing practical competencies.

PSYCHOSOCIAL AND PHYSICAL ENVIRONMENTS. Another target of academic services can be the environments of the institution. Arnold and Kuh (1999) point out that the various constituencies of higher education hold different mental models of what they consider important. For instance, faculty members perceive the core of the institution to be the curriculum, teaching, and scholarship. But for traditional-aged students, the core includes fitting in and making friends, having academic success (defined in terms of grades, progress toward a degree, and job credentials), and obtaining financial aid. Student affairs professionals value the means of promoting student involvement activities that foster student development. "Three intentionally designed learning sites—classrooms, student organizations and other co-curricular activities, and residence halls—are represented in the core" (p. 17). From this conceptualization, one can conclude that colleges and universities have multiple environments and that attempts to affect the psychosocial climate of an institution can produce important effects in students' educational experiences. Likewise, physical environments can be inviting, utilitarian, cold, hostile, or distracting, perhaps caused by confusing traffic patterns, echoing sound, or inappropriately sized rooms for the activities taking place within. Strange (1993) notes, "Although the physical environment may not directly cause specific behaviors or attitudes, its limitations present challenges that must be negotiated by those within" (p. 137).

Strange and Banning (2001) maintain that, for learning to take place, the institution must first have (create) an environment that is perceived to be safe, secure, and inclusive. Without a basic sense of belonging to the campus community, free from threat, fear, and anxiety, attempts to activate higher learning are difficult at best. Once safety and inclusion needs have been addressed successfully, however, the environment can then promote participation and engagement. As Astin (1985) notes, "Students learn from becoming involved" (p. 133). For him, "student involvement refers to the amount of physical and psychological energy that the student devotes to academic experience. A highly involved student is one who, for example, devotes considerable energy to studying, spending a lot of time on campus, participates actively in student organizations, and interacts frequently with faculty members and other students" (p. 134). Thus, Strange and Banning (2001) argue that the third condition needed to promote learning is an institutional environment that offers students a sense of belonging and full membership in an academic community. They maintain that "communities seem to thrive when space is available for (or dedicated to) a group of individuals who share characteristics and interests, when organizational designs invite participation, role taking, and decision making, and when artifacts of culture express and support a common vision and purpose" (p. 168).

Intervention Methods

A variety of methods can be used to accomplish educational purposes that are focused or targeted on individuals, groups and organizations, and environments. These methods include media, instruction, counseling and advising, and administrative policies and procedures.

MEDIA. With ever changing technology, an increasingly varied range of media interventions is available to promote an institution's educational goals. For hundreds of years in higher education, the printed word in numerous formats was used to inform students and other members of the academic community. By the mid-twentieth century, radio and television expanded the options available for informing students and the general public. The advent of the Internet expanded the alternatives for communicating with students and removed much of the editorial control exercised in the print media. The Internet and e-mail also provide opportunities for consumers to give and receive almost immediate feedback to the individuals who post material. Internet sites can contain massive amounts of information and use powerful search engines to assist in locating information. The media therefore cover the gamut of communication formats—from newspapers, magazines, pamphlets, and flyers to radio and television, as well as to the Internet and e-mail.

As Carroll (2002) notes, the traditional office conference between the student and the instructor is passé on many campuses, being replaced by the exchange of e-mail messages. Although some faculty members see the loss of face-to-face contact as depersonalizing the educational experience, Carroll (an adjunct faculty member) also points out that many "students feel as though they get 24/7 access to me, even though I protect my time and answer mail when it suits my daily schedule."

INSTRUCTION. For centuries in higher education, instruction was delivered primarily through face-to-face interaction between students and teachers. While this method of providing instruction still prevails, increasingly, formal classes are offered through asynchronous, computer-based instruction (which may include interactive communication between class members and the teacher). On many "traditional" campuses, face-to-face interaction between instructor and student is supplemented by use of the Internet and class listservs or bulletin boards. Informal instruction provided to students through their involvement in the cocurriculum remains principally face-to-face, although a variety of programs have been adapted for delivery over the Internet. For instance, the University of Minnesota has created a virtual town that is used to facilitate more active involvement by residential and commuter students (Elling and Brown, 2001).

COUNSELING AND ADVISING. When students encounter problems or experience difficult transitions in their personal or academic lives, an important means of providing assistance is through personal counseling and academic advising. Through interaction with a person who possesses well-developed helping skills and knowledge of higher education and institutional policies and procedures, students can be assisted in working through areas of concern—whether they be of an interpersonal nature, an academic nature, or a combination of the two (Ender, Winston, and Miller, 1984).

Counseling and academic advising in this model are appropriate interventions for helping students identify appropriate academic, life, and career goals, build or repair self-insight and self-esteem, broaden intellectual interests and curiosity, encourage the use of institutional resources and associated learning opportunities, establish meaningful interpersonal relationships with others, clarify personal values, examine the ethical implications of their behavior and beliefs, and enhance critical thinking and reasoning (Creamer and Creamer, 1994; Winston, 1996, 2003). These services may be provided by mental health professionals, such as counseling psychologists, professional or trained allied professional academic advisers, student affairs professionals, or some combination thereof.

ADMINISTRATIVE POLICIES AND PROCEDURES. It is through the development and implementation of policies and procedures that academic standards and integrity are codified and that much of an institution's social climate is shaped.

Hage and Aiken (1970) have identified factors that determine whether organizations are static or dynamic, resistant to change, or adaptive and efficacious. These factors may be viewed through the lens of an institution's polices and procedures. These include

- Complexity (number of units within the organization and the number of codependent interrelations)
- Degree of centralization (the extent to which power is distributed or shared among members of the organization)
- Degree of formalization (number and complexity of enforced rules)
- Degree of stratification (differential distribution of rewards)
- Degree of emphasis on quantity and quality of services or products (such as academic credit hours)
- Efficiency (relative emphasis on cost containment and high cost-benefit ratios)

Strange (1993) concludes that effective educational environments are those that exhibit the characteristics of a dynamic organization and where "individual differences are appreciated, participation is expected, interactions are personal rather than functional, and risk-taking is encouraged" (p. 173).

If an institution's leadership is primarily concerned about organizational efficiency, then it is most likely to adopt authoritarian policies that students (and faculty members as well) may perceive as being uniform but impersonal. If, however, the leadership is concerned about educational quality or maximizing individual development and learning—which frequently appears inefficient—then the policies and procedures will likely reflect a participative approach to policy development and are likely to be perceived as personalized and caring. In developing policies and procedures, leaders must be aware of both the goals of the policy and how those affected by the policy are likely to perceive its intent and means of implementation.

Use of the Model

This model is presented to help readers understand the scope and variety of academic services and to assist in developing and evaluating existing or proposed services. Many programs or services have multiple purposes, targets, and methods of intervention. This framework can be used as a template for viewing academic services. In my opinion, programs and services have a greater likelihood of being effective if the purpose is clearly conceptualized and unambiguously targeted and uses the intervention strategies that are best suited for the intended purpose and for the target population.

Baxter Magolda (1999a, 1999b, 2001) offers another approach to understanding the learning process and classroom instruction. She argues that the paramount goal of higher education should be to help students achieve self-authorship. This drive for self-authorship is founded on three core assumptions: (1) knowledge is complex and socially constructed (requiring contextual knowing in her model), (2) the self is central to knowledge construction (which reflects complex intrapersonal development), and (3) expertise and authority are shared in the mutual construction of knowledge among peers, which reflects complex interpersonal development and relationships (Baxter Magolda, 2001).

From these assumptions, Baxter Magolda (1999a) postulates three principles that should guide interventions that promote student learning, both inside and outside the formal classroom. First, *validate students as knowers,* by which she means "acknowledging their capacity to hold a point of view, recognizing their current understandings, and supporting them in explaining their current views. Validation as a knower helps students view themselves as capable of learning and knowing, heightening their engagement in learning" (p. 27). Second, *situate learning in students' own experience,* which means using students' previous experience and current knowledge as the starting point, which helps create a context that students can readily understand. Third, *define learning as mutually constructed meaning,* thereby making both the instructor and the students active players in the learning enterprise. "It suggests that the teacher and students put their understandings together by exploring students' experiences and views in the context of knowledge that the teacher introduces. Together they construct knowledge that takes experience and evidence into account" (1999a, p. 28).

Designing Academic Services

Generally, students are most vulnerable and therefore open to assistance from academic services during transition periods or while anticipating transitions. Such times include when they are first entering college, selecting an academic major, seeking entry into the job market or admission to graduate school, and experiencing stress (from such situations as parental dissension, financial crises, romantic breakups, or poor academic performance). Likewise, research has clearly documented that students who are more fully involved in the college experience (inside and outside the classroom) gain greater educational benefits and are more satisfied with the collegiate experience (Astin, 1977, 1993; Kuh, Schuh, and Whitt, 1991). As Tinto's landmark research (1993) has demonstrated, students are much more likely to leave an institution prior to completing degree requirements if they fail to become integrated academically and socially into the fabric of the college or university. In other words, the more students interact and form meaningful relationships with other students and faculty and staff members, the more likely they are to persist (Mallette and Cabrera, 1991; Tinto, 1998). Stage (1989) has found that students are more likely to persist when they are either academically or socially integrated, and they are even more likely to persist when both forms of integration take place.

Integrated Approaches

Students view their institution holistically. To a large extent, they are unaware of the administrative structures of institutions, unless they run afoul of a policy or rule or if they want special treatment, such as an exception to standing policy. For many students, faculty members teach (and at some institutions do research) and everyone else does something else (exactly *what* is unclear). Consequently, distinctions between academic affairs and student affairs, assistant and full professors, or deans and vice presidents do not have much meaning for most undergraduates.

The most powerful learning environments are those that integrate the curricular and cocurricular in purposeful and meaningful ways. Terenzini, Pascarella, and Blimling (1999) have reviewed the literature on cognitive development and cocurricular involvements and have found the following:

○ Even when students' precollege academic achievement and cognitive ability levels were taken into account, academic learning was positively shaped by a number of out-of-class experiences.

○ Not all out-of-class activities, however, exerted a positive influence on students' learning. Living at home, being a member of a fraternity or sorority, working full-time, and participating in intercollegiate athletics were negatively related to cognitive gains after the first year of college.

○ Living in residence halls does not in and of itself promote positive effects. Residential arrangements, however, that are built on the "living-learning" concept, such as residential colleges, shared interests halls (such as a foreign language), and service learning-focused units appear to have a substantially greater effect on resident students.

○ "In virtually all cases where students' out-of-class experiences were found to enhance academic or cognitive learning, those experiences required, or at least afforded, opportunities for active student involvement" (p. 619).

○ The most powerful influences on student learning appear to be students' interpersonal interactions with peers and with faculty and staff members. The more isolated a student is within the institutional environment, the fewer positive effects the collegiate experience seems to have.

○ The impact of out-of-class activities appears to be cumulative rather than catalytic. That is, individual activities do not seem to have powerful influences on student learning, but, taken together, they have a substantially positive impact.

Terenzini, Pascarella, and Blimling (1999) add, "The cumulative impact . . . is even stronger when those experiences are part of coordinated and mutually supportive and reinforcing sets of programmatic and policy interventions" (p. 620).

Examples of Integrated Curricular-Cocurricular Interventions

There are many interventions that meet the criteria for promoting student learning. This section briefly describes four examples: first-year experience programs, senior year experience programs, living/learning centers, and service learning.

About twenty years ago, John Gardner, at the University of South Carolina, started what has become something of a grassroots movement to assist students entering higher education, which has become known as "first-year experience" programs. This program was designed to cut the often high rates of attrition during and following the freshman year. Barefoot (2000) summarizes the six most salient objectives shared by most first-year experience programs: "(1) increasing student-to-student interaction, (2) increasing faculty-to-student interaction, especially outside of class, (3) increasing student involvement and time on campus, (4) linking the curriculum and co-curriculum, (5) increasing academic expectations and levels of academic engagement, and (6) assisting students who have insufficient academic preparation for college" (p. 14). A number of different formats have been used with some success, such as

- Using only experienced, senior faculty members to teach the seminar, team-teaching the seminar (faculty and student affairs staff) or faculty and trained undergraduate paraprofessionals—or some other combination of the three
- Making the seminar mandatory or voluntary
- Including participation in a service activity or attendance at one or more cultural events on campus
- Having students investigate institutional resources—such as counseling assistance, the academic advising process, or recreational facilities—and then informing classmates about them
- Having a topic such as oppression or civic responsibility as the integrating theme of the seminar
- Combining the seminar as part of a learning community (having a group of students share enrollment in at least two courses)

The possibilities are limitless. If the program focuses on the objectives outlined by Barefoot (2000), this intervention should qualify as an integrated curricular-cocurricular intervention for academic services.

A more recent kind of intervention on many campuses is the senior year experience. As Gardner and Van der Veer (1998) point out, the process of completing the undergraduate experience is a period of transition for most students. The senior year experience should facilitate the integration of students' total undergraduate academic experience, provide opportunities for reflection, assist students in finding closure to this phase of their lives, and aid in the postcollege transition to the world of work or graduate school. Gardner and Van der Veer (1998) promote programmatic themes for this experience, such as:

- A capstone experience designed to assist students in synthesizing what has been learned in the major and to establish connections between general education and the liberal arts (which may include internships, theses, recitals, or final projects)
- The linking of the liberal arts and the major in an effort to demonstrate coherence for the academic experience

- The provision of leadership education and the instilling of an understanding of educated citizens' responsibility to society
- Career planning
- Job search and transition planning or application to graduate school
- Alumni development
- The development of practical skills needs after college, such as an introduction to credit and financial management
- Preparation for adult life as a spouse, partner, parent, or community and political leader. One will recall that much of this experience is directly related to a number of items on Bowen's list (1977) of the goals of higher education.

Living-learning centers may take many forms. It may involve a group of volunteers who elect to live in a residence hall that focuses on developing academic skills through in-house workshops and programs. Or it may include a faculty member in residence who coordinates with a living unit to bring other faculty members to the residence hall for informal discussions of intellectual matters, perhaps focusing on a common theme. Other living-learning concepts include having all the residents (typically freshmen) take one or more courses together (either taught in the residence halls or elsewhere on campus). Other approaches include housing together student volunteers who share a common interest in a single topic, such as the culture and language of another country or protection of the environment. Centers may also be made up of majors in a single college (for example, education or agriculture) or a particular program, such as the honors program (Grimm, 1993).

Service learning is a much-used term in higher education that can mean anything—from requiring students as part of a class to devote a few hours of service to a community agency to including service as an integral part of a course or academic program. Engstrom and Tinto (1997) define service learning as a "pedagogical strategy that encourages students to make meaningful connections between content in the classroom and real-life experiences and that strives to increase students' level of civic responsibility and concern for social justice" (p. 10). The Wingspread Conference on service learning proposed ten principles of good practice for combining service and learning. An effective and sustained program that combines service and learning

- Engages people in responsible and challenging actions for the common good

○ Provides structured opportunities for people to reflect critically on their service experience

○ Articulates clear service and learning goals for everyone involved

○ Allows for those with needs to define those needs

○ Clarifies the responsibilities of each person and organization involved

○ Matches service providers and service needs through a process that recognizes changing circumstances

○ Expects genuine, active, and sustained organizational commitment

○ Includes training, supervision, monitoring, support, recognition, and evaluation to meet service and learning goals

○ Ensures that the time commitment for service and learning is flexible, appropriate, and in the best interests of all involved

○ Is committed to program participation by and with diverse populations (Porter, Honnet, and Poulsen, 1989, quoted in Engstrom and Tinto, 1997, p. 13)

Realizing the Student-Centric Institution

Institutions that subscribe to a mission of higher education that addresses all or most of Bowen's goals can only accomplish them if they create a "seamless" educational experience for their students. "The word seamless suggests that what was once believed to be separate, distinct parts (for example, in-class and out-of-class, academic and non academic, curricular and co-curricular, or on-campus and off-campus experiences) are now of one piece, bound together so as to appear whole or continuous. In seamless learning environments, students are encouraged to take advantage of learning resources that exist both inside and outside the classroom" (Kuh, 1996, p. 136). Within a student-centric institution, faculty members, academic administrators, student affairs professionals, and the top institutional leaders each have important contributions to make. If the primary goal of the institution is to ensure a high-quality learning experience for students, then all aspects of the institution must respect the others and cooperate. Otherwise, we will remain in our "functional silos" (Marchese, 1995), and students' educational experiences will remain fragmented. There are, however, obstacles to inplementing the goal of integrated learning on many campuses.

Obstacles to Student-Centric Academic Services

Despite the extensive research that supports the benefits of integrated approaches to student learning for students, there are powerful obstacles on many campuses to the implementation of these ideas. Some of the factors weighing against this approach include

○ The general lack of recognition and reward for faculty members' involvement outside their disciplines or academic departments. For neophyte faculty members, initial promotion and tenure decisions are made within the academic department or division. Those who devote a good portion of their time to involvement with students outside the traditional classroom may have difficulty documenting their disciplinary credentials.

○ Many campuses rely heavily on part-time instructors to meet their undergraduate teaching responsibilities. These individuals (no matter how capable) are not expected to engage in extensive outside-of-class interaction with students. At institutions with a heavy reliance on a part-time faculty, a weighty burden is placed on the shoulders of a dwindling number of full-time faculty members and student affairs professionals to be involved in providing academic services to students.

○ Programs and services that cut across traditional organizational lines of authority are often suspect and vulnerable to budget cuts because they lack powerful "champions" or "patrons."

○ When financial resources become scarce, the tendency is to cut back to the "basics," which is frequently defined as offering as few courses as possible with as large an enrollment as institutional or accreditation standards permit. Involvement with integrated academic services can make a faculty member feel vulnerable.

○ Student-centric approaches are often viewed by some within the institution as coddling students and watering down academic standards. High failure or attrition rates to such individuals are evidence of academic rigor.

○ Administrators in areas such as student affairs are sometimes hesitant to become too enmeshed in areas outside their usual activities because of a fear that functional units may be transferred or that control of personnel or facilities will be redirected.

○ On many campuses, only a few high-level institutional leaders have a broad institution-wide perspective. Administrators at lower levels are generally rewarded for pursuing their somewhat narrow institutional responsibilities; moving to larger perspectives may be viewed as threatening by a variety of institutional constituencies.

These obstacles can be overcome. To do so, however, requires senior-level leadership to affirm the values of a student-centric institution, redundantly focus the institution on individual students' educational experiences, insist on both the conceptual and functional integration of curricular and cocurricular learning, establish reward systems for individuals who contribute to integrated academic services, require frequent systematic evaluations of academic services in terms of student outcomes and base decisions about allocation of resources on the evaluations, and reward collaboration across organizational boundaries. It is also important to institutionalize successful academic service programs that support the idea of a student-centric institution so that a change in leadership or financial fortunes will not wipe them out overnight.

REFERENCES

American Association for Higher Education, American College Personnel Association, and National Association of Student Personnel Administrators. *Powerful Partnerships: A Shared Responsibility for Learning.* 1998. [http://www.aahe.org/teaching/tsk_force.htm]. Feb. 25, 2002.

Arnold, K., and Kuh, G. D. "What Matters in Undergraduate Education? Mental Models, Student Learning, and Student Affairs." In E. J. Whitt (ed.), *Student Learning as Student Affairs Work: Responding to Our Imperative.* Washington, D.C.: National Association of Student Personnel Administrators, 1999.

Astin, A. W. *Four Critical Years.* San Francisco: Jossey-Bass, 1977.

Astin, A. W. *Achieving Educational Excellence: A Critical Assessment of Priorities and Practices in Higher Education.* San Francisco: Jossey-Bass, 1985.

Astin, A. W. *What Matters in College? Four Critical Years Revisited.* San Francisco: Jossey-Bass, 1993.

Barefoot, B. O. "The First-Year Experience: Are We Making It Any Better?" *About Campus,* 2000 (Jan.–Feb.), 12–18.

Baxter Magolda, M. B. *Creating Contexts for Learning and Self-Authorship: Constructive-Developmental Pedagogy.* Nashville, Tenn.: Vanderbilt University Press, 1999a.

Baxter Magolda, M. B. "Defining and Redefining Student Learning." In E. J. Whitt (ed.), *Student Learning as Student Affairs Work: Responding to Our Imperative.* Washington, D.C.: National Association of Student Personnel Administrators, 1999b.

Baxter Magolda, M. B. *Making Their Own Way: Narratives for Transforming Higher Education to Promote Self-Development.* Sterling, Va.: Stylus, 2001.

Bowen, H. R. *Investment in Learning: The Individual and Social Value of American Higher Education.* San Francisco: Jossey-Bass, 1977.

Carroll, J. "Adjuncts, Students, and E-Mail." *Chronicle of Higher Education,* Aug. 5, 2002. [http://chronicle.com/jobs/2002/08/2002080501c.htm].

Creamer, D. G., and Creamer, E. G. "Practicing Developmental Advising: Theoretical Contexts and Functional Applications." *NACADA Journal,* 1994, *14*(2), 17–24.

Elling, T. W., and Brown, S. J. "Advancing Technology and Student Affairs Practice." In R. B. Winston Jr., D. G. Creamer, and T. K. Miller (eds.), *The Professional Student Affairs Administrator: Educator, Leader, and Manager.* New York: Brunner-Routledge, 2001.

Ender, S. C., Winston, R. B., Jr., and Miller, T. K. "Academic Advising Reconsidered." In R. B. Winston Jr., T. K. Miller, S. C. Ender, T. J. Grites, and Associates, *Developmental Academic Advising: Addressing Students' Educational, Career, and Personal Needs.* San Francisco: Jossey-Bass, 1984.

Engstrom, C. M., and Tinto, V. "Working Together for Service Learning." *About Campus,* 1997 (July–Aug.), 10–15.

Gardner, J. N., and Van der Veer, G. *The Senior Year Experience: Facilitating Integration, Reflection, Closure, and Transition.* San Francisco: Jossey-Bass, 1998.

Grimm, J. C. "Residential Alternatives." In R. B. Winston Jr., S. Anchors, and Associates, *Student Housing and Residential Life: A Handbook for Professionals Committed to the Goals of Student Development.* San Francisco: Jossey-Bass, 1993.

Hage, J., and Aiken, M. *Social Change in Complex Organizations.* New York: Random House, 1970.

Hurst, J. C., and Jacobson, J. K. "Theories Underlying Students' Needs for Programs." In M. J. Barr and L. A. Keating (eds.), *Developing Effective Student Service Programs: Systematic Approaches for Practitioners.* San Francisco: Jossey-Bass, 1985.

Kuh, G. D. "Guiding Principles for Creating Seamless Learning Environments for Undergraduates." *Journal of College Student Development,* 1996, *37,* 135–148.

Kuh, G. D., Schuh, J. H., Whitt, E. J., and Associates. *Involving Colleges: Successful Approaches to Fostering Student Learning and Development Outside the Classroom.* San Francisco: Jossey-Bass, 1991.

Mallette, B. I., and Cabrera, A. "Determinants of Withdrawal Behavior: An Exploratory Study." *Review of Higher Education,* 1991, *20,* 163–179.

Marchese, T. "It's the System, Stupid." *Change,* 1995, *27*(3), 4.

Morrill, W. H., Hurst, J. C., and Oetting, E. R. "A Conceptual Model of Intervention Strategies." In W. H. Morrill, J. C. Hurst, E. R. Oetting, and Associates. *Dimensions of Intervention for Student Development.* New York: Wiley, 1980.

Pascarella, E. T., and Terenzini, P. T. *How College Affects Students: Findings and Insights from Twenty Years of Research.* San Francisco: Jossey-Bass, 1991.

Sandel, R. H., and Sydow, D. "Advances—and a Retreat—in Student Retention." *Inquiry,* 1997, *1*(1), 61–70. [http://www.br.cc.va.us/vcca/illsydow.html]. Aug. 24, 2001.

Stage, F. "Reciprocal Effects Between the Academic and Social Integration of College Students." *Research in Higher Education,* 1989, *30,* 517–530.

Strange, C. C. "Developmental Impacts of Campus Living Environments." In R. B. Winston, S. Anchors, and Associates, *Student Housing and Residential Life: A Handbook for Professionals Committed to Student Development Goals.* San Francisco: Jossey-Bass, 1993.

Strange, C. C., and Banning, J. H. *Educating by Design: Creating Campus Learning Environments That Work.* San Francisco: Jossey-Bass, 2001.

Terenzini, P. T., Pascarella, E. T., and Blimling, G. S. "Students' Out-of-Class Experiences and Their Influence on Learning and Cognitive Development: A Literature Review." *Journal of College Student Development,* 1999, *40,* 610–623.

Tinto, V. *Leaving College: Rethinking the Causes and Cures of Student Attrition.* (2nd ed.) Chicago: University of Chicago Press, 1993.

Tinto, V. "Colleges as Communities: Taking Research on Student Persistence Seriously." *Review of Higher Education,* 1998, *21,* 167–177.

Winston, R. B., Jr. "Counseling and Advising." In S. R. Komives, D. D. Woodard Jr., and Associates, *Student Services: Handbook for the Profession.* (3rd ed.) San Francisco: Jossey-Bass, 1996.

Winston, R. B., Jr. "Counseling and Helping Skills." In S. R. Komives, D. D. Woodard Jr., and Associates, *Student Services: Handbook for the Profession.* (4th ed.) San Francisco: Jossey-Bass, 2003.

2

STUDENT ACADEMIC SERVICES

MODELS, CURRENT PRACTICES, AND TRENDS

Darlene Burnett, Diana Oblinger

HIGH-QUALITY STUDENT SERVICES are essential to higher education. The manner in which an institution provides support and services—from admissions and enrollment to financial aid, advising, and career planning—can distinguish an outstanding student experience from one that is mediocre, frustrating, or discouraging. Student services also reflect the importance an institution places on its students, on and off campus. Whether the experience is expedient and pleasant or drawn out and difficult has a direct impact on students'—and the public's—perception of the institution.

Like most other aspects of higher education, support services are undergoing a transformation. External and internal forces are having an impact. In the digital age, the traditional model of support services has some inherent limitations.

Based on changes in the expectations of our students, the tools available, and the competitive nature of higher education, there are new ways to look at the organizational, physical, and technical structure for service delivery. Alternative processes and technology exist that enable institutions to provide services that are more responsive, individualized, and integrated.

This chapter describes some of the current models in student support services. These models rely on multiple components: conceptual changes, physical facilities, staff skills, organizational structure, and Web-based resources. Also included are some vignettes of specific practices and institutions. Although not all models apply to every institution, common themes emerge.

Conceptual Changes

A major theme that is emerging in the delivery of services is the critical shift in the way institutions interact with students. More and more, institutions are moving service delivery away from a "transactional" focus and toward a "relational" one, with an emphasis on creating a positive experience and building a lasting relationship with the student (Pine and Gilmore, 1999).

A number of conceptual changes are associated with new models for support services, such as taking a student perspective. Rather than viewing processes from an internal organizational viewpoint, some institutions mobilize teams of faculty and staff members to "become a student for a day." Other institutions actively involve students in planning. This key conceptual change involves not only perspective but also the language used, from internal "bursar" to external "payments."

Institutions adopting new models are also taking a student-centered approach. They structure organizations, processes, facilities, and Web sites with the student as the prime customer. These services maximize convenience, accessibility, and consistency, and they treat the student in a holistic manner.

Another conceptual change is to focus on the experience. Many institutions have studied and adopted the philosophy and methods of commercial entities such as theme parks and successful retail stores to better understand how to make student experiences with the university outstanding. Although they often seem intangible, student experiences can be transformational, changing values and behaviors and having long-term implications for achievement and loyalty. This may translate to better retention and higher yield, two important institutional measurements.

For institutions to make the continual changes necessary to deliver outstanding services, they must be learning-centered, making learning an ongoing part of everyone's job. This requires a sustained investment in training, education, and mentoring. It also involves creating an environment of feedback, accountability, and empowerment.

A major conceptual change for organizations that have adopted new models deals with ownership. Rather than problems belonging to someone else or "not being in my job description," organizational cultures are moving toward accepting ownership and responsibility for resolving student issues. These trends are evident in the approaches James Madison University and Purdue University Calumet have taken to student services.

James Madison University

James Madison University (JMU) has established an intentional, integrated, experiential, action learning framework that has yielded positive results for the students and the institution alike. The campuswide initiative coordinates programs and services based on cohesive educational goals. The student success model at JMU is focused on

- Learning: providing programs and services that help students take responsibility for making educational transitions into, through, and beyond the university
- Service: making services available and accessible to students and removing obstacles that prevent students from accomplishing their educational goals
- Convenience: integrating functions in a central location so that students can make the best possible use of their time on campus
- Options: providing opportunities for students to conduct transactions with the university in the manner best suited to them
- Good advice: providing students with appropriate information, directions, and suggestions based on their educational needs
- Time: saving time and making the best use of time for students and staff members

To create conditions conducive to student success at JMU, the institution is pursuing three strategies. The first, *place improvement*, involves changing facilities to make them more accessible, flexible, and integrated in the delivery of programs and services. The second, *process improvement*, deals with studying, mapping, and changing processes to make them more efficient and effective for all university constituents. Finally, *performance improvement* integrates action learning, student learning, performance improvement strategies, instructional systems design, and continuous learning to improve the capacity of staff members to assist students in making educational transitions and developing self-motivation and responsibility.

JMU provides a model for the conceptual changes to staff learning. The mission for their Student Success Initiative is to "design, implement, coordinate and assess learning opportunities (programs and services) that help students complete seamless transitions into, through, and out of the institution; that develop the student's motivation to learn, engage in educationally purposeful activities, and assume self-responsibility; that are cohesive, supportive, and organized around common educational goals" (quoted in Foucar-Szocki, Harris, Larson, and Mitchell, 2002; Burnett and Oblinger, 2002).

Purdue University Calumet

Likewise, Purdue University Calumet rethought the enrollment process after discovering a number of flaws in its system. Between 10 and 12 percent of students' registrations were canceled for nonpayment at the start of each semester, only half of those reregistered, and even then, the university didn't receive state support because those students weren't enrolled by the deadline (the end of the first week of classes). Further study showed that about 20 percent of the students receiving financial aid did not know their next step in the enrollment process, even though they had just spoken with a financial aid clerk.

Taking a student-centered approach, Purdue University Calumet aimed to ease the process for students, making the steps clear and helping students develop positive relationships with faculty and staff members. The Enrollment Services Center consolidated a number of services, including registration, financial aid, and student accounts. The staff has received cross-training to answer a variety of questions from students. And several functions have been automated, allowing students to handle some requests themselves (Pellicciotti, Agosto-Severa, Bishel, and McGuinness, 2002; Burnett and Oblinger, 2002).

Redesign and Integration

One goal that is common to most best practice institutions is the redesign and integration of multiple functions. Many institutions have engaged in a process of redesign and integration. In many cases, the starting point is a reexamination of student needs, which results in conceptual changes as well as redesign, alternative facilities, and Web-based applications.

The focus of integration efforts can be different, centering on process, policy, organization, facilities, technology, or a combination of all of these (see Table 2.1).

Procedural consolidation. In procedural consolidation, a review and assessment of policies and procedures across all units is typically conducted. The goal is to ensure consistency of information, policies, and practices. Part of the process is to identify where and when students encounter inconsistencies in service and address those inconsistencies.

Table 2.1. Achieving Integration

Focus	Implementation Option	Considerations
Process/policy	Procedural consolidation	Appropriate when there is the need to ensure that students don't encounter inconsistencies in policy and practices as they receive services delivered by departments or offices that may report to different divisions.
Organization	Organizational consolidation	Appropriate for all campuses that believe that coordination between departments and offices that provide student services is hindered by virtue of their organizational structures and boundaries.
	Cross-training of staff	Appropriate for all campuses that believe staff members should be empowered to provide answers to basic questions outside their functional areas. The degree to which a formal program of cross-training is implemented may vary.
Facilities	One-stop centers	Appropriate for campuses that have or are planning a facility that can accommodate multiple service units.
Technology	Integrated information systems or portals	Appropriate for campuses whose student information data are currently scattered among different Web sites and housed on multiple systems.

Source: *University of North Carolina and PricewaterhouseCoopers, 1999.*

Organizational restructuring. Organizational restructuring brings together related departments or business units under one manager or division so that student services can be coordinated more easily. Many times, a redefinition of roles is necessary as organizations merge or restructure.

The cross-training of staff members. Cross-training gives staff members the tools they need to answer questions, locate resources, and make referrals for a broad range of topics. It also allows them to move beyond their organizational unit or area of expertise into broader areas. Cross-training staff members is a key way to reduce the runaround that students sometimes experience by being directed to multiple offices in search of information.

One-stop centers. One-stop centers house multiple functions in one or more centralized locations where students can transact campus business.

Typically, one-stop centers are staffed by cross-trained generalists who are supported by specialists. Staff members integrate information from multiple departments to solve students' problems.

Integrated information systems. Ensuring that information for students is consistent, integrated, and current can be achieved by integrating some or all of the information systems, databases, and shadow systems that contain student data. Care must be taken to ensure that data are accurate, updated regularly, and not entered multiple times. The Web is the typical delivery vehicle for integrated information systems, which may be used by students and staff and faculty members (Oblinger, 2002).

Following are three universities that have recently sought to redesign their processes and integrate various services.

Tufts University

Tufts University has engaged in an extensive redesign and integration process. The objectives of its student services project were threefold. The first was to create a student-centered environment by developing a collaborative process and organization. This would contribute to academic experiences that would emphasize interpersonal interaction and create a cohesive and distinctive undergraduate and graduate program.

The second objective was to create a physical and electronic environment to maximize student services. The staff would find ways to maximize technology to deliver self-service and core student services for all campus constituencies. Plus, students would receive value-adding, in-person assistance at just one location.

The third objective was to continually improve service by integrating human, process, and technological elements in the best interest of students and educational priorities, as measured by ongoing evaluation and input from students and faculty and staff members.

According to dean of academic services and student affairs Kristine Dillon (2002), Tufts must continue to respond to changes in society and student needs. With its new Student Services Center, Tufts has rededicated itself to strengthening student support and, in particular, faculty-student advising. For the first time, student administrative services will be integrated and performed in one place. Class teams, composed of class deans, career services, and the staff of the dean of students, will provide holistic support for students. All of this will be underpinned by new technology designed to speed access to academic and financial information (see Figure 2.1).

Figure 2.1. Tufts University's Student Portfolio Contact Records

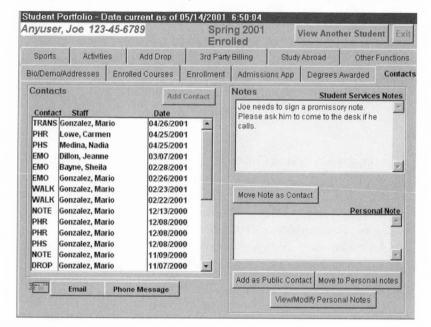

Johnson County Community College

Before beginning the design of a new student services building, Johnson County Community College (JCCC) initiated a planning process that involved more than 150 staff members, students, and faculty members. It addressed three vital questions: What do we value in student services? What are the processes we need to change to support our values? What does a building or facility need to look like to support these processes and procedures?

JCCC discovered that what its constituents said really mattered wasn't reflected in the way it did business. The major activities within student services revolved around the enrollment process, and the staff spent more energy registering students than assisting them in the life/education/career planning process.

As a result, JCCC has completely redesigned its processes. The focus is now on student development and learning, with an emphasis on engagement at the initial contact. The question is no longer Do you want to enroll? but rather Where are you headed, and how can we help you get started toward your goal? The new Student Success Center has become the entry point for all JCCC students. The center is an interactive, student-friendly area and is supported by staff members who have completed an extensive 240-hour training program. The goal is to encourage students to become active participants in their own educational and career planning processes. JCCC's student services model, LIFELINES, is targeted to a student's learning continuum for life, education, and career (Ramos and Vallandingham, 1999). (See Figure 2.2.)

Boston College

One of the goals of Boston College (BC) was to provide self-service capability to students via the Web and to create an organization to complement that self-service delivery mode. BC began by looking at how students were supported and specifically at how it could provide both better self-service and in-person service delivery.

BC formed a team from staff members in the major student service areas and charged them with examining all existing organizational boundaries and redesigning the work. Reviewing student financial services, for example, revealed the inconvenience of sending students from one office to another to track down a Stafford Loan problem. Simply putting loan information on the Web would not cause this problem to go away.

Figure 2.2. Johnson County Community College Lifelines

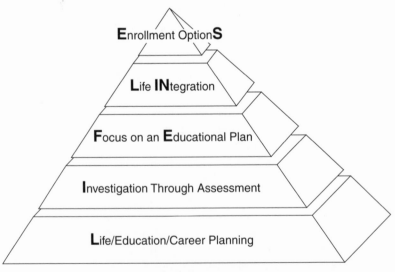

Note: *Courtesy of Dennis Day, JCCC.*

The team created a new design in which all services were part of a continuous process that began with an admissions inquiry and ended with a student's graduation. This high-level design structured services from the perspective of the student or parent and identified technology requirements for the new processes, both for "front-end" services (using the Web to transact business) and for "back-end" processing (providing the staff with better access to information and preparing for an electronic records system). Under this plan, the new Office of Student Services manages all the academic and financial processes relating to students and their families (Kreinbring, 2002).

Physical Facilities

The offices that support students are often scattered across campus, which can be inconvenient, confusing, and time-consuming for students, especially new students. And information is often inconsistent from office to office. Staff members and students equally feel frustrations from this environment—students because of the runaround and staff members because they aren't able to help students efficiently. For institutions seeking to create a single physical location where most student issues can be resolved, one-stop centers have become the dominant model.

One-stop center design and organization depend not only on the culture and values of each institution but also on the degree to which groups can work across the organizational lines. Services often integrated in a one-stop center may include but are not limited to

- Admissions
- Enrollment questions
- Registration
- Course add or drop
- Financial aid
- Bursar
- Housing
- Academic advising
- Career services
- Disability services
- Referrals to a specialist

No two institutions offer the same combination of services; one-stop centers are as individual as the institutions that implement them.

University of Delaware

At the University of Delaware, student services were scattered in offices in several buildings, making it inconvenient for students and confusing for those new to the campus. However, in 1991, a centrally located building that could house at least the front counter activities of the student services units became available. The university chose to go one step further in improving services: not only would it move functions to a single location, it would also modify the process to improve the overall delivery of student services. This was the genesis of Delaware's one-stop facility for student services, which provides registration, financial aid, billing and collection, student ID, housing, and meal plan services.

Key to the center's success was the cross-training of staff members, which allows one person to handle a variety of routine questions and transactions. The plan initially called for 70 percent of services to be handled by self-service means (using computer kiosks and self-service information), 20 percent by generalists in the center, and 10 percent by specialists located on site or elsewhere on campus. However, the goal quickly became to see how many services could be delivered by dealing with one (or no) service provider (Hollowell, 1999).

Staffing Changes

A critical component in one-stop centers and in most student support initiatives is the knowledge and skills of the staff. Student services staff members often have a long history with the institution, and change—particularly if not communicated clearly—can be stressful. Even when staff members are accepting of change, they may need additional skills to fill new roles. It may be advisable to create a staffing model that details the responsibilities of each individual in the new organization. A staffing model is the first step in assessing the strengths, weaknesses, and interests of the current staff.

It is critical that the staff members who will provide integrated services receive ongoing training and support that allows them to master new domains of knowledge as well as develop additional communication and problem-solving skills. The skills needed by the staff in one-stop centers go beyond transactional knowledge and incorporate a breadth of services. Training in customer service should also be provided because of the new emphasis on "service" attitude. The new skills will increase employees' empowerment, accountability, and responsibility.

The Generalist

Based on process redesign work, many institutions determined that they needed new job descriptions for the staff delivering new services. The term *generalist* is often used to describe the new service position. One could describe a generalist as having knowledge and responsibilities a mile wide, whereas a specialist's are a mile deep. As the one-stop source for information, the generalist interacts with students at the counter and handles a variety of job functions that have traditionally been included in such areas as admissions, registration, financial aid, and the bursar's office. The generalist is considered the front office person, whereas the specialist remains in the back office and interacts with students who have complex or exceptional cases. As employees become generalists, managers are required to make similar changes, broadening their existing areas of expertise.

At Seton Hall University, for example, the emergence of the one-stop concept for student services meant that employees needed to know *everything.* Customer-oriented work was found to be very different from the specialized, internal process-focused jobs staff members had previously held. In addition to good interpersonal and communication skills, generalists needed sufficient cross-functional skills and knowledge to handle about 80 percent of the ordinary business that comes their way (Green, Jefferis, Kleinman, 2002). The large amount of customer contact results in a very demanding job, whether the job is at a main service counter or in a call center. Not only do generalists provide services in one-stop physical centers, they also help create and staff call support centers and live chats, two outgrowths of the expanded services being offered on the Web. It is just as critical to provide the same level of expertise for a student electing to initiate services via the Web as it is for a student requesting services at a service desk. Both interactions should focus on providing a positive experience and creating a relationship.

Cybrarians

One concern expressed by institutions as they begin to create service delivery over the Web involves ownership of data and keeping information up-to-date and consistent. As a result, a new job has emerged—the "cybrarian." The cybrarian at the University at Buffalo, for example, has responsibility for the coordination, organization, classification, and review of content. She also monitors and maintains content by checking for broken links and by contacting content owners when replacement Web pages are needed. A content life cycle may be established for information that has a known life span or is time-sensitive (such as late spring interest in summer jobs or commencement details). The cybrarian works with various information stakeholders, including student service professionals and faculty members (Wright, Gorman, and Bernstein, 2002).

Human Resources Changes

In some institutions, the knowledge base and interpersonal skills that generalists need are those of a more highly skilled position. Often, this results in new position classifications, sometimes with higher pay rates. For example, at Seton Hall University, the position of enrollment services representative was reclassified and now has a higher level of pay than do previous student service positions.

Both the new generalist position and the administrators who manage them require different job skills that should be discussed with human resources. Skills and attributes that should be taken into account in the process of defining new job and skill requirements include customer service skills, a desire to help people, cross-functional skills for a variety of areas, the ability to teach students how to "serve themselves" if desired, and the ability to use information technology systems.

At the University of North Carolina at Greensboro (UNCG), changes to student services necessitated a change in staff training. In addition to ongoing training that focuses on the skills mentioned earlier, UNCG holds a one-day "immersion" experience for employees hired in the previous quarter. In a test environment, staff members apply for admission and financial aid, meet with an adviser, register for classes, receive a bill, are canceled for nonpayment, and have to reregister. This experience not only helps employees understand the process and potential obstacles a student might encounter but also helps them bond with the university (Black, 2002).

Web-Based Systems

Most students have significant experience with the Web. As a result, they bring a set of expectations to the services they receive from academic institutions. When using Web services, students typically expect to

○ Navigate the admissions process and become oriented to the campus

○ Identify financing options and manage financial obligations

○ Receive development, counseling, and decision guidance

○ Augment educational pursuits through extracurricular activities

○ Apply for basic services, including housing, meals, and health care

○ Access resources to support emotional well-being and cultural growth

○ Find internships, co-op programs, and full-time professional employment

○ Prepare to continue their education in graduate or professional programs and continuing education (University of North Carolina and PricewaterhouseCoopers, 1999)

Levels of Web Development

Many institutions now post significant amounts of student-related information on the Web. As institutions become more sophisticated in their use of the Web, they often move through four generations of Web development.

Generation I—content only. At this level, information is organized by the internal institutional view, and terminology and structures mirror the organizational silos. Information is posted to the Web and is read only. This information may cover such areas as admissions (scholarships, financial aid, housing, and orientation), academics (the calendar, courses, distance education, advising, enrollment and transcripts), school and department news (events, daily headlines, and calendars), and services and organizations (campus offices, student organizations, and policies).

Generation II—content within context. At this level, information is organized by customer segments and still reflects the institutional view and internal language. Information is posted to the Web and most is read only. Some transactions are available through multiple systems. The segments may include prospective students (admissions, orientation, and campus visits), current students (registration, financial aid, housing, and advising), family (safety, events, visiting the campus, and costs), alumni and friends (directories, the calendar, and giving), visitors and the community (children, community, and corporations), faculty (teaching, research, advising, and support services), and the staff (human resources, support services, and forms).

Generation III—Web portals. At this level, information is organized around individual needs and preferences, and the site provides students with the ability to perform transactions unique to personal data. The Web integrates multiple systems, providing one common ID and authentication. Features of this level include customization, personalization (information and data relating to the individual student), community (ability to connect with others with similar interests), and transactions (application, registration, personal data updates, billing/payment, housing assignments, clearing of holds, financial awards status, and student accounts balances).

Generation IV—high touch and high tech. At this level, information is organized in a personalized manner. Interactions go beyond the transaction and deliver an intangible experience that both engages and involves the student at an emotional level that helps build the relationship with the institution. Examples of this level of Web services include orientation step-by-step guides (Brigham Young University freshman adviser), decision-making guides (University of Minnesota financial aid estimator), personalized recommendations (Kent State *Collage* portfolio, University at Buffalo MyUB portal), proactive communications (UC Gateways portfolio, University of Texas Austin UT-Direct, Louisiana State University PAWS), enhanced community (UC Gateways), and real-time interactions with the institution (University of North Carolina Greensboro, Live Chat, Seton Hall University Call Support Center).

The Web has the potential to deliver services in a new and holistic manner. These redesigned, integrated services can create a positive experience and build lifelong relationships with students and other groups. As with physical one-stop centers, achieving truly student-centered services on the Web requires that processes be redesigned, with the student experience being the primary focus (Burnett, 2002).

Web-Based Services

High-touch, high-tech, Web-based services cover many areas. The following examples demonstrate how processes have been redesigned and services integrated to deliver personalized student-centered services on the Web.

LIVE CHAT SESSIONS. To support the services on the Web, several institutions have live chats that provide generalist services to students. Live chats are more common on commercial Web sites, such as that of retailer Lands' End, where a knowledgeable generalist is available when the customer needs help. UNCG was one of the first institutions to offer live chats with UNCG on-line personal assistants (see Figure 2.3). Weber State University is using live chats as part of its delivery of service for distance education students. It is critical that institutions consider the real-time support needs of students using Web services. Live Chats are an innovative way of delivering high touch in a very high-tech environment.

Figure 2.3. UNCG Online Personal Assistants

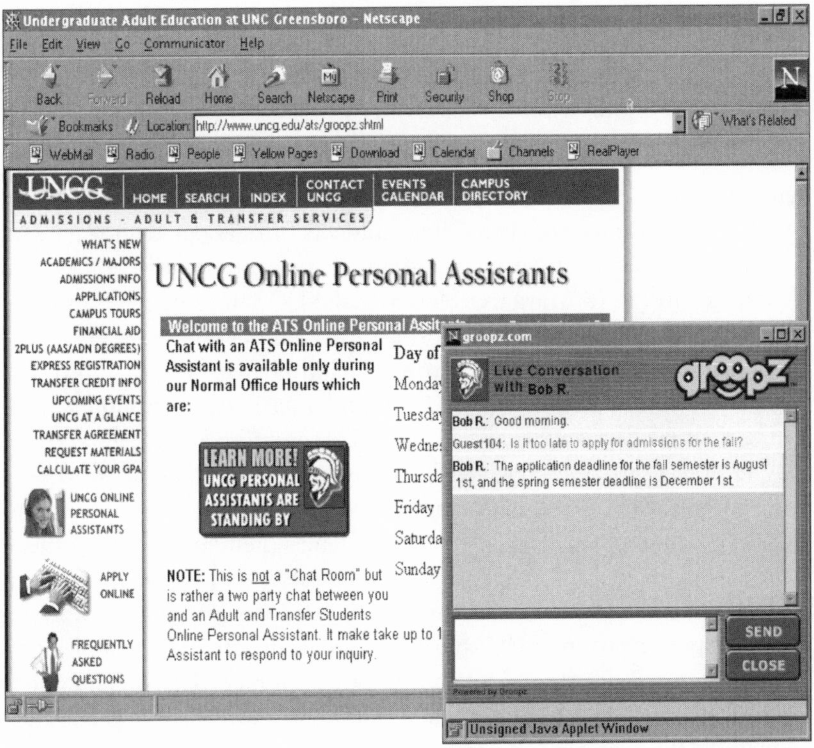

Note: *Courtesy of James Black, University of North Carolina at Greensboro.*

CALL SUPPORT CENTERS. Boston College, Seton Hall University, and Southern Alberta Institute of Technology are three institutions that have initiated call support centers. As more student services are delivered via the Web, it becomes critical that the same principles for in-person interaction apply to the Web, keeping service delivery student-centered and focused on the experience. Without those principles, Web services will not develop the student's relationship with the institution. One of the most common mistakes made during the redesign process is not to include all of the methods a student would use to contact an institution. Institutions commonly put an e-mail address on the Web site for contact, but, often, they haven't thought through the processes or the time required of staff members to support the new venue. Seton Hall University has created a customer response team that addresses all students who come to the university for assistance via phone, Web, or mail, or in person. Call support centers are critical when institutions achieve the higher thresholds for Web-services interaction. Many institutions have a target of 90 percent of service interactions taking place on the Web.

PROSPECTIVE STUDENT OUTREACH. The University of California System created a student portfolio, UC Gateways, to provide underrepresented middle school and high school students throughout California with an interactive tool that would encourage them as prospective college students. According to Margaret Heisel of the UC Office of the President, UC Gateways provides the platform for middle school and high school students to track their progress toward eligibility for admission to UC institutions on-line. Students build a multidimensional portfolio incorporating their academic work, extracurricular activities, and career and college interests into a single Web-based system. The academic portfolio incorporates the courses (with grades) that students have taken or plan to take at the middle and high school levels. The system includes the official list of all the courses that satisfy UC's admissions requirements for each high school. The activities portfolio accommodates information about a student's participation in UC-sponsored program activities, school-based activities, community service, and work experience. The social capital portfolio allows the students to take a series of on-line surveys designed to help them understand their personalities, interests, and learning styles. UC Gateways targets students as early as middle high to help establish a relationship with the university (Thompson, Heisel, and Caras, 2002). UC Gateways is an Internet-based tool that enables middle school and high school students to chart their progress toward higher education, at the same time, allowing university campuses and schools to guide and advise students appropriately (see Figure 2.4).

ADMISSIONS. In August 1998, the University of Texas at Austin debuted its Web site—www.applytexas.org. The site was built to provide a Web-based application for admission to any of the thirty-five public higher education institutions in Texas. The Web site is adaptive, based on the specific admissions rules, policies, and procedures of each institution. Applications are sent to the target institution over the Web. The site delivered more than thirty-nine thousand applications in its initial year, and in just three years, it tripled the number of applications to 120,000 for Fall 2001 (Stanfield and Rickard, n.d.).

Figure 2.4. UC Gateways

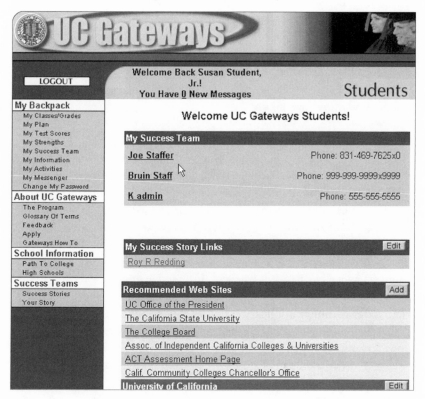

WEB-BASED ADVISING. Brigham Young University (BYU) takes Web-based advising to the next level with its program, aimed at freshmen. The goal of the Freshman Advising and Registration system is to help freshmen see "the big picture" and define and plan their educational goals. The primary features include a biographical summary of the student (including the major selected, advisement information, and the assigned registration time), five sequential steps to complete the advising process and registration, course options for each required area—based on the student's declared major and preparation, the option to change the major until the first day of school, a preliminary assessment for language proficiency, and instructions for making the transition from advising to registration.

In order to make the Freshman Advising and Registration system a reality, BYU established a required general education core to be completed during the first two semesters, simplified and combined information on freshman advising, orientation, registration, and other services into a single mailing, personalized academic advising, and provided a comprehensive, systems-integrated, Web-based freshman advising and registration system (Kramer, Peterson, Webb, and Esplin, 2002). At BYU, the Academic Information Management (AIM) System provides the Freshman Planning: First Semester Worksheet, which helps students with step-by-step "how to" directions, decision-making guides, and personalized recommendations (see Figure 2.5).

FINANCIAL PLANNING TOOLS. The College Foundation of North Carolina (www.cfnc.org) is designed to help students prepare for college and understand their financial alternatives. The hope is that by providing better information about college and its costs, North Carolina will increase its admissions rate. The site includes pages such as "You Can Afford College—We'll Show You How," where users can explore why college is important, its affordability, and how financial aid works. There are sections tailored to parents and students (high school, middle school, and younger) as well as to adult learners. Interactive applications allow users to estimate college costs based on the type of institution and the student's birth date. A similar application makes it possible to calculate the value of a college savings account based on user input for monthly contributions, estimated annual rate of return, and so on. The site also provides links to North Carolina colleges and universities, making it easy for users to get more information that is specific on the college of their choice. The College Foundation of North Carolina Web site provides a variety of information to help students and parents plan for college (see Figure 2.6).

BYU has developed a Web tool to help students and their families plan for college. The tool, "Financial Path to Graduation" (http://financialaid.byu .edu/bulletin2003/finPath.php), goes beyond discussion of loans and financial resources to help students analyze their career aspirations, determine the amount of debt they are considering incurring, the cost of borrowing money, and the impact of the debt on their future earnings. To support the Web services, BYU has trained financial aid officers as financial planners who can better help students and parents plan their educational finances.

Specific steps of the process include developing an academic path to graduation, estimating the total cost of attending college, identifying resources, determining the difference between costs and resources, evaluating the option of student debt, analyzing the cost of borrowing, and committing to a financial path to graduation. By following these steps, students are able to evaluate the total cost of their college education, evaluate the resources necessary to offset the costs, determine their unmet need, and determine the student loan debt that they can realistically assume.

Figure 2.5. Brigham Young University's AIM System

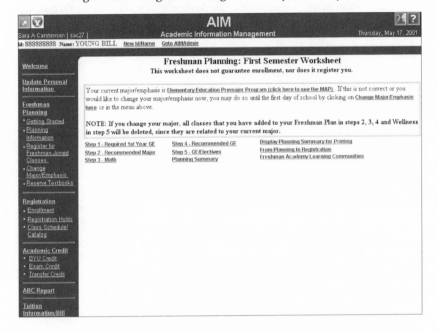

Figure 2.6. College Foundation of North Carolina

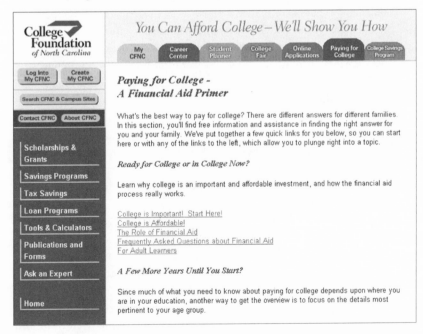

E-PORTFOLIOS. e-Portfolios are an emerging category of Web service. An example is Kent State University's *Collage*. *Collage* is a dynamic, Web-based learning tool designed to guide students in documenting their experiences at Kent State University and in their community through a reflective and meaningful process. *Collage* actively engages students in gaining self-awareness by helping them identify skills, interests, values, and goals. *Collage* gives students a fresh appreciation of how their collegiate and life experiences can help them realize their academic, professional, and personal aspirations. It provides them with a number of exercises to better know themselves and to help them plan their career (see Figure 2.7).

According to Charles Rickard, associate vice president for enrollment services:

> *Collage* serves as a road map or template for students who often desire, and require, the guidance provided by a structured yet self-designed plan to foster goal setting. Students begin on-line portfolios as freshmen and develop *Collages* throughout their undergraduate career, rather than waiting until their senior year to remember and record prior experiences and recognize, perhaps too late, unrealized opportunities and resources. Approved university faculty and staff members who assist students in the developmental process can also view *Collages* to broaden their understanding of students rather than rely on paper records. Students learn how to reflect on and articulate skills and experiences that will allow them to effectively develop a competitive résumé on which they document their well-rounded experiences and careful planning. Students easily link from *Collage* to the Career Services Center on-line registration system for connecting with employers seeking to hire Kent State graduates (Stanfield and Rickard, n.d.).

ALUMNI SERVICES. An increasing number of institutions are providing on-line services to alumni as a part of their effort to maintain a strong lifetime connection with their graduates. Beyond newsletters, fundraising campaigns, and vacation packages, institutions are offering lifetime e-mail accounts, on-line education, and career networks.

Stanford University is one institution that provides Web-based services for alumni. After logging on, users have access to e-mail and a host of services (such as downloading screensavers that show Stanford images) and information (such as news and current events). Users are invited to connect with other alumni, browse a list of alumni entrepreneurs, nominate or apply to serve as a trustee or adviser to the university, and so on. Another feature, the Stanford career network, available to alumni and students, is a searchable database of alumni volunteers who make themselves available to other alumni and students for information and career networking.

Portals

Portals represent the latest evolution of the Web. According to Howard Strauss (2002), portals "will turn the Web from an institution-centric repository of information and applications to a dynamic user-centric collection of everything useful to a particular person in a particular role. Instead of a single home page that proclaims identically to all who visit how grand the institution is, portals will give nearly every user a customized, personalizable, unique Web page" (p. 33).

A portal is much more than a home page. In a sense, portals are frameworks for personalized home pages that allow students to selectively view only the information that is useful and valuable to them. A student portal might include a personalized course schedule, this week's campus sports scores, today's weather, and an assignment calendar.

Figure 2.7. Kent State's Collage e-Portfolio

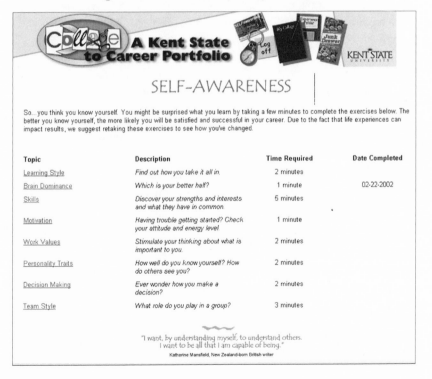

SELF-AWARENESS

So... you think you know yourself. You might be surprised what you learn by taking a few minutes to complete the exercises below. The better you know yourself, the more likely you will be satisfied and successful in your career. Due to the fact that life experiences can impact results, we suggest retaking these exercises to see how you've changed.

Topic	Description	Time Required	Date Completed
Learning Style	Find out how you take it all in.	2 minutes	
Brain Dominance	Which is your better half?	1 minute	02-22-2002
Skills	Discover your strengths and interests and what they have in common.	5 minutes	
Motivation	Having trouble getting started? Check your attitude and energy level.	1 minute	
Work Values	Stimulate your thinking about what is important to you.	2 minutes	
Personality Traits	How well do you know yourself? How do others see you?	2 minutes	
Decision Making	Ever wonder how you make a decision?	2 minutes	
Team Style	What role do you play in a group?	3 minutes	

"I want, by understanding myself, to understand others.
I want to be all that I am capable of being."
Katherine Mansfield, New Zealand-born British writer

Portals are sensitive to the role of the user. For example, a currently enrolled student needs information different from the information a prospective student needs; freshmen often need information that is distinct from that needed by graduating seniors. Sometimes called "vertical education portals," these portals deliver organization-specific information in a user-centric way. When the user logs on, a customized page is generated, tailored to that person's specific needs and requests. Based on the log-on, the portal "knows" where the cohort individual belongs (for example, student, faculty, or staff), the user's role (for example, student council member or employee), as well as specific information related to that person's identity and role (for example, when the next assignment is due or the amount of financial aid awarded) (Strauss, 2002).

Just as with one-stop centers, portals represent a shift in institutional philosophy from an institution-centric view to one that is user-centered. Often associated with this shift is the definition of an institution-wide portal strategy and Web strategy. Such user-centric approaches require that information be organized and structured in different ways, based on how individuals want to interact with the institution (Gleason, 2002).

Numerous institutions have created portals. Even though portals are customized and personalized, a number of functions are popular components (such as library tools, on-line forms, personal links, registration, student accounts, course guides, financial aid, scholarships, grades, drop/add functions, course searches, and housing).

UNIVERSITY AT BUFFALO. The University at Buffalo created MyUB as a personalized service portal for students. The goals behind the creation of MyUB include

○ Making it easy for students to find the information they need by providing an easy-to-navigate, personalized, and customizable portal

○ Creating a portal that coaches students from orientation through graduation, growing and changing with them

○ Building awareness of available virtual and physical campus services; encouraging the use of MyUB as a proactive university communication tool

○ Having a tool that helps retain students through learner communities (Wright, Gorman, and Bernstein, 2002)

The vision for the University at Buffalo Web portal, MyUB, was to create a personalized service portal that decreased the distance between students, faculty members, and student services and increased the sense of community (see Figure 2.8).

Figure 2.8. University of Buffalo's Web Portal

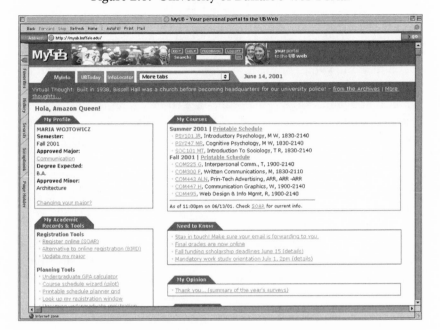

LOUISIANA STATE UNIVERSITY. Louisiana State University (LSU) established Personal Access Web Services (PAWS) as its digital infrastructure, with the overall goal of making technology relevant to students and faculty and staff members by giving them direct access to data. PAWS delivers sixty thousand unique intranet portals to members of the LSU community. Each portal is customized to reflect the individual's relationship to the university and dynamically adapts in real time when this relationship changes. Services accessed through the PAWS portal include enterprise, workgroup, and personal applications that meet the specific administrative, academic, and research needs of each user. Some of the most widely used PAWS applications include e-mail, registration, degree audit, grade and financial aid inquiry, library collections, and course tools.

PAWS, a secure site, facilitates connections between people, organizations, and content by providing databases of phone numbers and e-mail as well as on-line discussion groups. It also serves as a one-stop shop for university services that organizes information in such a way as to avoid information overload (Hadden, Borne, and Ethridge, 2002).

Conclusion

First-rate student services can serve as a differentiator in attracting and retaining students as well as a means of enhancing the institution's relationship with the student. How services are delivered often depends on the culture and values of the institution. A small liberal arts institution that focuses on personal attention might wish to start with a one-stop center that enhances the value of the face-to-face interactions, with an emphasis on the experience and relationship. A large public university might need to deliver more of its services via the Web, working to be both high tech and high touch.

In either case, the essential elements are ensuring that the services delivered are designed from the students' perspective, that the services delivered are student-centered, that there is a focus on the experience, and that a learning-centered environment is created.

There is no single correct model to which all institutions must adhere to deliver student services. Each institution must ask a series of questions, consider its unique culture and values, and then create services—in person and on-line—that bring the best possible value to learners.

REFERENCES

Black, J. "Creating a Student-Centered Culture." In D. Burnett and D. Oblinger (eds.), *Innovation in Student Services: Planning for Models Blending High/Touch and High/Tech*. Ann Arbor, Mich.: Society for College and University Planning, 2002.

Burnett, D. J. "Innovation Student Services: Best Practices and Process Innovation Models and Trends." In D. Burnett and D. Oblinger (eds.), *Innovation in Student Services: Planning for Models Blending High/Touch and High/Tech*. Ann Arbor, Mich.: Society for College and University Planning, 2002.

Burnett, D., and Oblinger, D. (eds.). *Innovation in Student Services: Planning for Models Blending High/Touch and High/Tech*. Ann Arbor, Mich.: Society for College and University Planning, 2002.

Dillon, K. E. "Student Service Standards: Valuing Contact." In D. Burnett and D. Oblinger (eds.), *Innovation in Student Services: Planning for Models Blending High/Touch and High/Tech*. Ann Arbor, Mich.: Society for College and University Planning, 2002.

Foucar-Szocki, D., Harris, L., Larson, R., and Mitchell, R. "Layers of Learning: Planning and Promoting Performance Improvements and Action Learning." In D. Burnett and D. Oblinger (eds.), *Innovation in Student Services:*

Planning for Models Blending High/Touch and High/Tech. Ann Arbor, Mich.: Society for College and University Planning, 2002.

Gleason, B. "Portal Technology Opportunities, Obstacles and Options: A View from Boston College." In *Web Portals and Higher Education: Technologies to Make IT Personal,* by R. Katz and Associates. San Francisco: Jossey-Bass, 2002.

Green, T., Jefferis, N., and Kleinman, R. "Change Beyond Change: The Next Iteration of Enrollment Services." In D. Burnett and D. Oblinger (eds.), *Innovation in Student Services: Planning for Models Blending High/Touch and High/Tech.* Ann Arbor, Mich.: Society for College and University Planning, 2002.

Hadden, C. M., Borne, J. C., and Ethridge, R. R. "Building the Digital Infrastructure Necessary to Transform University Services." In D. Burnett and D. Oblinger (eds.), *Innovation in Student Services: Planning for Models Blending High/Touch and High/Tech.* Ann Arbor, Mich.: Society for College and University Planning, 2002.

Hollowell, D. "Student Services: A Broad View." In M. Beede and D. Burnett (eds.), *Planning for Student Services: Best Practices for the 21st Century.* Ann Arbor, Mich.: Society for College and University Planning, 1999.

Kramer, G. L., Peterson, E. D., Webb, C., and Esplin, P. "A Web-Based Freshman Advising and Registration System." In D. Burnett and D. Oblinger (eds.), *Innovation in Student Services: Planning for Models Blending High/Touch and High/Tech.* Ann Arbor, Mich.: Society for College and University Planning, 2002.

Kreinbring, J. "Living with Change: The Implementation and Beyond." In D. Burnett and D. Oblinger (eds.), *Innovation in Student Services: Planning for Models Blending High/Touch and High/Tech.* Ann Arbor, Mich.: Society for College and University Planning, 2002.

Oblinger, D. "Integrated Services." Unpublished, 2002.

Pellicciotti, B., Agosto-Severa, A., Bishel, M. A., and McGuinness, P. "Integrated Service Delivery: In Person and on the Web." In D. Burnett and D. Oblinger (eds.), *Innovation in Student Services: Planning for Models Blending High/Touch and High/Tech.* Ann Arbor, Mich.: Society for College and University Planning, 2002.

Pine, B. J., II, and Gilmore, J. *The Experience Economy.* Boston: Harvard Business School Press, 1999.

Ramos, M., and Vallandingham, D. "Student Development Model as the Core to Student Success." In M. Beede and D. Burnett (eds.), *Planning for Student Services: Best Practices for the 21st Century.* Ann Arbor., Mich.: Society for College and University Planning, 1999.

Stanfield, V. S., and Rickard, C. "IBM Innovation in Student Services—Best Practice 2000." Unpublished abstract, n.d.

Strauss, H. "All About Web Portals: A Home Page Doth Not a Portal Make." In R. Katz and Associates (eds.), *Web Portals and Higher Education: Technologies to Make IT Personal.* San Francisco: Jossey-Bass, 2002.

Thompson, J. M., Heisel, M., and Caras, L. "Empowering Students Through Portfolio Management." In D. Burnett and D. Oblinger (eds.), *Innovation in Student Services: Planning for Models Blending High/Touch and High/Tech.* Ann Arbor, Mich.: Society for College and University Planning, 2002.

University of North Carolina and PricewaterhouseCoopers. *Information Technology Strategy Project: Services for Students Strategy.* Chapel Hill: University of North Carolina, 1999.

Wright, R. M., Gorman, J., and Bernstein, R. "MyUB: A Personalized Service Portal." In D. Burnett and D. Oblinger (eds.), *Innovation in Student Services: Planning for Models Blending High/Touch and High/Tech.* Ann Arbor, Mich.: Society for College and University Planning, 2002.

3

THE INTERRELATIONSHIP OF STUDENT ACADEMIC SERVICES

John H. Schuh

STUDENT ACADEMIC SERVICES have the potential to play an important role in developing comprehensive enrollment management and retention strategies for colleges and universities and can contribute to the growth and development of students. Here, student academic services refer to such institutional activities and entities as registration, academic advising, various student support programs—including tutoring services, financial aid, and the other services that are the focus of this volume. This chapter is designed to discuss how these services can contribute to an enrollment strategy, facilitate student learning, and add to an institution's vitality.

This chapter is organized around several themes. First, it examines contemporary thinking about institutional retention efforts. Second, it takes a look at current strategies that have been developed to link academic and student affairs into cohesive approaches for enhancing the experiences of students. Third, the chapter looks at how selected student services and programs can contribute to student growth and learning. Finally, it concludes with recommendations for practice, using an example of institutional collaboration.

A Theoretical Framework for Student Retention

Student retention has been an important topic in postsecondary education for at least the past two decades. For example, the report *Involvement in Learning* (Study Group on the Conditions of Excellence in American

Higher Education, 1984) points out that "only half of the students who start college with the intention of earning a bachelor's degree actually attain this goal" (p. 8). More recent reports have made similar observations. The Wingspread Group (1993) has also expressed concern about retention and graduation rates. Its report observes that "half of those students entering college full-time do not have a degree within five years" (p. 5). Even more recent data indicate that graduation rates are disappointing at many institutions (American College Testing Program, 1999).

In spite of the discouraging data about retention, models and recommendations have been developed that speak to how graduation rates can be improved. Perhaps the most significant of these was the study conducted by Tinto (1987), who concluded that "the more frequent and rewarding interactions are between students and the other members of the institution, the more likely are individuals to stay. When those contacts occur outside the formal domains of the institution and are seen as warm, receptive, and wide-ranging in character, that is, not restricted solely to the formalities of academic work, individuals are not only more likely to stay but [are] also more likely to grow both intellectually and socially while staying" (p. 150).

Other reports that have been released concerning retention (for example, Dey and Hurtado, 1999; Bowen and Bok, 1998; Berger and Braxton, 1998; Murtaugh, Burns, and Schuster, 1999) tend to reinforce the conclusions expanded upon by Tinto (1998). Kuh, Douglas, Lund, and Ramin-Gyurnek (1994, p. 71) put the commentary in other terms when they indicate that "'fitting in,' academic success and (making/having) friends" are at the center of the mental model of students. Regardless of the exact language, Tinto's model has provided an excellent framework for thinking about how institutions can address the challenge of improving graduation rates.

Using Tinto's work (1987) as a framework, then, student academic services can affect student retention rates by providing a point of contact for students with the academic aspect of their institution. With some creative thinking, these services can also facilitate students' interactions with each other. Before discussing ways of operationalizing retention efforts, the role of student affairs in student learning and the recent call for student affairs to collaborate with academic affairs and the faculty need to be explained.

Linking Academic and Student Affairs

The emergence of student personnel services is a relatively recent phenomenon on the higher education scene (Nuss, 1996). Nevertheless, student affairs has an important role on many campuses. From her vantage point as a president, Hughes (1999) points out, "When students exit the classroom, learning is not a spigot that may be turned off suddenly; likewise, when students participate in intentional learning activities organized by student affairs, learning does not cease because the program or activity ends" (p. 254).

Hughes (1999) takes both student affairs and academic affairs to task for artificially dividing student life, and, consequently, student learning. "The problem with the academic sector is that it devalues incidental learning," she observes. On the other hand, she suggests that "the problem with student affairs is that it hesitates to overtly affiliate with intentional learning" (p. 254). Her view is that academic and student affairs need to work together to enhance the overall experience of college students.

But the work of linking academic and student affairs is not one-sided. Faculty members should also understand the powerful influence collaborative relationships can have on student learning. Kuh (2001–2002), for example, recommends that faculty members "design cooperative learning activities that extend beyond the class hour and classroom building to bring students together to work on meaningful tasks elsewhere on the campus in order to encourage the continued adoption of academic norms and values and resist what are often anti-intellectual influences of their primary peer reference groups" (p. 35). In recent years, consequently, emerging trends in student affairs and academic affairs are to seek collaboration and identify ways the various units under these administrative structures can contribute to student learning.

Three Reports on Collaboration

Several reports have been released in recent years that speak directly to student learning and academic and student affairs collaboration. The next section highlights three of them.

THE STUDENT LEARNING IMPERATIVE. Student affairs practitioners and scholars realized that the issues identified in the various calls for reform, such as those previously cited, would require different ways of conceptualizing their work. One of their responses was to produce the document "The Student Learning Imperative" (American College Personnel Association, 1996). This document states, "Student affairs professionals must seize the present moment by affirming student learning and personal development as the primary goals of undergraduate education" (p. 121). The document recommends that "student affairs professionals collaborate with other institutional agents and agencies to promote student learning and personal development" (p. 120). The student learning imperative set the stage for other initiatives to refocus student affairs practice on student learning and development.

PRINCIPLES OF GOOD PRACTICE FOR STUDENT AFFAIRS. The document "Principles of Good Practice for Student Affairs" (Blimling and Whitt, 1997) put the circumstances in which student affairs finds itself this way: "We can pursue a course that engages us in the central mission of our institutions or retreat to the margins in the hope that we will avoid the inconvenience of change." The authors maintain that good practice in student affairs "forges educational partnerships that advance student learning." This means that student learning would be the organizing principle for establishing partnerships and that "partners for learning include faculty, academic administrators, staff and others inside and outside the institution." Among the practices suggested were that (1) student affairs staff members work with others outside student affairs to develop programs that increase student learning and that (2) faculty members, students, and student affairs staffers try to link academic programs with out-of-class learning experiences. In theory, this made perfect sense. But for the student affairs staff to link with the faculty would require the involvement of organizations other than those designed to serve student affairs practitioners. That occurred when the student affairs organizations formed a partnership with the American Association for Higher Education.

POWERFUL PARTNERSHIPS. The joint report published by the American Association for Higher Education (2002), the American College Personnel Association, and the National Association of Student Personnel Administrators, *Powerful Partnerships: A Shared Responsibility for Learning,* criticized the state of higher education, saying, "Most people on campus contribute less effectively to the development of students' understanding than they might." One of its principles was that "rich learning experiences and environments require and enable students to *make connections* (italics in original) through classroom experiences integrated with purposeful activities outside of class."

This document has the potential to have a profound effect on higher education, and it can provide direction by outlining how institutions and their members ought to behave. The document states clearly and unequivocally that student learning occurs in virtually all places on campus, potentially at all times. As a consequence, all members of an institution have a responsibility to devise ways of making sure that students' experiences are complementary and organized around a commitment to learning. The report adds, "Faculty and staff collaborators (should) design learning experiences that make explicit the relationships among parts of the curriculum and between the curriculum and other aspects of the collegiate experience."

In the context of student academic services, wonderful potential exists for a wide variety of learning experiences to emerge from this guidance. Examples are collaboration between the student financial aid unit (a student academic service) and courses in personal finance, or collaboration between tutoring services and academic support services for students.

Promoting Partnerships

Contemporary practice in student affairs includes partnerships with academic affairs designed to enhance and promote student learning. In this section, principles are identified that can guide practice in collaborative efforts involving student academic services.

Because student academic services often straddle major administrative units, at times being located in student affairs but at other times being assigned to academic affairs, administrative leaders for these groups need to be nimble in working across organizational lines. Schroeder (2001) indicates that competing perspectives have limited the ability of various units to work together. He calls for a new collaborative culture on college campuses. A way to start the process is to think in terms of one goal: How can students be best served so that they will graduate? This is not a novel idea. Masterson (1998) points out that "academic departments and student affairs units exist on our campuses so that students can learn. The learning objectives may differ from office to office, but learning remains at the core" (p. 3). When student learning is at the heart of activities in both academic and student affairs, relationships can be developed to better help students.

From a student perspective, the location of units that provide academic services on an organizational chart is of little importance. What is more important is that the distinct parts of a college or university are "of one piece, bound together so as to appear whole or continuous" (Kuh, 1996, p. 136). Students are served best when services, programs, and learning opportunities are linked so that they can be accessed easily and build on one another, resulting in a robust learning environment for students.

Kuh (1996) identifies a set of six principles that create seamless learning environments for students: (1) generating enthusiasm for institutional renewal, (2) creating a common vision of learning (3), developing a common language, (4) fostering collaboration and cross-functional dialogue,

(5) examining the influence of student cultures on student learning, and (6) focusing on systemic change. In the end, he indicates that mergers between academic and student affairs would be "sensible" at some institutions, but in other situations, having two distinct organizations makes more sense. He concludes that "all these components are needed if faculty and staff are to inspire and motivate students to integrate their classroom and out-of-class experiences, and to get faculty, staff and students to see their institution—and their collective experiences—as a connected whole" (p. 146).

Hirsch and Burack (2001) have identified a number of issues as points of contact between academic and student affairs. These can be used to initiate conversations between members of the two units. Instead of emphasizing the differences between academic and student affairs, these issues suggest shared concerns, problems, and challenges. Included in their set is an increasing interest in assessment, problems in understanding and applying technology, an effort to address the needs of a changing student population, a desire to deal with complex problems related to retention, and concern about how best to offer a coherent general education experience for students. To these, an increasing emphasis on student learning could be added. These points of common concern can form the basis for collaboration between academic and student services.

Engstrom and Tinto (2000) provide a number of suggestions for promoting collaborative relationships. Among these are having senior institutional leaders work together and call for collaboration, developing institution-wide task forces and design teams, initiating faculty and staff development programs, and building an infrastructure to support collaborative activities. Put into practice, these principles can provide an environment where collaboration that will enhance student learning can occur.

Suppose College X decides it wants to establish a residential learning community for a newly recruited group of students. Following the suggestions of Engstrom and Tinto (2000), the senior academic and student affairs administrators issue a joint statement indicating their interest in the project and asking key leaders to help develop the program. A task force cochaired by the dean of undergraduate academic programs and the dean of students then takes on the assignment of developing the learning community. A sequence of workshops are then offered for staff and faculty members who serve on the committee. Funds are provided for the staff to support the committee's work. The resulting learning community then has two permanent cochairs appointed from the task force—one from the student affairs unit and one a faculty member, who provide leadership for the community as it begins its operations. This simple example illustrates how collaborative activities can be developed following these principles.

Schroeder (1999) has identified several barriers to partnerships, the most significant of which is when the organizational culture of higher education does not encourage nor reward collaboration. He adds that "major obstacles to collaboration are fundamental differences in core assumptions and mental models exhibited by various campus constituencies" (p. 139). If various constituencies cannot agree on the value of the out-of-class experience, or if they wonder if their institutions might be better served if some students were "weeded out," then collaborating to enhance the student learning experience may not move past the conceptual stage. Leadership on the part of both academic and student affairs is required to chart institutional goals and identify specific objectives related to students.

Promising Examples of Partnerships

The good news is that a number of institutions have successfully established academic and student affairs partnerships, resulting in enhanced student learning. Several examples are included in this section that describe possible approaches.

LEARNING COMMUNITIES. Lenning and Ebbers (1999) have identified numerous examples of learning communities on college campuses. From their point of view, a learning community is an "intentionally developed community that will promote and maximize learning" (p. 8). They see a number of approaches to making learning communities work. Those developed around a curricular theme may include coordinated studies, such as having a cohort of students who take courses together (Potter, 1999). Other learning communities use students' residence as the organizing property, where they live together and take certain courses together. Lenning and Ebbers (1999) identify other forms of learning communities and conclude that these arrangements have enjoyed tremendous success in retaining students. They add that "it is clear that well-designed and -crafted cooperative and collaborative learning experiences within learning communities—as well as the existence and makeup of the learning communities themselves—greatly benefit both students and faculty" (p. 60).

Learning communities don't require a residential component. Warner and Dishner (1997), for example, describe a learning community for adult students—being defined as students twenty-one years of age or older. This program involves linked classes, specialized advisement, and personal counseling for a group of twenty-eight students. The authors say that students and faculty members reported great satisfaction with this program.

RESIDENTIAL PROGRAMS. Various forms of specialized residential arrangements have been available to students for many years, but the recent emphasis on student learning has resulted in recasting these arrangements. The living/learning center, which includes such features as students taking classes together, students interacting frequently with faculty members, cultural events and faculty lectures occurring in the residential facility, and classes being taught in the residence hall seems to be especially effective (Pascarella, Terenzini, and Blimling, 1994). Students who live in this form of housing are likely to perform better academically and are more likely to persist according to Pascarella, Terenzini, and Blimling (1994). To achieve this form of living experience, housing administrators, student affairs staffers, faculty members, student academic services units such as the registrar's office, and academic advisers must collaborate. Commitment to improving the students' experiences is necessary from the start. Reflecting on Tinto's elements for student success (1987), the living/learning center concept provides for the development of close student relationships and encourages student contact with faculty members outside the classroom. As a consequence of this experience, as Pascarella, Terenzini, and Blimling have found, students are more likely to persist to graduation.

Pike (1999) reports on the effects of living in a residential learning community (RLC), compared with living in a traditional residence hall (TRH). He says that RLCs "are designed to create environments that promote greater student involvement, improved faculty-student interaction, and a more supportive peer environment. They are also designed to assist students in integrating diverse curricular and cocurricular experiences" (pp. 270–271, citing Astin, 1993; Schroeder, 1994; Schroeder and Hurst, 1996). Pike (1999) reports that "students in RLCs had significantly higher levels of involvement, interaction and integration, and gains than did students in TRHs" (p. 280).

SERVICE LEARNING. According to Engstrom and Tinto (1997), "service learning is a powerful pedagogical strategy that encourages students to make meaningful connections between content in the classroom and real-life experiences and that strives to increase students' levels of civic responsibility and concern for social justice" (p. 10). Service learning is a programmatic development on many campuses that has been very successful. Eyler and Giles (1999) indicate that "service-learning should include a balance between service to the community and academic learning" (p. 4). They add, "Any program that attempts to link academic study with service can be characterized as service-learning" (p. 5). Astin and Sax (1998) studied the effects of service learning on 3,450 students from forty-two institutions of higher education and reported that service learning had a positive influence for all thirty-five outcome measures included in their study. They note that "participation in volunteer service during the undergraduate years enhanced the student's academic development, civic responsibility, and life skills" (p. 255). Bean and Eaton (2001) agree with this conclusion: "There seems to be ample evidence that service-learning programs offer opportunities for the kind of psychological growth that leads to increased academic and social integration" (p. 79).

Enos and Troppe (1996) have identified a number of examples of how to integrate service learning into the curriculum. They cite a wide range of institutions, from research universities to community colleges, that have integrated service learning into their curriculum. They point out that "service learning is by no means a panacea, but it does offer opportunities to fulfill important educational and service missions through its incorporation into the curriculum" (p. 181).

Organizing a service learning program requires a great deal of collaboration between the faculty, the student affairs staff, and academic student services. Rue (1996, p. 250) points out that "the costs of failing to coordinate efforts are compelling." The various elements of the institution that are involved in service learning programs need to agree on program goals, how to achieve them, who will handle various aspects of the program, and how the program will be evaluated. Faculty members will have to design course goals and ways of measuring learning. Student affairs staff members typically identify sites for service activities and provide assistance in the delivery of learning experiences. Academic student services provide an infrastructure for the experiences to be offered, including such elements as registration for the course(s), advising students to participate in these experiences, and providing logistical support when needed. Service learning programs have been successful student experiences for the same reasons that learning communities and living/learning centers have been successful: they provide an opportunity for students to connect with each other and for a special relationship to develop between students and faculty members. Student satisfaction increases, retention rates improve, and the institution benefits in immeasurable ways.

How Student Academic Services Can Enhance the Student Experience

We will now address how specific student academic services can work in partnerships with other institutional units to improve student experiences. Many of these units will be discussed in greater detail elsewhere in this book. Typically, the collaboration will be between student academic services and student services, but in other cases the partnership may involve faculty members. Tinto's retention model—as was the case in the previous examples, complemented by a commitment to student learning—continues to be the organizing framework for these collaborations.

Admissions

Typically, the first formal point of contact prospective students have at a college or university is with the admissions office. Admissions offices provide information to prospective students, arrange campus visits, conduct tours of facilities, and provide in-depth information to prospective students about the resources and assets of the institution. The Admissions staff can play an important role in introducing prospective students to the values of the institution (see Kuh, Schuh, and Whitt, 1991).

Being admitted is the first step in the process that culminates in students graduating from college. Braxton and McClendon (2001–2002) conclude that recruitment activities also have an influence on the persistence of enrolled students, so that the retention process actually begins with recruitment. Conceiving of their role in this way, admissions officers should work closely with academic advisers in providing appropriate academic experiences for new students, be they first-year students or transfers. Academic advisers can answer questions about appropriate courses for new students from admissions officers. Most important, admissions officers can provide a point of contact for students. New students will probably know few, if any, members of the campus community, and admissions officers can serve as a point of contact until students are connected with their academic adviser.

Orientation

The first intensive interaction between newly admitted students and the institution is orientation. Whether this occurs in the summer before enrollment or just before classes begin, orientation provides students with another important point of contact with the institution and begins the process by which they are connected to other students. Collaboration between orientation planners and academic advisers can yield individual and group meetings designed to provide information to students about general education requirements, any admission requirements for specific majors, and how to choose courses.

Pascarella, Terenzini, and Wolfle (1986) have found that participating in orientation has an indirect effect on persistence, so these activities need to be planned seriously by institutions and taken seriously by those who deliver them to students. Pascarella and Terenzini (1991), conclude that "orientation interventions linked with stronger direct effects on persistence tend to be longer in duration and more comprehensive in scope (freshman seminars or orientation courses). Nevertheless, even short, prefreshman orientations may exert a positive indirect effect on student persistence" (p. 404).

At a minimum, orientation planners need to link their activities with those responsible for residence hall administration and academic advising. Working with the residence hall staff helps students receive a strong orientation to both academic and out-of-class life. These introductions should complement each other by having similar goals for students and by having coordinated schedules.

An example of collaboration is reported in Boudreau and Kromrey's report (1994) on the effects of participation in a first-year orientation course on academic performance and retention. In this course, teachers and administrators from across the institution acted as unpaid course instructors. Analysis indicated that students who took the course were more likely to earn better grades and persist than those who did not take the course. House and Kuchynka (1997) found similar results in an analysis of the effects of an orientation course for first-year students in the health sciences. In this course, student affairs staffers were involved in the development of the course and an assessment of its effects.

Orientation staff members need to coordinate their work with academic advisers so that the induction process for students is as seamless as possible. This allows students to begin their relationship with their advisers and receive a careful, thorough introduction to the various components of the institution. Whether orientation is part of student affairs or academic affairs, working with other components of the institution will help students make important first connections to the collegiate life.

Academic Advising

As students complete orientation, they may have their first contact with their academic adviser. At some institutions, advisers are part of the support staff of the institution, whereas at others, paraprofessionals may advise students (see Ender and Newton, 2000); elsewhere, the faculty may advise students. Variations on these models reflect institutional needs and history and are explained in detail by Reinarz (2000). Regardless of who does the students' advising, these people play a critical role in the retention of students (see McGillin, 2000). From the perspective of Tinto's model (1987), academic advisers can be an important link in the student's integration with the academic side of the institution.

Academic advisers should help develop students' relationships with the teaching faculty (Upcraft and Stephens, 2000). This is especially important when professional academic advisers provide primary advising services to students. Upcraft and Stephens (2000) observe that "advisors can provide teaching faculty with valuable information about today's students, while teaching faculty can help advisors better understand the unique classroom challenges they present" (p. 81).

Kern and Engels (1996) report on a deliberate attempt to improve academic services in the business college at a large, metropolitan university. The dean proposed this change and sought assistance from the faculty in the college of education. The consequence of the collaboration was to add new staff members, enrich in-service training for academic advisers, and place greater emphasis on the professional involvement of the advising center staff. The authors report that the collaboration yielded "a vision, concept, goals and a plan of action for developmental advising" (p. 96). New ideas have been implemented, and students and staff members have responded positively to this collaboration.

Collaboration with the faculty is just one of several partnerships that academic advisers can develop. Academic advisers can develop other partnerships that can facilitate the overall goal of helping students succeed by taking a holistic approach to providing the best plan to help students achieve their academic goals. Among these are relationships with career services (McCalla-Wriggins, 2000), residence hall staff (King, 2000), multicultural efforts, first-year experience programs, capstone programs, and service learning (Gordon, 2000).

Financial Aid

Financial aid is becoming an increasingly important component of the college experience as students and their parents face growing challenges in paying for higher education (see Fossey and Bateman, 1998; National Center for Education Statistics, 2000; National Center for Education Statistics, 2001). As a consequence, financial aid officers need to work carefully with the admissions staff in the recruitment process of new students, as well as with many elements of the campus community, to provide opportunities for students to defray some of the cost of attendance.

Financial aid at some institutions is a student service, whereas at other institutions it might be part of an enrollment management unit that could be part of academic affairs or might even report directly to the senior officer of the institution (Coomes, 1996). Regardless of where financial aid is located organizationally, it touches many units in institutions of higher education, particularly through campus work programs.

The questions of whether students work, where students work, and how much they work have a major influence on their educational experiences (see National Center for Education Statistics, 1998). As a consequence, it is crucial for institutions to develop strategies to limit and target student work in such a way as to facilitate persistence. A comprehensive program suggests that financial aid staff members and business officers work closely with academic advisers and faculty members so that students can be guided into work programs that will facilitate persistence. Working full-time and working off campus take time away from the academic experience, so institutions should develop strategies to encourage part-time work on campus, since this activity is, according to Astin, "positively associated with attainment of a bachelor's degree and with virtually all areas of cognitive and affective growth" (Astin, 1993, p. 388).

Academic departments should develop ways for students to connect with faculty members as part-time research assistants or by working in other, similar positions. Besides the obvious monetary benefit to students, the relationships that develop can help students become integrated into the academic community. Such opportunities are made possible by the collaborative efforts of the financial aid office, academic advisers, and academic departments.

Gordon (2000) emphasizes how valuable these relationships will be in the future when she asserts that "the need for coordination and collaboration among the organizational components of our campuses has never been greater. Collaborative efforts are being encouraged across many campuses today and will continue because of pressures for higher education reform" (p. 390).

Creating a Collaborative Approach

Central City Metropolitan University (CCMU) is an institution that had services for students located in a number of administrative units spread throughout the institution. Such academic service units as the registrar's office, admissions, international student programs, and financial aid were located in the student affairs units. Academic advising, however, was located in the various colleges of the university. Adding to the complexity was that services for returning students, students who had not declared a major, and new student orientation were located in a student affairs division other than where the enrollment management units were. And finally, the controller's office was located in the Division of Business Affairs and Finance, further complicating the coordination of activities.

CCMU hit its enrollment peak in 1989, but shortly thereafter, its enrollment declined. Many reasons were offered for this decline, including a robust local economy, the relatively poor location of the institution (bordered on two sides by areas with substantial criminal activity), and aggressive recruiting by the other institutions in the local area. What was clear was that the uncoordinated student academic services did not make it easy for students to enroll in the institution.

CCMU senior leaders decided that far better coordination was needed at the operations level of the university. The vice presidents and president had mapped out a coordinated approach to dealing with enrollment issues, but at the level where services were offered, the units still went their own way. The senior leaders then decided it was time to bring people together to coordinate their activities and provide an improved set of services for students.

An associate vice president who had experience in virtually all the areas of the university was chosen to lead a group—called the Academic Operations Council—that would include the heads of all the departments listed earlier, as well as some others. The associate deans of every college were also included in the committee. The group met once each month, without fail, and devised ways to better understand each other's problems and to better collaborate to improve services to students. The registrar began talking with the computing staff about how to improve technology to make registration easier for students. Orientation staffers and the associate deans worked together to improve the academic orientation to the university. The international programs staff members were able to help other members of the committee understand some of the unique problems that international students faced with enrollment and the payment of fees.

The role of the associate vice president was to serve as the meeting convener and discussion leader and help resolve conflicts between members of the group. As discussions continued, members of the various units represented in the group not only began to understand the unique problems that the other units faced but also developed a team spirit in terms of trying to identify solutions to problems and improve services to students. The members began to realize that each unit had problems that could only be solved with the help of other units.

Over a few semesters, enrollment at CCMU began to rise—slowly, to be sure—but the trend was in the right direction. The extent to which the activities of the Academic Operations Council caused this is unknown, but this approach is consistent with operationalizing what Karl Weick (1984) has described as "small wins": "A small win is a concrete, complete, implemented outcome of moderate importance. By itself, one small win may seem unimportant. A series of wins at small but significant tasks, however, reveals a pattern that may attract allies, deter opponents, and lower resistance to subsequent proposals. Small wins are controllable opportunities that produce visible results" (p. 43). What resulted at CCMU was a change of the culture. These disparate units, all of which were competently led and providing good services to students, began to work together on a common agenda: to provide better academic services to students.

Conclusion

This chapter has been designed to discuss how student academic services can work together to enhance institutional retention efforts. Using Tinto's model (1987) as a framework, student academic services can play an integral role in helping students connect with their institution. Recent efforts by both academic and student affairs suggest that a collaborative approach to providing student services can be successful. What's more, contemporary practice indicates that anything less than a collaborative approach can have deleterious effects on students. The future suggests that student academic services units will continue to work closely with one another and that they may need to work even more collaboratively in the future. The techniques for this activity certainly are well known. All that is left is for institutions to have the will to make this happen.

REFERENCES

American Association for Higher Education, American College Personnel Association, and National Association of Student Personnel Administrators. "Powerful Partnerships: A Shared Responsibility for Learning." 1998. [http//:www.aahe.org.teaching/tsk_frce.htm]. Jan. 2002.

American College Personnel Association. "The Student Learning Imperative." *Journal of College Student Development*, 1996, *37*, 118–122.

American College Testing Program. "National College Dropout and Graduation Rates, 1998." 1999. [http//:www.act.org/news/releases/1999/04–01b99 .html]. Jan. 2002.

Astin, A. W. *What Matters in College? Four Critical Years Revisited.* San Francisco: Jossey-Bass, 1993.

Astin, A. W., and Sax, L. J. "How Undergraduates Are Affected by Service Participation." *Journal of College Student Development,* 1998, *39,* 251–263.

Bean, J. P., and Eaton, S. B. "The Psychology Underlying Successful Retention Practices." *Journal of College Student Retention,* 2001, *3,* 73–89.

Berger, J. B., and Braxton, J. M. "Revising Tinto's Interactionalist Theory of Student Departure Through Theory Elaboration: Examining the Role of Organizational Attributes in the Persistence Process." *Research in Higher Education,* 1998, *39,* 103–119.

Blimling, G., and Whitt, E. "Principles of Good Practice in Student Affairs." 1997. [http//:www.acpa.nche.edu/pgp/princple.htm]. Jan. 2002.

Boudreau, C. A., and Kromrey, J. D. "A Longitudinal Study of the Retention and Academic Performance of Participants in Freshmen Orientation Course." *Journal of College Student Development,* 1994, *35,* 444–449.

Bowen, W. G., and Bok, D. *The Shape of the River.* Princeton, N.J.: Princeton University Press, 1998.

Braxton, J. M., and McClendon, S. A. "The Fostering of Social Integration and Retention Through Institutional Practice." *Journal of College Student Retention,* 2001–2002, *3,* 57–71.

Coomes, M. D. "Student Financial Aid." In A. L. Rentz and Associates (eds.), *Student Affairs Practice in Higher Education.* (2nd ed.) Springfield, Ill.: Thomas, 1996.

Dey, E. L., and Hurtado, S. "Students, Colleges and Society: Considering the Interconnections." In P. G. Altbach, R. O. Berdahl, and P. J. Gumport (eds.), *American Higher Education in the Twenty-First Century.* Baltimore, Md.: Johns Hopkins University Press, 1999.

Ender, S. C., and Newton, F. B. *Students Helping Students: A Guide for Peer Educators on College Campuses.* San Francisco: Jossey-Bass, 2000.

Engstrom, C. M., and Tinto, V. "Working Together for Service Learning." *About Campus,* 1997, *2*(3), 10–15.

Engstrom, C. M., and Tinto, V. "Developing Partnerships with Academic Affairs to Enhance Student Learning." In M. J. Barr, M. K. Desler, and Associates (eds.), *The Handbook of Student Affairs Administration.* (2nd ed.) San Francisco: Jossey-Bass, 2000.

Enos, S. L., and Troppe, M. L. "Service-Learning in the Curriculum." In B. Jacoby and Associates (eds.), *Service-Learning in Higher Education.* San Francisco: Jossey-Bass, 1996.

Eyler, J., and Giles, D. E., Jr. *Where's the Learning in Service-Learning?* San Francisco: Jossey-Bass, 1999.

Fossey, R., and Bateman, M. (eds.). *Condemning Students to Debt.* New York: Teachers College Press, 1998.

Gordon, V. M. "Meeting the Needs of Tomorrow's Learners and Tomorrow's Workplace." In V. N. Gordon, W. R. Habley, and Associates (eds.), *Academic Advising: A Comprehensive Handbook.* San Francisco: Jossey-Bass, 2000.

Hirsch, D. J., and Burack, C. "Finding Points of Contact for Collaborative Work." In A. Kezar, D. J. Hirsch, and C. Burack (eds.), *Understanding the Role of Academic and Student Affairs Collaboration in Creating a Successful Learning Environment.* San Francisco: Jossey-Bass, 2001.

House, J. D., and Kuchynka, S. J. "The Effects of a Freshmen Orientation Course of the Achievement of Health Sciences Students." *Journal of College Student Development,* 1997, *38,* 540–541.

Hughes, M. S. "Student Affairs in the Next Century." In J. L. Bess and D. S. Webster (eds.), *Foundations of American Higher Education.* (2nd ed.) Needham Heights, Mass.: Simon & Schuster, 1999.

Kern, C. W., and Engels, D. W. "Developmental Academic Advising: A Paradigm Shift in a College of Business Administration." *Journal of College Student Development,* 1996, *37,* 95–96.

King, N. S. "Advising Students in Groups." In V. N. Gordon, W. R. Habley, and Associates, *Academic Advising: A Comprehensive Handbook.* San Francisco: Jossey-Bass, 2000.

Kuh, G. D. "Guiding Principles for Creating Seamless Learning Environments for Undergraduates." *Journal of College Student Development,* 1996, *37,* 135–148.

Kuh, G. D. "Organizational Culture and Student Persistence: Prospects and Puzzles." *Journal of College Student Retention,* 2001–2002, *3,* 23–39.

Kuh, G. D., Douglas, K. B., Lund, J. P., and Ramin-Gyurnek, J. *Student Learning Outside the Classroom: Transcending Artificial Boundaries.* ASHE-ERIC Higher Education Reports. Washington, D.C.: The George Washington University, School of Education and Human Development, 1994.

Kuh, G. D., Schuh, J. H., and Whitt, E. J. *Involving Colleges.* San Francisco: Jossey-Bass, 1991.

Lenning, O. T., and Ebbers, L. H. *The Powerful Potential of Learning Communities: Improving Education for the Future.* ASHE-ERIC Monograph Series, no. 6. Washington, D.C.: The George Washington University, Graduate School of Education and Human Development, 1999.

Masterson, J. T. "Learning Communities, the Wizard, and the Holy Grail." *AAHE Bulletin,* Apr. 1998, 1–3. [www.aahe.org/bulletin/Learning%Communities .htm]. Jan. 2002.

McCalla-Wriggins, B. "Integrating Academic Advising and Career and Life Planning." In V. N. Gordon, W. R. Habley, and Associates (eds.), *Academic Advising: A Comprehensive Handbook.* San Francisco: Jossey-Bass, 2000.

McGillin, V. A. "Current Issues in Advising Research." In V. N. Gordon, W. R. Habley, and Associates, *Academic Advising: A Comprehensive Handbook.* San Francisco: Jossey-Bass, 2000.

Murtaugh, P. A., Burns, L. D., and Schuster, J. "Predicting the Retention of University Students." *Research in Higher Education,* 1999, 40, 355–371.

National Center for Education Statistics. *Undergraduates Who Work.* (NCES 98–137). Washington, D.C.: U.S. Department of Education, 1998.

National Center for Education Statistics. *Low-Income Students: Who They Are and How They Pay for Their Education.* (NCES 2000–169). Washington, D.C.: U.S. Department of Education, 2000.

National Center for Education Statistics. *Middle Income Undergraduates: Where They Enroll and How They Pay for Their Education.* (NCES 2001–155). Washington, D.C.: U.S. Department of Education, 2001.

Nuss, E. M. "The Development of Student Affairs." In S. R. Komives, D. B. Woodard Jr., and Associates (eds.), *Student Services: A Handbook for the Profession.* (3rd ed.) San Francisco: Jossey-Bass, 1996.

Pascarella, E. T., and Terenzini, P. T. *How College Affects Students.* San Francisco: Jossey-Bass, 1991.

Pascarella, E. T., Terenzini, P. T., and Blimling, G. S. "The Impact of Residential Life on Students." In C. C. Schroeder, P. Mable, and Associates (eds.), *Realizing the Educational Potential of Residence Halls.* San Francisco: Jossey-Bass, 1994.

Pascarella, E. T., Terenzini, P. T., and Wolfle, L. "Orientation to College and Freshman Year Persistence/Withdrawal Decisions." *Journal of Higher Education,* 1986, 57, 155–175.

Pike, G. R. "The Effects of Residential Living Communities and Traditional Residential Living Arrangements on Educational Gains During the First Year of College." *Journal of College Student Development,* 1999, 40, 269–284.

Potter, D. L. "Where Powerful Partnerships Begin." *About Campus,* 1999, 4(2), 11–16.

Reinarz, A. G. "Delivering Academic Advising: Advisor Types." In V. N. Gordon, W. R. Habley, and Associates, *Academic Advising: A Comprehensive Handbook.* San Francisco: Jossey-Bass, 2000.

Rue, P. "Administering Successful Service-Learning Programs." In B. Jacoby and Associates (eds.), *Service-Learning in Higher Education: Concepts and Practices.* San Francisco: Jossey-Bass, 1996.

Schroeder, C. C. "Forging Educational Partnerships That Advance Student Learning." In G. S. Blimling, E. J. Whitt, and Associates (eds.), *Good Practice in Student Affairs: Principles to Foster Student Learning.* San Francisco: Jossey-Bass, 1999.

Schroeder, C. C. "Collaboration and Partnerships." [http://www.acpa.nche.edu/seniorscholars/trends/trends7.htm]. Sept. 2001.

Study Group on the Conditions of Excellence in American Higher Education. *Involvement in Learning: Realizing the Potential of American Higher Education.* Washington, D.C.: National Institute of Education, 1984.

Tinto, V. *Leaving College: Rethinking the Causes and Cures of Student Attrition.* Chicago: University of Chicago Press, 1987.

Tinto, V. "Colleges as Communities: Taking Research on Student Persistence Seriously." *The Review of Higher Education,* 1998, *21,* 167–177.

Upcraft, M. L., and Stephens, P. S. "Academic Advising and Today's Changing Students." In V. N. Gordon, W. R. Habley, and Associates (eds.), *Academic Advising: A Comprehensive Handbook.* San Francisco: Jossey-Bass, 2000.

Warner, C. E., and Dishner, N. L. "Creating a Learning Community for Adult Undergraduate Students." *Journal of College Student Development,* 1997, *38,* 542–543.

Weick, K. E. "Small Wins: Redefining the Scale of Social Problems." *American Psychologist,* 1984, *39*(1), 40–49.

Wingspread Group on Higher Education. *An American Imperative: Higher Expectations for Higher Education.* Racine, Wisc.: Johnson Foundation, 1993.

PART TWO

PROFILES OF STUDENT ACADEMIC SERVICES

PART ONE DESCRIBED the historical, philosophical, and contemporary context of student academic services in the higher education milieu. In this section—in Chapters Four through Twelve, we describe, from a systems perspective, individual functional units—from enrollment to graduation, which allows readers to evaluate and align their work with the overriding goal of student success. The authors in this section recommend creating convenient services, cross-training staff members, and consolidating services. The overriding emphases that stem from these chapters are on unifying staff members, simplifying services, enhancing systems, and, overall, providing students with better services. Thus, the primary objective of these chapters is to thoughtfully describe and interweave the features and functions of student academic support into a collaborative system of services. Beginning with Chapter Four on enrollment management, Jim Black illustrates this notion of collaboration as a service that focuses not only on attracting students to apply for admission to an institution but also on retaining them to graduation. This chapter concentrates on these aspects of enrollment management and their interrelationship with other student academic services. No matter how elaborate or well connected the institution's academic services, a key factor in college success, as Gary Peterson, Janet Lenz, and James Sampson Jr. advance in Chapter Five, is "the state of readiness for student learning." They propose that students should have immediate and easy access to a comprehensive and structured readiness assessment experience immediately upon entry into college. Equipping students with an individual "readiness needs" plan for how these needs can be met within the institutional environment is the focal point of this chapter. Bonita Jacobs, in Chapter Six, points out that freshmen orientation is an excellent and comprehensive colloquy designed to deliver—in addition to advising, registration, and readiness assessment—sessions on academic success, career and life goals, campus adjustment, housing, financial aid, and campus life. This chapter takes a look at new student orientation as an interconnected array of student academic services. In Chapter Seven, Louise Lonabocker and J. James Wager describe academic scheduling and registration not only as being available 24/7 but also as being a service that bridges other student academic services described in the following chapters. Building on the foundations of enrollment management, student readiness assessment, and registration services, Robert Reardon and Jill Lumsden, in Chapter Eight, connect career planning services with career placement, academic internships, academic advising, and counseling. They focus on a career portfolio program that is student-centered and uses the Internet and campus-based information systems. Such a program enables students to conceptualize university experiences as strategic learning events that, over time, will help them prepare for varied life and career roles. This chapter is fundamental and sets the stage for Chapter Nine, authored by Virginia Gordon and Gary Kramer, which is about student planning, and the integral and pervasive role of academic advising is discussed in Chapter Ten by Elizabeth Creamer, Don Creamer, and Kimberly Brown. These two chapters focus on campus venues of academic, career, and financial planning. They emphasize the importance of students achieving success with the college experience, particularly in student (graduation) planning. Thus, these two chapters emphasize a systemic and strategic view of connected student academic services.

Finally, this section concludes with the two institutional mainstays: the student academic record and student financial aid. W. W. (Tim) Washburn and Gene Priday describe, in Chapter Eleven, the student academic record, with its accompanying processes and its interrelationship with other student academic services. This chapter discusses these critical academic record functions and other related matters essential to the faculty's, departments', and students' needs for accurate, secure, and accessible academic records. In Chapter Twelve, Rita Owens and Bernie Pekala review student financial aid and scholarship services. Like some of the chapters preceding it, this chapter describes the "gold standard" philosophy of providing maximum support for students, and it concentrates on the emerging need for financial counseling and academic planning, as well as the ever-growing importance of connecting academic plans with financial resources.

4

ENROLLMENT MANAGEMENT AND CONCEPTUAL UNDERPINNINGS

Jim Black

PART TWO OF THIS VOLUME focuses primarily on the functional dimensions of student academic services. Equally important, however, is the organizational, political, and cultural context. Enrollment management provides a construct for exploring these various dimensions. One reason for applying an enrollment management construct is that it often is the organizational home for student academic services or, at the very least, an institutional driver for related change. Thus, the enrollment lens is frequently used to set priorities, measure effectiveness, and structure academic services.

If used as an organizational filter or lens rather than as an opportunity for empire building, enrollment management can make it apparent how otherwise fragmented student services can function for a common purpose. Increasing enrollment, reducing student attrition or dissatisfaction, streamlining services, enhancing student success, or gaining competitive advantage are some of the banners flown in the name of enrollment management. Alone, student academic services are often relegated to a marginal position within the institutional food chain. But when enrollment, the lifeblood of most colleges and universities, becomes a lever for improving student services, they suddenly and almost magically become central to the academic enterprise and essential to institutional vitality. Leadership support, funding, technology infrastructure, staffing, quality space, and the like become more easily obtainable. Previously impenetrable barriers seemingly melt away.

Like any relationship, the marriage between enrollment management and student academic services requires work and sacrifice. Silos must crumble, deeply ingrained organizational behaviors must be challenged, long-standing policies and practices must be scrutinized, conflict must be embraced and overcome, and the will of an individual or a department must be supplanted with the will of the institution. Indeed, it must be a relationship built on mutual trust and sacrifice for the common good. Anything less will result in a loose confederation of student academic services—each with its own mission—and no synergy or comprehensive approach to enhancing student success will emerge.

Though academic services are vital to student success, they play a relatively minor role, compared with the students themselves and the faculty. Students must be motivated, self-disciplined, organized, and committed to their pursuit of knowledge. They also must manage their time effectively, ask for help when needed, and prepare appropriately. Students must be active participants, fully engaged in the learning experience.

Partnering with students, faculty members can foster success inside and outside the classroom. They are in a unique position to guide the student from rote learning to higher learning. Faculty members assist many traditional-aged students' transition into adulthood and challenge them to consider new possibilities, broaden their thinking, and develop a passion for learning. They serve as mentors who help students imagine their future and become self-actualized.

The probability of students being successful increases significantly when the institution, the students, and the faculty work together with a common purpose. Enrollment management provides a vehicle through which this three-way partnership can be forged. From the point of admission to graduation, the enrollment manager's sole focus is student success. The astute enrollment manager recognizes the importance of this partnership and thus develops interfaces between the institution, the students, and the faculty. By strengthening existing connections between this trinity and, where necessary, proactively creating new connections, the enrollment manager engineers an environment in which student retention and satisfaction are enhanced.

Definitions for Enrollment Management

Student recruitment and retention are centerpieces of most widely accepted definitions of enrollment management. Both naturally fit within the "cradle to endowment" model commonly used to describe the enrollment continuum. However, it would be a gross oversimplification to assume that recruitment and retention fully define the construct. From its origin at Boston College in the early 1970s, enrollment management has had a strong marketing orientation. Jack Maguire, dean of admissions at Boston College during the 1970s, described this new phenomenon as having five goals: (1) marketing, (2) research and information flow, (3) market prediction and institutional response, (4) financial aid strategy, and (5) retention transfer (Henderson, 2001).

In the late 1980s and early 1990s, Don Hossler and John Bean began describing enrollment management in terms of shaping the characteristics of a student body and systematically addressing the factors that influence student choice (Hossler, Bean, and Associates, 1990). They extended the construct beyond initial enrollment to include student retention and student outcomes. Through strategies such as recruitment, financial aid, student support services, and curriculum development, Hossler and Bean believed that colleges and universities could exert influence over their enrollments (Kalsbeek, 2001).

Later in the 1990s, Michael Dolence introduced into the enrollment management lexicon such phrases as *optimal enrollments* and *within the academic context*. Dolence also brought a higher level of thinking regarding the connection between enrollment management and strategic planning. As a result of Dolence's insights, key performance indicators, also known as critical success factors, became a mainstay of the enrollment planning process on many campuses. By removing some of the mystery about what works and what does not, enrollment management gradually evolved from an art to a science. Dolence described the construct in five evolutionary stages: (1) *precognition*—there is no institutional understanding or awareness of enrollment management concepts, (2) *nominal*—enrollment management is seen as a quick fix to an enrollment problem, resulting in modest organizational changes, usually combining admissions and financial aid, (3) *structural*—the institution integrates recruitment and retention under a single plan typically directed by an enrollment management committee with some interface with the academic enterprise, (4) *tactical*—the institution begins to look outward to the external environment and collaborates with academics, and (5) *strategic*—enrollment management is aligned with the institution's goals and objectives, imbedded in institutional planning, fused with the academic enterprise, and forward-thinking (Henderson, 2001).

The Current State of Enrollment Management

Most enrollment management enterprises are wavering between Dolence's structural and tactical stages. Efforts are generally focused inward on improving processes, procedures, and policies and on increasing efficiency or effectiveness. The critical success factors are usually short-range enrollment targets, but, occasionally, campus leaders have the foresight to scan the environment for opportunities and threats and develop a long-range enrollment strategy. Constantly vacillating between being proactive and being reactive, one might call this "schizophrenic" enrollment management. In this confused state, enrollment management shows sporadic signs of becoming a comprehensive, institutionalized operating modality. Touch points between enrollment planning and academic, revenue, and facility planning are inconsistent yet are increasingly seen as valuable.

Seasoned enrollment managers recognize that this construct is most effective when it is inclusive. Integrated marketing, viral marketing, one-on-one recruiting, relationship management, intervention strategies, one-stop services, and a host of other enrollment-related initiatives do not work unless embraced by those outside of enrollment management. Unfortunately, many enrollment management divisions have not ventured out beyond their own organizational boundaries. Successful organizations have intentionally blurred the boundaries in order to integrate services and streamline processes for students.

To achieve a seamless service experience for the student, enrollment management must first align with the institution's mission and vision. For others to buy in, enrollment strategies must be linked to these broader institutional aspirations and strategic directions. More and more, enrollment leaders are actively involved with institution-wide planning. Having a voice at the table provides the politically savvy enrollment manager with opportunities to position enrollment-related requests and concerns among those on the institution's priority list. Where appropriate, an enrollment crisis can be used to create a sense of urgency (Black, 2001).

Though enrollment management is gaining prominence on college campuses, as a profession, it is still in its infancy. Henderson (2001) characterizes enrollment management as being "on the brink of a profession" (p. 3). Symbolic of the growing pangs of this maturing profession is a dearth of literature in the field—a small but growing body of research, emerging models, best practices, established ethical standards, and formal training and educational opportunities, as well as limited certification options and a high turnover rate.

The Future of Enrollment Management

Although the precise future of enrollment management is uncertain, it will not quickly fade away as so many other management fads have. Escalating competition will ensure that enrollment management does not disappear from the higher education landscape in the foreseeable future. After all, the construct is essentially an eclectic patchwork of the best practices found in business and industry.

The business sector tends to be a few years ahead of higher education, so university administrators have a glimpse into the immediate future. Some emerging trends in business and industry include mass customization, customer relationship management, partnerships with former competitors, increased outsourcing, bundled services and products, business intelligence, knowledge management, and the integration of various technologies. Many of these trends have begun to surface in the hallowed halls of academe.

Of course, it is impossible to accurately predict the future. Demographic, economic, political, social, military, and technological changes in the environment can and do alter the path we choose. Nonetheless, it is clear that the future of enrollment management and academic services will continue to be influenced by our customers—primarily the students. Students are increasingly demanding convenience. They expect easily accessible services (available 24/7), accurate and timely information, decision-making tools that guide their academic choices, flexible course offerings, relevant and stimulating course content, teaching styles that match their learning styles, and vastly enhanced marketability upon completion of a degree or certificate.

Younger students have grown up in a culture of immediacy. Hence, institutions that adopt speed itself as a strategic direction will be positioned to gain market share (Schnaar, 1998). However, speed alone is not enough. Students also expect quality, affordable costs, and customization. Customization to students relates to the delivery of course content, student services, and information. Using portal technology and course development software, a level of customization is possible.

Finally, students want greater control over their educational experience. Students will select and combine courses from multiple educational providers in order to fit their busy lifestyles and meet their educational needs. Course length, delivery mode, availability, and cost—not location—will drive their choices in the future. Program completion will be increasingly defined by mastery of skills and content rather than credit hours (Wallhaus, 2000). Consequently, academic services will become unbundled and increasingly Web-based. Blending high-tech with high-touch service solutions will be essential to meet the needs of these nomad-like students. Face-to-face interactions on campus as well as at remote locations, caller-authenticated phone assistance, Web chats, two-way video counseling or advising sessions, and on-line tutorial assistance are examples of a blended delivery model for student services.

Enrollment Management Concepts

The concepts that undergird the enrollment management construct are simple to understand yet difficult to actualize. The difficulty is possibly in the detail. Attention to even the most granular level of detail is often necessary for successful execution. Mired in the details, it is all too easy to focus on the urgent matters of the day, to the exclusion of the important, "big picture" issues. Though enrollment management is about execution, it is not about micromanagement or crisis management. Its focus is primarily on strategic management.

Another potential difficulty is the complex nature of change in enrollment management. By design, enrollment management involves taking calculated risks, solving perplexing problems, dealing with difficult people, thriving in the midst of chaos, and reaching across departmental and divisional lines. It requires campuswide investment from a legion of recruitment and retention agents. Due in part to the magnitude of effort, enrollment management is resource-hungry. Crossing sacred boundaries, challenging calcified practices and policies, or draining away scarce resources generally does not yield institutional allies. Often, the need to involve others and the work of enrollment management are at cross-purposes. The best way to relieve this natural tension, of course, is to demonstrate success. Indeed, living on the "bleeding edge" is a precarious position but one that is part of the enrollment management buzz (see Figures 4.1 and 4.2).

Figure 4.1. Enrollment Funnel

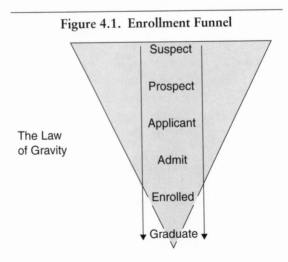

Figure 4.2. Enrollment Pyramid

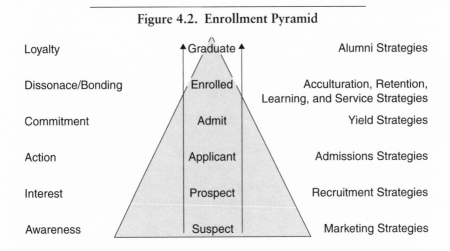

Loyalty	Graduate	Alumni Strategies
Dissonace/Bonding	Enrolled	Acculturation, Retention, Learning, and Service Strategies
Commitment	Admit	Yield Strategies
Action	Applicant	Admissions Strategies
Interest	Prospect	Recruitment Strategies
Awareness	Suspect	Marketing Strategies

Enrollment Management as a Continuum

A common myth among campus administrators is that enrollment management is simply a numbers game. Following this faulty logic, more prospects and applicants equal more newly enrolled students, and more newly enrolled students yield more graduates. Put more in at the top of the enrollment funnel, allow gravity to work, and, presto, more students emerge at the bottom of the funnel. Numbers do matter, but the people reflected in the numbers are more important. Are certain prospects more likely to enroll than others? Are some applicants a better fit with the institution than others? Are some admitted students more likely to be successful than others? Are some enrolled students predisposed to transfer or drop out? An institution's ability to gather and analyze information about individual students at various stages in the enrollment process and then use the knowledge gained to discriminate between prospects, applicants, and enrolled students will determine the degree of effectiveness in predicting and actually managing enrollments. A one-size-fits-all approach will yield minimum results and can be extremely costly.

SUSPECT LEVEL. The enrollment continuum, previously referred to as the cradle to endowment model, begins with an institution identifying potential students, who may consider enrolling. At the suspect level, potential students are at various stages of awareness—from intimate awareness of the institution's brand to some name recognition or even no awareness at all. *Marketing strategies* such as newspaper, radio, television, and Web advertising, direct-mail campaigns, guidebook listings, billboard postings, and promotional products are used to enhance visibility and therefore increase awareness. This broadcast approach to marketing tends to be the most expensive and yields the fewest results. The return on investment is difficult to measure partially because of the medium but also because of the uncertainty of the cause-and-effect relationship. Direct responses to an advertisement, for example, can be tracked by using unique phone numbers or Web addresses. However, the relationship between an individual's decision to enroll and an impression produced by an advertisement is much more difficult to assess. Time elapsed between the initial impression and the decision, the cumulative effect of contacts from the college or university, and external variables that influence the decision make direct correlations nearly impossible to derive.

PROSPECT LEVEL. At this level, a potential student has expressed some level of interest in the school by responding to a broadcast marketing effort, completing an inquiry card at a college fair, submitting test scores, or initiating a request for information in person, in writing, or via the Web, e-mail, or a phone call. The prospective student is then added to a database for further cultivation.

Recruitment strategies such as promotional and informational brochures, tailored e-mails, telecounseling calls, alumni contacts, private visits with admissions representatives, campus events, and the like are used to convert initial interest into a desire to apply for admission. Effective cultivation requires frequent and relevant contact points. These contacts are designed to convey information but, more important, they are intended to establish and develop a relationship. Recruiters and volunteers become the "trust agents" of the institution—over time, working to persuade the prospect to take action and apply.

Because the recruitment of prospects can be both labor- and cost-intensive, it is critical to distinguish between those who are most likely to enroll and those who are extremely unlikely to enroll. Efforts and resources should be allocated accordingly. A large, identifiable portion of any institution's prospect pool will never apply. Contacts for this portion should be limited to acknowledgment of their interest, a viewbook or other general information piece, an application, and any contact that does not add cost, such as e-mail. Likewise, some in the prospect pool will apply, regardless of contacts from the institution. Unlike the students who will never apply, this population should not be ignored. Cementing an already strong relationship reduces the risk that a bad experience for the student in the recruitment process will result in a change of plans. In between these two extremes exist prospects who are uncommitted and can be swayed. These are the prospects who should be the focal point of recruitment efforts. They represent the margin of success or failure in any new student enrollment campaign.

APPLICANT LEVEL. At this level, the institution must make a decision about the admissibility of the student. *Admissions strategies* are designed to meet institutional goals and predict student success. As a general rule, selection criteria are based on factors that have been statistically tied to student success at a particular institution—for example, standardized test scores, high school grades, course difficulty, or class rank. The selection process can be driven by an institutional desire to manage capacity—channeling enrollments toward programs with available capacity or, conversely, constraining enrollments in programs with little or no capacity. With recent court decisions, selection criteria are less likely to favor specific ethnic groups; nonetheless, ethnic diversity remains an imperative for most colleges and universities. Aggressive minority recruitment initiatives, the elimination of standardized test scores in the admissions review, automatic admission of students in the top percentage of their graduating class, and preference for economically disadvantaged students are but a few of the tactics adopted by institutions and states to ensure minority representation. To attract some of the best and brightest students, many selective institutions have early admissions programs. This strategy encourages students to commit early to ensure their spot in the entering class. On the opposite end of the selectivity continuum, open-admissions institutions are mainly interested in determining whether or not the applicant has met the prerequisites.

Regardless of the admissions strategy, institutional fit should always be a factor. Matters of fit begin with "truth in advertising" and may extend to admitting only those students who have a reasonable chance of succeeding. For the admissions professional, these fundamental ethical distinctions represent the difference between calculated, quota-driven sales and educational counseling. Institutional fit is not only an ethical issue but also a retention opportunity. When there is incongruence between prospective students' perceptions of an institution and the reality they find once they are enrolled, they are prone to leave. When student needs and interests are aligned with what the institution has to offer, the chance of continued enrollment is higher.

ADMIT LEVEL. *Yield strategies,* sometimes called *conversion strategies,* are aimed at increasing the psychological, emotional, and eventually financial commitment of the student to enroll. Events such as admitted student open houses, area receptions, information sessions, hosted Web chats, and orientations are common yield strategies. During these events, tactics such as issuing student IDs, providing disposable cameras to chronicle campus visits, attending classes, staying overnight with a current student, meeting an adviser, and registering for courses are used to bond the student with the institution.

At the admit level, telecounseling is also a frequently used tactic. Current student callers may discuss student life or encourage attendance at an event. Faculty volunteers may call admitted students who have indicated an interest in their respective majors to convey the strengths of the program, and, more important, to establish rapport with the student. Academic advisers may call to begin the advising process prior to orientation. The focus of the contact is typically on exploring the student's educational, career, and life goals. Alumni contacts are generally designed to congratulate the student on his or her admission and to welcome the new student to a special university or college community. The more mundane, procedural calls are completed by admissions or financial aid professionals. Contacts of this nature might include reminders of deadlines or missing documentation, a review of steps to enrolling, a scholarship offer, or simply a call to confirm continued interest in enrolling. Others, such as college presidents, academic deans, parents of current students, and coaches (contingent upon athletic recruiting restrictions), may be included in the mix of phone contacts orchestrated by the Admissions Office, but this is less prevalent.

Customization, relevancy, and relationships are among the primary ingredients needed to influence yield. Emerging tools such as vertical portals (Web content designed around the self-defined preferences and information needs of a single individual), tailored Web mail, and digital publications allow for mass customization at minimal or no cost. A few institutions have gone so far as to send personalized video messages to admitted students. One has even sent text pagers to all confirmed students in order to send periodic messages related to orientation and the semester start-up. Direct mail and e-mail are often used as tools to affect yield. However, neither is effective at this level unless highly personalized and relevant to the student's interests. Relationships are best developed and cultivated through personal interactions. Face-to-face encounters, phone contacts, e-mail dialogues, and Web chats promote relationship building.

Another yield influencer is the financial aid package. The timeliness of the aid award, the award amount, and the mix of gift aid versus loans and work study are all important factors in the student's decision-making process. Many campuses use computer modeling or financial aid leveraging to optimize the allocation of institutional dollars. The strategic use of institutional aid is designed to find the optimal amount required to recruit and retain each student. Typically, such a strategy consists of analyzing a student's ability to pay and his or her willingness to pay. Ability to pay is estimated on the basis of the student's documented financial need, whereas willingness to pay is usually based on academic criteria such as standardized test scores or high school grade point average.

ENROLLED LEVEL. There are multiple enrollment management strategies that occur, once the student has enrolled. As students transition into an institution, effective *acculturation strategies* are critical. From a programmatic perspective, acculturation is commonly achieved through orientation experiences, welcome weeks, opening convocations, freshman reads, freshman transition courses, and, occasionally, service projects or group outings. The objectives of these activities include proactively connecting students with their peers and faculty and staff members, showing them how to navigate the campus and student services, introducing them to campus traditions and rituals, teaching them the fundamentals of being a successful college student (time management, effective study habits, note-taking skills, and so on), and involving them in the life of the campus. Assuming that the objectives are met, students are more likely to feel a sense of belonging and comfort with their new campus home.

Beyond the initial acculturation strategies, student retention becomes a priority. Effective *retention strategies* incorporate a multifaceted approach. Focusing solely on high-risk students is not the answer. The retention strategy should consider high-risk experiences as well. Gateway courses with high failure and withdrawal rates, harsh policies and difficult processes, ineffective placement testing, inadequate financial assistance, a lack of academic planning, chronic problems with class availability, inaccurate advising, parking difficulties, language barriers, and diversity issues entail high risk.

A comprehensive approach to retention should begin with the recruiting and admissions process. Create a profile of successful persisters and find more like them. The profile should include academic variables that have a high correlation with academic success and persistence. At most institutions, the variable that best predicts future academic success is past academic success—performance in high school or at other colleges and universities. Sophisticated tools have been developed to help institutions find students who are likely to be successful and graduate. Geodemography, predictive modeling, and data-driven admissions algorithms are but a few. Regardless of the tool used or the variables selected, the goal is usually to maximize student enrollments, shape the class, or enhance student success.

Finally, effective retention strategies do not simply focus on why students leave; they also focus on why students stay. By identifying positive factors associated with persisters and, where possible, replicating those factors, an institution is positioned to attain maximum retention levels, given the mission, service region, admissions selectivity, and characteristics of the school and the characteristics of its students.

At the core of the academic experience is student learning. *Learning strategies* such as learning communities, service learning, supplemental instruction, acculturation courses, capstone experiences, and academic support services have become prominent fixtures on college campuses across the United States and abroad. Unfortunately, progress in shifting from a teacher-centric model to a learner-centric model has been gradual and sporadic. Most college classes are still delivered in the traditional lecture mode, even though there is convincing evidence that most students are visual, not auditory, learners. Generally, students learn best through active participation and reflection rather than passive listening. An increasing number of faculty members have adopted instructional approaches that take into account the individual student's learning style. Often, such approaches incorporate technology by using e-mail, PowerPoint presentations, Web-based resources, two-way video, CD-ROMs, and software that tracks individual student responses to instructor-prompted questions and indicates when important concepts have not been grasped. E-learning has emerged as a dominant learning modality. Ranging from 100 percent online to a blended model that includes some portion of classes meeting in person, e-learning options provide the student with convenience that is often customized to his or her learning needs.

Accompanying the various learning strategies is an array of *student services strategies*. Like the learning strategies, these service strategies are student-centered. They are designed to facilitate a student's painless movement through the institution while providing information and decision-making tools to enhance student success. Attributes of student-centered services often include seamless processes, 24/7 access to services and information, high levels of service reliability, customized and convenient services, a robust technology infrastructure, a focus on staff learning, a high priority placed on managing institutional knowledge, and, where appropriate, standardization of processes and responses. Emerging models blend high-tech, high-touch, and sometimes high-show service delivery. Components of these service models may consist of automated services that occur without the student taking any action, self-service options—usually Web-based, services provided by generalists in an office or one-stop center, and services provided by specialists. Institutions engaged in some variation of this blended model have found that students largely prefer self-service options but do want easy access to a professional when they have questions or special circumstances. Well-trained generalists are capable of handling the bulk of questions and special circumstances that arise, leaving specialists free to spend time with students who really need their expertise. Having human help ensures service reliability.

Though not widespread in higher education, another approach that is commonplace in the corporate sector is a *brand-loyalty strategy*. During the recruitment process, on the front end of the student's experience with the institution, there is an intense courtship (Hayek and Hossler, 1999). Similarly, on the back end of the student's experience, the alumni and development offices court her. In the middle, however, when the student is closest to the institution, the dance ceases. There is no active marketing effort to influence the student's image of the school. There are few relationship-building strategies in place. And there are minimal efforts at most colleges and universities to romance the brand.

This courtship should begin by delivering on the promise of the brand made during the recruitment phase—every day and in every encounter with a student (Wheatley, 1999). By effectively managing these "moments of truth," the institution sends a clear message that the individual student matters (Carlson, 1987). Much as the recruitment strategy does, a brand strategy should include a tailored communications plan designed to address the unique needs of the student at the various developmental and academic stages of enrollment. Such communications might also include recognition of life events and accomplishments such as birthdays, making the dean's list, receiving scholarships, or even tragic events. Direct mail, e-mail, vertical portals, phone contacts, face-to-face encounters, and the school newspaper provide multiple mediums through which such a communications plan could be implemented. Regardless of the medium, the purpose of the communications is to cultivate a relationship and engage the student in the life of the university. Every opportunity to engage a student is an opportunity to enhance institutional commitment. John Gardner, founder of the First-Year Experience and senior fellow with the Pew Foundation, suggested a simple formula for enhancing commitment: time plus involvement equals commitment.

GRADUATE LEVEL. If brand loyalty is cultivated while the student is enrolled, the graduate will be much more likely to contribute time or money back to the institution. There are numerous *alumni strategies* designed to solicit monetary donations. While donations are important for institutional vitality, the physical facilities, and scholarships, the alumni strategies discussed here are specific to contributions of time. First and foremost, ongoing enrollment opportunities exist with alumni, particularly those who have indicated an interest in graduate or professional school—or other lifelong learning possibilities. A simple business axiom applies: the best way to expand market share is not by extending to new markets but by extending participation rates among existing or former customers. Alumni can also contribute time through involvement in student recruitment. Corresponding with admitted students, providing testimonials for publications, hosting area receptions, and presenting scholarship awards at local honor's day programs are illustrations of ways in which alumni can contribute to the recruitment effort.

Alumni contributions need not be limited to enrollment as a student or work in student recruitment. They have much to contribute to the academic experience of current students. For example, they can sponsor internships or job shadowing opportunities, supplement classroom instruction by serving as a guest lecturer or an adjunct faculty member, and provide "real-world" insights by serving on an advisory board for an academic department or school. All of these contributions enhance the learning environment and the academic reputation—the two most important institutional assets in terms of influencing student enrollment choices.

Enrollment Management Within the Academic Context

The fusion of enrollment management with the academic enterprise is necessary to optimize enrollments. That is not to suggest that enrollment objectives should drive academic priorities. To the contrary, enrollment objectives should flow from the academic strategic plan. Within the context of the academic plan, optimum enrollments should be identified. The definition of optimum will depend upon the academic mission, faculty interests and expertise, capacity constraints, market demand, student selectivity, diversity objectives, and institutional incentives and support.

Opportunities to connect with and add value to the academic enterprise are abundant. The discipline of enrollment management prepares enrollment professionals to complement the expertise of academics. By collecting and analyzing information for strategic decision making, offering assistance with marketing academic programs, providing academic student services, and supporting retention efforts, an enrollment manager becomes an invaluable asset on the academic leadership team.

SHARING INFORMATION. Timely and relevant information is absolutely essential for academic planning. Deans and department heads need current and historical data on the number of applicants, admits, and newly enrolled students, along with enrollments by classification and retention rates between years. That data should be segmented by school and academic program and provided in a Web-based report that is updated at least twice a month. Ideally, the Web report would depict real-time data. Other internal reports reveal information about such things as credit hour production, classroom space use, net revenue, return on investment, attrition factors, and the impact of academic policies.

As previously mentioned, strategic enrollment management goes beyond an inward analysis. It looks outward. To secure and sustain competitive advantage, academic units must know the strengths and weaknesses of their competitors, the market demand for potential programs and courses, and the opportunities and threats within the environment. The enrollment manager is in a unique position to conduct an environmental scan, a demand analysis, or a competition analysis.

MARKETING ACADEMIC PROGRAMS. Before launching any new academic program, the aforementioned external analysis should be conducted. In addition, a pricing analysis may be appropriate. From the data collected, enrollment managers can work with the academic leadership to develop a rollout strategy. Among the many considerations in a rollout strategy is the identification of a market niche or cohort groups, a marketing message, a promotional campaign, a pricing strategy, a course delivery model, instructional support, academic student services, and a technology infrastructure, as well as the development of a business plan.

The effective marketing of existing programs is equally important. In reality, most academic programs are generically marketed by the admissions office without an in-depth understanding of the distinctive features of the program or knowledge of competitor programs. With few exceptions, academic departments do not engage in extensive marketing. A crudely designed brochure or antiquated Web site is all too often the extent of departmental marketing efforts. In fact, neither the department nor the admissions operation typically does effective academic program marketing. It is viral, word-of-mouth marketing that carries the day—producing satisfied students and employers who share their experiences with others. Whereas positive viral marketing is a welcomed phenomenon, it is far too unpredictable to rely solely on it as the primary marketing thrust. Consequently, academic units are well served by capitalizing on the experience and, in some instances, resources of the enrollment management organization to develop effective publications, Web pages, recruitment events, and cultivation plans.

PROVIDING ACADEMIC STUDENT SERVICES. Whether offered on campus, completely on-line, or at a satellite location, no academic program can function without some level of student services. Matching academic services with the needs of students is the first step. Admissions, financial aid, advising, registration, orientation, fee payment, book purchasing, and library services are core ingredients, regardless of the location or instructional medium. However, the delivery method may vary. For example, students who are taking courses remotely will not want to purchase books from a brick and mortar store some distance away. Either a mobile bookstore or on-line ordering with door-to-door delivery best serves these students. Soon, a mushrooming e-book industry will make downloading full texts on PDAs or computers a practical option as well.

Services that have traditionally been delivered in a face-to-face mode, such as academic advising, counseling, and tutoring, pose interesting challenges in the age of e-learning. Outsourcing tutorial services or providing Web-based academic advising or counseling through two-way video at a remote location represents some emerging methods of academic service delivery. Inherent in these delivery methods are concerns about confidentiality and user authentication. Also, technology-driven service solutions like these have imbedded within them issues of infrastructure, technical support, and financial resources. In many ways, the traditional mode of service delivery is less complex and certainly more comfortable for professionals who have always delivered in-person services. But the landscape has changed. Services must be engineered to meet students where they are.

SUPPORTING RETENTION EFFORTS. Though tactical plans and retention initiatives are essential to improving student persistence, the most important element is human interaction. At its most basic level, improving retention is about changing the culture. The role of enrollment management in such a culture shift is, first, to orient faculty members to the dynamics of retention issues and then to help them see how they can make a difference.

Often, the reasons students leave a college or university are quite appropriate or outside the control of the institution: they have met their intended educational goal, they have changed majors or career objectives, they did not find a good institutional fit, or they have experienced a change in life circumstances such as the loss of a job, the death of a parent, or the contracting of a medical condition. The enrollment manager should identify the retention dynamics that an institution can and should attempt to control or at least influence. For example: What are the persistence rates by school, department, ethnic group, gender, age, and admissions type? What is the profile of a successful persister versus a suspended or withdrawn student—in terms of academic background, standardized test scores, demographic patterns, socioeconomic factors, placement results, course selection issues, academic major, first-semester grade point average, participation in campus activities, usage of existing academic support services, and residency status (living on or off campus)? What are the high-risk experiences? What initiatives are currently in place to address retention issues? What can individual faculty members and departments do to improve retention rates?

Actually, faculty members and academic departments have the most impact on students' academic success and their decision to stay or leave. When academic advising, for instance, goes beyond once-a-semester course scheduling to regular mentoring, students create an academic plan and possibly a career path. More important, they have an individual with whom they have developed a relationship based on trust and mutual respect. They become anchored and focused.

Likewise, interactions with faculty members inside and outside of class have the potential to bond students to the school and enrich their learning experience. Active learning, clearly articulated expectations, service learning projects, class social functions, e-mail exchanges, and individual meetings to discuss academic progress are among the virtually infinite ways faculty members can have an impact on the lives of students. Even something as simple as knowing the names of students in a class can make a difference. Most students want to be noticed. They want to make significant contributions, and they need to be challenged and supported where they are intellectually, emotionally, socially, and spiritually.

Enrollment Management and Systems Thinking

In enrollment management, decisions made in isolation can have dire consequences or produce minimal results. Like an intricate spider web, each piece of the enrollment management enterprise must be carefully constructed and spun together into a tightly intertwined web of enrollment initiatives. Understanding how various strategies fit together and how each affects another will yield synergistic efforts that can withstand internal and external pressures.

As enrollment strategies are constructed, it is prudent to view the enterprise through the *student lens*. All too often, institutional research related to student characteristics, enrollment patterns, behaviors, values, and satisfaction are absent from enrollment planning. There seldom is a review of literature or even solicitation of student input into the planning process. When students are removed from the equation, the result is often misguided decisions that have no grounding in reality. What successful company develops a business plan without focusing on its customers? The student perspective is ultimately the most important.

To illustrate, consider how students prefer to have academic services provided. Basically, they expect services to be seamless and intuitive. They do not care how schools are organized and are frustrated when they are left to aimlessly navigate institutional structures, policies, and procedures. So the enrollment management organization that is student-centered and incorporates systems thinking will work to make organizational boundaries invisible to the student and will devise cross-functional teams to streamline processes that span multiple departments or divisions.

The organization that employs systems thinking will consider all facets of academic service delivery, including what Bolman and Deal (1991) call organizational frames:

1. The *human-resource frame* consists of staffing patterns, skill assessment, training, knowledge management, employee incentives, staff morale, and the enhancement of human capital. This frame represents the capacity to produce enrollment results. Without an emphasis on this frame, it is virtually impossible to engage in systems thinking. Only organizations that regularly invest in individual and team learning will have the intellectual capital necessary to effectively sustain a competitive advantage within an increasingly complex system.

2. The *structural frame* is composed of organizational structure, policies, procedures, and processes. On many college campuses, extremely student-centered staff members are greeted every day by dissatisfied students. If the employees are so friendly and caring, why are the students discontented? Simply put, in a battle between good people and bad systems, the people always lose (Black, 1999). Systems are highly dependent upon structural issues and, thus, the structural frame plays a significant role in the delivery of quality academic services.

3. The *political frame* is particularly relevant to the higher education environment. After all, we are highly political organisms. We thrive on discourse, collegiality, and, often, conflict. All three are necessary to produce change of any significance. However, when pushed to the extreme, this trinity can paralyze higher education. The effective enrollment manager understands the political climate, identifies power brokers, plans for inevitable conflict, and leverages opportunities to influence key decision makers.

4. In the fourth and final frame—the *symbolic frame*, stories, rituals, traditions, and actions shape the culture. Consistency is imperative to managing the symbolic frame. People will watch to see if actions, and even inaction, reflect the rhetoric. They will not believe the message unless they believe in the messenger (Black, 1999).

Systems thinkers continually reach out to others within the organization. They fervently work to influence perception and behavior so that staff members will embrace the organizational vision and view success of the organization as being synonymous with their own success. Equally important, system thinkers strive to integrate processes and related systems. They see the organization as a disjointed jigsaw puzzle that longs to become a unified whole. But there are seemingly endless options and no picture of the completed puzzle to aid in linking the right combination of pieces together. Correct assembly requires vision, trial and error, ongoing communication, teamwork, multiple perspectives, and patience. There are no quick fixes.

Strategic Enrollment Management

Enrollment management becomes strategic when it looks outward and forward. Exclusively introspective approaches leave institutions vulnerable to external elements. By regularly scanning the environment, the enrollment manager can warn the institution of impending danger, or he can forecast potential opportunities. Institutions that look beyond their own ivy-covered towers are better positioned to manage change. They tend to be proactive rather than reactive and more strategic than tactical.

Once the environmental terrain has been mapped, an enrollment management vision can be created. The vision should reflect the realities of the environment while being grounded in the institution's mission. It should go beyond the institution's immediate horizon and consider possibilities that force the organization to stretch. The vision is less about what the organization is and more about what it aspires to be.

The overall integration of the planning process under a single vision will help to ensure a focused approach to institutional improvement. Of course, it takes more than planning to prevent vision drift. Campus leaders, including those in academic service units, must perpetuate the vision through their words and actions. The vision must be institutionalized by supplying incentives for desired behavior and by connecting budget allocations to the implementation of the strategic plan. Furthermore, effectiveness measures should be developed for each component of the comprehensive plan, and successes should be broadly touted.

Critical Success Factors

Critical success factors are milestones that represent progress. Generally, critical success factors are broad categories or goals with incremental objectives supporting them. In the realm of enrollment management, critical success factors might focus on student head count or credit hours, the academic quality of the entering class, diversity issues (such as gender, race, age, state and county of residence, or intended major), student satisfaction, retention rates, graduation rates, and institutional image. To illustrate, the underlying objectives for the critical success factors related to academic quality of the entering class might include:

- ○ Increase the average SAT score by fifty points within the next five years
- ○ Raise the average high school grade point average from 3.2 (on a 4.0 scale) to 3.5 by 2005
- ○ Lower the acceptance rate by 2 percent annually for the next five years
- ○ Increase scholarship offers by 20 percent immediately
- ○ Raise the minimum admissions requirement from a 1.8 predicted grade point average to 2.2 by 2004

Along with these standard critical success factors, there should be several that demonstrate return on investment. Common among private institutions are success factors related to net revenue—comparing the investment of institutional aid dollars with the total revenue produced by students whose decision to enroll was positively influenced by the aid award. Another example of return on investment would be to compare the revenue generated by additional enrollments with that generated by new investments in the recruitment or retention strategies that led to the enrollment increases.

Regardless of the identified success factors, benchmarking, tracking, and reporting results shift the institutional focus from semester-to-semester, bottom-line enrollments to an incremental, multifaceted enrollment approach. It allows the campus community to see the big picture as well as the relative parts. In essence, critical success factors suggest a calculated enrollment journey, not crisis management or a "flavor of the month" frenzy. Such regular assessment implies accountability and builds confidence in the enterprise.

Enrollment Management and Student Academic Services

Calling student academic services a subset or component of enrollment management would understate the critical importance of academic services to the enrollment mission. For it is these services that facilitate a student's transition from prospective student to enrolled student and through each classification on to graduation. This transition represents the yardstick by which enrollment management is measured.

Enrollment management and student academic services share two common characteristics. First, they both function best in a student-centered culture. When students are the central focus of the academic enterprise, the institution makes student services a priority. Similarly, student recruitment and retention are seen as being critical to the institution's vitality. Every institutional decision and endeavor is considered within the student-centered context. Second, both revolve around student success. If students are successful, they are more likely to persist and graduate. And successful graduates promote the school to others and give of their time and money.

A Student-Centered Culture

Service providers who view each interaction with a student as an institutional "moment of truth" and an opportunity to influence a student's life are fully aligned with the objectives of enrollment management. Managing moments of truth is largely a mind-set. When academic services staffers think of students as customers and place the needs of students ahead of their own, they perform job tasks and make decisions within a student-centered context. This mind-set, combined with a "servant's heart," can be a powerful force in an academic services unit. It becomes infectious. Others want to align with it, particularly if it is rewarded and counterproductive behavior is not. By transforming the underlying assumptions and values governing behavior within the organization, it is possible to create an enduring culture that values students (Cummings and Worley, 2001).

To be a student-centered college or university requires more than employees with service-oriented attitudes. Academic service systems must be accessible, convenient, and intuitive. They also must add value to the student's experience. As the society shifts from a service economy to an experience economy, services must even be entertaining—the "high show" mentioned earlier in this chapter. Admittedly, our primary business is student success, not entertainment. But we must recognize that quality services are irrelevant if students choose not to use them. Innovative approaches to service delivery can enhance student success and, at the same time, be entertaining. The two are not mutually exclusive.

Having student-centered services is tightly coupled with having successful enrollment management. Institutions that adopt a student-centered culture are, in fact, building brand loyalty, enhancing word-of-mouth recruiting, and reducing student attrition.

Student Success

Traditionally, both enrollment management and student academic services have student success as a core value. It is important to remember that many students enter academe highly capable but unprepared. For twelve plus years, they have been programmed to memorize and regurgitate information on demand, to practice for the test, to sit up straight and be quiet during class, not to collaborate with their peers, not to write in textbooks, and to follow the rules. Teachers often provide lecture outlines to supplement instruction, thus eliminating the need to develop note-taking skills. Most of the tests they have taken are multiple choice or true/false, and seldom have they been asked to apply information learned. In most cases, they have had minimal practice writing, and the average student reads only what is required for class.

Obviously, there are exceptions to these indictments of K–12 education, but the truth is, many students enter college as dependent learners who are without the necessary critical thinking, analytical, problem-solving, and communication skills to be successful students. Our job as faculty members or academic service providers is to help students become independent and, when appropriate, interdependent learners. We should help them see connections between academic disciplines, the relevance of learning to life and career interests, and the application of knowledge to the world around them. Most important, we should help them open their minds to new possibilities. Ideally, we should aspire to develop within them an unquenchable thirst for learning.

Students are also unprepared to navigate our complex systems. We are the first bureaucracy many of them have ever encountered. Foolishly, we expect students to understand our organizational structure, know what forms need to be completed and where to find them, remember a dozen deadlines, and even read the catalogue. They come to us with little exposure to and tolerance for red tape, delays, and runaround treatment. Yet we often thrust them into a vortex of disjointed service obstacles without teaching them how to successfully accomplish necessary tasks. As service providers, we have an opportunity to teach them not only the mechanics of financial aid or academic planning but also the importance of managing one's time, establishing priorities, setting goals, organizing information, attending to details, building justifications, balancing responsibilities with consequences, and even successfully navigating a bureaucracy.

Problem solving, planning, seeking information, evaluating options, and making decisions are among the life skills academic services staff members can impart to the students they encounter. Clearly, this assumes that staff members embrace their role as educators, not just as guardians of the rules.

Finally, we have a responsibility to help younger students mature into adulthood. For many of them, their freshman year will be the first time they have ever shared a room with anyone. Notions of compromise and sacrifice in relationships may be foreign to them. Most will grapple with their newfound freedom. Whereas many will readily accept the responsibilities that come with this freedom, others will pursue more hedonistic tendencies or flounder without any clear direction or sense of purpose. They have left behind a highly structured, rule-driven life for one that is untethered to the demands of parents and the expectations imposed by high school teachers and administrators. To a degree, higher education still embraces the Darwinian survival of the fittest model of education. We rightfully expect students to take responsibility for their actions, come to class prepared, study outside of class, and seek help when needed. But the reality is, these are learned behaviors, and many new college students have not been taught these lessons.

Academic service providers will have a significant impact on student success if they do not fall prey to commonly held myths about student preparedness and if they meet students where they are. By focusing on the developmental needs of the whole student, academic service professionals can facilitate student growth while enhancing academic performance.

Conclusion

The enrollment management construct provides a unique view of student academic services. It is results-oriented but at the same time very much about people. Students are at the center of enrollment management. Their success and migration through the institution represent the primary task of enrollment managers as well as that of student service providers. Staff members are not lost in the amalgamation of enrollment strategies; in fact, their intellectual contributions fuel the metabolism of the organization. Their ability to learn and manage knowledge dictates the rate and, to an extent, the direction in which the organization evolves.

Enrollment management brings a strategic focus, along with an internal and external perspective of the institution's strengths, weaknesses, opportunities, and threats to academic services. In the enrollment paradigm, competition propels student services units to heightened levels of performance by demanding thoughtful planning, "outside the box" think-ing, and near-perfect execution. Metrics associated with this methodical construct are used to assess tactical and strategic initiatives and are then incorporated into a continuous improvement cycle.

The field of enrollment management has introduced academic service operations to proven business practices and principles. For example, the notion of integration is imbedded in enrollment management—not integration for its own sake but for the distinct purpose of streamlining student processes and sharing student information. Integration may require reengineering, restructuring, or migrating to new technology. Though often painful, these changes typically yield a stronger, more efficient organization.

Efficiency and effectiveness are hallmarks of sound organizations. By bringing to academic services the tools and conceptual underpinnings needed to better serve students and the institution, enrollment management has had a profound impact on the profession. Since the advent of enroll-ment management, academic services have become increasingly student-oriented, marketing conscious, and analytical. More than ever before, academic services are well-oiled machines adding immense value to the organization.

REFERENCES

Black, J. *Navigating Change in the New Millennium: Enrollment Leadership Strategies*. Washington, D.C.: American Association of Collegiate Registrars and Admissions Officers, 1999.

Black, J. "Garnering Resources and Building Infrastructure." In J. Black (ed.), *The SEM Revolution*. Washington, D.C.: American Association of Colle-giate Registrars and Admissions Officers, 2001.

Bolman, L. G., and Deal, T. E. *Reframing Organizations*. San Francisco: Jossey-Bass, 1991.

Carlson, C. *Moments of Truth*. New York: HarperCollins, 1987.

Cummings, T. G., and Worley, C. G. *Essentials of Organization Development and Change*. Australia, Canada, Mexico, Singapore, Spain, United King-dom, and the United States: South-Western College Publishing, 2001.

Hayek, J., and Hossler, D. "The Information Needs of Prospective Students: I Want What I Want When I Want It." Presentation at the annual meeting of the American Association of Collegiate Registrars and Admissions Officers, Charleston, S.C., Apr. 1999.

Henderson, S. E. "On the Brink of a Profession." In J. Black (ed.), *The SEM Revolution*. Washington, D.C.: American Association of Collegiate Regis-trars and Admissions Officers, 2001.

Hossler, D., Bean, J. P., and Associates. *The Strategic Planning of College Enrollments*. San Francisco: Jossey-Bass, 1990.

Kalsbeek, D. H. "Strategic Enrollment Management." Presentation at the American Association of Collegiate Registrars and Admissions Officers' Strategic Enrollment Management Workshop, Chicago, June 2001.

Schnaar, S. P. *Marketing Strategy: Customers and Competition*. New York: Free Press, 1998.

Wallhaus, R. A. "E-learning: From Institutions to Providers, from Students to Learners." In R. N. Katz and D. G. Oblinger (eds.), *The "E" Is for Everything*. San Francisco: Jossey-Bass, 2000.

Wheatley, C. "Delivering on the Promise of the Brand." Plenary address at the American Association of Collegiate Registrars and Admissions Officers' Strategic Enrollment Management Conference, Orlando, Fla., Nov. 1999.

5

THE ASSESSMENT OF READINESS FOR STUDENT LEARNING IN COLLEGE

Gary W. Peterson, Janet G. Lenz, James P. Sampson, Jr.

SEVERAL SOCIOLOGICAL THEORETICAL MODELS have been advanced to explain student retention in college. In his student social integration model, Tinto (1987) asserts that academic and social integration and institutional and goal commitment are related to persistence in college. Bean's student attrition model (1985) emphasizes such factors as the intent to persist, attitudes, institutional fit, family approval, the encouragement of friends, financial attitudes, and the opportunity to transfer to other institutions. Borrowing from these two models, Cabrera, Nora, and Castaneda (1993) subsequently developed a comprehensive integrated model of student retention. They found that the most powerful direct effects in predicting persistence one year after enrollment were the student's intent to persist and his or her academic performance (grade point average). The intent to persist was predicted by the indirect effects of institutional commitment, encouragement, and goal commitment. The model accounted for 47 percent of the variation in whether students persisted after their freshman year.

Psychological models of retention relate student traits to student persistence. For example, Bean and Eaton (2000) related the theories of attitudinal behavior (Fishbein and Ajzen, 1975), coping behavior (Lazarus, 1966), self-efficacy (Bandura, 1982, 1986, 1997), and attribution (Weiner, 1986) to persistence. They hypothesized that normative beliefs about the likelihood of success and one's ability to control outcomes, one's ability to cope with stress, and one's self-confidence all contribute to academic success. Stage and Hossler (2000) advanced a sequential student-centered model, in which school persistence is based first on family background characteristics (family self-efficacy, parents' education, and parents' encouragement), second on primary and secondary school experiences (feedback from peers, teachers, and counselors), third on students' intentions and engagement (taking college-prep classes, seeking advice and information about college, and volunteering), fourth on college entry (goal setting, motivation, and intellectual and social involvement), and finally on the decision to persist or drop out. According to Stage and Hossler (2000), at entry to college, successful students initiate behaviors that help them adapt to a school environment, such as engaging in intellectual and social pursuits, establishing study patterns, and interacting with the faculty. Such adaptive behaviors are predicated on "getting ready" behaviors engendered in the first three stages, which involve prior family and school experiences.

A limitation of these theoretical models is that they do not provide clear guidelines for application in the design and implementation of student assessments and services that would enhance student learning and the likelihood of success and persistence. For example, variables such as academic and social integration, commitment to goals, family self-efficacy scale or education, and primary and secondary school experiences may have explanatory or predictive power, but, unfortunately, they are backward-looking and do not suggest how to create student service interventions in the present.

Furthermore, although students are typically introduced to available services on campus through orientation procedures, they often must "self-diagnose" their strengths and limitations in an unfamiliar and challenging environment. Students often do not become aware of their limitations until well into the first or second semester. Moreover, at the point of awareness, they must then locate appropriate services to help them. What is needed is a way to expedite the early identification of strengths and weaknesses so that students can address them sooner.

This chapter presents a model of student readiness for learning in college and demonstrates how readiness can be assessed at the point of entry. Our intention is that readiness assessments be incorporated within the normal freshmen-orienting mechanisms of most postsecondary institutions. The intended outcome of readiness assessment is a profile with local and, if appropriate, national norms that identify areas of student strength and areas for growth and development according to key readiness dimensions related to subsequent performance and persistence. Students and their advisers or counselors can then use this information to identify student services to address identified readiness needs. Furthermore, because cost considerations in the delivery of services are becoming increasingly important, the readiness model incorporates the concept of level of readiness (high, moderate, or low) to suggest the intensity of assistance required to meet individual needs.

The Nature of Readiness

Readiness for learning in postsecondary education refers to a student's ability to successfully engage in academic programs and to use student services in ways that enhance learning within a social context. Students who are ready for learning and successfully engaging the academic and social environment are more likely to attain educational, career, and life goals.

Based on our work in helping individuals solve career problems and make career decisions (Peterson, Sampson, Reardon, and Lenz, 2002), we have found that the state of readiness can be conceptualized in terms of a relationship between two fundamental dimensions: *capability* and *complexity* (Sampson, Peterson, Reardon, and Lenz, 2000). The capability dimension refers to the possession of knowledge, skills, and attitudes (KSAs) that enable students to engage a college environment academically and socially in ways that enhance learning. The complexity dimension refers to contextual factors in the environment that influence an individual's learning—namely, family, social, organizational, and economic factors.

Capability for Learning

The capability dimension entails the KSAs, which comprise internal factors in learning. Key attributes of the capability for learning, derived from a review of the literature, include several domains, which will be described in the section that follows. Principal sources of theory and research undergirding this section are drawn from Peterson, Sampson, Reardon, and Lenz (2002) and Crockett and Levitz (1988).

KNOWLEDGE DOMAIN. One aspect of the knowledge domain is curricular knowledge—or the mastery of disciplinary facts, concepts, rules, and operations—that freshmen bring with them from high school (Pascarella, Terenzini, and Wolfle, 1986; Stage and Hossler, 2000). Another is knowledge of the school environment, which includes familiarity with the policies, regulations, physical location of classrooms and services, service providers, and places to buy food and health supplies (Hamrick and Hossler, 1996; Pascarella, Terenzini, and Wolfle, 1986). Self-knowledge refers to having a clear perception of one's interests, abilities, and values. To make career choices, students also need occupational knowledge, or familiarity with labor market structure and conditions, as well as familiarity with the educational and credentialing requirements for entry onto a chosen career path.

SKILLS DOMAIN. The skills domain includes skills necessary for success inside and outside the classroom. The most obvious are academic skills—the traditional "learning skills" involved in mastering academic program goals and classroom objectives—namely, reading, writing, mathematics, and study and test-taking skills (Pascarella and Terenzini, 1991; Stage and Hossler, 2000). Students also need problem-solving and decision-making skills that are unique to their individual academic disciplines, career development, and everyday, real-life situations (Gordon, 1988; Woditsh, 1977). The capacity for thinking clearly through problems and decisions can be constrained by dysfunctional thoughts and beliefs (Krumboltz, 1991; Sampson and others, 1998).

Other skills may be less directly tied to performance in the classroom but are also essential for college success. Self-regulation and self-management are metacognitive skills (Flavel, Miller, and Miller, 1993; Meichenbaum, 1977)—such as self-talk, self-awareness, and control and monitoring in the executive processing function of cognition, which regulates lower-order problem-solving and decision-making skills. These skills enable one to maintain focus and direction toward the attainment of educational goals, all the while resisting distractions and temptations (Bandura, 1997; Zimmerman and Bandura, 1994). Also important are social skills, or the capacity to communicate effectively with peers and faculty members, and to maintain social relationships. They include such capabilities as self-disclosure, active listening, assertiveness, and conflict resolution (Cabrera, Nora, and Casteneda, 1993; Pascarella and Terenzini, 1991; Pascarella, Terenzini, and Wolfle, 1986). Finally, students need financial management skills. Freshmen are often forced to learn how to develop and use a budget to manage their limited monetary resources. They must also be able to use credit wisely if they are to leave college without burdensome debts (Combs, 1994). Students with these skills develop budgets and live within them (Cabrera, Stampen, and Hansen, 1990).

ATTITUDINAL DOMAIN. One attitude that leads to success is *self-efficacy*—self-confidence and belief in one's ability to formulate and attain educational, career, and life goals (Bandura, 1997; Lent, Brown, and Larkin, 1987; Peterson, 1993; Wilhite, 1990). Another is *locus of control*, which refers to the belief that rewards are the result of planning and effort rather than luck or chance (Perry, Hechter, Verena, and Weinberg, 1993; Wilhite, 1990).

Readiness Needs

Readiness needs are the gap between an existing level of proficiency or attainment and the level desired. Proficiency in any KSA connotes a sufficient level of attainment such that it facilitates rather than interferes with learning. A gap in any of the aforementioned dimensions could deter students from effectively coping with their academic and social environments.

Complexity of the Learning Environment

Complexity refers to environmental factors in learning. Such factors are external to the student and indirectly bear on student learning. Key factors—which may range from being supportive to being detrimental to academic success—include influences from family and partners, society and social networks, economic considerations, and organizations (Sampson, Peterson, Reardon, and Lenz, 2000).

Family and Partners

On one hand, family encouragement is a key variable in theoretical models of student performance and persistence (Cabrera, Nora, and Castaneda, 1993); on the other hand, some aspects of family relations, such as attending to the needs of children, partners, and incapacitated parents, may impose demands on a student's time and attention. Furthermore, students who enroll at a school located a long distance from their family may find adjusting to school particularly difficult. Dysfunctional family and personal relationships can also hinder or distract students. For example, parents may want to be more involved in helping their son or daughter make academic and social decisions than is helpful or desirable to him or her. Students in committed relationships can also encounter stress due to conflict over relationship goals, finances, household duties, leisure activities, sexual behavior, and future career plans.

Society and Social Networks

Positive and negative social forces, both within and without postsecondary institutions, can exert influences on learning. On one hand, positive societal factors—such as modeling, mentoring, networking, and peer support and caring—can exert a facilitative function in learning; on the other hand, negative social influences—such as discrimination in any form—may interfere with learning and access to educational opportunities. Stigmatizing, stereotyping, harassment, and a lack of role models also negatively influence learning.

Economic Considerations

Ultimately, the amount of financial resources available to a student has a direct bearing on both the amount of time an individual can devote to learning and the rate of progress he or she can make toward attaining educational goals. If the amount of financial assistance is insufficient to meet their needs, students often hold part-time or even full-time jobs. While employment may provide positive benefits of helping students acquire work experience and money on which to live, it also demands time and draws concentration away from academic pursuits. When the economy is thriving and new technology jobs lure students away with promises of early wealth, some students may choose to forgo higher education altogether or leave early to pursue a job.

Institution

Postsecondary institutions vary widely in size, culture, climate, curricular offerings, academic expectations and standards, access to faculty member, peer support, and availability of student services. And various academic disciplines within an institution may have different expectations of and influence on students, which can be positive or negative (Smart, Feldman, and Ethington, 2000). Some college environments are large and complex, with highly differentiated academic programs and services; others are small and less complex, offer basic academic programs, and provide general global services. The more complex and differentiated the college environment, the greater the challenge for entering students to negotiate it to meet their educational and life needs. The next section will focus on how these dimensions of capacity and complexity can be used in relating levels of student readiness to the provision of services.

The Two-Factor Readiness Model and Required Levels of Service

A student's state of readiness may be portrayed in terms of a two-factor model—capacity and complexity, with four quadrants (see Figure 5.1). The respective quadrants indicate high, moderate, and low states of readiness for learning. In terms of complementary student services, the quadrants can be seen as zones of enrichment, improvement, and remediation. The nature of these student services will be described in greater detail later in the chapter.

Quadrant I: High Readiness

Students falling into this quadrant possess high levels of KSAs relative to the complexity of their personal, social, and academic environment. None of the capability dimensions present severely limiting barriers to learning. In terms of student services, they are in the zone of enrichment. Thus, upon entry into college, these high-capability students likely require only low-cost interventions, such as an orientation experience and self-help services.

Quadrant II: Moderate Readiness

Students in this quadrant possess high capability in terms of KSAs but are also typically coping with a complex situational environment. The complexity of their academic and social situation is at parity with their ability to cope, which may place them at risk, should the complexity in their lives increase. In terms of student services, these students are in a zone of improvement and may require some staff-assisted services to help them manage the complexity in their lives.

Figure 5.1. A Two-Dimensional Model of Readiness for College

| | **Complexity** | |
	Low	High
High	**I** **High Readiness** *Zone of Enrichment* (Self-Directed Services)	**II** **Moderate Readiness** *Zone of Improvement* (Brief Staff-Assisted Services)
Capability		
Low	**III** **Moderate Readiness** *Zone of Improvement* (Brief Staff-Assisted or Case-Managed Services)	**IV** **Low Readiness** *Zone of Remediation* (Case-Managed Services)

Quadrant III: Moderate Readiness

Although students in this quadrant are in a low-complexity environment, they lack KSAs and may have a limited capacity to cope with their environment. Thus, even though complexity is low, should they encounter increased social and academic demands (which is likely due to maturation and more difficult courses), their academic performance may be immediately affected. These students are in a zone of improvement and typically require some staff-assisted services.

Quadrant IV: Low Readiness

Students in this quadrant are in an academic and social environment that clearly exceeds their capability to cope effectively. These students possess several or more deficits in key capability dimensions. Therefore, they are in the zone of remediation, needing to quickly acquire KSAs to meet academic and social demands. In terms of the delivery of student services, they require intensive case-managed services.

Readiness Assessment

The goal of readiness assessment is to identify students' readiness needs and link them with the appropriate services. Using the two-factor readiness model, readiness assessment involves the appraisal of both capability and complexity. From this preliminary assessment, a student can be tentatively located in one of the quadrants.

Capability Assessment

The objective of capability assessment, as a component of readiness assessment, is to identify gaps in any of the student's KSAs that may present constraints or barriers to learning. As a starting point, the desired state in any dimension can be derived through establishing local freshman norms. Low scores relative to the norm in a dimension could point to an area that students and their advisers or counselors would focus on in follow-up meetings. The methods, measures, and instruments listed later for each of the dimensions are not meant to be exhaustive. Further exploration of assessments at local institutions is encouraged. Moreover, with cost-effectiveness in mind, many of the assessments are in the form of self-report or proxy measures.

KNOWLEDGE DOMAIN. The mastery of curriculum content could be measured in terms of high school grade point averages in designated mathematics, science, language, and social science courses. Scores earned on national or local departmental placement tests also provide readiness information for specific courses.

School environment. Familiarity with the school environment could be determined through a self-report on whether students have read the college catalogue, student handbook, and student honor code and have attended general, school, college, or department orientation sessions.

Self-knowledge. The extent to which individuals possess accurate knowledge of their own interests, abilities, and values may be assessed through formal instruments, such as *Self-Directed Search* (Holland, 1994) and *Strong Interest Inventory* (1994), or through the use of less formal measures, such as on-line career guidance systems, card sorts, workbooks, and checklists.

Occupational information. A gap in this dimension may be identified through a student's self-report of his or her need for information. *My Vocational Situation* (Holland, Daiger, and Power, 1980) and *Career Factors Inventory* (Chartrand, Robbins, and Morrill, 1997) are examples of instruments that measure students' perceived need for occupational and training information.

SKILLS DOMAIN. *Academic skills.* Academic aptitude may be assessed through scores earned on college entrance examinations such as the Scholastic Assessment Test (SAT) and the American College Test (ACT). Study habits and attitudes may be assessed through a brief, locally developed questionnaire or through comprehensive formal instruments such as *Learning and Study Strategies Inventory* (Weinstein, Palmer, and Schulte, 1987).

Problem-solving and decision-making skills. In terms of general problem solving, *Problem Solving Inventory* (Heppner and Petersen, 1982) is an example of a self-report measure that identifies strengths and weaknesses. In the career realm, *Career Thoughts Inventory* (Sampson and others, 1996) and *Career Beliefs Inventory* (Krumboltz, 1991) are examples of instruments that identify a variety of factors that inhibit career problem solving and decision making. *Career Thoughts Inventory* (Saunders, Peterson, Sampson, and Reardon, 2000) also helps assess general anxiety and depression, thereby providing an indicator of general psychological adjustment. The "occupational alternatives" question, "What occupations are you now considering and which is your first choice?" (Slaney, 1980, pp. 122–129) can also be used to measure career decidedness.

Self-regulation and self-management. Here, a brief self-report questionnaire could be developed from *Diagnostic and Statistical Manual of Mental Disorders* (American Psychiatric Association, 1994) for attention deficit hyperactivity disorder (ADHD), in which students respond to items pertaining to distractibility, inattention, impulsiveness, lack of concentration, and emotional liability, in terms of pervasiveness across life settings and levels of severity. This dimension is also related to dimensions such as study, test taking, social skills, and financial management.

Social skills. On the one hand, the extent to which students have a tendency to become isolated, withdrawn, and depressed is a concern. Sometimes, social isolation is associated with alcohol and substance abuse, as well as with absenteeism from classes. Shy students may avoid peers, advisers, faculty members, and campus social events and opportunities. On the other hand, there are students who are unable to curtail their social activities as needed, such as when they need to study for examinations or produce papers. Although formal personality instruments, such as the NEO PI-R (Costa and McRae, 1992) and the MMPI-2 (Minnesota Multiphasic Personality Inventory) (Butcher and others, 1989), measure social introversion and extroversion, and others, such as the College Adjustment Scale (Anton and Reed, 1991), identify interpersonal adjustment problems, peer and other campus advisers and resident assistants could play a role in identifying and approaching students whose social behavior may be interfering with learning.

Financial management. This dimension may be assessed through a self-report checklist regarding whether students have independently managed money—that is, such as owned a checking account, maintained a credit card, held or paid off a loan, or formulated or lived within a budget.

Attitudes

Self-efficacy. The extent to which students possess self-confidence in their ability to attain their educational, career, and life goals may be assessed through self-report measures such as the Self-Efficacy Scale (Sherer and others, 2000)—a measure of generalized self-efficacy, or domain-specific self-efficacy, such as the math self-efficacy expectations measure (Betz and Hackett, 1983), and the occupational self-efficacy expectations measure (Betz and Hackett, 1981).

Locus of control. General locus of control, the extent to which individuals believe rewards are obtained by internal or external control, may be measured by Rotter's I-E Scale (Rotter, 1966). Career locus of control, the extent to which individuals believe they are in charge of their career decisions, may be assessed by scales within *Career Thoughts Inventory* (Sampson and others, 1996) or *Career Factors Inventory* (Chartrand, Robbins, and Morrill, 1997).

Complexity Assessment

The objective of complexity assessment is to determine the extent to which environmental factors impose stress on students and whether they interfere with or place barriers on learning. An important aspect in assessing complexity is that the student's internal perception of the extent to which environmental factors impose stress is more salient than the apparent reality to an external observer. Thus, we use the term *problem space* (Newell and Simon, 1972; Peterson, 1998; Sinnott, 1989) to connote all cognitive and affective components contained in working memory as individuals approach a problem-solving task. The amount of space available in working memory to devote to a problem-solving task can be considered a finite amount (Kahnaman, 1973). Therefore, individuals can only think about so many issues at a time, including academic and nonacademic factors.

An assessment procedure used in career problem solving and decision making is to first have a student list all academic and environmental factors (such as family and partners, societal and social network, economic considerations, and organizational factors) that can potentially influence his or her academic performance. Next, the student draws a large circle on a blank sheet of paper that represents one's total amount of attentional space. Now the student draws circles within the large circle in proportion to the amount of stress or attention these factors occupy within the wider circle. This figure represents a cognitive map of the problem space and provides a perceptual representation of the complexity of issues in their lives. Cognitive maps with low complexity typically have considerable open spaces and broad circles related to academic issues, whereas cognitive maps, totally consumed with contextual factors and small circles related to academic pursuits, suggest high complexity. An adviser can then help the student explore the respective issues on the map and develop a strategy for managing them effectively.

An Organizational Strategy for Comprehensive Readiness Assessment

Readiness assessment for learning may be seen as a three-stage process. The first stage is a preliminary screening process targeting the capability dimension that is proactive in nature and can be administered at orientations, at freshman seminars, and even on-line. The second stage involves students and their advisers engaging in a complexity assessment. Here, readiness needs are identified and referrals are made to appropriate student services and programs. The third stage entails a thorough diagnostic procedure and a plan for interventions, which can be provided at various campus locations.

STAGE 1: CAPABILITY SCREENING. Any capability screening device should not take more than one hour (so that it can be easily administered at orientation experiences, at freshman seminars, or on-line) and should provide information with respect to the status of the respective KSAs in the capability dimension. It should also be benign and nonthreatening in appearance so as not to discourage students from taking it. Finally, all subtests measuring the respective dimensions should possess adequate psychometric qualities of reliability and validity to serve as an effective screening device.

In this discussion of capability screening, we will use the Comprehensive College Assessment Inventory (CCAI), a hypothetical screening device. Following orientation, the results of the CCAI are sent to student advisers for review. Together, students and their advisers incorporate the findings from the CCAI as they discuss first-year course scheduling. The hypothetical CCAI provides the following information about student capability:

1. Curricular content: high school GPAs in selected subject areas, scores on placement tests

2. School environment: attended orientation (yes or no); if yes, date of attendance

3. Self-knowledge: student interest in exploring career interest areas and values (yes or no)

4. Occupational information: student interest in knowing more about occupations and training, determined by the My Vocational Situation Need for Information Scale (4 items)

5. Academic skills: SAT or ACT scores; results of short-form Study Skills and Test Taking Skills and Attitudes Survey (30 items)

6. Problem-solving and decision-making skills: My Vocational Situation (26 items); Occupational Alternatives Question (2 items)

7. Self-regulation and self-management: checklist of ADHD behaviors (10 items)

8. Social skills: omit in screening measure; use observation and self-report

9. Financial management: checklist of money-management experiences (6 items)

10. Self-efficacy: Self-Efficacy Scale (30 items)

11. Locus of control: I-E Scale (29 items)

After receiving a signed release from the student, a summary of scores with local norms is reported to the adviser. All of the aforementioned measures can be used by trained paraprofessionals.

STAGE 2: CAPABILITY ASSESSMENT. At a scheduled advising session, an appropriately trained adviser and the student review the results of the CCAI in light of the student's unique complexity status. A determination concerning capability is then made, using the two-dimension readiness model as a framework. Questions that are discussed may include the following: Are there any readiness scores among the key dimensions that suggest potential learning difficulties? What is the degree of complexity that may exacerbate potential limitations and place students at risk for early academic difficulty? What campus services and programs are available to assist students with respect to identified readiness gaps? Advisers must possess the communication, counseling, and referral skills to help students become fully aware of their state of readiness and the areas that possibly need immediate attention. With a student's permission, a referral can be made to appropriate student services for further diagnostic assessment and follow-up.

The system necessitates the effective selection and training of advisers who are highly committed to the role. At Florida State University (FSU), the Council of Informed Advisors, which includes staff members from the undergraduate studies office and the Center for Advising Undeclared Students, oversees the training and support of student advisers.

STAGE 3: DIAGNOSIS AND PRESCRIPTION. For dimensions in which readiness needs have been identified and agreed upon in stage 2, students report to the appropriate student service to complete the referral. At the service, an appropriately trained staff member reviews the screening measure and assigns additional diagnostic appraisals as needed. The staff member also assesses the extent to which any of the four complexity factors may impose disabling stress on the student. On the basis of further diagnostic assessment of capacity and complexity, the student is assigned to an appropriate level of services.

For such assessment to be successful, there must be sufficient coordination among the components of the readiness assessment system. The administration and scoring of high-quality assessments, the use of assessments by advisers to inform, counsel, and refer students, and the delivery of quality support services and programs to address individual readiness needs must be integrated almost to the level of a symphony orchestra. A cross-functional team, such as an enrollment management task force— composed of test developers, advisers, and student services staff members, faculty members, and administrators—must be formed to design, develop, and implement the system. Once implemented, the team must continue to function to maintain and improve it. Again, at FSU, the Enrollment Management Committee, chaired by the assistant provost, coordinates the activities of two teams—the student enrollment team and the student retention team. The former team is responsible for recruiting, orienting, and enrolling students; the latter administers and coordinates student services involved in the care and maintenance of students—from their arrival on campus to their graduation. The readiness assessment system herein presented would be implemented and coordinated under the aegis of the Enrollment Management Committee.

Student Services and Programs to Address Readiness Needs

This section addresses the kinds of student services and interventions that could be offered on a college campus to address identified readiness needs. Self-directed, brief staff-directed, and case-managed services are described later. Examples of the kinds of interventions that could be offered to address key readiness dimensions by level of service are presented in Table 5.1.

Self-Directed Services—High Readiness

Self-directed approaches have been a part of service delivery on college and university campuses for a number of years. One example from FSU is the creation of career-related modules (Reardon and Minor, 1975), which provided a self-guided experience for locating and using career information resources and interventions. In early years, print materials and face-to-face contact were the primary means for disseminating information to individuals. Now, the Internet has become a primary mechanism for those students seeking information. Students at high levels of readiness can seek out many of the resources and services they need simply by accessing various campus Web sites.

Table 5.1. Examples of Student Services and Programs

Readiness Dimensions	High Readiness Enrichment (Self-Directed)	Moderate Readiness Improvement (Brief Staff Assisted)	Low Readiness Remediation (Case Managed)
Knowledge Domain			
Curriculum	Honors classes, colloquia, Web-based instruction	Special topic study sessions, workshops	College-prep courses
School environment	Study abroad, FYE, campus virtual tours	Freshmen seminars or courses	Freshmen courses
Self-knowledge	On-line career assessments, Web-based portfolio	On-line career assessments, Paper-and-pencil inventories	Individual counseling in career center, special abilities testing
Occupational information	On-line occupational information, multimedia presentations, internships	Career resource center, career and job search workshops, shadowing/externships, internships	Individual career counseling
Skills Domain			
Academic	DIS/independent study, faculty research projects	Reading/writing center, math lab, test-taking workshop	Retention center, prep courses, reading/writing center, tutoring
Problem solving and decision making	Discipline-specific or topic-specific print guides to problem solving	Counseling center groups (such as stress/anxiety management), peer education programs	Mentoring, individual counseling
Self-regulation and self-management	CDs/videos on time management and study skills	Study skills and test anxiety workshops, group counseling, drop-in sessions with advisers	Peer education programs
Social/interpersonal	Student activities and leadership programs	Committee work with student organizations; course team projects	Group counseling
Financial management	CD/video-based financial management information	Financial aid workshops	Individual meeting with financial aid specialist
Attitudinal Domain			
Self-efficacy and locus of control	Honors courses, participation in faculty research, seeking leadership opportunities, volunteering for community service, becoming peer mentors	Short-term self-esteem group, mentoring	Individual counseling using cognitive and behavioral techniques, mentoring

Enrichment experiences available to students cut across all aspects of campus life. These experiences may include opportunities to do research with the faculty or to be involved in leadership, community service, and related activities. Students at the high-readiness stage may successfully navigate campus systems via the Web and rarely require face-to-face contact with student services officers. In the academic realm, students can review their course options, register for their courses, pay for their courses, and, in some cases, complete their courses on-line. With the availability of voice and video technology, offices can create Web-based orientations and virtual tours that don't require students to physically set foot on campus. Other campuses have used kiosk technology to deliver information to students and allow them to conduct business with the university, such as pay for classes and housing and review their transcript.

Students may also seek enrichment activities through campus living/learning communities (Johnson and Romanoff, 1999). Students in these types of residence halls look beyond meeting basic needs of room and board to the possibilities in joining a smaller intellectual community within the larger institution. These students may also seek to further hone their academic skills by participating in research projects, even at the undergraduate level. A section of FSU's Web site is devoted to this endeavor and includes the following message: "Florida State University believes that a student's ability to participate in a 'hands-on' fashion is key to a complete education. Undergraduate students at FSU can be actively involved in research under the direction of a distinguished professor or through jobs and internships in various departments" (http://www.research.fsu.edu/students.html). These students may seek out leadership roles through student government and other campus organizations. And they may become peer advisers to other students through academic departments, orientation, and related programs.

Brief Staff-Assisted Services—Moderate Readiness

Students in this category of readiness may, like many other students, participate in the array of campus activities that are designed to assist them in becoming oriented to the college campus and in enrolling in classes. While they are also likely to access print and Web-based resources, it is often the case that simply providing information does not resolve the gap they are experiencing, be it in academic, career, or social areas. They would be more likely to follow up by phone or through a face-to-face contact to gain further information or assistance. Although FSU is considered to be one of the most technology-accessible campuses in the nation, the institution is very concerned about creating a "welcoming environment" for students and thus maintains "Students First" information desks to provide easily accessible one-on-one assistance. Even before students matriculate, their "welcome" begins with a series of sessions for admitted students and their families called "New Student Previews," which are designed to acquaint students early on with the academic and service components of the institution.

Some campuses have created "drop-in" academic advising services in high student traffic areas such as the student union, the library, and the recreation center. Many individual schools and colleges have created peer advising centers, where students can get answers to questions and related forms of brief assistance. FSU has maintained a successful "drop-in" career advising service for many years (Reardon, 1996). These kinds of service delivery formats allow students with moderate levels of readiness to quickly secure help for a specific concern or question, oftentimes from a paraprofessional staff member. These interactions are typically brief (fifteen to thirty minutes) and don't require making an appointment with a highly trained professional. We often describe this aspect of our career services as the "fast food drive-through approach," where students generally wait no more than five to ten minutes before they are seen. A related concept, "career shopper," was described by Reardon, Sampson, and Lenz (2000) and suggests that students want the freedom to browse, much as they would in a store, before they receive specific services. For students at a moderate level of readiness, an individual learning or action plan (Peterson, Sampson, Reardon, and Lenz, 2002) can be written in collaboration with them. The plan lists activities that are designed to help them address their concern, such as choosing a major. The student then executes the plan in a self-directed manner, with periodic brief follow-up by a staff member when the student initiates a request for further assistance.

Students at a moderate level of readiness may also find that participating in workshops or short-term group activities focused on their needs may further enhance their ability to learn and successfully navigate the learning environment.

Case-Managed Services—Low Readiness

As indicated earlier, students at low levels of readiness may have needs that cut across a variety of concerns, including academic, career, financial, and social ones. These students may be targeted through programs that start even before the normal academic year. For instance, institutions may offer summer programs that address the specific needs of first-generation college students and other at-risk populations. These summer enrichment programs are designed to give such students a head start on becoming familiar with the demands of college courses and negotiating a complex learning environment. At FSU, the Center for Academic Retention and Enrichment (CARE) is an academic support unit that assists undergraduate students "who may be disadvantaged due to economic, educational or cultural circumstances. CARE provides programs and services targeted to first-generation college students, and helps facilitate their preparation, recruitment, adjustment, retention and graduation from college" (http://www.fsu.edu/~care/).

More traditional programs that address the needs of low-readiness students include support groups run by the counseling center on topics such as study skills, test anxiety, self-esteem, and stress management. Some campuses have used summer orientation assessment data to target students with special needs through follow-up mailings. The mailings are used to inform them of campus programs and services that may assist them. Students receive specific invitations to meet with an adviser to obtain further assistance.

One key aspect of services targeted to low-readiness students is the focus on individual appointments, usually on a weekly basis. These appointments may be with a tutor in the writing or math lab, a counselor in the counseling center, a career counselor in the career center, or a full-time professional academic adviser. Although a service provider may use print- and computer-based materials in assisting these students, the focus of service delivery is on specific strategies that will help students improve their capability in one or more areas and increase their ability to cope with individual, family, and organizational complexity. It is not unusual to find students who are doing poorly in classes, combating both physical and mental health issues, dealing with a family crisis, or facing relationship issues. One of the retention issues we faced at FSU involved students in their junior year who had completed the general education requirements but who had not yet been accepted into a school or college, often because the program the students were interested in had limited access. These students were found to be at risk of dropping out. Consequently, a specific academic advising position was created to meet the needs of these students.

Some schools have also used a curricular approach for low-readiness students. At FSU, some students are required by the undergraduate studies dean's office, as a condition of their being allowed to stay in school, to take a three-credit-hour career development course to clarify their educational and career plans and, it is hoped, to improve their grade point average. The class provides a great deal of support for low-readiness students through small group meetings and one-on-one instructor conferences.

Conclusion

This chapter has described a model of readiness based on the assessment of key dimensions related to academic performance and retention. In effect, we have designed a system for identifying discrepancies in knowledge, skills, and attitudes necessary for successful adaptation to an academic environment and the ways they can be assessed and developed through effective advising and complementary student services. The intent is that deficiencies in preparation for college-level work can be identified and addressed early so that all students may experience a successful beginning to their college careers. Although the requirements to implement such a system may seem formidable, with effective leadership, we believe they are attainable. With the use of appropriate levels of service delivery with respect to specifically targeted dimensions of readiness, economies in the delivery of student services can be achieved so that readiness assessment and best practices in student advising do not become costly add-ons (Reardon, 1996). At the same time, the effectiveness of student services will be enhanced through the early identification of students' specific areas of growth that require immediate attention to foster successful academic performance and social adjustment.

REFERENCES

American Psychiatric Association. *Diagnostic and Statistical Manual of Mental Disorders.* (4th ed.) Washington, D.C.: American Psychiatric Association, 1994.

Anton, W. D., and Reed, J. R. *College Adjustment Scale.* Odessa, Fla.: Psychological Assessment Resources, 1991.

Bandura, A. "Self-Efficacy Mechanism in Human Agency." *American Psychologist,* 1982, 37, 122–147.

Bandura, A. *Social Foundations of Thought and Action: A Social Cognitive Theory.* Englewood Cliffs, N.J.: Prentice Hall, 1986.

Bandura, A. *Self-Efficacy: The Exercise of Control.* New York: Freeman, 1997.

Bean, J. P. "Interaction Effects Based on Class Level in an Exploratory Model of College Student Dropout Syndrome." *American Educational Research Journal,* 1985, 22, 35–64.

Bean, J. P., and Eaton, S. B. "A Psychological Model of College Student Retention." In J. Braxton (ed.), *Reworking the Student Departure Puzzle*. Nashville, Tenn.: Vanderbilt University Press, 2000.

Betz, N. E., and Hackett, G. "The Relationship of Career-Related Self-Efficacy Expectations to Perceived Career Options in College Women and Men." *Journal of Counseling Psychology*, 1981, *28*, 399–410.

Betz, N. E., and Hackett, G. "The Relationship of Mathematics Self-Efficacy Expectations to the Selection of Science-Based College Majors." *Journal of Vocational Behavior*, 1983, *28*, 149–162.

Butcher, J. N., and others. *MMPI-2 (Minnesota Multiphasic Personality Inventory): Manual for Administering and Scoring*. Minneapolis: University of Minnesota Press, 1989.

Cabrera, A. F., Nora, A., and Castaneda, M. B. "Structural Equation Modeling Test of an Integrated Model of Student Retention." *Journal of Higher Education*, 1993, 64(Mar.- Apr.), 123–141.

Cabrera, A. F., Stampen, J. O., and Hansen, W. L. "Exploring the Effects of Ability to Pay on Persistence in College." *Review of Higher Education* 1990, *13*(3), 303–336.

Chartrand, J. M., Robbins, S. B., and Morrill, W. H. *Career Factors Inventory*. Palo Alto, Calif.: Consulting Psychologists Press, 1997.

Combs, P. *Major in Success*. Berkeley, Calif.: Ten Speed Press, 1994.

Costa, P. T., and McRae, R. R. *NEO PI-R: Professional Annual*. Odessa, Fla.: Psychological Assessment Resources, 1992.

Crockett, D. S., and Levitz, R. S. "Current Advising Practices in Colleges and Universities." In R. B. Winston, T. K. Miller, S. C. Ender, T. J. Grites, and Associates (eds.), *Developmental Academic Advising*. San Francisco: Jossey-Bass, 1988.

Fishbein, M., and Ajzen, I. *Belief, Attitude, Intention and Behavior: An Introduction to Theory and Research*. Reading, Mass.: Addison-Wesley, 1975.

Flavel, J. H., Miller, P. H., and Miller, S. A. *Cognitive Development*. Englewood Cliffs, N.J.: Prentice Hall, 1993.

Gordon, V. N. "Educational Planning: Helping Students Make Decisions." In R. B. Winston, T. K. Miller, S. C. Ender, T. J. Grites, and Associates (eds.), *Developmental Academic Advising*. San Francisco: Jossey-Bass, 1988.

Hamrick, G., and Hossler, D. "Active and Passive Searching in Postsecondary Education Decision Making." *Review of Higher Education*, 1996, *19*(2), 179–198.

Harmon, L. W., Hanson, J. C., Borgan, F. H., and Hammer, A. L. *Strong Interest Inventory and Application Guide*. Palo Alto, Calif.: Consulting Psychologists Press, 1994.

Heppner, P. P., and Petersen, C. H. "The Development and Implications of a Personal Problem-Solving Inventory." *Journal of Counseling Psychology,* 1982, *29,* 66–75.

Holland, J. L. *Self-Directed Search.* Odessa, Fla.: Personality Assessment Resources, 1994.

Holland, J. L., Daiger, D. C., and Power, P. G. *My Vocational Situation.* Palo Alto, Calif.: Consulting Psychologists Press, 1980.

Johnson, J. L., and Romanoff, S. J. "Higher Education Residential Learning Communities: What Are the Implications for Student Success?" *College Student Journal,* 1999, *33,* 385–399.

Kahnaman, D. *Attention and Effort.* Englewood Cliffs, N.J.: Prentice Hall, 1973.

Krumboltz, J. D. *Career Beliefs Inventory.* Palo Alto, Calif.: Consulting Psychologists Press, 1991.

Lazarus, R. S. *Psychological Stress and Coping Process.* New York: McGraw-Hill, 1966.

Lent, R. W., Brown, S. D., and Larkin, K. D. "Comparison of Three Theoretically Derived Variables in Predicting Career and Academic Behavior: Self-Efficacy, Interest Congruence, and Consequence Thinking." *Journal of Counseling Psychology,* 1987, *34,* 293–298.

Meichenbaum, D. *Cognitive-Behavior Modification.* New York: Plenum, 1977.

Newell, A., and Simon, H. A. *Human Problem Solving.* Englewood Cliffs, N.J.: Prentice Hall, 1972.

Pascarella, E. T., and Terenzini, P. T. *How College Affects Students.* San Francisco: Jossey-Bass, 1991.

Pascaralla, E. T., Terenzini, P. T., and Wolfle, L. M. "Orientation to College and Freshman Year Persistence/Withdrawal Decisions." *Journal of Higher Education,* 1986, *57*(Mar.-Apr.), 155–175.

Perry, R. P., Hechter, F. J., Verena, H. M., and Weinberg, L. E. "Enhancing Achievement Motivation and Performance in College Students: An Attributional Retraining Perspective." *Research in Higher Education,* 1993, *34*(6), 687–723.

Peterson, G. W. "Using a Vocational Card Sort as an Assessment of Occupational Knowledge." *Journal of Career Assessment,* 1998, *6,* 49–67.

Peterson, G. W., Sampson, J. P., Jr., Reardon, R. C., and Lenz, J. G. "A Cognitive Information Processing Approach to Career Problem Solving and Decision Making." In D. Brown (ed.), *Career Choice and Development.* (4th ed.) San Francisco: Jossey-Bass, 2002.

Peterson, S. L. "Career Decision Making Self-Efficacy and Institutional Integration of Underprepared College Students." *Research in Higher Education,* 1993, *34*(6), 659–685.

Reardon, R. C. "A Program and Cost Analysis of a Self-Directed Career Decision-Making Program in a University Career Center." *Journal of Counseling and Development,* 1996, *74,* 280–285.

Reardon, R. C., and Minor, C. "Revitalizing the Career Information Service." *Personnel and Guidance Journal,* 1975, *54,* 169–171.

Reardon, R. C., Sampson, J. P., Jr., and Lenz, J. G. "Career Assessment in a Time of Changing Roles, Relationships, and Contexts." *Journal of Career Assessment,* 2000, *8,* 351–359.

Rotter, J. B. "Generalized Expectancies for Internal Locus of Control of Reinforcement." *Psychological Monographs,* 1966, *80,* 1–28.

Sampson, J. P., Jr., and others. *Career Thoughts Inventory.* Odessa, Fla.: Personality Assessment Resources, 1996.

Sampson, J. P., Jr., and others. "The Design and Use of a Measure of Dysfunctional Career Thoughts Among Adults, College Students, and High School Students: The Career Thoughts Inventory." *Journal of Career Assessment,* 1998, *6,* 115–134.

Sampson, J. P., Jr., Peterson, G. W., Reardon, R. C., and Lenz, J. G. "Using Readiness Assessment to Improve Career Services: A Cognitive Information Processing Approach." *The Career Development Quarterly,* 2000, *49,* 146–174.

Saunders, D. E., Peterson, G. W., Sampson, J. P., Jr., and Reardon, R. C. "Relation of Depression and Dysfunctional Career Thinking to Career Indecision." *Journal of Vocational Behavior,* 2000, *56,* 288–298.

Sherer, M., and others. "Self-Efficacy Scale." In K. Corcoran and J. Fisher (eds.), *Measures for Clinical Practice, Volume 2.* (3rd ed.) New York: Free Press, 2000.

Sinnott, J. D. "A Model for the Solution of Ill-Structured Problems: Implications for Everyday and Abstract Problem Solving." In J. D. Sinnott (ed.), *Everyday Problem Solving.* New York: Praeger, 1989.

Slaney, R. B. "Expressed Vocational Choice and Vocational Indecision." *Journal of Counseling Psychology,* 1980, *27,* 122–129.

Smart, J. C., Feldman, K. A., and Ethington, C. A. *Academic Disciplines: Holland's Theory and the Study of College Students and Faculty.* Nashville, Tenn.: Vanderbilt University Press, 2000.

Stage, F. K., and Hossler, D. "Where Is the Student? Linking Student Behaviors, College Choice, and College Persistence." In J. Braxton (ed.), *Reworking the Student Departure Puzzle.* Nashville, Tenn.: Vanderbuilt University Press, 2000.

Tinto, V. *Leaving College: Rethinking the Causes and Cures of Student Attrition.* Chicago: University of Chicago Press, 1987.

Weiner, B. *An Attributional Theory of Motivation and Emotion.* New York: Springer-Verlag, 1986.

Weinstein, C. E., Palmer, D. R., and Schulte, A. C. *Learning and Study Strategies Inventory.* Clearwater, Fla.: H&H Publishing, 1987.

Wilhite, S. "Self-Efficacy, Locus of Control, Self-Assessment of Memory Ability, and Student Activities as Predictors of College Course Achievement." *Journal of Educational Psychology,* 1990, *82*(4), 696–700.

Woditsh, G. A. *Developing Generic Skills: A Model for Competency-Based Education.* Bowling Green, Ohio: Bowling Green State University, CUE Project, 1977.

Zimmerman, B. J., and Bandura, A. "Impact of Self-Regulatory Influences on Writing Course Attainment." *American Educational Research Journal,* 1994, *31*(4), 845–862.

6

NEW STUDENT ORIENTATION IN THE TWENTY-FIRST CENTURY

INDIVIDUALIZED, DYNAMIC, AND DIVERSE

Bonita C. Jacobs

PERHAPS NO SINGLE ACTIVITY can do more to set the academic tone of the collegiate experience and establish a comprehensive approach to student academic success than new student orientation. A well-planned orientation program accentuates the interrelationship of the classroom experience with student development initiatives, and a well-conceived program exposes the student to the importance of techniques for academic success and individual development.

New student orientation requires an institutional interweaving of objectives in order to provide students with (1) access to testing, advising, and registration, (2) information on housing, financial aid, commuter life, and student activities, (3) exposure to mentoring, wellness issues, decision making, and career exploration, (4) an underscoring of institutional values (for example, diversity issues, acceptance of others, and honor codes), and (5) a focus on campus identity and pride. This comprehensiveness requires departments to interact with one another beyond administrative divisions and institutional separations.

Although Harvard was the first to implement an orientation program (of sorts) by assigning returning students to assist new students in their transitions to college, new student orientation in the United States began in 1888, with the first official program being at Boston University. By

1925, there were more than twenty-five orientation programs throughout the country, often taking the form of a "welcome week" (Johnson, 1998; National Orientation Directors Association, 2000). During the early twentieth century, faculty members were at times assigned responsibilities to orient students to the campus. And with the influx of students after World War II, campuses struggling to provide individualized services began to offer formal orientation services. The stately convocations and lectures common during that era gave way to small group meetings and precollege clinics during the 1960s (Johnson, 1998).

Today, new student orientation can take the form of a traditional one- to three-day summer program, a drive-in workshop, a welcome week activity, a yearlong program, or a combination of all these. It is increasingly commonplace to find interactive and virtual orientation programs, particularly with the growth in adult, transfer, and distance education populations and with the increased need for campuses to categorize attendees in order to accommodate diverse transitional issues. A part-time adult student with a full-time job and a family has different orientation needs from those of a full-time traditional-aged residential student, and a student transferring a large number of credits may have different needs from those of one transferring only a few credits.

The components of a successful new student orientation, whether a one-day, one-week, or yearlong program, will include a wide range of services, activities, and opportunities. It is mutually important, for example, for students to learn about adjusting to campus life, achieving in the classroom, and making responsible decisions, since lack of success in one can have devastating effects on the others. Orientation can help students set more realistic academic, personal, and social expectations (Krallman and Holcomb, 1997) and thus aid in the development of the "whole" student.

Orientation has not always been so ambitious in new student transitions. Once little more than a sort of party for new students, with a limited menu of advising, registration, and campus tours (Bergman, McClelland, and DeMont, 1999), the orientation agenda has evolved into a rich array of seminars on academic survival and life choices (Clayton, 1998). One of the many challenges for a quality orientation program is to educate the campus on the objectives of the program in order to overcome the image some have of the orientation as being limited to fun and games (Gonzales, Hill-Traynham, and Jacobs, 2000; Mann, 1998).

Even though students may remain on campus for a semester or two, they make a decision to leave or stay within the first few weeks. Orientation is a key factor in this decision process; it is the first chance students have to evaluate their college decision firsthand. They size up the institution and how well they can make satisfactory academic progress, crystallize their career or life goals, integrate successfully into campus life, and meet their personal and social anticipations.

Furthermore, connecting students with the faculty is a proven retention strategy. Any such involvement during orientation can help students feel more connected to the academic process and to the college environment. Clearly, orientation can be a powerful tool for systematic transitioning of students into college.

A Programmatic Guide to Orientation

The following programmatic guide is designed to include the most commonplace components of new student orientation programs. Although not intended to provide a comprehensive blueprint, this overview of new student issues can be overlaid against an institution's mission to create an individual campus plan. Each issue is important to the first-year experience, and each should be included in orientation, the freshman seminar, campus programming, or mentoring programs. It is increasingly evident that the orientation agenda must by its very nature consider the components of the freshman seminar, mentoring, and other transition initiatives, in order to prevent gaps and duplications in services.

Advising

Quality advising during orientation is imperative, not only because of the obvious need to initiate the academic planning process appropriately but also because it provides intervention at a high-stress, unsure period in the transition process. There is a "significant correlation between quality academic advisement, student satisfaction, and enhanced persistence and graduation" (Gardner and Kerr, 1995, p. v).

Quality advising relationships can "enhance students' academic progress; improve students' emotional state; aid in guiding students to form sensible long-term plans; and assist institutions by reducing many avoidable problems" (Petress, 2000, p. 598). New initiatives in technology, academic progress tracking, extended articulation agreements, and assessment programs have aided the advisement process (Francis and Hampton, 1999), thus allowing the adviser to focus more on the student relationship and less on the mechanics of advisement.

Registration

Orientation directors have long touted registration as the incentive to attract students to the "real purposes" of orientation. Nonetheless, an efficient registration process is imperative to a quality orientation, and care should be taken to ensure that the entering student is given a wide range of appropriate course selections from which to choose. When one considers that entering students are faced with multiple transitional issues and are thus "at risk," it becomes nonsensical to provide them with anything other than optimal course selections during the registration process. Yet some campuses have limited orientation course options, giving new students access to only a few seats in the more popular classes.

Registration will shortly become—and already has become on many campuses—"a very passive on-going procedure. Students will be able to register any time and for all four years if they wish. . . . Students will be assured that at the end of their sessions, their enrollments will be complete and their bills paid by electronic transfer" (Stedman, 1995, p. 76). Thus, the streamlined registration process will require collaborative pre-planning between the registrar and the orientation director. It is no longer feasible to defer registration problems until they are detected during the orientation process.

Student Assessments

Most campuses offer a variety of testing for students, including academic placement tests, personality inventories, learning and reading skills inventories, lifestyle assessments, and career placement tests. A carefully selected testing program can be an important retention tool, provided it is used to assist students in their advisement and learning skill assessments. Care should be taken to ensure that orientation is not consumed with the testing process; to do so would leave students with little information and with even less of a campus connection. The most comprehensive student assessment program with the most detailed information indices fails the orientation process if it is used as a substitute for a humanistic, pragmatic approach to new student orientation and retention.

Physical Orientation

Although orientation is reduced in the minds of some to little more than a campus tour, it is nonetheless important to include both physical and academic orientations to campus. Without a clear understanding of services and academic assistance available to them, students are at risk of dropping out even though excellent services may be in place. Incoming students who are familiar with the physical layout of a campus feel acclimated and more in charge when classes begin; students who are aware of and comfortable with resources available to them are more apt to take advantage of retention interventions.

Campus Services

Provided that campus services are efficient and friendly, orientation can instill in students a trust in the institution. Students expect top-quality services, and the time it takes to provide them with such services can yield positive results. "Prospective students who trust a college are more likely to enroll or make noncontractual precommitments to attend the college. Current students are less likely to transfer or drop out if they are trusting, thereby easing retention problems" (Amit, Thomas, and Glenn, 2001, p. 322). Orientation has an opportunity to build such a trust in the institution's services and thereby in the institution itself.

Financial Aid and Financial Management

With more than 50 percent of all students enrolled in higher education receiving grants, loans, and work-study employment, it is crucial for the orientation director to have basic knowledge of financial aid (Pope, 2001). In addition, many students receive scholarships and will be concerned about getting their overall financial package in order. A quality orientation program will work diligently to ensure that information is clearly, accurately, and completely presented to students and their parents.

The number of orientation programs offering workshops on financial management has increased as students have experienced heightened difficulties with financial management, in part as a result of the increased exposure to credit card offers. Some students presume that by accepting financial aid they can afford all college expenses. Yet the level of aid is not always sufficient to accommodate the entire cost, particularly if a student opts for more expensive housing, a large clothing or entertainment budget, or a car with its accompanying expenses. It is important that orientation help students realize the full cost of education, even to the point of having each student list personal income and expenses. Outside employment, family support, parent loans for undergraduate students, and the reduction of expenditures are options to help students handle the finances of college and thereby increase their odds of managing debt and remaining in school.

Housing and Commuter Life

Students living in campus residence halls tend to have easier access to campus opportunities than their off-campus counterparts. Research indicates that, compared with commuting students who live at home, residential students persist and graduate at higher rates, are more involved in extracurricular, social, and cultural events on campus, interact more frequently with faculty members and peers, and are significantly more satisfied with college (Schroeder, Mable, and Associates, 1994). Nonetheless, residential students and their parents may have myriad questions and concerns, ranging from the size of the windows and roommate assignments to safety and programming, all of which need to be addressed during orientation.

Commuter students can face a greater risk of attrition if they lack the opportunity to become involved in informal contacts available to residence hall students (Wolfe, 1993). Therefore, it is important that orientations focus on networking opportunities for commuter students and provide them with mechanisms for maneuvering the college system as off-campus students. Breakaway sessions specific to commuter and residential issues are particularly effective (Jacobs, 1993).

Health and Wellness Issues

New students are faced with challenging decisions about alcohol, tobacco, illegal drug use, sexual health, stress management, nutrition, and fitness. These decisions can have enormous impact on students' academic success—so much so that most orientation programs incorporate these issues into the orientation agenda (Strumpf, 2000). Orientation directors typically provide information via flyers, brochures, skits, and games. In addition, wellness directors may be invited to incorporate surveys into orientation with follow-up activities, and some institutions require students to take a one-hour course on health issues during the first semester (Axiotis, Symons, Pepe, and Dubick, 1991).

Campus Pride

Orientation has been instrumental on many campuses in initiating or building school spirit and campus pride and therefore campus identity. In fact, one of the ways to alter a campus culture is to incorporate these programs into orientation. Many of the orientation activities are interactive and specifically designed to help students become acquainted with their new environment, and student orientation leaders are typically trained to help connect students with one another and with the university. Schools that foster high campus identity tend to also have high retention rates, and an emphasis on campus connection ought not be underestimated.

Orientation Sessions for Specific Populations

Orientation programs can have sessions specifically tailored for student-parent or student-family sessions or unique orientation activities for certain populations, including transfer students, adult students, graduate students, international students, students with disabilities, and student athletes. It is important to individualize orientation to the extent necessary to address the needs of each of these groups. This may take the form of special programs, breakaway sessions, or extended orientation.

Parent and Family Orientation Programs

Because students remain interconnected with their families, involving parents and spouses can be an important component in the orientation process. Families are partners in the education of the student; after all, both the family and the institution want the student to succeed academically, and they are willing to go to great lengths to assist in that process.

Parents are generally eager to be part of the orientation process. They ask questions, guide the student, and reinforce the tenets of academic demands. In addition, "there are a number of reasons why it makes educational sense for the college to provide clearly defined opportunities for parents to stay involved in their son's or daughter's academic experience. The underlying aim in student development theory and practice is to provide an educational environment that acknowledges the multidimensional aspects of human development and strives to enhance the growth process" (Austin, 1993, p. 98).

Parent programs should include a wide range of individuals who can provide accurate and detailed information on financial aid, scholarships, housing, academic success, career planning, immunizations, business services, and wellness issues. Parents are attentive to and benefit greatly from informal activities that allow them to network with faculty and staff members, students, and other parents. At the same time, they are generally both anxious and eager to know that the school will take seriously its commitment to assist the student. Only when parents begin to feel comfortable with the student entering college can they release their long-used protective umbrellas.

Likewise, families of adult students can enhance the orientation process. Adult learners "seek associations with peers and families whose intentions are congruent with their own" (Hatch, 2000, p. 43). The networks formed between families during orientation can be particularly helpful, and workshops, discussions, and forums on coping with the multiple demands of college, family, and careers are beneficial to both the student and the family. Spouses of students, in particular, need an opportunity to discuss the demands that will be placed on the students and to explore avenues for the family to cope with these changes.

Many orientations, especially those specific to adult learners, offer children's or siblings' programs during orientation. This allows the children to have a positive campus experience, but it primarily affords the orientation participants an opportunity to focus on the program. Noting that the age ranges of children will vary greatly, it is important to include a number of activities to involve them in different ways, regardless of whether orientation is a one-time event or a yearlong endeavor.

Parent and family associations are often a part of the orientation office. Membership can be automatic or elective and usually involves newsletters, e-mail information, campus athletic and cultural event discounts, and scholarship contribution opportunities. Parents are particularly adept at reinforcing the need for students to seek campus resources that can help them in their transition process, and it is in the orientation director's interest to maintain contact with them.

Transfer Students

Most of the research and literature on transfer students centers on the community college transfer student (Harrison, 1993). Community colleges make up more than one-fourth of all postsecondary institutions and are the fastest growing segment of higher education (Pascarella, 1999). In addition, a significant number of minority students and older college students enroll first in the community college system.

Students also transfer to and from a wide range of four-year institutions and for a variety of reasons, and recent studies indicate that transfer students tend to have similar adjustment issues as incoming first-year students. Some of these issues, commonly referred to as "transfer shock," include a decrease in grade point average the semester following transfer (Rhine, Milligan, and Nelson, 2000) and transitional issues similar to incoming first-semester students.

Because transfer students tend to be so diverse in their demographic makeup and academic backgrounds, it can be difficult to provide a quality orientation program for them. In addition, they transfer a wide range of courses, an issue that presents a unique challenge for advisers, registrars, academic deans, and orientation staffers.

Increasingly, orientation directors are understanding the need to individualize transfer orientation programs, particularly those with large numbers of students, to accommodate the academic and demographic diversity of the transfer population. It is not feasible to assume a "one size fits all" mentality when orienting these students.

Adult Students

It is often difficult to convince adult students that they need orientation programs, and they tend to be less satisfied with orientation than are traditional-aged students (Kasworm, 1980). This is in part because adult students often feel that they have life experiences that offset any orientation needs; also, transfer students may not feel the need for orientation because they attended one at a previous institution. Nonetheless, adult students typically have concerns about studying, managing time, writing papers, taking tests, and coping with campus life (Copland, 1989; Kasworm and Blowers, 1994), all of which are addressed in new student orientation. It is important that programs for adults include developmental sessions, information on student rights and responsibilities, and information about what students might realistically expect from an adviser (Creamer, Polson, and Ryan, 1995).

Because so many adult learners and their spouses work, it is particularly important to provide orientation on varying days, evenings, and weekends to accommodate schedules. In addition, it is important that orientation directors and advisers make themselves aware of the characteristics of the adult population and the developmental issues faced by adult students (Creamer, Polson, and Ryan, 1995), especially when one considers that, since 1970, adults have made up roughly half of all college enrollments (Aslanian, 2001).

It should be noted that community and junior colleges are seen as leaders in educating both adult and at-risk students (Green and Miller, 1998) and, as a result, have an especial obligation to seek creative ways to provide a meaningful orientation to a diverse population. In addition, community colleges are attracting the majority of first-year higher education students (Rhine, Milligan, and Nelson, 2000), and these institutions' responsibility for providing meaningful new student orientations is enormous.

Graduate Students

Orientation programs for new graduate students are most often organized through the graduate school rather than through the office of new student orientation, and they are distinct programs that are designed specifically for graduate students (Strumpf, 2000). Respondents to a recent informal e-mail survey indicate that most colleges have Web sites; however, the majority of the ones who responded do not have information that highlights an orientation program separate from other new student enrollment requirements.

There is little literature specific to graduate student orientation; nonetheless, a substantial number of schools do offer such programs. Obviously, the orientation needs of these students will be different from those of undergraduates, as they will have great concern with graduate expectations and requirements. It will be interesting as data emerges to see whether graduate student orientation can have as much effect on the transitioning postbaccalaureate student as undergraduate student orientation has on the beginning college student.

International Students

Orientation programs for new international students can range from a distinct program organized out of the international office to a workshop in conjunction with other new student orientations. Typically, the larger the institution, the more likely it is to host a separate program designed for international students (Strumpf, 2000).

International students typically need information on regulations, including insurance requirements, American customs, academic expectations, immigration responsibilities, financial management, and other issues specific to the individual region or campus. With all these extra focuses, it is important not to overlook the presentation of the material that native students receive in their orientations—for example, residence and commuter life, quality advisement, academic success, safety issues, and campus resources.

For international students, the events of September 11, 2001, and increased security have brought additional concerns about immigration policies and procedures, acceptance by American students, and receiving finances from home countries. This angst serves as a reminder to the orientation director that it is as important to help students from another country to feel welcome (and some would argue more so) as it is to acclimate those from within the United States.

Students with Disabilities

In 1998, more than four hundred thousand students with disabilities were enrolled in postsecondary education, primarily at public two-year and four-year schools and most often at medium and large institutions (National Center for Educational Statistics, 2000). There has been unprecedented growth of this population over the last two decades, primarily due to four factors: (1) because of legislation passed in 1973, services now exist for those who qualify, (2) there is better academic preparation in high school, (3) students with disabilities are entering professions that require a postsecondary education, and (4) the Americans with Disabilities Act of 1990 has increased the opportunity for adults in higher education (Hitchings and others, 1998).

It is important to ask both the orientation participant and anyone who may be attending with the student (for example, parents, siblings, spouses) if they will need accommodations during orientation. Accommodations might include provision of the following:

o Sign language interpreters, closed captioning, captioning in real time (CARTs), and assisted-listening devices for students and family members with severe hearing loss

o Enlarged print, scribes, readers, and Braille for those with severe visual impairment

o Adjustable desks and wide aisles for students with mobility impairments

o Extended time on tests for students with learning disabilities and attention-deficit disorders

Each campus will need to determine the most appropriate and feasible accommodations based on students' documented needs. It should, however, be a matter of course that all rooms used for orientation are in accessible locations with accommodating restrooms and other necessary facilities nearby.

Student Athletes

Student athletes have a unique set of challenges as they adjust to college life, and getting off to a good start is critical (Denson, 1994). Their schedules require them to spend numerous hours in practice and athletic events, and since they are typically not able to work, financial management is often an issue. They are sometimes more focused on athletics than academics, they may miss classes because of game schedules, and they must learn to deal with media and public attention that is afforded few nonathletes (Jacobs, 1993; Simons, Van Rheenen, and Covington, 1999).

The added advantage that most athletic programs bring is tutoring and other support services for athletes (Simons, Van Rheenen, and Covington, 1999). Staff members have an opportunity to build on the resources already available for athletes but must often adjust the orientation program around athletes' schedules and differing needs. Student athletes are typically part of the general orientation program, but there is a growing trend to provide a session especially geared to the athlete. The National Orientation Directors Association Data Bank found that, in 1996, 43 percent of the reporting institutions provided some sort of special orientation for scholarship athletes, whereas 95 percent distinguished them in some way in 2000 (Strumpf, 2000; Strumpf and Sharer, 1996). Although some might consider this a result of "big school athletics," there was no difference in the trend based on the size of the institution, although large schools do tend to be more likely to provide special programming.

Other Student Populations

A number of institutions present distinct sessions, special orientation programs, or workshops for particular student populations. The most frequently mentioned of these groups include the academically disadvantaged students, honors and academically talented students, ethnic minority students, and veterans (Strumpf, 2000). The decision to provide special orientation programming for a specific population is based on the campus mission, institutional values, the resources available, campus interest, the level of student interest, political considerations, and the desire to improve data (for example, yield rates, persistence, and satisfaction levels) for that population.

Trends in New Student Orientation

Originally designed as a registration period for first-year students, new student orientation has evolved into an individualized, targeted program to transition a diverse, ever-changing population. Once colleges began to see the advantage of providing programs for parents, transfers, and other targeted populations, orientation programs began to take on a new look. Today, an evolving understanding of the transition process, factors influencing retention, the impact of orientation on the overall college experience, and competing demands on students' time have translated into emerging trends in the profession.

Technology

Technology is allowing for more individualization of orientation programs. Registration and orientation information is often Web-based, and financial aid, student resources, academic information, and housing sites are typically connected to orientation Web sites. Class scheduling is no longer offered through touch-tone phone registration alone; Internet access is often available as well. At many institutions, virtual orientations and videoconferencing are available for distance education students and for those who attend school a long distance from home, and virtual social opportunities are included to allow students to make friends and select roommates (Lask, 1998; "Virtual Orientation Pairs Friends, Roommates," 2001). Students receive CD-ROMs chock-full of reference information, allowing the actual orientation session to be more dynamic and less focused on covering a plethora of facts (Greenlaw and Kaplan, 1998; Rielley, 2000). The new orientation is designed to hold the attention of a generation accustomed to video games, multimedia entertainment, and immediate feedback.

In addition, distance education, class chat rooms, on-line libraries, video tutoring, and Web-based information demand that incoming students possess technological savvy, and some orientation programs provide a series of interactive teaching workshops designed to prepare students for video instruction and e-mail classroom addendums (Thompson, 2000). Whereas half-day to three-day orientations cannot provide the requisite time for more than the most basic instruction, welcome-week and year-long programs are now offering much-needed workshops in technology. Nonetheless, conveying technological knowledge to students attending orientation is of the utmost importance (Miller and Viajar, 2001).

Outdoor Activities

Ropes courses, summer spirit camps, and wilderness outings are often an optional, or sometimes even required, part of orientation. These outdoor activities are designed to increase self-esteem and self-confidence as well as provide an opportunity for students to become quickly acquainted with their peers (Brown, 1998; Devlin, 1996). Originally used to build teamwork among orientation leaders, many outdoor activities now include the incoming class as a way of introducing the new students to the campus community. An added benefit is the creation of a group of leaders who are committed to one another and to the college or university (Henton and Smith, 1998). Although not heavily researched, some studies indicate that students who have participated in wilderness programs have increased levels of retention (Fears and Denke, 2001).

Extended Orientation Periods

Orientations continue to expand. Mentoring programs and yearlong orientations are found in all sizes and types of colleges. Learning communities, formed during orientation, include common class schedules and, in some cases, common housing assignments (Fried, 1999; Gordon, Young, and Kallanov, 2001; Schroeder, 1997). First-year seminars have been found to be effective in improving freshman retention rates (Howard and Jones, 2000) and are excellent tools for expanding transition initiatives beyond orientation. As institutions have realized that significant, positive retention gains in a strong first-year experience program can be snuffed out with a dismal sophomore slump, many orientation programs have instituted a sophomore year experience that focuses primarily on career exploration and development. In addition, four-year institutions frequently have a senior year experience program to ease students out of college and into the career world, and postbaccalaureate institutions have realized that graduate students can also benefit from orientation (Miller, Miles, and Dyer, 2001).

Reading Lists

Students today often receive a reading list prior to arrival on campus. This is not a new concept, but unlike past generations of reading lists, the content today is often focused on during current orientation programs (Gracie, 1997; Tifft, 1990). The book author is frequently brought to campus for fall convocation—another reincarnated phenomenon—and he or she is asked to deliver the address, using the book discussed during orientation. By combining the reading requirement with writing assignments, an institution's commitment to creative writing is highlighted. Likewise, by selecting a book with an acceptance theme, the institutional commitment to diversity is underscored ("New Student Orientation: Don't Wait," 2001; Spann, Smith, and Buchanan, 1998).

Service Learning

A growing trend for both orientations and welcome week programs is service learning ("New Student Orientation: Don't Wait," 2001). Hours or days are carved out for students to work on a Habitat for Humanity house, serve in a soup kitchen, or help in a homeless shelter. Orientation students report that the activities help them become an integral part of the campus, feel good about their service role in the new community, and get to know other students quickly in positive circumstances. Students are entering colleges with a high interest in volunteerism, and connecting community service to orientation programs provides a welcoming environment and a tool for helping a group of students feel comfortable and connected (Geelhoed, 1999). The 2001 CIRP survey found "a record high level of volunteerism, with 82.6 percent of incoming freshmen reporting frequent or occasional volunteer work, compared [with] 81 percent last year and a low of 66 percent in 1989" (Higher Education Research Institute, 2002). Contributing in part to this rise is the requirement of community service for graduation from many high schools, which has increased from 23.2 to 28.2 percent since the idea was first broached in 1998 (Higher Education Research Institute, 2002).

Other Trends

Increased scholarship opportunities and expanded financial aid packages translate into an increase in the number of students receiving some type of financial assistance. This will greatly enhance the amount of information and time devoted to financial aid issues during orientation.

Privacy and the appropriate use of the Internet will become of more concern as abuses become public knowledge (Greenlaw and Jacobs, 1999)—for example, such security issues as published crime statistics.

Budget crunches, coupled with a desire to pack more perks into orientations, have sent directors to private companies and the corporate world for funding. T-shirts and notebook covers often advertise a fast food or display a department store logo in addition to the campus logo. Banks, airlines, cell phone companies, shopping malls, bookstores, and restaurants are all eager to get their names in front of students. This translates into huge funding opportunities for orientation programs and a more generously funded event for students, complete with free food, prizes, and giveaways. This funding bonanza is, of course, not without its critics (Marcus, 1999), and the campus must be careful in the kinds of messages it gives to incoming students via its corporate partnerships.

Significant demographic and sociological shifts will create additional concerns for orientation in the future. The growing minority population will enter colleges in record numbers, creating more diverse student bodies, and orientation programs must be able to respond to cultural individuality and diverse student needs.

These trends underscore the fact that orientation offices must continue to collaborate with other campus departments, sometimes taking the lead and sometimes the back seat. Orientation is more than a program or an activity; it is a college's virgin initiative in retention efforts and campus milieu management for each new class of students. It is an endeavor that involves everyone from the computing center to the police department, from the academic dean to the registrar, and from the adviser to the upper echelons of the administration.

REFERENCES

Amit, K., Thomas, W., and Glenn, A. "Student Trust and Its Antecedents in Higher Education." *Journal of Higher Education,* 2001, 72(3), 322.

Aslanian, C. B. *Adult Students Today.* New York: The College Board, 2001.

Austin, D. "Orientation Activities for the Families of New Students." In M. L. Upcraft, R. H. Mullendore, B. O. Barefoot, and D. S. Fidler (eds.), *Designing Successful Transitions: A Guide for Orienting Students to College.* Columbia, S.C.: The National Resource Center for the Freshman Year Experience, 1993.

Axiotis, I. R., Symons, C. W., Pepe, M., and Dubick, C. "Health Promotion Programming for Freshmen: A Campus-Wide Strategy." *Wellness Perspectives,* 1991, 8(2), 76–80.

Bergman, B., McClelland, S., and DeMont, J. "First-Year Confidential." *Maclean's,* 1999, 112(46), 86–89.

Brown, D. A. "Does an Outdoor Orientation Program Really Work?" *College and University,* 1998, 73(4), 17–23.

Clayton, M. "Getting to Know You." *Christian Science Monitor,* 1998, 90(195), B1–B5.

Copland, B. A. "Adult Learners." In M. L. Upcraft and J. N. Gardner (eds.), *The Freshman Year Experience.* San Francisco: Jossey-Bass, 1989.

Creamer, E. G., Polson, C. J., and Ryan, C. C. "Advising and Orientation Programs for Entering Adult Students." In M. L. Upcraft and G. L. Kramer (eds.), *First-Year Academic Advising: Patterns in the Present, Pathways to the Future.* Columbia, S.C.: National Resource Center for the Freshman Year Experience and Students in Transition, 1995.

Denson, E. I. "Developing a Freshman Seminar for Student Athletes." *Journal of College Student Development,* 1994, 35, 303–304.

Devlin, A. S. "Survival Skills Training During Freshman Orientation: Its Role in College Adjustment." *Journal of College Student Development,* 1996, 37(3), 324–334.

Fears, G., and Denke, M. S. "Wilderness Pursuit Programs: An Orientation Paradigm." *Journal of College Orientation and Transition,* 2001, *9*(1), 5–12.

Francis, J., and Hampton, M. "The Adaptive Research University and the Drive to Market." *Journal of Higher Education,* 1999, *70*(6), 625.

Fried, J. "Steps to Creative Campus Collaboration." *Journal of College Orientation and Transition,* 1999, *7*(1), 11–19.

Gardner, J. N., and Kerr, T. "Foreword." In M. L. Upcraft and G. L. Kramer (eds.), *First-Year Academic Advising: Patterns in the Present, Pathways to the Future.* Columbia, S.C.: National Resource Center for the Freshman Year Experience and Students in Transition, 1995.

Geelhoed, J. "Capitalizing on Student Interests: Community Service and Orientation." *Journal of College Orientation and Transition,* 1999, *7*(1), 30–32.

Gonzales, T. V., Hill-Traynham, P. S., and Jacobs, B. C. "Developing Effective Orientation Programs for Special Populations." In M. J. Fabich (ed.), *Orientation Planning Manual.* Pullman, Wash.: National Orientation Directors Association, 2000.

Gordon, T. W., Young, J. C., and Kallanov, C. J. "Connecting the Freshman Year Experience Through Learning Communities: Practical Implications for Academic and Student Affairs Units." *College Student Affairs Journal,* 2001, *20*(2), 37–47.

Gracie, W. J. Jr. "Summer Reading and an Intellectual Community." *Liberal Education,* 1997, *83*(4), 39–43.

Green, J. T., and Miller, M. T. "A Comparison Study of Enrollees and Non-Enrollees in an Orientation Course at a Two-Year College." *Journal of College Orientation and Transition,* 1998, *5*(2), 14–20.

Greenlaw, H., and Jacobs, B. "Trends in Orientation." Paper presented at the annual conference of the National Orientation Directors Association, Tampa, Fla., Oct. 1999.

Greenlaw, H., and Kaplan, S. "Using Compact Discs as a Supplement to an Orientation Program." *Journal of College Orientation and Transition,* 1998, *6*(1), 36–37.

Harrison, C. H. "Orienting Transfer Students." In M. L. Upcraft, R. H. Mullendore, B. O. Barefoot, and D. S. Fidler (eds.), *Designing Successful Transitions: A Guide for Orienting Students to College.* Columbia, S.C.: The National Resource Center for the Freshman Year Experience, 1993.

Hatch, C. "Parent and Family Orientation." In M. J. Fabich (ed.), *Orientation Planning Manual.* Pullman, Wash.: National Orientation Directors Association, 2000.

Henton, M., and Smith, K. P. "Joining Team Building and Experiential Learning in an Orientation Leader Training Program: The Quest Training Model." *Journal of College Orientation and Transition,* 1998, *5*(2), 32–38.

Higher Education Research Institute. "College Freshmen More Politically Liberal Than in the Past, UCLA Survey Reveals." [http://www.gseis.ucla.edu/heri/heri.html]. Jan. 2002.

Hitchings, W. E., and others. "Identifying the Career Development Needs of College Students with Disabilities." *Journal of College Student Development,* 1998, *39*(1), 23–32.

Howard, H. E., and Jones, W. P. "Effectiveness of a Freshman Seminar in an Urban University: Measurement of Selected Indicators." *College Student Journal,* 2000, *34*(4), 509–515.

Jacobs, B. C. "Orienting Diverse Populations." In M. L. Upcraft, R. H. Mullendore, B. O. Barefoot, and D. S. Fidler (eds.), *Designing Successful Transitions: A Guide for Orienting Students to College.* Columbia, S.C.: The National Resource Center for the Freshman Year Experience, 1993.

Johnson, M. J. "First-Year Orientation Programs at Four-Year Public Institutions: A Brief History." *Journal of College Orientation and Transition,* 1998, *5*(2), 25–31.

Kasworm, C. E. "Student Services for the Older Undergraduate Student." *Journal of College Student Development,* 1980, *21,* 163–169.

Kasworm, C. E., and Blowers, S. S. *Adult Undergraduate Students: Patterns of Learning Involvement.* Knoxville, Tenn.: The University of Tennessee, College of Education, 1994.

Krallman, D., and Holcomb, T. "First-Year Student Expectations: Pre- and Post-Orientation." Paper presented at the annual meeting of the Association of Institutional Research, Buena Vista, Fla., May 1997.

Lask, T. "Orientation from a Distance: Connecting New Students to Campus by Utilizing Video Conferencing." *Journal of College Orientation and Transition,* 1998, *5*(2), 21–24.

Mann, B. A. "Retention Principles for New Student Orientation Programs." *Journal of College Orientation and Transition,* 1998, *6*(1), 15–20.

Marcus, D. L. "Next Up: Corporate Logos on the Pennants?" *U.S. News & World Report,* 1999, *12*(8), 75.

Miller, M., Miles, A. S., and Dyer, B. G. "Graduate Student Orientation Through a Professional Seminar: A Case Study of Doctoral Students, 1997–2000." *Journal of College Orientation and Transition,* 2001, *8*(2), 22–31.

Miller, M., and Viajar, P. "The Integration of Technology in New Student Orientation Programs." *Journal of College Orientation and Transition,* 2001, *9*(1), 33–40.

National Center for Educational Statistics. *Stats in Brief.* Jessup, Md.: National Center for Educational Statistics, 2000.

National Orientation Directors Association. *NODA New Member Handbook.* Pullman, Wash.: National Orientation Directors Association, 2000.

"New Student Orientation: Don't Wait Until the Honeymoon's Over." *National On-Campus Report,* 2001, *29*(14), 1, 6.

Pascarella, E. "New Studies Track Community College Effects on Students." *Community College Journal,* 1999, *69,* 8–14.

Petress, K. "How to Be a Good Advisee." *Education,* 2000, *120*(3), 598.

Pope, M. L. "Why Knowledge of Student Financial Aid Is Important to Orientation Professionals." *Journal of College Orientation and Transition,* 2001, *9*(1), 41–43.

Rhine, T. J., Milligan, D. M., and Nelson, L. R. "Alleviating Transfer Shock: Creating an Environment for More Successful Transfer Students." *Journal of Research and Practice,* 2000, *24,* 443–453.

Rielley, D. F. "The Growing Trends of Orientation Web Pages." *Journal of College Orientation and Transition,* 2000, *7*(2), 41–42.

Schroeder, C. C. "Developing Learning Communities." In Elizabeth J. Whitt (ed.), *College Student Affairs Administration.* Needham Heights, Mass.: Simon & Schuster, 1997.

Schroeder, C. C., Mable, P., and Associates. *Realizing the Educational Potential of Residence Halls.* San Francisco: Jossey-Bass, 1994.

Simons, H. D., Van Rheenen, D., and Covington, M. V. "Academic Motivation and the Student Athlete." *Journal of College Student Development,* 1999, *40*(2), 151–162.

Spann, N. G., Smith, J. R., and Buchanan, H. C. "Building a Sense of Community Through a Summer Reading Program." *Journal of College Orientation and Transition,* 1998, *5*(2), 39–40.

Stedman, J. B. "The Driving Force of Technology in Enrollment Management." In R. R. Dixon (ed.), *Making Enrollment Management Work.* New Directions for Student Services, no. 71. San Francisco: Jossey-Bass, 1995.

Strumpf, G. *NODA Data Bank 2000.* College Park, Md.: National Orientation Directors Association, 2000.

Strumpf, G., and Sharer, G. *NODA Data Bank 1995–1997.* College Park, Md.: National Orientation Directors Association, 1996.

Thompson, R. "A Passport to Flexible Learning: An Orientation Program Designed to Introduce First-Year University Students to Interactive Teaching Technologies." Paper presented at the Technological Education and National Development Conference, Abu Dhabi, United Arab Emirates, Apr. 2000.

Tifft, S. "College Days: Then and Now." *Time,* 1990, *136*(14), 23–24.

"Virtual Orientation Pairs Friends, Roommates." *National On-Campus,* 2001, 29(14), 5.

Wolfe, J. S. "Institutional Integration, Academic Success, and Persistence of First-Year Commuter and Resident Students." *Journal of College Student Development,* 1993, *34,* 321–326.

7

COURSE PLANNING AND REGISTRATION

Louise Lonabocker, J. James Wager

FROM AN OUTSIDE PERSPECTIVE, it seems fairly obvious that all colleges and universities operate in the same manner. After all, how complicated can it be? Students are admitted, choose a major, enroll in a few dozen courses, and graduate. Pretty straightforward! Or so it often appears to parents, taxpayers, and the general public. But from an inside perspective, higher education has many more complexities than those just described. Of the thirty-eight hundred or so institutions of higher learning in the United States, it may be fair to say that there are perhaps as many "systems" of course planning and student registration. Regent boards, state legislatures, faculty governance, politics, tradition, and technology sometimes mandate these differences. Best practices that work well at one institution may not equally apply to another. This reality is often recognized in a very tangible way as externally developed academic record systems are purchased and installed. Frequently, the assumptions and rules inherent to the software differ from the assumptions and rules in place at the institution. Therefore, a change is necessary, either to the purchased software or to the institution's business rules (often to the chagrin of the faculty).

It is within this context that this chapter presents the concepts of course planning and student registration. These two separate but highly related student services will be examined from both practical and theoretical perspectives. Best practices, emerging technologies, and student-centered services are themes discussed in this chapter. The approach taken will be descriptive, not prescriptive. The focus will be on the strategic issues, with a vision to the future and grounded by practical examples of exemplary applications in place today.

Course planning refers to the broad topic of the institution's delivery of its core competency, courses, and academic programs. This arena includes the courses that the faculty members teach, where and when these courses are taught, the method of publishing the course schedule, and pertinent curricular issues, such as general education, writing, and quantification requirements. Course planning also includes future planning as driven by enrollments, time-to-graduation issues, and the physical capacity of the instructional facilities.

Student registration refers to the mechanical process of physically associating a student with a course. Inherent in this process is identifying the student as an eligible and qualified enrollee, confirming the registration action to both the student and the course instructor, monitoring the registration over the course of the semester, and providing support to the course instructor. Finally, the registration process provides critical information to academic planners involved with future course planning cycles.

Course Planning

Course planning is the higher education equivalent of the process a manufacturing operation follows to decide which products to manufacture and sell through its wholesalers and retailers. Courses and programs are the institution's equivalent of inventory. Good course planning is a complicated process. At many schools, including Penn State University and Boston College, this planning process begins a year or more in advance of the actual first day of class.

The goal of course planning may be simply stated as to provide the appropriate courses at the appropriate time to the students so that they may achieve normal progress in completing graduation requirements. The courses need to be made available in the correct sequence, be offered at times that do not result in scheduling conflicts, and provide for adequate academic preparation, including prerequisites and corequisites. Pretty straightforward!

Time Allotments

Course scheduling typically begins with the distribution of time allotments to academic departments. Different schools perform this in different ways. Some use an actual time period allotment (for example, *x* number of classes in total, with *y* number offered first period on Monday, Wednesday, and Friday). Other schools use a distribution formula (for example, 15 percent of all courses must be offered during the last period of the day). Time allotments may be distributed evenly across departments or they may take into consideration the needs and preferences of each department. Some departments, such as foreign language departments, may prefer to schedule most of their courses to meet three times a week for 50 minutes, whereas other departments may prefer to meet twice a week for 75 minutes or once a week for 150 minutes.

A basic requirement of all course planning systems is to properly distribute the offered courses across the days of the week and periods during the day. Although many students, and perhaps some faculty members, would describe the perfect schedule as being from 10:00 A.M. to 2:00 P.M. on Tuesday and Thursday, such a condensed scheduling arrangement would result in two specific difficulties. First, students would not be able to register for a full array of courses needed to maintain full-time status and thus maintain normal degree progress. Second, the institution would not be efficiently using teaching facilities, which are generally a scarce resource to begin with.

Scheduling courses over a broad range of times within each department will also help students construct schedules that are interwoven with other responsibilities and interests, such as child care arrangements, work, extracurricular activities, or athletic practice. It is also a good practice to schedule courses within a department at various times throughout the day so that majors will have several courses available in a semester.

At Boston College, academic departments are given a specific number of course allotments for each time allotment. The distribution is based on past history and new requests from the department, all of which are balanced against other needs of the institution. The time allotments are distributed to the academic departments electronically. A time allotment must be linked to a course in order to activate the course for a specific semester. If the department wishes to change time allotments or add additional time allotments, it must do this through the course administration specialist. This automated process ensures that courses are distributed throughout the day in all departments and it eliminates the step of manually verifying observance with allotment allocations.

At Penn State, course scheduling is a decentralized process monitored and supported by a central scheduling system. Academic departments are encouraged to plan well in advance of the semester, taking into consideration such issues as the number of continuing students, the anticipated number of new freshmen, curricular changes within the academic unit, and degree program changes in other departments that will influence the consumption patterns of courses offered by the department. Departments are encouraged to collaborate with each other and with the registrar's office to best plan the upcoming semesters' course offerings.

This desired distribution of course offerings presents a serious challenge in teaching and learning models. In other environments, this would be appropriately referred to as the effectiveness versus efficiency dilemma. It is much more efficient to require that all courses follow a fixed-period arrangement. Using such a model, classrooms have no downtime—no periods when the classroom is unused—maximizing the number of students who can occupy the classroom. Although efficient, a fixed-period scheduling arrangement is not effective. The actual number of minutes students occupy a classroom seat does not determine how much they learn. It is often better to provide opportunities to engage the student in learning activities outside the classroom.

Classroom Types

The size and type of classroom is also key to successful course planning. Course sections differ in size. Certain courses may be better suited to a classical lecture delivery in a large auditorium. Other courses that include active learning competencies require smaller rooms. Those courses that use information technologies need instructional space that is connected to the Internet, is capable of computer projection, and has lighting controls and windows that can be shaded.

Classroom seating is another critical scheduling constraint. The best way to maximize the square footage of instructional space is to install fixed seating. Yet such seating is often exactly the wrong approach to foster and promote interactive learning styles. To provide maximum student-instructor interaction, seating should be movable and flexible. Again, the scheduling must balance effective and efficient uses of limited instructional space.

The number of technology-equipped rooms continues to increase on most campuses. This opens discussion about which particular technologies will be supported. Is there a computer in every classroom? What type? Does it support current software? Does the instructor need to bring his or her own laptop to the classroom? Is there a backbone connection to the Internet? Should some classrooms be equipped with workstations or laptop connections at every seat? Most colleges and universities are struggling to keep ahead of the technology classroom curve, especially as faculty members adopt course management software to improve the delivery of instruction. There can be high costs associated with equipping a technology classroom, keeping the equipment physically secure and in good working order, and upgrading the technology over time.

Classroom Control

Classrooms, laboratories, and other learning space need to be controlled. This control refers to proper usage, physical security, maximum scheduling, and maintenance. An important question is, who does the controlling? Are classrooms designated as general-purpose classrooms with control centrally coordinated by the registrar's office? Or is classroom control decentralized to each academic department for its own courses? Central control will likely provide for a higher degree of scheduling use, whereas decentralized control will likely provide for a higher level of satisfaction among the faculty. (The English and economics departments won't compete for the same classroom.)

Taking this one step further, which office is responsible for physical renovations, the normal replacement of seating and furniture, technology installation and upgrades, and other costs associated with classrooms? Are funds allocated from central administrative budgets to provide for ongoing classroom upgrades? Is the growth rate of technology classrooms a function of budget or of faculty needs? Is the audiovisual office responsible for classroom computers, or is this an information technology responsibility?

Master Schedule

As previously indicated, the master schedule is generally constructed at least a year in advance of the first day of class. The schedule, which may appear in print, on-line, or both, normally includes such information about the course as

- Course title
- Section title
- Instructor
- Days of week and time of day
- Building and room location
- Credits
- Maximum size and current enrollment

○ Special enrollment restrictions

○ Special registration

○ Department/college center

○ Special fees

Requests for computer projection, preferred location, or classroom configuration (such as fixed or moveable seats) are generally included at the time the master schedule is created, to ensure that the instructors obtain classrooms suitable for their teaching methods and, in some cases, physical limitations.

Course description information may also be gathered at this time. At most institutions, this information is available on the Web, allowing students to browse the master course schedule and link to the course description, the course syllabus, the textbooks required for the course, the textbook inventory in the bookstore, and other relevant information, such as the location of the classroom building and the closest parking lot.

The responsibility of developing the academic schedule is typically distributed among academic departments, colleges, and the registrar's office. The mechanical process of collecting, summarizing, and publishing the detail associated with the scheduling process typically rests with the registrar's office. Historically, this has been a "roll forward" process that used the previous semester as the base, which was updated for the new semester. The update process deletes courses and sections that will not be offered, adds new courses and sections, and updates other information, including instructor names, technology delivery, and course syllabus.

Distributed processing allows master course information to be captured at the source, specifically the academic department responsible for the course. Department administrators enter the data locally while the registrar's office reviews the information to ensure that it complies with the standards established for the listing of titles, locations, and instructor identification. Adherence to time allotments is also verified. Comparing the anticipated size with enrollment in previous semesters will also help ensure that the course is scheduled in an appropriate room and that anticipated enrollment is not inflated for purposes of obtaining the best classrooms.

Imagine being faced with as many as three thousand course options and asked to select four or five. Students narrow these options, based on general education requirements, their major and minor, and their general interests, but the prospect is nevertheless daunting. Most students get down to eight or ten but struggle to make a final decision. One scheduling feature that will allow students to sample courses during the first week of class and maintain registration flexibility is the displaying of the maximum size of the course and the current enrollment. This will help students determine whether the course will close early or remain open throughout the registration period and whether they should register for courses with limited openings or gamble on courses that have many seats still available.

The traditional method of informing both students and academic advisers of the semester course offerings has been to consult either "Timetable" or "Schedule of Courses." These paper-based documents are quickly being replaced with Web documents that are frequently updated, or operated in real time. At Penn State, the document "Web Schedule of Courses" is updated each day and is driven by a powerful set of search parameters that enable students and advisers to check on available sections, courses that meet at a particular time of day or on certain days of the week, courses taught by specific instructors, and courses that satisfy special curricular requirements. This Web tool also provides links to the course descriptions, the course syllabus, and faculty curriculum vitae. These search and information capabilities have greatly enhanced students' ability to formulate a registration schedule that satisfies their individual needs.

In addition to maximum and actual size, the academic schedule should include as much information about the course as possible to allow students to make informed choices during registration. Course location may be unimportant at a small college but it could be a critical piece of information at a large institution, where the amount of time required to reach a building may need to be taken into consideration. Identifying the course instructor will allow students to take courses from a variety of instructors and viewpoints during their degree program. And information on corequisites and prerequisites is essential to ensuring that students have the necessary preparation for the course, as well as the knowledge of associated requirements, such as labs, discussion sections, or work groups.

Planning for the academic schedule also requires an examination of the institution's curricular patterns. Which courses fulfill a degree program requirement? Which courses fulfill a general education or general elective requirement? A writing requirement? Quantification, language, diversity, or other specific institution or academic program requirements? Are there multiple courses that may be substituted for each other in the fulfillment of these requirements, or must a specific course be completed? Are there enough seats in required courses to ensure that all students are able to maintain normal progress toward their degree? Are faculty teaching loads based on such mandatory courses, or do faculty members offer topics courses that represent findings from their research but do not contribute toward fulfilling a degree requirement?

Several issues of coordination are inherent in most course planning environments. For example, if the school supports cross-listing the same educational experience under multiple course titles (a common approach used to satisfy external accrediting organizations), all cross-listed courses must be updated if a change is made to one component. Although this type of editing logic should be incorporated into the course scheduling software, it often is not, with the notification requirement falling to the scheduling or department staff. Similarly, someone must be responsible for ensuring that corequisite courses are properly scheduled to avoid time conflicts, enabling the student to register for both courses during the same semester.

Another practical matter is to notify academic advisers and students of course offering changes, such as course cancellations and additions and time and room changes. This becomes especially acute for schools that follow an early registration cycle. Does the institution have an obligation to notify students who completed their registration weeks or months before the start of the semester of changes to their course schedule? The commonsense answer is yes, but many schools cannot provide this notification, either because of limited technical support or cost.

Examination Scheduling

Some students may want to schedule courses in a way that will allow them to space out their final examinations. The final examination schedule should therefore be available to students at the time of registration. This may be especially important for learning-disabled students or students with inflexible scheduling obligations.

At Boston College, the schedule of examination times is determined by the starting time of each course. Each course time block is randomly assigned to a final examination module. Exams take place over a period of seven days, with final examinations scheduled at 9:00 A.M. and noon each day. Courses taught on Monday, Wednesday, and Friday at 11:00 A.M., for example, may be assigned to final examination module one, which is the first final examination time module on the first final exam day. The linking of course time to final examination modules ensures that students do not have two exams scheduled at the same time. Other institutions have developed algorithms that schedule final examinations randomly and minimize the number of students who have two exams scheduled at the same time.

Exceptions to this rule include common exams, which are offered for multiple-section courses, such as accounting. At Boston College, all common examinations are administered at 4:00 P.M. and are spaced out throughout the final examination period. Other exceptions include courses that do not fit into a course time block and so assume the module corresponding to the closest class meeting time. All courses that meet once a week starting at 4:00 P.M. or later have final examinations on the first regular class day that occurs during the examination week.

Students are not expected to have more than two final examinations in one day. If a student has three examinations scheduled in one day and one of these is a common examination, it is the responsibility of the instructor holding the common examination to give a makeup examination. If a student has three regularly scheduled examinations because he or she is taking a course that meets once a week at or after 4:00 P.M., the instructor teaching the course outside of the standard time block must provide a makeup examination.

Enrollment Management

As new curricular programs are being considered, questions need to be raised. What is the total number of credits or courses required to complete the program? What are the core educational competencies to be mastered and demonstrated by the graduates? Will the array of offered courses develop these competencies? If the content of a particular course is modified, or if the course is not offered, will there be a negative impact on other academic programs? Have course prerequisites changed, leading to a reduction in enrollments in the formerly required course(s)? All of these questions are critical and should be examined during the planning cycle. The more that can be identified before publishing the course schedule and before students begin registering for courses, the less disruption will be experienced by the students, their advisers, and the faculty members.

It is during the planning process that anticipated enrollment management issues must be examined. Fundamentally, the issue to be clarified is the number of students who will be enrolled during the target semester. How many new freshmen will be admitted and how many will be arriving with advance placement credits that may be used to satisfy degree requirements? What is the anticipated enrollment of transfer students, and will their previously completed courses fulfill degree requirements? Will exchange students enroll, and when will they be allowed to register? What about students cross-registering from other institutions? Does the institution's enrollment policy permit nondegree students to enroll? If so, to what extent, if any, may degree-seeking students be shut out of course enrollments? Will there be an extraordinary shift in the number of students participating in study abroad programs? How many students will be entering degree-seeking majors, and what are the resulting demands on courses required for the major? Are student patterns in the selection of majors changing in significant ways? These and similar enrollment-level questions define the demand side of the course planning equation. The answers to these questions come from a variety of sources, including admissions, study abroad, and continuing education, and the registrar can play a valuable role by compiling the information and providing it to deans and academic departments for course and enrollment planning.

With the demand understood, the supply side requires a response. Will adjunct faculty members need to be hired to fill the correct number of course sections? Classroom and laboratory availability will also have a strong influence on the course planning process. Will classrooms be temporarily lost because of renovations or technology improvements, or will they be permanently lost because of conversion to office space? Will new classrooms that are being built or renovated be ready by the start of the semester being planned? These are all necessary questions that must be asked during the academic planning process.

Time to Degree

During the past decade, colleges and universities across the country have been required to respond to time-to-degree issues. There is growing evidence that students are taking longer than four years to graduate from four-year degree programs. There are at least two leading contributors to delayed graduation. First, students may choose to learn at a slower pace, taking lighter credit loads each semester (they may be working to earn money to fund their education, placing greater emphasis on grades, participating in varsity athletics, and so on), or they spend a semester or more in foreign study programs, enroll in multiple majors and minors, or engage in some other activity that leads to delayed time to graduation. The second contributor, which is sometimes considered suspect by the public, governing bodies, and parents, is that the institution minimizes the sufficient quantity of courses to delay student progress toward graduation. Many colleges and universities have established on-time graduation requirements to alleviate such concerns. Although the details of such contracts differ, they all guarantee the student's ability to graduate by ensuring that required courses are available. Under such contracts, institutions must ensure that their course planning process will result in the scheduling of the correct courses in sufficient quantity so that students can register for the required courses without administrative intervention.

Registration

If course planning is the equivalent of a manufacturing operation, registration provides student consumers with the mechanism to select from the inventory of courses offered. Some departments market their courses with interesting titles, such as Shop 'Til You Drop, whereas others stick with standard favorites like Introductory Psychology. The selection process is based on a variety of factors related to course requirements, work, extracurricular activities, instructor, topic, and time. All registrars yearn to discover the secret ingredient that will draw students to early morning classes.

It is common practice that currently enrolled students register in advance of the upcoming semester. For example, students typically register during the spring semester for the upcoming fall semester. Some institutions allow students to register for two or more future semesters, which helps students lock in selected courses and plan their time to graduation. At most institutions, this takes the form of early or advance registration, which gives students the opportunity to simulate various scheduling options, complete a schedule on-line, view the schedule, and leave with a completed schedule. Students may even be able to immediately view the resulting tuition and fee charges generated based on the registration. Both on-campus and off-campus students have ready access to advising resources through interactive Web applications and personal communication with their academic adviser. This is often confused with and referred to as preregistration. Preregistration occurs when students submit course selections that are then fed through a batch scheduling program. The actual selection of courses takes place electronically or manually, based on the requests submitted by students, who ultimately receive a completed schedule, which may or may not include the right mix of courses.

Through the act of registration, new students establish a connection to the university. They select a set of courses and begin to prepare for their intellectual journey. They may become involved in undergraduate government, volunteer activities, or athletics, but obtaining a degree is their primary goal, and registration is the first step toward that goal. Registration also provides a connection to a range of other people and services, including faculty members, advisers, learning resource staff, career services, study abroad, and extracurricular activities. Students begin to engage in activities, attend class, and make use of university services after they register.

New students often register as part of the orientation process. At Boston College, new students take part in one of seven freshman orientation sessions during the summer months. Groups of approximately 325 students come to orientation for two full days of advisement, tours, and meetings with deans and information sessions with other campus officials. They are led by upper-class orientation leaders, who shepherd groups of ten students through the process. Orientation concludes with registration, which helps ensure that students remain engaged and goal-oriented throughout the program.

Today's registration seems effortless, compared with the days of arena registration. It takes students minutes to register, but the planning that goes into the process, including creation of the master schedule, course and enrollment planning, advisement, and registration appointment scheduling, begins well in advance of the event. Registration via either the Web or interactive voice response is almost invisible on campus, and the automation of the process frees the staff to concentrate on enrollment planning, demand analysis, and the maximization of classroom space.

Advisement

Getting students off to a good start is critical, so it is especially important to assist entering students with their initial course selections. Some students come from high schools where the choices were made for them, and so, in the college environment, the baffling array of majors, minors, requirements, and prerequisites may be overwhelming. Orientation programs should include components to assist students through the process of academic advisement, course selection, and educational planning. Students may be guided by faculty advisers, the freshman year experience staff, student peers, program directors, the learning center staff, deans, and other campus experts. Enrolled students often come to rely on a network of peers, faculty members, and advising center staff members for course and degree planning, but entering students may lack awareness of these resources or may be too intimidated to make the initial contact.

There are many factors that may complicate registration for new students. Entering students, exchange students, and transfer students may have earned advanced placement or college credit, which will alter the typical program and require more individual attention. Pass/fail courses, honors programs, and cornerstone options may require additional interpretation.

The registration period at many institutions begins with the distribution of degree audits to students and advisers. A period of advisement conducted by faculty members, advisers, and student peers normally follows.

The students and advisers use degree audits to track progress toward the degree. Core or general education requirements and the student's major, minor, and concentration are displayed, and completed courses as well as courses in progress are matched to these requirements.

This comparison adds value to the advisement process by giving students a clear picture of completed and outstanding requirements and by allowing advisers to broaden the advising session to encompass a discussion of personal, educational, and career goals. Freed from the chore of determining what requirements have been fulfilled and what remain to be completed, advisers have the opportunity to assess student success and identify, encourage, and refer students who may be considering study abroad, senior theses, undergraduate research, or postgraduate fellowships. Degree audits also help rectify mistakes that may have occurred when well-meaning advisers miscalculated or misread completed courses and outstanding requirements. The degree audit provides a road map to graduation and reassures the student and the adviser that courses and requirements have not been omitted.

Institutions that want to be certain students have obtained advisement prior to registration can distribute a registration access code or a Personal Identification Number (PIN) to advisers, who give each student his or her PIN after the advisement session. The PIN, or access code, which changes each semester, allows students to enter registration at their scheduled appointment time. After the assigned registration appointment, students can usually reenter the registration transaction and drop or add courses through the last day of the registration and drop/add period. This is referred to as continuous registration.

Registration Holds

In advance of registration, holds are usually set for students with unpaid balances, outstanding academic requirements, incomplete immunizations, or other unfulfilled administrative obligations. Students should be notified of the holds in advance of registration. Holds should be used judiciously because they may prevent students from obtaining desired or required courses. Holds are often a last resort when all other forms of notification and prodding have failed.

Study Abroad

In recent years, many institutions have witnessed significant increases in the number of students participating in study abroad programs for one or more semesters. Each institution has its own procedure for recording study abroad and for making students' exit and reentry as seamless as possible. This may include leave of absence and readmission in the case of programs sponsored by other institutions or the entry of a course and program for students who are attending programs sponsored by the institution.

Students planning to study abroad should plan early by scheduling courses that must be taken prior to departure, determining the required courses that can be taken while on study abroad, and preparing for the courses or theses that will have to be completed upon their return. At Boston College, where 30 percent of the junior class participates in study abroad, with more than forty partner institutions, each academic department publishes study abroad guidelines in the university catalogue. The guidelines include predeparture recommendations, the number and type of courses that may be taken abroad, recommended programs for majors, and preapproved courses. A separate study abroad catalogue is published, with additional information about programs, preparation, and time lines.

Students on study abroad have benefited from systems that allow them to register anytime, anywhere via the Web. Web-based systems provide the most convenient access, and 24/7 systems allow students to register at their scheduled appointment time, giving them the same access to courses as their on-campus classmates.

Registration Scheduling

Registration is normally scheduled by class year or number of credits earned, starting with graduate students and ending with entering freshmen. Some institutions choose to give priority to selected groups of students, including honors students, student athletes, learning-disabled students, and commuter students. If priority registration is used, there is the risk that high-demand courses will be filled at the end of priority registration. The educational experience will be enhanced if all classes contain a mix of students, so priority registration should not be used unless there are clear reasons for doing so.

Students are usually assigned specific registration appointment times and are allowed to register at that time or at any time after the assigned appointment. The appointments may be scheduled to avoid conflicts with current classes, or the algorithm may ensure that students who receive an undesirable time one semester will receive a desirable time the following semester. Some institutions limit the registration session time to control the number of simultaneous users on the system and to ensure that students are able to access the system at their scheduled time. Others have taken the approach that students should be given as much time as they need to construct a complete and satisfactory schedule. Some students, especially those in majors that are in demand, may encounter numerous closed courses, whereas others, with early appointment times or obscure majors, may receive all of their preferred courses. Registration, especially for the former group, can be stressful, so providing students with an unlimited time frame will allow students to explore various scheduling options without the pressure of completing the process within a defined period of time.

Registration Systems

Most registration systems are now Web-based, and some are supplemented by interactive voice response systems. Web-based systems are ideal for constructing complicated schedules and simulating various options, whereas interactive voice response may be preferred by students attempting to drop or add a course or by part-time students registering for just one or two courses.

Web search features assist students both when they prepare to register and during the registration process. Many systems allow students to search for open courses within a department, limit their search to general education courses, or view all sections of specific courses within the department. Students may also search for courses by semester, time, instructor, or title, or they may enter their own search criteria. For example, students interested in the Renaissance may search on that keyword and discover courses in departments that they ordinarily might not have considered.

Web-based systems may include a shopping cart feature, which gives students an opportunity to select courses that interest them, simulate various options, and finalize a schedule that best suits their needs and interests. Other systems allow students to enter course selections and block out specific times. The system then returns various scheduling options to the student. This can be especially helpful when students are also attempting to manage other activities, such as labs, performance ensembles, extracurricular activities, volunteer experiences, and student employment.

On-line systems allow students to determine at the time of registration whether the course is closed, restricted, or in conflict with a course already selected, or whether it has a prerequisite or corequisite. Some systems inform the student about alternate sections or cross-listed sections if the course is closed. In some cases—such as in the case of, notably, student athletes, who are registered and certified for practice and play, edits may be added to ensure that they cannot reduce their course load to less than full-time status.

Academic departments normally enter restrictions on courses that are in demand in order to reserve seats for majors or minors, for students in specific schools or colleges, or for students in various class years. Seats can also be held for release at various points throughout the registration period. The hold and release feature may be used to distribute seats throughout registration, ensuring that a course is not populated by seniors only. Held seats may also be released throughout the summer to ensure that students who attend the first orientation sessions do not have an advantage over international students and others who are more likely to attend the last session.

Most institutions are limited in the range of courses they offer and may form consortium arrangements with other institutions to expand their course offerings. Some consortiums, such as the twelve-college exchange in New England, offer students an opportunity to study at another campus for a semester or a year. Others allow students to cross-register for one course each semester at a neighboring institution, such as one of the six colleges of Colleges of the Fenway in Boston.

Course Evaluations

On-line access to course evaluation information has been offered at some institutions through a formal process or through informal mechanisms such as student government Web sites. At Boston College, students can enter the Undergraduate Government of Boston College Web site, provide anecdotal comments about a course and instructor, and submit an overall rating on a 1 to 5 scale. The site includes examples of appropriate and inappropriate entries, and all submissions are edited by the students responsible for maintaining the site. Each class that has been evaluated includes an overall score and a short summary of the instructor's strengths and weaknesses. The site is heavily used in conjunction with registration, and registration results have been affected by ratings at extreme ends of the scale.

Waitlists and Rain Checks

The number of students who approach academic departments during registration in their quest for overrides can be discouraging. Indiana University has developed a system that automates the process, determines course demand, and limits foot traffic in the academic departments. Their Automated Course Exchange system is composed of three components: waitlist, rain checks, and continuous schedule adjustment.

The objective of the system is to have the student register for all courses that can be confirmed, identify on the waitlist system those that cannot, and identify the confirmed course that is to be dropped if the desired wait-listed course is added. Departments and schools can see the number of requests and respond by adjusting the schedule of offerings to meet demand.

Rain checks provide a guarantee of course registration in the following semester to a waitlisted student if the course request is not fulfilled for the current semester. This component of the program is intended to show the university's commitment to fulfilling student course requests, reducing the number of closed courses, and avoiding student problems with progress toward degree completion.

Student Access Systems

Although there have been many technological developments over the past twenty years, the turning point for registrars occurred when Brigham Young University introduced touch-tone registration to its students in the early 1980s. Placing data entry and data management in the hands of students was a dramatic change in the way business had been conducted, and it started a transformation that led to transactional systems and, eventually, Web-based systems.

By the mid-1980s, institutions such as the Georgia Institute of Technology were developing transactional systems that allowed students to conduct business by using terminals and personal computers. But it wasn't until the introduction of the Web, with its ubiquitous access and unlimited real estate, that students were able to link to the master schedule, course descriptions, and faculty home pages, as well as conduct complex searches.

Today, Web portals provide customized views of information for specific audiences, including students, faculty members, parents, prospective students, alumni, and athletic fans. The following is a sampling of transactions that allow students to register and see the immediate effect of that registration on their degree audit or student account. These transactions also inform the student of any outstanding obligations that have resulted in a hold on the registration. They include

- View course history, current schedule, and grades
- View financial aid application status and awards
- Process medical insurance waiver
- Submit graduation form
- View/change addresses and directory preferences
- View or simulate a degree audit

○ View student account; request a copy or refund

○ View classmate photo roster and directory info

○ Create/add money to meal plan account or view balance

○ View status of Stafford Loans

○ Complete Stafford Loan entrance or exit counseling requirement

○ Complete Stafford borrower authorization statement

○ Request enrollment certification

○ Request replacement ID

Integrated Student Services

In 1998, Boston College consolidated the offices and functions of the registrar, financial aid, student accounts, student loans, student employment, credit and collections, ID card services, and parking permits into an Office of Student Services. In this office, general service staff members are cross-trained, and students with questions about academic, financial, or auxiliary services can come to one place for help, whereas previously they may have had to visit several offices. For example, a student whose registration has not cleared may be unaware of whether the problem resides in the registrar's office, the financial office, or the student account office. The general service staff members have access to information that will allow them to either resolve the issue or relay it to an expert in financial services or academic services. The consolidation of services brought staff members into physical proximity and resulted in greater collaboration among them, as they constantly look for ways to simplify processes, enhance systems, and provide students with better service.

Penn State has taken a different approach to the integration of student services. Rather than the physical integration of numerous student support offices, the specific services of these offices are provided in a secure Web-based environment called eLion (after the school mascot, the Nittany Lions). The Penn State eLion system is designed as the university's premier academic advising system and provides dozens of services to students, advisers, faculty members, and new and prospective students. The services are developed by numerous university offices, including those of the registrar, the bursar, undergraduate education, and student aid. Each Web application is developed following standards that create a seamless approach to the user and downplay attribution to the office that developed the application. This anytime, anyplace set of services has become the primary mode of responding to many student needs.

Related Services

Students are not the only ones served by this transformation. For example, the Penn State eLion system and the Boston College Agora system also provide secure Web services to the faculty and advisers. Faculty and staff members have information at their fingertips when students are preparing for registration or seeking advice. Faculty members use Web-based systems to browse the campus directory, the schedule of courses, and the catalogue, as well as to retrieve class rosters (including student photos), submit grades, and send e-mail or voice mail to all of their advisees or to all the students in their classes. Faculty members can also access degree audits and course history for their advisees.

Faculty members can also use course management software systems to post syllabi and class notes, administer exams and quizzes, provide threaded discussions and newsgroups, and deliver technology-enhanced course material to their students. The real benefit of course management systems is that faculty members do not need in-depth knowledge of HTML or Web-authoring software to use them.

The Web has also simplified the process of providing information to staff members who advise and serve students. Staff members who work in learning centers, advisement centers, minority student support services, and athletic learning resource offices can access student records with appropriate security clearance. Deans and academic departments also have access to information for students in their respective schools and majors. At Boston College, class lists of high-risk students are provided to learning resources staff members at the midpoint of the semester. The lists are used to encourage faculty members to monitor student progress in the course. This allows staff members to identify students who are not making use of their services and to invite them to seek help. It also provides them with the information they may need to provide better assistance to students who have been making use of their services.

Students at the time of enrollment set privacy preferences in compliance with the Family Educational Rights and Privacy Act. These privacy preferences permit them to withhold the release of all or selected elements of directory information. Students may not, however, prevent the release of directory information for university business; for example, they cannot withhold their name or photograph from the class list of the instructor teaching the class or their degree audit from the academic adviser responsible for their progress. Most institutions permit students to request a new adviser.

Systems are also in place that permit deans and academic departments to easily communicate with students. Academic departments frequently communicate with all students in their major via e-mail to announce meetings, canceled courses, new courses, preregistration information about restricted enrollment courses, and the promotion of low-enrollment courses in which students might have an opportunity to work in a seminar-like environment in a specialized field.

Conclusion

Years ago, students arrived on campus and received a prescribed set of courses that would lead them for the next four years. As this chapter illustrates, those days are gone. Students arrive with previous educational experiences, intense educational goals, and ambitious postgraduation plans that necessitate the personal involvement of faculty and staff members—and the students themselves—in the educational planning process. Students welcome the interactivity provided by today's Web-based systems, which open up an array of information about courses and the faculty members teaching those courses, which was previously unavailable.

What lies ahead? Certainly, a great deal of speculation. For example, as more and more institutions adopt distance learning modes of delivering their capstone courses and programs, will future students enroll in courses across many institutions instead of just one? If so, which institution will certify the educational experience and award the degree? Will distance learning technologies eliminate the traditional residential campus? Probably not, but these technologies are likely to transform the instructional space on campuses away from lecture halls toward learning laboratories. Will the e-business approach heighten the concern of fraudulent records and identity theft? In all likelihood, this will occur. Institutions will need to make significant infrastructure investments to ensure computer and network security that will protect the integrity of institutional databases and student records. Will future technologies tempt faculty members to become independent entrepreneurs, selling their coursework to the highest bidder? The issue of intellectual property rights has recently emerged as a strategic concern as many institutional presidents are examining this very topic.

From a technology perspective, what comes next? In the 1980s, the emerging technology was the touch-tone telephone. In the 1990s, the Web emerged along with its powerful capabilities, including e-business. The speculation is that the next decade will likely include wireless networks, both local and wide-area, personal digital assistant devices replacing laptop computers, and high bandwidth availability. Theses changes, along with more technology-comfortable students and faculty and staff members, will provide both new challenges and opportunities to enrollment managers. But, hey, how complicated can it be?

8

CAREER INTERVENTIONS

FACILITATING STRATEGIC ACADEMIC
AND CAREER PLANNING

Robert C. Reardon, Jill A. Lumsden

CAREER PLANNING, ALONG WITH ACADEMIC ADVISING and financial counseling, is part of a triad of interrelated student academic services. As explained in Chapter Fourteen these services represent a seamless array of broad educational counseling and advising services that support students' academic retention and postgraduate achievements. In this chapter, we explore the varied ways in which career planning services operate on college campuses across the nation, focusing on the student-centered nature of contemporary services and the impact of technology on service delivery. We think of *career services* as including career planning and development interventions, cooperative education and experiential career education programs, and job placement and employment services. *Career planning services,* in contrast, are concentrated in the areas of career development (not placement), counseling, advising, assessment, information, and decision-making interventions. In this chapter, we describe career planning services as a complex array of career development interventions that span many organizational boundaries in a typical postsecondary educational institution. Finally, we describe the career portfolio as a meta-approach for promoting student strategic educational and career planning.

Organizational Models

Career services have a long history in higher education, and offices from orientation to placement have had organizational responsibility for these functions. In colonial times, instruction about work might have been the subject of a collegewide convocation, along with discussions of health, morals, deportment, and other life adjustment topics. Maverick (1926) reports that freshman orientation courses, which appeared as early as 1911, included several hours of instruction on vocational guidance. At the beginning of the twentieth century, career services often functioned as appointments offices for college graduates, arranging job placements in government, business, health care, or educational organizations. The appointments secretary served as a broker between employers and the school in arranging job placements, probably after the faculty tired of making such arrangements. Herr, Rayman, and Garis (1993) provided a good synopsis of the development of career services programs in American higher education institutions. They noted that in 1924 the first professional organization devoted to career placement in the United States was established in Chicago and was called the National Association of Appointments Secretaries. This organization continued to evolve during the 1930s and eventually became the American College Personnel Association, which is now a comprehensive organization of varied student services professionals.

Career Centers

Over time, career placement offices tended to become separate from counseling centers and other student affairs offices, because placement was conceptually linked to business, employment, and economics rather than psychology, emotions, and student development (Herr, Rayman, and Garis, 1993). The location of career planning services on the campus in either the placement office or the counseling center became a territorial issue on many campuses. If career planning was located in the counseling center, it was more likely process- or clinically oriented, provided by trained psychology specialists, offered over a longer time period, and focused on the remediation of students' academic or emotional distress. If career planning was offered in a placement office, it was more likely focused on matching students' traits or preferences with jobs, providing employment information and assistance with job search strategies, offered over a shorter time frame prior to graduation, and provided by staff members trained as generalists.

At present, there is no single institutional model for providing career planning services, and the administrative location of these services is associated with the organizational history of each institution. However, the National Association of Colleges and Employers published a monograph, *Professional Standards for College and University Career Services* (1998), which identifies areas such as program components, management, organization, human resources, facilities, and employer relations as critical areas.

Vernick, Garis, and Reardon (2000) suggest that the delivery of career services in college or university settings can be categorized along four continua (see Figure 8.1). The first continuum reflects the degree to which a career center holds the mission for providing career development services through career advising, counseling, assessment, and information. At many institutions, the mission for career counseling and assessment resides in the student counseling center rather than the career center. In such instances, the career center may provide assistance with employability skills but will not offer programs for academic or career choice. Such a career center would fall at the far left of the career development continuum. The issue of assessment is pivotal because the use of tests, computer-based guidance systems, and other assessments (for example, the Strong Interest Inventory, the Myers Briggs Type Indicator, Self-Directed Search, DISCOVER, and SIGI PLUS) is a key factor in the delivery of career planning services. At other institutions, counseling and assessment for career choice may be shared among a variety of offices (for example, the student counseling center or the academic advising center). Such offices would fall in the middle of this continuum. Finally, some career centers include advising, counseling, assessment, and the provision of information supporting career decision making in their mission, falling on the right side of this continuum.

The second continuum addresses the degree to which a career center provides experiential career education services—for example, externships, internships, and cooperative education programs. Part-time, work-study, volunteer, or summer job programs could also be included in this area. At many institutions, internship and cooperative education programs reside in academic units rather than career centers, placing them to the left on this dimension. Commonly, the institutional mission for delivering experiential education is shared among colleges, academic departments, financial aid, and career centers. For example, the financial aid office administers part-time jobs and work-study programs, whereas a volunteer service office assists students in locating volunteer opportunities. Such programs would fall in the middle of the dimension. Finally, schools that fall on the right side of the model have career centers shouldering the complete responsibility for experiential career education programs.

Figure 8.1. Career Center Mission Continua

Involvement in Career Development

Low	High

Placement Advising Only
with Career Counseling in
the Counseling Center or in
Academic Advising

Comprehensive Career
Counseling, Programming,
and Assessment

Involvement in Experiential Education

Low	High

Decentralized
Experiential Education
Services

Mission for Cooperative
Education, Internships, and
Part-Time Employment

Locus of Placement

Low	High

Decentralized

Centralized

Locus of Placement

Low	High

Self-Supported Through
Client and Employer Fees

State/Institutional
Appropriated

Source: *Vernick, Garis, and Reardon, 2000, p. 9. Reprinted with the permission of the Career Planning and Adult Development Network.*

Placement, or employer relations services, shown on the third continuum, range from decentralized to centralized. About 20 percent of institutions have decentralized placement offices residing in academic colleges and would fall to the left on this dimension (National Association of Colleges and Employers, 1999). Other institutions have fully centralized career centers charged with the college or university-wide mission for placement. More frequently, schools fall toward the middle of this dimension, with the career center providing most of the placement and campus recruiting services, whereas certain "vocationally oriented colleges," such as business or engineering, would have their own placement office. It is common for professional schools (for example, law or M.B.A. programs) to have separate placement services.

Finally, the degree to which the career center is funded by the institution can be plotted on a continuum. At some colleges and universities, the operating budget for career services is not funded by the institution. These career centers must generate their funding through charges and fees to students, alumni, and employers, as well as through fundraising. At other institutions, the career center operating budget is fully supported by the institution, and any income from fees or contributions are used as enhancement funds. A further breakdown of institutionally based budgeting for career planning services could involve budgeting based on student fees, instructional support funds, or administrative monies.

College and university career services falling on the right side of the four continua reviewed earlier would generally be considered *comprehensive career centers* and would offer the following core programs and services:

- Career advising, intake, and referral services
- Individual and group career counseling
- Assessment and computer-assisted guidance
- Career information (educational, occupational, and organizational)
- Career courses for credit
- Career education outreach
- Experiential career education
- Career expositions
- On-campus recruiting
- Graduate school services
- Job listings and résumé referral services

The first five of these services are typically viewed as career planning services, as we defined them earlier in this chapter. It is beyond the scope of this chapter to provide details about the development, operation, and management of core programs and services related to career planning. Textbooks such as those by Isaacson and Brown (2000); Herr and Cramer (1996); Sampson, Reardon, Peterson, and Lenz (forthcoming); and Zunker (2001) provide extensive descriptions of career planning programs.

Career Planning Services

This review of varied administrative arrangements for providing career planning services on a campus suggests an array of political and policy issues that affect the provision of such services. However, in our view, there are five essential components of an effective career planning services program, no matter where it is administratively located.

STAFFING. Career planning services should be administered by professional counselors—ideally, those with recognized credentials and academic training. For example, the Council for Accreditation of Counseling and Related Educational Programs accredits programs that prepare professional counselors and the National Board for Certified Counselors certifies professional counselors with established competencies in career counseling. The National Career Development Association (NCDA) recognizes three special membership categories: fellow, master career counselor, and master career development professional. The NCDA has also developed a model for training career development facilitators—paraprofessionals who provide career services. The Center for Credentialing in Education credentials the global career development facilitator. We fear that many institutions have not viewed career planning services in a way that prioritizes the hiring of appropriately trained staff members to lead such programs.

ASSESSMENT. Career planning services require the assessment of students' interests and other personal characteristics related to varied educational and occupational options. Holland's typological theory (1997) provides a sophisticated way to link student and environmental characteristics, the latter including occupations and work and educational environments (fields of study). Many assessment instruments are based on this theory. Ideally, assessment should also develop information about student readiness for career planning and decision making as outlined in Chapter Two.

We view assessment instruments that have good psychometric characteristics as an essential component of academic and career planning services.

INFORMATION. Career planning services provide information about
fields of study, occupations, and jobs. Educational and career decision
making are integrally related for many students, and decisions about a
major field of study are directly tied to decisions about occupations and
work organizations or graduate and professional training. Ideally, this
array of information would be coordinated and managed by a professional librarian (Epstein and Kinsley, forthcoming). Indeed, career planning occurs within the context of information, and an office providing
such services requires the necessary materials and resources to carry out
this function.

LOCATION. Ideally, career planning services are housed in adequate space
that is contiguous to other related student services, including academic
advising, financial aid, counseling and psychological services, placement
or employment services, and experiential career services. The location of
the service in contiguous space would at least facilitate the referral of students among related programs. Location may be more important than the
administrative lines on the organizational chart.

TECHNOLOGY. Career planning services are increasingly dependent upon
computer technology, and appropriate hardware, software, and technical
support are essential. For example, information about educational and
career opportunities, including job openings, financial aid, and graduate
school, are increasingly available on the Internet and incorporated into
computer-based career guidance programs such as DISCOVER, FOCUS,
and SIGI PLUS. Information can be readily explored through many different Internet-based providers. The telephone is also finding new life as
a medium for career education service delivery. Some students increasingly
rely on such technological innovations in seeking career planning services
because they do not have to leave their home or office to seek assistance.

In Chapter Five, Peterson, Sampson, and Lenz describe a readiness
model for student learning that includes three levels of intervention based
on the capability of the student (for example, high academic ability, positive attitude, or clear career goals) and the complexity of the student's situation (for example, strong family support, low financial needs, or few
conflicting life roles). At level one, students who are well prepared and
ready to engage in student learning and career planning use self-help
services. Students at level two have moderate needs and require medium

levels of intervention. At level three are students who are not well prepared and therefore require individual case-managed services. (See Chapter Two.)

We believe that the career planning services on most campuses are offered at levels two and three and that systemic interventions at level one have been slighted. Interventions at levels two and three require direct student contact in workshops or individual counseling by appointment—something that counselors like to do. But this type of intervention is not cost-effective in meeting the career planning needs of most students. Systems-level interventions (level one) are initially more costly to establish but operate at lower unit costs over time (Reardon, 1996).

Now that we have explored some of the organizational and policy issues affecting career planning services, we want to focus on service delivery that is student-centered and technology-enhanced. The vehicle we have chosen to use as an example is the career portfolio. We view the career portfolio as primarily a level-one career planning intervention, with the option of also using it as a level-two or -three intervention.

Career Portfolios

A portfolio is generally considered to be a set of pictures, drawings, or photographs used to present evidence of one's skills and accomplishments. With advances in technology related to computers and the Internet, portfolios are increasingly appearing in electronic formats. Indeed, Young (2002) has reported that "e-portfolios" could be the next big thing in campus computing, as more and more institutions are encouraging, even requiring, students to create them to highlight their academic work and reflect upon their campus experiences.

While portfolios can be used for multiple purposes (for example, as a personal or professional history), a career portfolio is generally used to present evidence of work-related skills and accomplishments to employers or college admissions committees. A student's career portfolio is tangible evidence of career planning in action. In recent years, career portfolios have become popular as a device for helping students focus on the acquisition of new skills, and they present evidence of those skills to potential employers or graduate school admissions committees. There is evidence of their increased use in high schools and in many other settings (Perry, 1996–1997). An e-portfolio (Young, 2002) may be thought of as a comprehensive résumé that links to an electronic storehouse of a student's reports, products, work samples, presentations, or works that document skill sets or accomplishments. In the following two sections, we examine the importance of articulating philosophical principles and design and the use of principles in portfolio development.

Philosophical Principles

It is important to be as clear as possible about the meaning, purpose, and values that provide the foundation for an on-line career portfolio program. Such clarity helps ensure that requirements for portfolio implementation, such as staff training, advertising, budget, and space, follow from the philosophical premises on which the program is based. The philosophical basis of a career portfolio program can grow out of a desire to link the various constituencies of a college—such as faculty members, students, parents, public officials, employers, contributors, and citizens—into a common purpose that promotes the core teaching/learning mission of the undergraduate program.

The philosophy guiding an on-line career portfolio can be summarized as *career preparation,* which we view as an outcome of career planning interventions. In this regard, it is important to define two terms: *career* and *work* (Reardon, Lenz, Sampson, and Peterson, 2000). A *career* is the "working out of a purposeful life pattern through work undertaken by a person" (p. 6). This is not simply a matter of choosing an occupation or finding a job; career is a much broader concept. A career is unique to a person; it is a process of balancing life roles—such as the role of student, parent, spouse or partner, citizen, or worker. *Work* is "activity that produces something of value for one's self or others" (p. 7). This includes unpaid, volunteer work as well as paid employment. We believe that career preparation, given these definitions, is consistent with the core educational mission of an undergraduate liberal arts curriculum. Indeed, career preparation enables students to live as contributing citizens in a global community.

PRINCIPLE 1: DEVELOP STUDENTS' STRATEGIC CAREER VISIONS. The first philosophical principle of an on-line career portfolio program is that it should enable students to develop and pursue a strategic career vision. Therefore, a career portfolio program should

- ○ Help students select and pursue learning activities within and outside of the formal curriculum to achieve personal and professional goals
- ○ Be a student-centered program, with student learning throughout the undergraduate years as the primary focus
- ○ Be initiated, managed, and sustained by student involvement, with assistance from college resources, throughout the undergraduate years
- ○ Be available to students in all majors and at all ability levels

- Use sophisticated technology to provide a method for selecting, developing, and documenting career skills

- Be initiated by students at all levels (lower-division or upper-division)

- Provide potential employers with documentation regarding students' specific learning activities undertaken to advance in a strategic educational and career plan

PRINCIPLE 2: PREPARE QUALIFIED GRADUATES. The second philosophical principle is that the university should be dedicated to producing the kinds of graduates that are needed in an emerging global economy that is characterized by lean production, information technology, and alternative ways of working (Reardon, Lenz, Sampson, and Peterson, 2000). A university-based career planning program should therefore

- Address the needs of students, faculty members, employers, citizens, and parents

- Increase the economic productivity and career satisfaction of graduates

- Increase public support for higher education

- Involve many different university agencies and programs (such as service learning, academic advising, student recruiting, job placement services, cooperative education, classroom instruction, student activities and organizations, liberal arts courses, and preprofessional training programs) to develop students

PRINCIPLE 3: PROVIDE EVIDENCE OF STUDENT PREPARATION. The third philosophical tenet is that the career portfolio program should provide employers of college graduates with evidence that students are ready to make effective contributions in the workplace. Employers—including market, governmental, and service organizations—will likely appreciate the career portfolio program, primarily because it can provide evidence of skills that can be used in various work settings. Admissions committees and others selecting students for postgraduate studies may come to view the career portfolio as a value-added component of the admissions process.

PRINCIPLE 4: LINK EDUCATION, WORK, AND COMMUNITY. The fourth principle is that career planning services should span boundaries, linking education and employment and providing for connections between education, work, and community organizations. By using an on-line career portfolio program, career preparation can be infused into every phase of the university undergraduate educational experience, making it an indirect system-level intervention and not just a one-time appointment at the career center. Indeed, the on-line career portfolio provides a new scheme for introducing the concepts of career and work to the university and its constituents. Using a career portfolio should create a developmental and learner-centered emphasis for educational and career planning services at the university.

In summary, an on-line career portfolio program should help college students develop a strategic career vision that reflects the realities of present and future workforce needs in the nation and the world. A career preparation program can provide a way for students to develop skills that provide a foundation for success in their career and life. Such a program could also provide a shared vision of the undergraduate teaching and learning mission for faculty members, employers, public officials, parents, and friends of the university—a vision around which they could coordinate their efforts.

Design and Use Principles

Three steps are involved in making career portfolios a focal point of career planning services in higher education institutions.

PRINCIPLE 1: REFLECTION. To prepare a career portfolio, a student must first engage in reflection regarding past accomplishments and future life and career goals. Whereas some students are ready to engage in this goal-setting activity at the time of admission, others require career planning assistance in the form of assessment, counseling, advising, and information. As Young (2002) notes, reflection may involve consultation with a counselor, a friend, an academic adviser, a teacher, a parent, or a trusted mentor. This reflection process could involve a review of career goals and an analysis of curricular and cocurricular learning activities. Many people on and off campus can help students in this reflective process; it is a primary intervention that is not limited to the career center. This point will be elaborated later in this chapter.

PRINCIPLE 2: SKILL IDENTIFICATION. Portfolio preparation requires a student to identify the array of skills and attitudes associated with career behaviors in targeted occupations, employing organizations, or training programs. Research in these areas will enable a student to specify the skills and attitudes related to career success. To identify activities that would most likely lead to career success, younger students need to think in a strategic way about academic and occupational goals. For example, a student interested in management would want to build a portfolio featuring leadership and teamwork skills and would identify courses and activities in which such skills might be developed. As with reflection, personnel from many academic services on the campus are in positions to help students build a strategy for their career development.

PRINCIPLE 3: COURSE, ACTIVITY, AND JOB SELECTION. After reflecting on career and life goals and identifying needed skills, a student can begin to identify appropriate academic courses, cocurricular activities, and jobs. Courses, volunteer work, and other activities take on additional meaning when seen as opportunities to build and document skills and behaviors congruent with the student's career goals. As with reflection and skill identification, it is the responsibility of many different personnel in the college to help students become informed about the varied activities that could provide experiences for developing desired skills and behaviors.

Career portfolio development, then, becomes a lifelong, goal-directed activity. Staff members in many different student academic support offices can provide guidance and direction in helping students develop their career portfolios. In the following paragraphs, we briefly describe the operating features of the program, how the program connects with other academic support offices, and how the program supports student learning and strategic academic and career planning.

Profile of an On-Line Career Portfolio System

What are the possibilities regarding career portfolio development and career planning? Young (2002) reports that several consortia of colleges and universities are collaborating to design e-portfolio systems. Several schools have already developed Internet-based career portfolios, and others have adopted standard paper-based portfolio systems (see the American Association of Higher Education's "Portfolio Clearinghouse," 2002, for a listing of portfolio systems). In this section we will highlight what Florida State University (FSU) has done in developing an on-line system that empowers students in the career planning and employment process (Lumsden and others, 2001). We believe that this Web-based, student-centered career planning program may provide a new paradigm for systemic educational and career services.

Although programs such as an on-line career portfolio can be initiated in different ways, we believe that top-level support is the optimum situation for the development of a systemic career planning program. In FSU's case, the concept of the career portfolio was initially created by encouragement of the university president, who challenged a comprehensive career center to consider developing an on-line system that would enable students to develop and chronicle skills valued by employers. This resulted in the formation of a task force that included staff and faculty members from all units of the career center and a representative from the university office responsible for developing Web-based applications. The task force initially researched portfolio systems developed by other universities and private vendors. Failing to find a suitable system, and given a desire to create a program with university-wide applications the task force ultimately initiated the development of a new system at FSU.

Systemic interventions such as this on-line career portfolio have significant start-up costs, the most significant of which is staff time. For this program to be successful, it was necessary to have dedicated staff members in both the career center and the information technology office. In this example, staffing was first provided to the career center to develop the program concept. With a part-time representative from the technology office and the work of the career center task force, an on-line career portfolio prototype was created over a period of approximately eighteen months. The system was frequently demonstrated throughout the university community in order to receive initial feedback and evaluation of the concept. It was especially important that academic advisers and administrators throughout the university and personnel in student affairs review system development work and provide feedback. As a result of these demonstrations, the career portfolio was endorsed as a university-wide program priority and funding was provided to enable the technology office to develop the technical infrastructure necessary for system implementation. FSU's career portfolio system represents a joint effort between the career center and the academic information technology office on campus. This collaborative effort between a student services office and a university technology office was one of the early accomplishments of this project.

It is important to understand how each feature of the career portfolio system applies to students' educational and career planning. (A preview of this career portfolio is available at http://www.career.fsu.edu/portfolio/index.html.) A key ingredient of the career portfolio is the identification of skills that are valued in the workforce and in many other life roles as well. These skills, which later became the Career/Life Skills, include communication, creativity, critical thinking, leadership, life management, research/project development, social responsibility, teamwork, and technology (Lumsden and others, 2001). This list was developed by the portfolio task force and was based on research regarding the skills that employers look for in their prospective employees. The development of a consensus within the university community about this list of career and life skills—including faculty members from across the campus in professional schools and liberal arts areas as well as the advising staff from various offices—was another important accomplishment of this career portfolio program. Although a few liberal arts faculty members were uncomfortable in identifying skills outcomes of a college education, the prevailing consensus was that these skills were highly compatible with a liberal arts education and should be at the core of this on-line portfolio.

The home page of the career portfolio provides users with three selection options: (1) First-Time User: Start Here, (2) FSU Students: Enter Portfolio, and (3) Referred User: View Portfolio. Each of these three options is described as follows.

First-Time User: Start Here

This selection is intended to provide an introduction or overview of the system and to motivate students to become involved in the program. This "tour" also provides information about the nine career and life skills and the five experience categories through which students develop their skills. The experience categories are courses, jobs/internships, service/volunteer work, memberships/activities, and interests/life experiences. Because this system is on-line, it can be previewed in classes, workshops, residence halls, or individual offices by advisers, counselors, or teachers. It can also be previewed directly by students themselves on the Internet.

FSU Students: Enter Portfolio

The second selection takes the user to the main menu. At the main menu, students can choose to build, manage, or learn in relation to their portfolio.

BUILD. Within the build section, students can begin building their skills matrix, profile, résumé, references, and artifacts. Each of these provides an option for an additional tour if students would like more information. Tours provide students with guidance and assistance on an "as needed" basis. The remainder of this section provides details about the five methods students can use to build their portfolio.

Skills matrix. The skills matrix is the heart of this on-line career portfolio (see Figure 8.2). In the skills matrix, students build their portfolio by documenting the experiences that have contributed to the development of the nine skills areas identified earlier, plus one skill area of the student's choice. Each cell within the matrix contains data entry screens that give students a framework for entering information about their skill development. Through the skills matrix, students can access all courses on their academic transcript by a link with the university registrar database and then import the information directly into the data entry screens. This feature demonstrates one of the ways the career portfolio is integrated with many different academic support services of the university.

An important component of this portfolio-building process is that students are asked to reflect upon their experiences. They are encouraged to describe specifically how a particular experience led to the development of a career and life skill. As noted earlier, this reflective process is valuable for students when they engage in the job search or graduate school application process, because it helps prepare them to market their skills to potential employers or admissions committees. Many different personnel within the university assist students with this process.

Figure 8.2. Skills Matrix

Skills	Courses	Jobs / Internships	Service / Volunteer Work	Memberships / Activities	Interests / Life Experiences
Communication	Add/Edit (1)	Add/Edit (0)	Add/Edit (0)	Add/Edit (0)	Add/Edit (0)
Creativity	Add/Edit (0)	Add/Edit (4)	Add/Edit (0)	Add/Edit (0)	Add/Edit (0)
Critical Thinking	Add/Edit (1)	Add/Edit (1)	Add/Edit (0)	Add/Edit (0)	Add/Edit (0)
Leadership	Add/Edit (0)	Add/Edit (0)	Add/Edit (0)	Add/Edit (2)	Add/Edit (0)
Life Management	Add/Edit (1)	Add/Edit (0)	Add/Edit (0)	Add/Edit (0)	Add/Edit (0)
Research/Project Development	Add/Edit (0)	Add/Edit (0)	Add/Edit (2)	Add/Edit (0)	Add/Edit (0)
Social Responsibility	Add/Edit (0)	Add/Edit (0)	Add/Edit (0)	Add/Edit (1)	Add/Edit (0)
Teamwork	Add/Edit (0)	Add/Edit (0)	Add/Edit (0)	Add/Edit (0)	Add/Edit (0)
Technical/Scientific	Add/Edit (1)	Add/Edit (0)	Add/Edit (0)	Add/Edit (0)	Add/Edit (0)

Add your own Skill

Note: *Reprinted with permission from Florida State University.*

Profile. The profile section enables the user to present a biographical sketch. The profile allows students to say a little about their personal interests, background, and plans. The profile might include a photograph or other special personal material. Students are encouraged to include items such as goals, qualifications, and career objectives.

Résumé. The résumé section allows students to upload their résumé directly into the career portfolio. Students are encouraged to create their résumé in a generic format that can be used for other purposes and are able to maintain multiple versions of their résumé.

References. The reference section allows students to enter contact information for people who can provide references for them. This section encourages students to be proactive in developing and maintaining relationships with such persons both on the campus and in the community.

Artifacts. In the artifacts section, students upload samples of their work in a variety of formats. For example, students may want to include writing samples, PowerPoint presentations, research papers, artwork, links to Web sites, or other artifacts that show the scope and quality of their work.

These five subsections of the build section of this on-line career portfolio provide a rich variety of methods for students to construct an e-portfolio. The remaining two sections of the main menu of this on-line portfolio—manage and learn—are described as follows.

MANAGE. The manage section of the main menu allows students to personalize their portfolios (users are allowed to have up to three versions of their portfolio). Because students will be documenting their skills and experiences for an extended length of time (ideally, from freshman to senior year), they may have a large number of items in their career portfolio. Students can customize each of their three portfolio versions to target specific career objectives. In addition, students can view their career portfolio through the manage section and send e-mails with access information to people they want to have view their career portfolio. Finally, students can track data to know if or when referred users have accessed their career portfolio.

LEARN. The learn section of the main menu allows students to access all of the tours in the career portfolio, view sample portfolios, and access the help menu. Most important, students can access Opportunities for Experience, where they can find out about opportunities on campus and in the community that will help them develop their career and life skills. This section includes links to more than three hundred campus organizations and Web pages of almost all student affairs and academic support offices on campus. In this regard, the career portfolio is a systemic career planning intervention for students.

Referred User: View Portfolio

The third selection from the home page of this career portfolio is called Referred User: View Portfolio. In this section, those persons referred by students can access a particular portfolio and examine the information provided there. The output of a particular portfolio is organized by tabs across the top of the screen, which first opens to the profile screen, where students briefly summarize the information that they want the referred user to see. By clicking on the tabs, referred users can then view a student's résumé, skills, unofficial transcript, references, and artifacts. Through the referred user option, students can also obtain consultation with and assistance from faculty members, academic advisers, and career counselors regarding the development of their career portfolios. In this way, many varied university personnel can become an active part of this career planning intervention if a student so desires.

Connections with Other Academic Services

This on-line career portfolio is targeted to students, employers, administrators, and faculty and staff members. Besides direct, self-help use, students are encouraged to develop their career portfolio within the context of the first-year experience course, academic advising, career planning classes, outreach presentations, and one-on-one career advising. Each of these interventions involves faculty and staff members working with students in their respective roles and relationships.

Academic advisers can use the career portfolio when meeting with students to develop programs of study and establish educational goals, particularly in conceptualizing generic skills drawn from learning activities in the liberal studies curriculum and other courses. Advisers should encourage students to find courses and activities that will help in the development of desired career and life skills. As Young (2002) notes, some faculty members and administrators believe that e-portfolios will breathe new life into the academic advising process and help students conceptualize how various activities relate to career and life skills development.

At FSU, the career center offers multiple sections of a career planning class, and building a career portfolio is incorporated into the course. The career portfolio is marketed through presentations around the campus and in career advising, where students drop in to get assistance with their career planning and employment needs. Internship, cooperative education, and volunteer work experiences also provide learning events that can be categorized into one or more of the career and life skills categories. Reflection upon the meaning of these learning experiences with a mentor or adviser facilitates portfolio development.

The on-line career portfolio may be a way for some students to engage in career planning who would not ordinarily come to the career center for assistance. For example, Murray (2002) notes that male students are presently underserved in career centers. Our own experience is that 57 to 67 percent of those seeking career services at our center are Holland's "Social and Enterprising" personality types (1997) (see also Reardon, Lenz, and Strausberger, 1996; Wright, Reardon, Peterson, and Osborn, 2000). Indeed, the on-line career portfolio could become a trigger mechanism for some students to seek existing career planning and academic advising services. Ultimately, it could lead some students to begin to evaluate academic courses and cocurricular experiences with respect to the development of career and life skills as embodied in the career portfolio system. This would be the essence of a self-help, systemic career planning intervention (see Peterson, Sampson, and Lenz, Chapter Two in this book).

University administrators and faculty and staff members at FSU have been exposed to the on-line career portfolio through demonstrations, and they are also encouraged to develop their own career portfolio to further their understanding of the process. Some academic degree programs have expressed interest in the program as an aid in their accreditation processes—in, for example, engineering, dietetics, or athletic training. Continuing education about the value of the career portfolio system and how it can be used effectively is critical to the adoption of the program university-wide. It is important for faculty members and administrators to understand how the career portfolio supports the mission of the university.

The success of the career portfolio hinges upon all constituencies adopting and supporting the program. Follow-up studies will be conducted to evaluate the usage and effectiveness of this tool, and we will seek to learn more about student characteristics associated with the successful application of the on-line career portfolio. For example, do students with low vocational identity or self-efficacy develop on-line career portfolios? Do their specific dysfunctional career thoughts impede their development of a career portfolio?

Conclusion

This chapter has explored career interventions—particularly educational and career planning—as one of the essential academic support programs in higher education, and has focused on organizational arrangements that affect such programs. The on-line career portfolio has been highlighted as a systemic, student-centered intervention that uses new information technologies that are connected horizontally across the campus and can advance developmental student career planning.

REFERENCES

American Association of Higher Education. "Portfolio Clearinghouse." [http://www.aahe.org/teaching/portfolio_db.htm]. July 2002.

Epstein, S., and Kinsley, K. "The Career Resource Library: Development and Management Issues." In J. Sampson, R. Reardon, G. Peterson, and J. Lenz (eds.), *Career Counseling and Services: A Cognitive Information Processing Approach*. Pacific Grove, Calif.: Wadsworth-Brooks/Cole, forthcoming.

Herr, E., and Cramer, S. *Career Guidance and Counseling Through the Life Span*. (5th ed.) New York: HarperCollins Publishers, 1996.

Herr, E. L., Rayman, J. R., and Garis, J. W. *Handbook for the College and University Career Center*. Westport, Conn.: Greenwood Press, 1993.

Holland, J. L. *Making Vocational Choices*. Odessa, Fla.: Psychological Assessment Resources, 1997.

Isaacson, L., and Brown, D. *Career Information, Career Counseling, and Career Development*. (7th ed.) Needham Heights, Mass.: Allyn & Bacon, 2000.

Lumsden, J., and others. "Developing an On-Line Career Portfolio." *Journal of Career Planning and Employment*, 2001, 62(1), 33–38.

Maverick, L. A. *The Vocational Guidance of College Students*. Cambridge, Mass.: Harvard University Press, 1926.

Murray, N. "Engaging Male Students in Career Planning—How Practitioners Can Bridge the Gender Gap." *Journal of Career Planning and Employment*, 2002, 62(2), 25–27.

National Association of Colleges and Employers. *Professional Standards for College and University Career Services*. Bethlehem, Pa.: National Association of Colleges and Employers, 1998.

National Association of Colleges and Employers. "The 1998 NACE Career Services Benchmark Survey." *Journal of Career Planning and Employment*, 1999, 59(3), 41–44, 58–63.

Perry, N. S. "Life Career Portfolios across a Life Span." *Career Planning and Adult Development Journal*, 1996–1997, 12(4), 41–46.

Reardon, R. "A Program and Cost Analysis of a Self-Directed Career Decision-Making Program in a University Career Center." *Journal of Counseling and Development,* 1996, *74,* 280–285.

Reardon, R., Lenz, J. P., Sampson, J., and Peterson, G. *Career Development and Planning: A Comprehensive Approach.* Pacific Grove, Calif.: Wadsworth-Brooks/Cole, 2000.

Reardon, R., Lenz, J. P., and Strausberger, S. "Integrating Theory, Practice, and Research with the Self-Directed Search: Computer Version (Form R)." *Measurement and Evaluation in Counseling and Development,* 1996, *28,* 211–218.

Sampson, J. P., Jr., Reardon, R. C., Peterson, G. W., and Lenz, J. P. *Career Counseling and Services: A Cognitive Information Processing Approach.* Pacific Grove, Calif.: Wadsworth-Brooks/Cole, forthcoming.

Vernick, S., Garis, J., and Reardon, R. "Integrating Service, Teaching, and Research in a Comprehensive University Career Center." *Career Planning and Adult Development Journal,* 2000, *16*(1), 7–24.

Wright, L., Reardon, R., Peterson, G., and Osborn, D. "The Relationship Among Constructs in the Career Thoughts Inventory and the Self-Directed Search." *Journal of Career Assessment,* 2000, *8,* 139–149.

Young, J. R. "'E-Portfolios' Could Give Students a New Sense of Their Accomplishments: Online Archives of Educational Experiences May Help Graduates Land Jobs." *Chronicle of Higher Education,* Mar. 8, 2002, A31–32.

Zunker, V. *Using Assessment Results in Career Counseling.* (6th ed.) Pacific Grove, Calif.: Brooks/Cole, 2001.

9

SUPPORTING STUDENT PLANNING

Virginia N. Gordon, Gary L. Kramer

MANY TRADITIONAL-AGED STUDENTS and even some older adult students enter college with little thought as to how they are going to reach that day when they will don cap and gown and receive their diploma. Some realize the importance of the long-range planning it takes to reach that goal, but others cannot see beyond the first year or even the first semester. Some students also think of financial planning as a separate issue from the academic and career planning that will carry them to graduation and their life beyond.

The integration of academic, career, and financial counseling is probably the most critical aspect of successful graduation planning. Most students fail to realize how the achievement of their goals and aspirations is based on the interaction of all three. On many campuses, these three critical student services operate autonomously and are often separated physically, thus perpetuating the impression in students' minds that they are independent agencies. Although technology has made information about these resources more available to students, this information is almost always in three separate databases or sites. Often, there is no institutional attempt to integrate the information that could help students understand the critical interrelationships of these three areas and how they apply to practical planning and decision making.

The purpose of this chapter is to demonstrate why integrating knowledge about academic, career, and financial services is so vital to student graduation planning and to suggest vehicles for incorporating it into practical application. Administrators and faculty and staff members must work together if students' knowledge and behaviors are to be directed to the long-range academic planning that establishes a definitive path to graduation. Just as it has been discussed in previous chapters that the cooperation and coordination of many academic services are essential for students to derive the optimum benefits from their college experience, so, too, the interaction of these three areas in particular is key to ensuring student success.

What Is Academic Planning?

Academic planning for college begins before students are in high school, even though they may not realize it. Most students make their choice of college based on their interests, abilities, values, and goals. Most are very much aware at this point of how financial considerations influence their decision to enroll at a certain institution. Even during orientation, some students and their parents are still shopping for a college to see if it offers the type of academic programs, academic counseling, campus climate, and financial resources they are seeking. Older students, who are often confined geographically to their choices, base their decision to attend (or perhaps *whether* to attend) college on a variety of factors, including family, financial considerations, and career change or advancement. These factors have an effect not only on what college they select but also on the type of academic planning that could determine when or if they graduate.

Many students are ready to confront the tasks that come with academic planning when they arrive on campus. They are not only eager to learn how to create a course schedule but are also ready to accept a broader perspective that plots future demands of the academic area they have chosen. Other students are content to plan a course schedule one semester at a time. They may have selected a major but are unaware of the need, or they are not ready to take the responsibility to spend the time and energy that long-range planning requires.

As outlined in Chapter Eight, academic advising is the one academic service that brings all aspects of academic planning together. The authors of this chapter explain that academic advising programs and services are at the heart of the institution's education practices of ensuring student success. Academic advisers either have the knowledge and skills to help students with the myriad tasks involved in choosing a major, registering and scheduling courses, examining career implications, and formulating a graduation plan or they can play a vital collaborative role on behalf of the students. For example, although they are not experts in financial planning, advisers are aware of how finances can affect students' lives in the number of work hours needed, how class times may conflict with work schedules, and the stress associated with time management. In addition, they can assist students by coordinating academic and financial planning with the financial aid office.

Academic advising presents an excellent model for how many services must come together if students are to successfully negotiate the sometimes complex institutional and financial policies and procedures that are involved. Advising encompasses the entire gamut of services offered on campus, from registration to career advising. Advisers are often the only personnel on campus who can discern the range of students' needs and concerns and know the wide variety of resources to which they can refer for specific assistance.

What Is Career Planning?

The mission of career planning services on a campus may be very limited, all-encompassing, or many shades in between. They often include career counseling, career information resources, and job placement services. As discussed in Chapter Eleven, career planning services have expanded their focus to include helping students with many types of career concerns, from typical first-year exploration to the senior job search process. As Reardon and Lumsden state in Chapter Eleven, career planning, along with academic advising and financial counseling, is part of a triad of interrelated student academic services. Their discussion on career planning services concentrates on the integration of the areas of career development, advising, assessment, and decision-making interventions. Their discussion of the "career portfolio" and its usefulness to advisers in helping students develop programs of study and establish educational goals is particularly related to this chapter's emphasis on the integration of planning services.

Career planning is an example of how confusing the lack of integration can be for students. For example, some may need personal counseling for self-assessment (which is often provided in a counseling center), career information to explore viable alternatives (which is often provided through course work, the library, and computer resources), or job placement assistance (which is provided in a career center or placement office).

The level of services students will need depends on their readiness. *Career readiness* is a concept that career theorists have discussed for many years. Donald Super (1970) is especially clear about how student differences in vocational maturity affect the career choice process. This maturity involves an awareness of the importance of planning and the ability to take responsibility for it. Since students (especially first-year students) are at so many levels of readiness for career choice and planning, any program or service working with them must focus on these individual differences. Moreover, Peterson, Lenz, and Sampson, in Chapter Five, explain that readiness in postsecondary education refers to a student's ability to successfully engage academic programs and use student services effectively. They go on in their chapter and present a practical "how to" two-factor readiness model that helps determine students' needed level of service.

Successful career planning must be built on information. Career information services provide "educational, occupational, and psychosocial information related to work" (Isaacson and Brown, 1993, p. 159). On some campuses, this information might be available in academic advisers' or departmental offices or in the campus library. Although some libraries concentrate their career resources in one place, many still locate them according to library designation, where they are difficult for students to access easily. The growing trend is to install a career library that includes printed materials, computerized career exploration programs, and Internet access as part of a center where most career-related activities for students take place.

Although most personal career counseling is still delivered through individual contact, it is sometimes provided in group or computerized modes. One aspect of career counseling is the "information gathering" step, which is when students must use many types of materials to explore academic and career alternatives. However, collecting information, without interpretation or applying it in a personal context is not that useful. Gathering data and interpreting it in a personal context are important components of career services. On campuses where these two functions (career counseling and information resources) are separate, students must figure out not only how to find these services but also how to apply the information they have gathered into realistic and satisfying educational and occupational choices.

There is great disparity among colleges and universities as to the depth and breadth of the career services they offer students. This disparity may also exist between academic colleges and departments on large campuses, leaving the quality of service uneven for many students. The importance and priorities set by an institution for the integration of academic and career planning will have great impact on the quality of the educational and career-related decisions that students make. College administrators who place high value on this integration and view it as a student-centered approach will provide the leadership and resources to make it happen. This priority or value will be manifest in their making sure that both academic and career services are physically close, organized to share staff training and materials, or actually combined into one operation (McCalla-Wriggins, 2000). Chapter Eleven contains a more elaborate discussion of career interventions and facilitating strategic career and academic planning.

What Is Financial Planning?

As stated in Chapter Ten, the need for financial planning has grown tremendously over the past four decades. The authors of this chapter state that, of the many academic services delivered in higher education in the United States, none are more critical to a student's success than effectively delivered and integrated financial aid services. The need for financial counseling is a result of the many complicated sources for financial assistance available to today's college students. Students aren't always aware of the long-range ramifications of the decisions they make about financing their education and how these decisions inherently affect academic planning and graduation prospects. Students who receive many types of financial aid (federal, athletic scholarships, military, and so on) are made aware of the conditions of their aid and that their academic progress is being monitored accordingly. Many academic advisers can relate stories of students who created course schedules according to their understanding of financial aid requirements, which put them in academic jeopardy. Satisfactory academic progress is a condition that cannot be negotiated, and it must be the critical guide to how many credit hours students carry, the way they schedule their courses, and what major they choose. Students must not only be aware of how academic and financial planning are interrelated but must also understand the impact these choices have on achieving desired career goals.

Students have responsibility not only for their academic path to graduation but for their financial obligations as well. If they accept loans or grants, for example, they need to carefully monitor and fulfill the terms of these awards and view them as an integral part of graduating. It is the students' responsibility to notify their financial aid office of any changes, such as their changed address, their dropping below the required point hour or number of credit hours, their withdrawal from school, or their transferring to another institution. It is also students' responsibility to understand the requirements for repaying loans. A commitment to financial obligations is part of being a mature and successful student. These important commitments should be explained in materials designed by the financial aid office in conjunction with graduation and advising services. As Finlinson and Stevenson (2000) point out, poor academic choices can cost students thousands of dollars and place them in financial jeopardy after graduation.

Most students need structure to engage in the complex type of planning that ultimately leads to graduation. Furthermore, student development theorists claim that individuals vary in their maturity and cognitive readiness to perform the tasks involved in this type of planning. Thus, faculty members and academic administrators share the responsibility with students to make sure systems are in place to assist them in this integrative process.

The Students' Perspective

Approaching graduation planning from the students' perspective is imperative. How do we impress upon them the importance of a task that is so fundamental to their success as college students? They must be made aware that planning for graduation is not a one-time event—happening only when they begin college, but that it is an ongoing, cyclic process that requires assistance from many campus offices and resources. Graduation planning is not a linear process that travels a straight path from orientation to graduation. It requires that students and the institution form a partnership that is committed to a common goal. To describe the process from the students' perspective, one decision-making theory suggested by Vincent Harren (1979) helps to emphasize the developmental nature of individual students as they progress through the myriad decisions involved in this critical planning (Figure 9.1).

Harren's model (1979) describes how students engage in the decision-making process. It suggests four stages that students experience, moving from (1) an *awareness* of the need to create a plan to (2) gathering information upon which *planning* is based to (3) *committing* to a plan of action to (4) *implementing* the decisions they have made. These four steps have significance for students involved in graduation planning.

Figure 9.1. Student Stages of Graduation Planning*

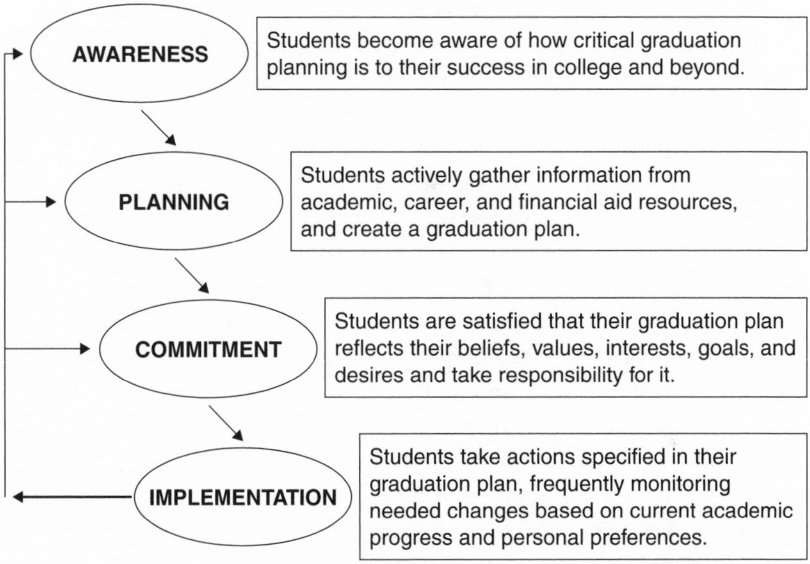

Suggested by Harren's decision-making process model (1979).

Awareness

Many students don't appreciate the impact that careful graduation planning can have on their lives during and after college. Because it may seem like an elusive, abstract concept, it is ignored by some. Beginning students may have a vague anxiety about the future when they enter college but have no firm ideas about how to prepare for it. Some are not aware of the information they need for graduation planning, where to find it, or how to use it when they do find it. Some may have unrealistic expectations of what the institution can provide, and they assume that if they follow the catalogue they will graduate without a problem. A campus program created to ensure that students formulate a graduation plan must make them aware of its importance, motivate them to take an active role in the planning process, and provide the structure for accomplishing it. Some students are mature enough and have the confidence to seek the sources they need for planning assistance. These students may skip the awareness stage altogether and begin to master the tasks required in the planning stage. But many more need to be made aware of the importance of this type of planning and how to become involved at many levels.

Planning

In the planning stage, students begin to understand what elements make up a personal graduation plan and the tasks associated with each facet of planning. Academic, career, and financial aid offices need to recognize that every student's situation is unique. Students' ability to engage in planning—and their planning needs—is varied and often complex. Integrated planning services offered by the institution need to provide students with easily accessible and visible resources to gather information, reflect on that information in the context of their personal interests and goals, and integrate the information into a usable, realistic plan.

Different populations of students may view graduation planning from different perspectives. Some undecided students, for example, can't imagine confronting this task and so they try to put it off until the day they select a major. If first-year undecided students aren't taught to build even a temporary graduation plan, they will not know how to engage in the process when they are required to do so for academic or financial reasons. Honors students, athletes, minority students, and adult students may have different expectations about what it takes to reach graduation and how to prepare for it.

Commitment

When students make a commitment to a plan, they must really *believe* that it is the best possible route for moving toward graduation. They must be satisfied that their plan reflects their values, goals, and desires. As they accept responsibility for their current plan, they must acknowledge that future events may call for changes or revisions. Counselors must emphasize that every plan is temporary and that it may need to be adjusted, reshaped, or even completely redone over time. This is probably the most difficult concept (especially for new students) to accept, since many will want assurances that their initial plan is final and obtainable.

Academic, career, and financial aid counselors will need to help students understand what is involved in these commitments. Both academic and financial aid offices need to develop checklists with time lines and other written materials to assist students in meeting these commitments. Although monitoring academic progress is the responsibility of students and their academic advisers, financial aid counselors need to be consulted regularly.

Implementation

Once a commitment is made, the graduation plan must become action-oriented. Each time students engage in the scheduling process, they should monitor how their progress is affecting their graduation plan.

If unexpected events such as a family crisis or academic difficulties interfere with normal progress, some students may need to recycle back to another stage of Harren's decision-making process (1979). Circumstances may dictate that they return to the planning stage for more information gathering, for example, if other academic majors need to be researched. When initial career decisions are no longer viable, more career exploration is inevitable. Some changes may require committing to and implementing a new or different type of financial aid package.

A natural flow through the decision-making stages that Harren (1979) espouses means that students and counselors are involved in a planning process that embraces the best expertise of all three campus areas working in unison on the student's behalf. A unified approach focuses on each student's abilities, interests, goals, and personal situation. Students are oftentimes left on their own to unscramble the services they need to devise an academic plan composed of the elements described earlier. The purpose of this book and chapter is to present and show how, under effective management and leadership, academic, career, and financial planning services can come together as an integrated and collaborative system of services that support student development, planning, and—above all—a successful college experience. The next section provides application examples of how this can be done.

Academic Services Interaction

One obvious argument for making sure that academic, career, and financial planning is provided through cooperative services is student convenience. Physical proximity of the offices and the support of cooperative staffing can encourage students to take advantage of these resources more often. It may also help to reinforce the fact that every academic, career, and financial decision they make over their entire college experience is a step toward the goal of graduating. When students understand how these three areas interact, they will be more apt to incorporate the critical information provided by them into their educational decision making.

Once campuses understand the importance of actively changing the way they assist students with graduation planning, certain questions need to be raised. How efficiently are these services performing and interrelating now? What information sources do each of these services currently provide and how much of this information concerning graduation planning is duplicated or inadequate? How do staffers working in each of these three areas approach students about graduation planning? Who is accountable for making sure student outcomes are defined and accomplished?

On most campuses, academic advising, career services, and financial aid services perform very well in their assigned mission, and even cooperate on occasion to resolve a particular student's problem. Formalizing this cooperation for all students, however, may require new ways of performing everyday tasks and disseminating information. Some staff members who work in these traditionally autonomous services only refer students to another office when there is a problem beyond their area of expertise. All three services probably have evaluative procedures to monitor their individual goals but have not examined how their stated purposes and outcomes overlap or whether they adequately address graduation planning.

What are the essential components, tools, or resources that must be available if collaborative academic services are to be successful? What critical features of each of the three areas can be shared and made interactive?

Levels of Interaction

Working together on the part of academic, career, and financial aid services for the purpose of student graduation planning can take place at several levels (Plant, 2000). These include

o *Communication.* This is the basic level at which many campus service offices interrelate today. Each service understands what the others offer and refers students, based on this knowledge, when questions need to be answered or problems need to be resolved.

o *Cooperation.* Academic advising and career services may interact in varying degrees, but on occasion, they cooperate with each other on certain projects (for example, career fairs or lecturers in career classes), or they meet to discuss common problems.

o *Coordination.* Although still functioning as separate services, planning offices can alter certain working patterns to bring about a closer relationship for certain functions (for example, library resources, interstaff training activities, and student workshops).

○ *Integration.* Academic and career functions are joined to work across former boundaries and are sometimes performed by the same individuals. On a few campuses, the staff in one office performs both academic advising and career functions (McCalla-Wriggins, 2000).

Regardless of what level of cooperation exists, better linkages between all offices can eliminate overlapping in the services provided, create easier access to these services for students, and improve how individual students are involved in graduation planning.

One approach might be to create a program within current retention efforts to coordinate the activities involved in graduation planning—from orientation to the senior year. Many of the activities and resources that are currently on most campuses are involved in graduation planning, but they are rarely pulled together into one concerted program that has that specific responsibility. This mission fits with the intent of most retention efforts, and if an institution already has a retention office, this may be the campus service most able to coordinate such a program. Regardless of the type of coordinating group or office designated, until the importance of this function is acknowledged, students will not receive the integrated assistance they need. To accomplish such a goal will take commitment from the highest administrators to the academic and student services professionals who work with students on a daily basis. In some cases, this may demand change that has enormous implications for how certain functions are traditionally performed.

Interacting with Other Academic Services

Although this chapter has concentrated on the interaction of academic, career, and financial services, students' contact with many other offices will influence their plan for graduation. Recruitment, orientation, and job placement services are by necessity interrelated in the way they assist students in their progress toward a degree.

As students are admitted and attend their new student orientation, academic planning and financial planning are their biggest concern. As is indicated in Chapter Six, students are often unaware of how important the office of academic scheduling and registration is to the ease and accuracy of course scheduling. Lonabocker and Wager, the chapter's authors, observe that today's students arrive with previous educational experiences, intense educational goals, and ambitious postgraduation plans that necessarily involve students and faculty and staff members in the educational planning process. Furthermore, students' knowledge of academic policies and procedures is critical to planning a smooth and uninterrupted academic path. Monitoring academic progress is the responsibility of both the students and the institution.

Technology is another important service for career planning. Technology is often taken for granted on college campuses today, both by the administration and by students. More than half of all institutions have a mandatory student fee to support information technology (Green, 1996). Students today can interact with peers, faculty members, and others through e-mail, electronic libraries, and the Internet. Harasim, Hiltz, Teles, and Turoff (1995) describe other technological resources often used in distance learning, such as electronic libraries, whiteboards, digitized movies, voice and chat tools, debate forums, and student opinion polls. Kuh and Hu (2001) found that the use of these sources appears to be positively related to learning and personal development in a variety of areas. They emphasize that institutional policies must ensure that all students have access to these resources. As stated in Chapter Eleven, the delivery of on-line student services is critical to providing students with reliable, consistent, and timely information. Technology can now create a system for displaying and monitoring students' progress toward a degree in an accurate, consistent, and user-friendly way.

Implementing Change

In Chapter Four, Burnett and Oblinger call our attention to how the manner in which an institution provides student planning services determines whether students gain from the services an outstanding experience or one that is mediocre and therefore frustrating and discouraging. In their chapter, these authors thoughtfully present models and trends that enable institutions to provide responsive, individualized, and integrated student academic services.

Levine and Cureton (1998) have observed that "students are bringing to higher education the same consumer expectations we and they have for every other commercial enterprise they deal with. Their (and our) focus is on convenience, quality, service, and cost" (p. 4). Historically, most campus departments have defined themselves in a hierarchical model, which tends to create barriers to student planning efforts. Well-designed and -implemented student planning services, however, are often linked to a flatter organizational structure (such as one-stop centers), bringing multiple units together to solve student planning problems and to lend support. Oftentimes, such student planning systems are manifested through Web technology that is connected to and preserves the human face of the institution, as illustrated by the institutional examples that follow.

Campuses that have taken no steps to integrate these vital and related services but acknowledge their importance must plan carefully for reorganizing or coordinating these functions. Because colleges and universities traditionally value continuity, they are sometimes reluctant to change when new directions are needed. Change should be built around an institution's functions, values, and rules. Change and continuity need to be balanced so that the value of the old is preserved while creating the new. The services most affected must be directly involved in planning and implementing these changes. This sometimes requires a redefinition of the purposes of campus services, which might fundamentally change the very nature and structure of the organization (Drucker, 1999).

Academic services function best when they have a clear purpose that guides the professionals involved. When those professionals (such as, faculty members, advisers, counselors, and student services staff members) believe that they are making a contribution to a worthwhile purpose, whether rewarded tangibly or intangibly, they will feel satisfaction with being a part of the change (Haworth and Levy, 2001).

The scenarios that emerge from these different levels of interaction will depend on the structure and culture of the institution. McCalla-Wriggins (2000) describes the many ways these interactions can take place. Faculty liaisons from academic departments can be invited to advise career services about faculty needs, and career counselors can act as liaisons to departments. Inviting faculty members into career classes and using career counselors as guest speakers in academic courses are other ways to share information and perceptions. Advisory boards made up of the faculty, career and financial aid services personnel, administrators, and students can offer suggestions for how linkages might take place. A central repository for printed materials (both academic- and career-related), computerized career information systems, and Internet resources can offer convenient access to the rapidly changing information that students need.

Some institutions offer academic and financial planning materials to first-year students. The materials, however, generally do not integrate academic, career, and financial resources in one document and often do not reach beyond the first year. Other institutions have placed interactive programs on campus Web sites that provide activities, exercises, worksheets, checklists, and lists of resources that students can use as they progress through their college years. Here again, very few institutions combine academic, career, and financial planning in one interactive document. With new technology, there are many creative ways students can be encouraged to take part in long-range planning that is permanent and easily accessible through a process that begins their first term in college and continues to graduation. Completing parts of these student planning documents could be built into certain courses that all students are required to take. For example, students could be introduced to a graduation planning Web site, create their own file, and be instructed in its continuing use in a first-year experience course or workshop. Essays on various topics related to career exploration and planning could be assigned in an English course. How financial planning and budgeting can have an impact on graduation planning and beyond could be built into a math or statistics course. As stated earlier, these efforts require an awareness of the critical need to help students with this type of planning, a commitment to the goal of designing exciting, creative approaches that foster student success, and a willingness on the part of the administration and all academic services to be involved in a collaborative effort.

Application Examples

There are many superior student planning initiatives currently in operation for both the human interaction and the technology interface. We refer the reader to Chapter Four, wherein Burnett and Oblinger review several institutional models and methods of delivering student academic services. In particular, the reader should note that chapter's description of the student-centered approaches that specifically focus on student planning through Web technology, person-to-person service, or both. Different forms of integrating a student's academic, career, and financial advising, including his or her selection of a major and classes, financial planning, and the establishment of personal and career goals, are represented in the following institutional examples:

- *James Madison University's Success Center.* (See Chapter Nineteen by Foucar-Szocki, Larson, and Mitchell for details about the staffing and performance aspect of this model.)
- *Tufts University One-Stop Student Center.* This is an integrated student academic and career services model underpinned by technology on academic and financial aid.
- *Johnson County Community College's Lifelines.* JCCC's emphasis is on personal contact, student learning, and development in the educational and career planning processes.

- *University of Delaware's One-Stop Facility.* This model focuses on connecting student academic registration and financial aid services.

- *Seton Hall University's Customer Response Team and Boston College's Call Support Center.* Both these universities emphasize a highly trained and collaborative student academic services staff.

- *Brigham Young University's Financial Path to Graduation.* As Burnett and Oblinger note in Chapter Four, this program goes beyond discussion of loans and financial resources, to help students analyze their career aspirations and academic goals. It is supported by trained financial aid counselors.

- *University at Buffalo's MyUB.* This is a personalized Web service portal that coaches and guides students—from orientation to the campus through graduation.

- *Boston College's Gold Standard Philosophy.* As discussed in Chapter Ten by Owens and Pekala, the gold standard is applicable to all student academic services and has specific meaning to student planning because it promotes all processes and services that are designed to provide maximum support for the student.

- *Florida State University's On-Line Career-Portfolio System.* This student educational and career planning program is detailed in Chapter Eleven and is accessible through fsu.edu/portfolio/index.html.

- *Kent State University's* Collage. As a way to help students select the right major, connect it to career options, and, overall, enhance the college experience, Kent State University has designed, developed, and implemented *Collage*. *Collage* is a Web-based career exploration tool that consists of interactive exercises and a place to track and reflect on academic, career, and personal experiences. It actively engages the student in gaining career self-awareness and connects academic and personal experiences. Specifically, students are able to bring together various aspects of campus services in goal setting, and, just as important, *Collage* helps students establish a personal place to collect, organize, and review academic and career information. It also provides faculty members and advisers with an interactive venue with which to connect with students, and it helps students connect with university resources as they develop their academic and career plan. In addition, *Collage* is designed to encourage student ownership of the major selection process and to complement academic advising as well as foster student development (Rickard and Motayar, 2002).

Conclusion

As indicated earlier, effective graduation planning is dependent on the quality of the interaction between academic, career, and financial aid services as students move from admissions to commencement. It is especially important for academic advising and career services to do more than just "cooperate." They must combine their expertise to assist students at every step in their journey to graduation. They must also recognize that financial planning can have an impact on what courses are scheduled, the number of credit hours taken each term, and even a student's decision to remain in school. All must work together to ensure that students are treated as whole individuals and that their graduation plan reflects their dreams and goals as well as a realistic projection of what is possible. As students' interests and goals change, their plan must be flexible enough to accommodate these changes. Professionals helping students with this task must take into account students' different stages of maturity and decision-making ability as they move through their awareness of the need to plan and commit themselves to the implementation of their plan.

Peter Drucker (1993) offers a framework for student services providers to consider as they organize academic services from the student point of view (see Figure 9.2). As the top sequence of the figure shows, strategic planning begins with the customers (students) and the services we provide them, rather than beginning with organizing departments, as the bottom sequence depicts, which is higher education's general inclination to do first—that is, reorganize. Drucker's framework, however, centers on the key issue of this chapter: integrating, collaborating, and humanizing the service environment for providers and students. Namely, the authors conclude that student career, academic, and financial planning services will be effective when planning processes are viewed from the student perspective and not primarily from the institutional or organizational perspective. A systemic and strategic view of these student planning services from the student point of view, which tends to be more organizationally horizontal than vertical, will provide institutions with more appropriate and well-defined—even connected—business processes that support student learning, growth, and success. Indeed, reengineering student academic services along technology lines or physical one-stop locations, or a combination of both, as the previous application examples illustrate, calls for a transformation not only of organizations and technology but also of the student academic services provider.

Figure 9.2. Sequence of Questions to Ask in Strategic Planning

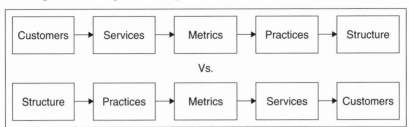

Professionals involved in these services must examine how well they interact with other critical campus functions. Evaluating their combined efforts to help students with graduation planning may result in changes in policies and procedures, and even in reframing their missions and collective goals.

REFERENCES

Drucker, P. F. *The Five Most Important Questions.* San Francisco: Jossey-Bass, 1993.

Drucker, P. F. *Management Challenges for the 21st Century.* New York: Harper-Collins, 1999.

Finlinson, N. B., and Stevenson, F. L. "Expanding Our View." In G. L. Kramer and M. W. Childs (eds.), *The "e" Factor in Delivering Advising and Student Services.* NACADA Monograph Series, no. 7. Manhattan, Kans.: NACADA, 2000.

Green, K. C. "The Coming Ubiquity of Information Technology," *Change,* 1996, *28,* 24–28.

Harasim, L., Hiltz. S. R., Teles, L., and Turoff, M. *Learning Networks: A Field Guide into Teaching and Learning Online.* Cambridge, Mass.: MIT Press, 1995.

Harren, V. A. "A Model for Career Decision Making for College Students." *Journal of Vocational Behavior,* 1979, *14,* 119–133.

Haworth, C. L., and Levy, P. E. "The Importance of Instrumentality Beliefs in the Prediction of Organizational Citizenship Behaviors." *Journal of Vocational Behavior,* 2001, *59,* 64–75.

Isaacson, L. E., and Brown, D. *Career Information, Career Counseling, and Career Development.* Needham Heights, Mass.: Allyn & Bacon, 1993.

Kuh, G. D., and Hu, S. "The Relationships Between Computer and Information Technology Use, Selected Learning and Personal Development Outcomes, and Other College Experiences." *Journal of College Student Development,* 2001, *42,* 217–232.

Levine, A., and Cureton, J. S. "What We Know About Today's College Student." *About Campus,* 1998, *3*(1), 4–9.

McCalla-Wriggins, B. "Integrating Academic Advising and Career and Life Planning." In V. N. Gordon and W. R. Habley (eds.), *Academic Advising: A Comprehensive Handbook.* San Francisco: Jossey-Bass, 2000.

Plant, P. "Wall-to-Wall or Patchwork? Linkages: Vehicles of Partnership." *Career Development Quarterly,* 2000, *48,* 348–353.

Rickard, C., and Motayar, A. "*Collage:* Delivering High-Touch Services to a High Tech Generation." A presentation given at the IBM Innovation in Student Services Forum, University of California, Berkeley, July 24–26, 2002.

Super, D. E., and Bohn, M. J. *Occupational Psychology.* Belmont, Calif.: Wadsworth, 1970.

APPLYING QUALITY EDUCATIONAL PRINCIPLES TO ACADEMIC ADVISING

Elizabeth G. Creamer, Don G. Creamer, Kimberly S. Brown

ACHIEVING EXCELLENCE IS A GOAL of all educational institutions, and quality educational practices are an essential part of this pursuit. Academic advising programs and services are at the heart of educational practices that help institutions achieve their purposes of promoting student learning and development and ensuring student success. From an institutional perspective, academic advising programs and services are second only to the instructional mission in most colleges and universities in their pervasive reach to all students throughout their time at the institution. Because academic advising crosses academic departments and academic and student services, it offers a unique site for collaboration, which is essential to achieve excellence. Academic advising programs and services are a key component of any educational institution's quest for excellence.

There is considerable debate in higher education about the meaning of excellence and quality and whether they can be defined to cover a broad spectrum of institutional types and missions. For purposes of this discussion, excellence will refer to the full achievement of institutional goals, as it is often used in accreditation reviews (Commission on Higher Education, 1994). Quality will refer to meeting or exceeding the expectations of stakeholders (Fife, 2000; Fife and Janosik, 1999; Freed, Klugman, and Fife, 1997). This chapter focuses mainly on quality, as this concept is most directly associated with educational practice and is most sought after by policymaking agencies, such as state coordinating or governing bodies, and other oversight groups, such as boards of trustees.

Identifying principles of quality in educational practices in academic advising is particularly challenging, given that there is considerable variability in the organizational models for the delivery of academic advising services. These vary by institutional size and mission but are often categorized, using a model developed by Habley (as cited by Pardee, 2000), as ranging from centralized to decentralized, or being a combination of both. Centralized services are administered by a central administrative unit, whereas decentralized services are based in academic departments where advising is supplied by either the faculty or a combination of the faculty and staff. The majority of colleges and universities use a model that combines centralized and decentralized services where, for example, undeclared students receive advising from a centralized office, whereas students with a declared major look to advisers in their departments as the primary source of academic advising. Because academic advising's purpose is similar, whether centralized or decentralized, it is possible to define principles of good practice that span different organizational models.

The primary audience for this chapter is college and university administrators responsible for academic advising. This includes administrators who oversee advising services at the departmental, college, or university level. It also includes administrators who are responsible for a range of academic services, such as vice presidents of academic services, associate academic deans, and directors and coordinators of academic support services such as retention programs targeted to address the needs of high-risk student populations.

Many resources describe academic advising programs and services and demonstrate their connection to student development (Creamer, 2000; Creamer and Creamer, 1994; Thomas and Chickering, 1984; Miller and Alberts, 1994; Winston and others, 1984), goal setting and student success (Frost, 1991), and positive educational outcomes (Ender, Winston, and Miller, 1982). The purpose of this chapter is not to reiterate or synthesize these works but to demonstrate how promoting student development can be incorporated into a wider view of quality practices in academic advising.

This chapter proposes a conceptual model of quality principles of good practice in academic advising and illustrates how these principles apply to advising practices. One of the principal arguments put forward in the chapter is that advising administrators should establish a strategic vision that is grounded in quality principles that reflect both the goal of student learning and the development and enhancement of institutional effectiveness. Particular emphasis is placed on the effective use of technology and collaboration as central components of the application of quality educational principles in academic advising.

The chapter is organized into two major sections. In the first part, a conceptual model for principles of good practice in academic advising is proposed. The second half of the chapter builds on the principles identified in the first part to provide an in-depth discussion of the importance of collaboration among educational leaders. It discusses advantages and barriers to cross-unit collaboration and uses the principles of good practice in academic advising to conceptualize what an integrated model of academic advising might look like. Recommendations are made in this section for using technology to enhance cross-unit collaboration to promote student learning and development.

The Application of Quality Principles to Academic Advising

Multiple groups and associations close to the delivery of educational programs and services in higher education have been working for years to articulate a shared view about what constitutes quality educational practices. Foremost among these groups is the Council for the Advancement of Standards in Higher Education (CAS). CAS has been promulgating standards and guidelines for academic and student services for more than twenty years (Miller, 2001). CAS is a consortium of professional associations—including the National Academic Advising Association (NACADA)—that are devoted to the promulgation of standards for educational practice and quality assurance practices in higher education. The CAS view of quality emphasizes two dimensions: (1) excellence—believing that all people in the organization must function at optimum levels, and (2) collaboration—believing that educators and students work together to achieve educational outcomes. The CAS view of quality also underscores the role of ethics in educational practice and places the focus of educational programs and services on student development.

Other groups and professional associations have also been involved in articulating principles of good educational practice. These include the Baldrige National Quality Program (BNQP) (2001), the North Central Association's Academic Quality Improvement Program (AQIP) (Commission on Institutions of Higher Education, 2000), the American College Personnel Association (ACPA) (2001), and the National Academic Advising Association (NACADA) (2001). There are many similarities among the various quality-related statements of these groups and associations; however, each one has its own perspectives and adds important dimensions to the issue under discussion here.

Established by Congress in 1987, in recognition of former secretary of commerce Malcolm Baldrige for managerial excellence that contributed to long-term improvement in efficiency and effectiveness of government, the BNQP (Baldrige National Quality Program, 2001) takes an institutional perspective. Its emphasis is on quality practices that include leadership, student and stakeholder focus, the use of information in measuring institutional performance, a focus on faculty and staff members' work systems and training and development, quality educational processes, and institutional results.

The AQIP builds upon the BNQP and the emphasis on an institutional perspective. It stresses that quality institutions help students learn, accomplish distinctive objectives, understand stakeholder needs, value people, lead and communicate, support its institutional operations, plan for continuous improvement, and build collaborative relationships.

The quality-related statements developed by professional associations like the ACPA and the NACADA are considerably more focused on standards related to student development and their respective practice arenas than they are to issues of administrative leadership. The ACPA's "Principles of Good Practice in Student Affairs" resembles the "Seven Principles of Good Practice in Undergraduate Education" (Chickering and Gamson, 1991). These encourage active learning, the development of coherent values and ethical standards, high expectations, systematic inquiry, the effective use of institutional resources, partnerships in advancing student learning, and supportive and inclusive communities.

Similarly, the NACADA (National Academic Advising Association, 2001) explores quality practice by articulating its core values and beliefs about students. As with the ACPA's principles of good practice, the central focus is on goals related to student development rather than administrative leadership. The NACADA Statement of Core Values of Academic Advising asserts the responsibilities of advisers—to students, institutions, and the advising process. It affirms, as does the ACPA statement, that students are responsible for their learning, vary in their motivations, needs, and interests, and can be successful with the appropriate assistance.

A comparison of the quality principles of three of these groups is instructive to the creation of principles of good practice in academic advising. Table 10.1 depicts principles of CAS, BNQP, and AQIP.

Table 10.1. Distinctive Quality Principles of CAS, BNQP, and AQIP

CAS	BNQP	AQIP
Organizational Principles		
Excellence	Leadership	
Collaboration	Collaboration	Collaboration
Ethical Behavior	Staff Development and Training	
	Measuring Effectiveness	Measuring Effectiveness
		Planning for Continuous Improvement
Student-Directed Principles		
Student Development		Promoting Student Learning
Student Responsibility for Learning	Student Responsibility for Learning	
	Knowledge of Student Needs, Expectations, and Satisfaction	Knowledge of Student Needs, Expectations, and Satisfaction

Table 10.1 illustrates both the distinctive and the overlapping principles found in the CAS, BNQP, and AQIP statements about the principles of quality in educational practice. These principles go significantly beyond the standard of promoting student development and learning that has been the bedrock of professional practice in student affairs, to include strategic organizational principles as well. Organizational principles address issues that affect institutional effectiveness. Student-directed principles focus on dimensions of the relationship with the students that promote student learning and development. Collaboration is the single quality principle that crosses the CAS, BNQP, and QIP statements of quality educational practice.

Principles of Good Practice in Academic Advising

Developed by the authors from the quality practices identified by a number of organizations and summarized in Table 10.1, the following are principles of good practice in academic advising. These principles capture a systematic and strategic view of academic advising. The principles give equal weight to the role of academic advising administrators in providing institutional leadership and to working effectively with students.

Organizational Principles

Academic advising

- Provides leadership to students and other members of the institutional community, including administrators, faculty and staff members, and other stakeholders
- Is grounded in the mission of the institution and its values and culture
- Collaborates with related administrative units in methods of delivery, by sharing information, and by developing and implementing policies that promote student learning and development
- Uses technology to promote student learning and development and to facilitate effective collaboration among related units
- Provides effective training, development, evaluation, and reward of advisers
- Abides by professional standards of good practice
- Conducts systematic student outcome assessment and uses other measures of organizational performance to determine the institution's effectiveness in achieving its goals

Student-Directed Principles

Academic advising

- Provides leadership about effective ways to promote student learning and development
- Values student interests and their educational needs and expectations
- Is conducted ethically, with full respect for students and colleagues

The principles of good practice in academic advising as asserted here form the foundation for academic advising that will help institutions achieve excellence and high-quality educational practices. Because it provides the link between organizational principles and student-directed principles of quality practice, the next section of the chapter explores the role of cross-unit collaboration in achieving quality educational practices. It underscores the obligation of leaders in academic advising to take a perspective that moves beyond the individual student to consider both organizational culture and standards established by national professional associations.

Collaboration and Quality Educational Practice

As indicated in Table 10.1, collaboration is the single quality principle identified by all three leading professional groups' standards of good educational practice. Administrative collaboration refers to a shared commitment of effort and resources to a common goal that generally requires a high level of interaction. To be effective in the delivery of comprehensive services that provide continuity from preenrollment and enrollment through graduation, academic advising units must be at the center of a web that has strong links to other services. These services include orientation, career services, financial aid, and programs for student populations with special needs, including minorities, women majoring in fields where they have traditionally been underrepresented, students with disabilities, and athletes. This is a way to limit duplication in services, to provide consistent information to students, and to ensure that policies are applied equitably.

This section of the chapter discusses how cross-unit collaboration can enhance the quality of academic advising services. Barriers to this kind of activity, often deeply embedded in institutional culture, will also be discussed. The discussion focuses on collaboration among administrative units.

Glennen and Vowell (1995) edited a monograph regarding the comprehensive nature of academic advising. Its purpose is to "describe ways people in all parts of the institution may serve as advisers and the kinds of interaction to be expected" (p. 1). Specifically, section three of the text explores the linkages between various student support services and academic advising. Although Glennen and Vowell do not use the term collaboration frequently, similar concepts such as mutual cooperation and communication can be found. In addition, potential barriers and conflicts to establishing collaborative relationships between these entities are discussed. The current text picks up where this text has left off by focusing on why collaborative relationships may not exist between academic advising and various academic support services.

An excellent example of administrative collaboration can be seen in the academic advising system of Valencia Community College. The system is called LifeMap and is a fully integrated arrangement involving all aspects of the college, including marketing. A visit to the home page of Valencia Community College shows the LifeMap link prominently displayed among features of the site's primary navigation scheme, which introduces any visitor to a complex web of advising activity. The home page of LifeMap contains two slogans that are used both as student attention-getting devices for the advising system and as commitments to internal marketing (designed to improve the retention of students): "Life is a trip. You will need directions" and "Taking life one semester at a time? Students who succeed have a plan." These are good examples of dual-purpose slogans. Not only do they appear on the college's Web pages, especially in the LifeMap section, they also appear physically all over the four main campus sites of the college. Valencia Community College takes its academic advising responsibilities seriously and has involved everyone in the system, all of whom make significant contributions to the system's goals. Advising has been defined broadly to provide a differentiated but significant role for everyone at the college. The LifeMap staff works hard to collaborate with teaching faculty members by helping them know why individual students are enrolled at the college, what their motivation for learning is, and how each class can help students meet their goals.

A second example of how administrative collaboration can contribute to expanding the scope of the commitment to academic advising is illustrated by a planning effort undertaken by Virginia Tech. During Fall 1998, a university task force was established to review undergraduate advising practices. Representatives from the entire campus community served on the task force and were instrumental in developing the institution's framework for advising undergraduate students. The framework included six components: (1) a definition of advising, (2) a philosophy statement regarding advising, (3) a developmental model for advising students, (4) the university statement of responsibility, (5) the adviser statement of responsibility, and (6) the student statement of responsibility.

Implementation of the proposed framework for advising undergraduate students is currently under way and its success has yet to be fully assessed. The endeavor is noteworthy, however, for several reasons. First, it attempts to have multiple stakeholders focus on a common goal. Second, it enhances services provided to students in a cost-effective manner by having more departments of the campus community take ownership of the project. Finally, it seeks to symbolically change the institutional climate regarding advising by eliminating communication barriers that hinder collaboration.

Using Organizational Theory to Understand Cross-Unit Collaboration

Both the advantages and the barriers of cross-unit collaboration to achieve quality educational practice become more than a mere list when framed within the context of organizational theory. Organizational theory provides a mechanism to understand, explain, and manage issues of an organization. Bolman and Deal (1997) proposes a widely recognized conceptual framework for understanding organizations from four different perspectives. The four conceptual approaches are (1) structural, (2) human resources, (3) political, and (4) symbolic. Although each approach is discrete in nature, a complete analysis of any organization requires that analysts employ multiple approaches, or lenses, for a more accurate and realistic assessment.

A structural approach to organizations focuses on how institutions, like colleges and universities, are structured or organized to accomplish identified goals. In this approach, organizational problems are best addressed through shifts in the organizational or administrative structure. The human resource approach to organizations places emphasis on individuals and their fit within the organization. From this perspective, organizational problems can best be resolved through the training, development, evaluation, and reward of advisers. A political interpretation of organizational issues highlights the role of resources and the distribution of financial, personnel, and physical resources as a reflection of organizational power. From this perspective, organizational problems can best be addressed through a realignment of resources to expand advising services. The symbolic approach to organization is the final conceptual approach to organizations proposed by Bolman and Deal (1997). This approach acknowledges the central role of symbolic actions and rituals in how members of an organization make meaning of their experience within the organization. In this approach, organizational problems can best be addressed by careful attention to what events—such as a convocation ceremony for new students—communicate to students and other stakeholders.

Advantages of Cross-Unit Collaboration

The theoretical framework for understanding organizations offered by Bolman and Deal (1997) provides a way to conceptualize some of the major advantages of collaboration among academic and student services units. The structural perspective points to the cost efficiencies gained by collaboration that could result from streamlined, or "seamless," student services and the reduction of the duplication of services. A more efficient use of personnel, such as shifting staff members across units to adjust to the different types of student services needed during the academic calendar, is an advantage of collaboration that would be highlighted in the human resource perspective. Using a political perspective, collaboration can be enhanced, conflict can be more productive, and competition for resources can be reduced by a shared commitment to a common goal and by the ongoing exchange of information among unit members. This exchange of information can bring enhanced accountability, as well as a more comprehensive and cohesive plan, for outcome assessment. The presentation of a unified image to students about the culture and priorities of the institution is an advantage of cross-unit collaboration that the symbolic perspective on organizations might emphasize.

This symbolic dimension of cross-unit collaboration may have the greatest impact on student outcomes. Tinto's frequently cited theory (1987) explains that students who voluntarily leave college often do so because they are not academically or socially integrated into the activities and dominant culture of the institution. This is akin to Astin's argument (1984) that student involvement is related not only to satisfaction with the college experience but also to knowledge acquisition and social and cognitive gains. Students who leave college without completing a degree often feel alienated and uninvolved. Institutions that have cross-unit collaboration built into the culture are likely to present a more unified image of institutional culture than are institutions with relatively autonomous academic and student service units. When the institution presents a consistent view of its culture, values, and mission, student outcomes may more closely match those established in the institutional mission.

Barriers to Cross-Unit Collaboration

As with the advantages of collaboration, the four conceptual frameworks for understanding organizations proposed by Bolman and Deal (1997) can also provide a way to understand the root of many of the obstacles that discourage or inhibit collaboration among administrators in higher education. The lack of leadership that models and initiates collaborative efforts and the lack of administrative structures to facilitate communication across units are barriers to cross-unit collaboration underscored by the structural perspective. The lack of agreement or commitment to common goals in the units' and institution's mission statements is an additional barrier to collaboration underscored by this perspective. The security provided by specialization, insecurities about the goal of seamless student services, concern for the loss of autonomy, apprehension about change, and the expectation of heightened accountability are obstacles to collaboration that the human resources perspective would highlight. The political perspective of the organization would point to the competition for resources and the power to shape policy as major barriers to collaboration. With its emphasis on resources, the political perspective would also point to the barriers to collaboration created by the geography of college campuses, particularly the physical distance between offices that supply student services. Symbolic barriers to collaboration include an institutional climate and culture that values individual achievement and therefore fails to provide incentives for collaboration.

Envisioning an Integrated Model of Academic Advising

The principles of good practice in academic advising identified earlier in the chapter, and the aspects of colleges and universities that inhibit or foster collaboration, as seen through the different organizational perspectives, provide a basis for identifying strategies that can enhance cross-unit collaboration. First listed by the organizational principles and then by the student-directed principles, these strategies provide a framework for an integrated model for academic advising. The discussion in the following section provides concrete suggestions about ways administrators responsible for academic advising services can develop collaborative relationships with key units that provide related services. It also highlights ways technology can help accomplish the goal. For a more general discussion of how technology can advance academic advising practice, refer to Kramer and McCauley (1995) and Kramer and Childs (1996).

Organizational Principles and Strategies

Involve multiple constituencies in the planning, development, and continual enhancement of academic and student services.

This strategy addresses a structural issue and relates to the first principle of good practice: providing institutional leadership. It requires the collaboration of numerous offices involved in providing student academic services, as well as the registrar's office, personnel from student information systems and orientation programs, and units that serve students with special needs, such as learning assistance centers and disability support services.

Collaborating on the development and enhancement of student information systems is a central way technology can enhance the effectiveness of student and academic services. It not only enhances student access to services but also adds to the quality of these services by promoting the sharing of accurate and timely data about students across units. Degree audit systems that provide students with a way to evaluate the progress they have made toward the completion of degree requirements is one element of a comprehensive student information system.

Incorporate collaboration among academic and student service units as a goal in both the institution's and the units' mission statements and make these statements widely available to stakeholders.

This strategy relates to the second administrative principle for good practice in academic advising and, like the first goal, addresses a structural element of the organization of colleges and universities. Visibility of the mission statements can be enhanced not only through printed materials, such as catalogues and brochures, but also through Internet resources. Integrating the mission statement into the organizational culture can be best achieved by linking it to departmental goals and objectives and internal evaluation processes.

Establish an officially recognized administrative structure that is part of the college or university governance system, like a commission on academic and career advising. Such a commission can promote dialogue among stakeholders, including students, and initiate the creation or revision of collegewide policies involving academic matters.

This strategy relates to the third administrative principle for good practice in academic advising and, like the previous two, suggests a strategy that involves a structural issue. The creation of such a commission would require collaboration among units, as well as the involvement of influential faculty members who have demonstrated a commitment to academic advising. Such an administrative structure would help provide not only a platform for dialogue but also a way to promote consistency and fairness in the implementation of academic policies and to determine exceptions to those policies. Having representatives from across a college or university achieve consensus about a policy can prevent a situation in which a student is held to one standard in one setting and to another standard in another setting on the campus. The academic eligibility policy for continued enrollment is one of many polices that would be within the purview of this commission.

Use technology to promote regular dialogue among involved stakeholders, such as through an advisers LISTSERV or chat room. Encourage stakeholders to participate in similar dialogues that are occurring nationwide, such as on the NACADA LISTSERV.

This strategy relates to the fifth administrative principle for good practice in academic advising and focuses on the human resource dimensions of organizations. It underscores the way that technology can promote collaboration through dialogue, sometimes diluting the impact of physical isolation or limitations in resources, which may restrict advisers from participating in professional development activities held at distant locations.

Provide training about the policies and practices of other units, possibly as part of the agenda for an advisers network.

This strategy relates to the sixth administrative principle of good practice in academic advising and addresses the human resources dimension of a college or university. Many administrators support continuous training of their staff but struggle with balancing the time required for such activities with the time to maintain routine services. These concerns can be addressed by hosting a university-wide workshop. The timing of such an event is critical. For example, some institutions have developed annual workshops where both new information and updates on existing policies are provided in preparation for new student orientation. Preparation for new student orientation is an ideal setting for such an activity because, usually, both student and academic units are involved.

Establish evaluation criteria and rewards for academic advising and cross-unit collaboration.

Like the previous one, this strategy relates to the sixth administrative principle for good practice in academic advising, which involves providing effective training and evaluation of academic advisers—and reward for excellent performance. It also focuses on the human resource dimension of organizations. A natural place to coordinate training opportunities are Centers for Teaching Excellence, where professional and faculty advisers may interact. Depending on the computer literacy of its advisers and the availability of computers, some colleges may find that on-line instructional activities are an effective strategy for cross-training.

Earmark resources to support participation in professional development activities for advisers that occur off campus, and allow networking among advisers at a state, regional, and national level.

This strategy relates to the seventh administrative principle for good practice in academic advising, which involves becoming familiar with and abiding by professional standards of good practice, as promulgated by related professional associations such as the ACPA and the NACADA. It acknowledges both the political and the human resource dimensions of college and universities. As most of these statements are available on-line, events on campus can be organized to ensure that advisers and others working in related areas are aware of accepted standards of professional practice, including those regarding ethical principles and practices.

> Coordinate a plan for the collection of outcomes assessment data pertinent to academic advising, and find ways for related units to share this information with stakeholders and to use it in long-range planning.

This strategy relates to the eighth and last principle of administrative practice. Such a strategy would avoid a situation in which multiple units are collecting similar data from students, such as data about satisfaction with services. Students are oversurveyed, reducing the quality of the data they supply. Technology can contribute here, too, by providing a way to track student outcomes and providing a readily accessible way for units to share outcomes data with current and prospective students, their parents, and other stakeholders.

Student-Directed Principles and Strategies

The final three principles of good practice in academic advising relate to promoting student development. This is the dimension that has been most widely discussed in advising literature. A strategy that enhances collaboration between academic and student services and addresses the three student-directed principles is listed as follows.

> Promote student learning and development by using a variety of delivery models to provide advising services that can be combined to serve the needs of diverse student populations.

This recommendation for promoting integrated academic advising services embraces many of the elements of organizations identified by Bolman and Deal (1997). This recommendation underscores the importance of using multiple methods of delivery to acknowledge diverse needs of students. These can range from one-on-one advising to small- and large-group advising, to advising through electronic and digital means.

Following a counseling model, a commitment to one-on-one advising as a primary method of delivering advising has been the common denominator shared by advising services in many colleges and universities. This is supported by the literature from the early 1970s and 1980s that demonstrated the connection between interaction with the faculty and student achievement and retention (Astin, 1984). Light (2001) has found that the informal interactions with faculty members and academic advisers have a significant impact on student success. As the demographics of student populations have changed so that the traditional eighteen- to twenty-one-year-old full-time student is no longer the norm, more recent literature has attested to the value of a more diverse palette of delivery methods, including those that reach students participating in distance education programs. Braithwaite (1997) argues, for example, that electronic forms of communication may be particularly helpful to Native American students attending nontribal colleges, both in communicating with their families and in initiating contact with faculty members and advisers whose cultural backgrounds differ from theirs. Similarly, Kramer and Childs (1996) argue that information technology enhances the likelihood of students taking responsibility for planning and decision making. Integrated information systems that provide ready access for students to move among the Web pages of different academic units can enhance the image of the institution as providing coherent, integrated services that are grounded in common values.

Conflict in Collaboration

It is unrealistic to tout the virtues of collaboration without acknowledging conflict. Conflict is endemic to organizations. Conflict can arise from a lack of familiarity related to low levels of interaction, but conflict is also likely to occur when, through frequent interaction, faculty members, advisers, and administrators grow conscious not only of the values they hold in common but also of fundamental and sometimes deeply rooted differences. To maintain collaborative relationships, the acceptance of diverse viewpoints must be embedded into the administrative culture. A second way is to discuss and reach agreement about systematic ways to deal with differences of opinion and competing views about the best ways to address new challenges.

Conclusion

Promoting student learning and development is the foundation of the standards of practice established by a number of professional associations, including the ACPA and the NACADA. This is understandable, given the stakeholders in these associations, as well as the educational training of many of its members and of those who are hired at college and universities to serve as academic advisers. This chapter has proposed a set of guidelines for professional practice in academic advising that takes a broader perspective than the standards established by these professional associations. Combining quality principles and organizational theory, institutions of higher education can move beyond an individualistic focus on student-directed principles to offer a strategic focus that acknowledges interaction not only within the institution but also at the national level.

REFERENCES

American College Personnel Association. "Principles of Good Practice in Student Affairs." 2001. [http://www.acpa.nche.edu/pgp/principle.htm]. June 2002.

Astin, A. "Student Involvement: A Developmental Theory for Higher Education." *Journal of College Student Development,* 1984, *25,* 287–300.

Baldrige National Quality Program. *Education Criteria for Performance Excellence.* Gaithersburg, Md.: Baldridge National Quality Program, 2001.

Bolman, L. G., and Deal, T. E. *Reframing Organizations: Artistry, Choice, and Leadership.* San Francisco: Jossey-Bass, 1997.

Braithwaite, C. A. "Helping Students from Tribal College Succeed." *About Campus,* 1997, *2*(50), 19–23.

Chickering, A. W., and Gamson, Z. F. "Appendix A: Seven Principles for Good Practice in Undergraduate Education." In A.W. Chickering and Z. F. Gamson (eds.), *Applying the Seven Principles for Good Practice in Undergraduate Education* (pp. 63–69). New Directions for Teaching and Learning, no. 47. San Francisco: Jossey-Bass, 1991.

Commission on Higher Education. *Characteristics of Excellence in Higher Education: Standards for Accreditation.* Philadelphia: Middle States Association of Colleges and Schools, 1994.

Commission on Institutions of Higher Education. *Academic Quality Improvement Project.* Chicago: North Central Association of Colleges and Schools, 2000.

Creamer, D. G. "Use of Theory in Academic Advising." In V. N. Gordon, W. R. Habley, and Associates (eds.), *Academic Advising: A Comprehensive Handbook.* San Francisco: Jossey-Bass, 2000.

Creamer, E. G., and Creamer, D. G. "Practicing Developmental Advising: Theoretical Contexts and Functional Applications." *NACADA Journal,* 1994, *14*(2), 17–24.

Ender, S. C., Winston, R. B., Jr., and Miller, T. K. "Academic Advising as Student Development." In R. B. Winston Jr., S. C. Ender, and T. K. Miller (eds.), *Developmental Approaches to Academic Advising.* San Francisco: Jossey-Bass, 1982.

Fife, J. D. "From Quality Promised to Quality Certain: Creating a Systematic Approach to Mission Fulfillment." In S. M. Janosik, D. G. Creamer, and M. D. Alexander (eds.), *International Perspectives on Quality in Higher Education.* Educational Policy Institute of Virginia Tech Monograph Series on Higher Education, no. 1. Blacksburg: Virginia Tech, 2000.

Fife, J. D., and Janosik, S. M. *Defining and Ensuring Quality in Virginia Higher Education.* Educational Policy Institute of Virginia Tech Policy Paper no. 3. Blacksburg: Virginia Tech, 1999.

Freed, J. E., Klugman, M. R., and Fife, J. D. *A Culture for Academic Excellence.* ASHE-ERIC Higher Education Report, vol. 25, no. 1. Washington, D.C.: The George Washington University, 1997.

Frost, S. H. *Academic Advising for Student Success: A System of Shared Responsibility.* ASHE-ERIC Higher Education Report, no. 3. Washington, D.C.: The George Washington University, 1991.

Glennen, R. E., and Vowell, F. N. (eds.). *Academic Advising as a Comprehensive Campus Process.* Manhattan, Kans.: National Academic Advising Association, 1995.

Kramer, G. L., and Childs, M. W. (eds.). *Transforming Academic Advising Through the Use of Information Technology.* Manhattan, Kans.: National Academic Advising Association, 1996.

Kramer, G. L., and McCauley, M. "Degree Progress Report (Degree Audit)." In R. E. Glennen and F. N. Vowell (eds.), *Academic Advising as a Comprehensive Campus Process.* Manhattan, Kans.: National Academic Advising Association, 1995.

Light, R. J. *Making the Most of College.* Cambridge, Mass.: Harvard University Press, 2001.

Miller, M. A., and Alberts, B. "Developmental Advising: Where Teaching and Learning Intersect." *NACADA Journal,* 1994, 14(2) 43–45.

Miller, T. K. (ed.). *The Book of Professional Standards for Higher Education, 2001.* (2nd rev. ed.) Washington, D.C.: Council for the Advancement of Standards in Higher Education, 2001.

National Academic Advising Association. *NACADA Statement of Core Values of Academic Advising.* [http://www.nacada.ksu.edu/Profres/corevalu.htm]. Nov. 2001.

Pardee, C. F. "Organizational Models for Academic Advising." In V. N. Gordon, W. R. Habley, and Associates (eds.), *Academic Advising: A Comprehensive Handbook.* San Francisco: Jossey-Bass, 2000.

Thomas, R. E., and Chickering, A. W. "Foundations for Academic Advising." In R. B. Winston, T. K. Miller, S. C. Ender, T. J. Grites, and Associates (eds.), *Developmental Academic Advising.* San Francisco: Jossey-Bass, 1984.

222 STUDENT ACADEMIC SERVICES: AN INTEGRATED APPROACH

Tinto, V. *Leaving College: Rethinking the Causes and Cures of Student Attrition.* Chicago: University of Chicago Press, 1987.

Winston, R. B., and others (eds.). *Developmental Academic Advising.* San Francisco: Jossey-Bass, 1984.

11

THE ESSENTIAL ACADEMIC RECORD

W. W. (Tim) Washburn, Gene F. Priday

WHAT IS A STUDENT ACADEMIC RECORD? Is it more than a transcript? More than a ledger card in a file cabinet? Certainly, academic records have been both of these things, but today's academic records reach far beyond the file room. They reside in large, legacy computer databases, in client servers scattered like small information engines across the campus, and in personal computers parked on desks, doing the daily work that makes the modern college and university function. Data stored in academic records provide the grist for the detailed analyses that help us understand and shape the teaching/learning mission of our institutions. What is the history of the student academic record, what has it become, and what will it be? These questions and other issues related to the academic record will be covered in this chapter. One thing is certain: the student academic record of today will continue to evolve to reflect our institutions' ever-changing information needs.

History of the Academic Record

Student academic records have been maintained in many different forms. In the nineteenth century, academic records were generally maintained in ledger books, with a page for each course showing the term and year, students' names, and the grades awarded. Another ledger book contained information about each student, including name, birth date, high school, high school subjects completed, religious affiliation, and parents' names and address. These two ledgers constituted the institution's academic record system. Transcripts were seldom needed, because students studied a common curriculum, and statements of academic accomplishment generally included only the date a degree was awarded and the student's dates of attendance. The secretary of the faculty, who was also the registrar, prepared these statements (American Association of Collegiate Registrars and Admissions Officers, 1996, p.2).

The Permanent Record Card

In the early twentieth century, universities began offering students the freedom to select courses that led to different degrees and majors, and the common course ledger system could not support these variations. A new approach was needed, and institutions began entering courses and grades directly onto each student's demographic ledger page. This method was subsequently modified to use individually filed paper ledger cards instead of the ledger book. This card eventually came to be called the permanent record card (American Association of Collegiate Registrars and Admissions Officers, 1996).

The methods historically used by Brigham Young University (BYU) and the University of Washington (UW) to store academic data and to reproduce transcripts have only basic similarities.

BYU moved from large ledger books to hand-recorded paper ledger cards in the early 1920s. In the late 1940s, course and grade entries were typed on the card. Later, keypunch cards were created to contain course data. These cards were used in connection with a card reader and typewriter to type courses and grades directly onto the transcript card stock. In the 1960s, mark-sensed grade cards were read into the computer, and a transparent, sticky-back label was printed for each student, showing courses attempted and grades earned. These labels were then manually applied to the student's transcript card.

UW changed from hand-printed paper ledger cards to hand-inked velum sheets (transparent paper) in the 1920s, to take advantage of a photo-reproduction process used to copy architectural drawings. Although copies could be made for transcripts, drafting the original records in ink must have been another matter.

Manually printed velum sheets were used by UW until the late 1950s or early 1960s, when punched cards and accounting machines led to a method that used heat transfer to record grades on a paper ledger card. Heat transfer used continuous-form printers to print courses and grades on paper that was backed by a reversed carbon paper. The reversed carbon paper printed courses and grades on the back of the original form, which was fed into a heat transfer machine. An operator then placed the academic ledger card under the paper, and heat and pressure were applied to transfer the carbon from the back of the paper onto the ledger card. This was an automated but slow process that required that academic record cards be in exactly the same sequence as the grades on the carbon paper—or Nancy's permanent record card received Betty Jo's grades.

Limitations of the permanent record card. Permanent record cards were easily retrieved for posting grades and making transcripts, but they were filed centrally and were not accessible to anyone outside the registrar's office. Although early data processing accounting machines could sort marked-sensed grade cards to print grade labels for the academic record, they could not store data. Even early computers fed by scanned bubble sheets could not store large amounts of easily retrievable data. Disk storage was too expensive to hold large data files, and magnetic tape did not lend itself to the random access required for grade maintenance and transcript production. Consequently, the paper ledger card continued to be the most satisfactory academic record. Students and advisers were provided with quarterly or semester grade reports, but obtaining a comprehensive student record required photocopying the ledger card—a time-consuming process if copies were to be made for the entire campus. The file room in the registrar's office was at the center of an information-starved campus. Institutional researchers, academic advisers, and students all had to place their transcript orders with the registrar's office and wait in line.

The Computerized Academic Record

Eventually, in the late 1970s and early 1980s, the cost of computing and disk storage declined enough so that it became economically feasible to store the entire academic record on magnetic disk. Once on disk, student records were more easily updated, and they became more accessible for institutional research. Computerized student records did not become readily available to advising offices, however, until campuses developed distributed data networks that connected "dumb" terminals and, subsequently, PCs to the central mainframe computer. The integration of student demographic data with the computerized transcript system provided the foundation for contemporary data systems that, today, provide instantaneous, decentralized access to student records. Although computerized academic record systems were initially designed to replace paper academic records, current record systems are comprehensive and include detailed academic and personal information. Clearly, the use of computer technology has increased the quality and accuracy of academic information.

Academic Record and Transcript?

At one time, the permanent record card represented the entire academic record, and transcripts were therefore copies of the complete academic record. Today's student academic records are more comprehensive, however, and only a subset of the record is printed to create a transcript.

The academic record includes, on hard copy or electronically, all pertinent information about a student, from the student's classes (with grades) to qualitative learning experiences to demographics for institutional purposes. As space and materials are of less concern in the digital age, today's academic record may include a wide variety of information beyond what is needed for the transcript. This information may include personal information about the student's interests, family, educational background, skills, entrance exam scores, and honors and achievements. The transcript is a complete or partial copy of the information in the academic record that can be sent to people or agencies to give proof of the student's academic experience and performance. The transcript will also include some identifiers to match it with a specific student (American Association of Collegiate Registrars and Admissions Officers, 1996).

The Essential Elements of a Transcript

The "official" transcript is designed to be an external record of a student's academic work, and "all entries should be neat, readable, and, perhaps most important, readily and completely understandable. These requirements are based on the basic purpose of the permanent record: to provide a record of academic progress and achievement to be transferred from the institution to prospective employers, other institutions and others to whom the student presents his or her records" (Quann and others, 1979, p. 188).

At a minimum, a transcript should include the name and address of the institution issuing the transcript, the institution's accreditation, the student's name, birth date, class, and major, and a chronological list of courses taken each semester, including the number of credits associated with each course and the grades and credits earned. A summary should follow each semester's entry to indicate credits earned and the grade point average (GPA). The last semester should be followed by both the semester grade summary and a cumulative GPA and the credits earned. Quarterly high scholarship or dean's list notations are also appropriate. Some universities elect not to print low scholarship or academic probation warnings on official transcripts, letting the grades speak for themselves. It is recommended, however, that academic suspensions be recorded. In addition, degrees and certificates should be clearly noted with the dates they were awarded. A detailed listing of transfer course information is not required on official transcripts, but the identification of previous institutions attended and the number of credits transferred from each institution should be included.

Printed transcripts generally include the items in the following list. An asterisk (*) indicates the items that are described as "essential" by the American Association of Collegiate Registrars and Admissions Officers (1996, pp. 4–10).

- Name of educational institution*
- Address of educational institution*
- Accreditation status of educational institution
- Student's legal name*
- Student's birth date*
- Student's Social Security number
- Student number
- Student's gender
- High school location, name, and graduation date
- Previous colleges attended, dates attended, and total credits transferred*
- Advanced placement and international baccalaureate credits awarded*
- Degrees awarded by previous colleges
- Intended major(s) and minor(s)
- Class (for example, nonmatriculated, freshman, sophomore, and graduate)
- Terms enrolled*
- Courses and credits taken and grades earned each term*
- Term and cumulative grade point information*
- Probationary scholastic standing
- Courses in progress
- Degrees, certificates, and dates awarded*

- Honors awarded*
- Academic suspension or dismissal*
- The seal of the university and signature of the registrar or issuing authority*
- Identifying code of the institution (FICE, CEEB, and so on)
- A last-entry notation so that recipients will know if information has been added
- A legend explaining symbols, grading systems used, and the academic calendar

The electronic student academic record is more detailed and may also include the following:

- Student's religious preference
- Addresses (local mailing, permanent mailing, e-mail, and so on)
- Phone number(s)
- Adviser's notes
- Waivers or substitutions for degree requirements
- Name and address of next of kin (for example, father or mother)
- Name and telephone number of emergency contact
- Admissions test scores
- Placement test scores
- Residency information
- Visa status and immigration SEVIS number
- Internships completed
- Portfolio of student's accomplishments
- Degree progress for major(s) and minor(s)
- Career information (such as service learning experiences and work experiences)
- Course information (such as syllabi and instructor name)
- Course section type (for example, day school, continuing education, seminar, and distance learning)
- Memorandum (a free formatted area of the academic record for recording thesis or dissertation titles and any other information deemed important by the university or college)

MULTIPLE TRANSCRIPT FORMATS. In addition to the official transcript, some universities print an internal or adviser's copy that includes more detailed academic information, such as specific courses and grades transferred from other colleges and the receiving institution's course equivalencies. The internal transcript may also show the student's major each quarter, in addition to the current major, to provide a history of the student's academic journey. Probationary scholarship notations are included as well, to provide detailed information to the student and advisers. The internal transcript may serve as the unofficial copy that is issued to students in person or from the Web. Another format for an unofficial transcript copy is a degree progress report showing requirements that have been completed and those that remain.

The American Association of Collegiate Registrars and Admissions Officers recommends against printing partial transcripts that show only courses taken for graduate or professional degrees when the student has also completed a bachelor's degree at the same institution. "Because the academic record reflects the total academic experience of a student at that institution, the undergraduate and graduate transcripts of a student should be part of the same document. The courses that apply to the undergraduate degree should be clearly identified and distinguished from courses leading to a graduate degree" (American Association of Collegiate Registrars and Admissions Officers, 1996, p. 11). Students can be very persuasive, however, in requesting separate transcripts for graduate and professional work. Institutions may wish to plan their transcript systems to print either comprehensive transcripts or transcripts that include only graduate or professional work. If partial transcripts are printed, they should clearly note that only courses associated with the particular program are included.

NARRATIVE EVALUATIONS. Some colleges and universities use narrative evaluations instead of grades, and transcripts from these colleges may require multiple pages for each course, including a description of the course, expected educational outcomes, and both the instructor's and the student's narrative evaluation of his or her performance. Universities awarding transfer credit for these courses must review the narratives and determine the number and quality of credits and grades to be transferred. Since these determinations are made subjectively, it is advisable to validate decisions periodically by comparing the student's subsequent academic performance with the initial admission GPA. The original evaluation may be either too conservative or too liberal.

DISTANCE LEARNING. The extensive development of the World Wide Web has created the ability to deliver rich educational content to students away from the traditional campus. Unique student record considerations are associated with distance learning (DL) courses. To avoid confusion, these courses must be identified as "DL" in curriculum listings or registration schedules so that students know the kind of instruction that will be offered. In addition, institutional, state, or federal requirements may require identification of the kind of DL delivery used for each course—for example, prerecorded videotapes, correspondence, correspondence with e-mail, television broadcast, or the Internet. These codes need not appear on the transcript but should reside in the computer record for analysis and reporting. Financial aid regulations are important considerations for DL as well. Some DL courses may qualify for federal financial aid, whereas others may not.

The number and kind of DL courses offered may affect an institution's eligibility for federal student financial aid (SFA). A college is not eligible for SFA participation if, during the school's latest complete award year, more than 50 percent of its courses are taught through correspondence. Correspondence courses are home study courses that do not meet the definition of *telecommunication,* below.

Telecommunications courses are those offered through television, audio, or computer transmission, including open broadcast, closed circuit, cable, microwave, satellite, audioconferencing, computer conferencing, and videocassettes or disks when the same cassettes and disks are used for students who are physically attending classes on campus.

Institutions are advised to review these requirements with their financial aid officers for the latest regulations. Formal audit requirements exist to verify the percentage of students taking correspondence courses if such students are made eligible for financial aid.

There are two basic instructional formats for DL courses: synchronous and asynchronous. Synchronous DL courses are similar to regular classroom courses in the sense that all students begin the course at the same time, and instructional content is delivered to all participants on the same schedule. Synchronous courses are the most economical to offer, because a single instructor can deliver simultaneous instruction to a large number of students. This type of instruction may also be more effective, because students and instructors can communicate electronically and exchange ideas with each other on the Internet. Asynchronous DL courses allow students to begin a course at any time, and each student interacts independently with the instructor. Assignments may be accelerated or delayed, depending on the student's progress.

Synchronous DL courses that begin and end with an institution's traditional academic calendar may be recorded in the usual way on the permanent academic record and transcript. Asynchronous courses that begin and end at any time should be recorded with the beginning and ending dates of the course.

To support financial aid distribution, tuition collection, and enrollment reporting, DL courses should be entered on the chronological transcript according to the date the student begins the course. The course completion date reflects the date the final grade is assigned. An in-progress grade should be recorded at the end of the initial term for asynchronous courses not completed. Institutions will want a policy specifying the amount of time students have to complete asynchronous DL courses and the grading consequences for not finishing the course on time.

Record Security and Confidentiality

Institutions issuing transcripts and those accepting transcripts for transfer credit must guard against forgery and illegally reproduced transcripts. Whereas official transcripts were formerly embossed with seals and signatures to provide authentication, many transcripts today include seals and signatures printed directly on the paper, making forgery and reproduction easier. To prevent transcript alteration, colleges should use colored transcript paper that is specially treated to show erasures. When possible, emboss the seal and issuing signature. Preprinted seals and signatures are acceptable, however. Official transcripts should be placed in sealed envelopes for mailing to a second party. Transcripts issued directly to students should be stamped "Issued to Student" and should not be used for final admission decisions or to award transfer credit.

PROTECTING THE STUDENT'S IDENTITY AND SECURITY OF THE TRANSCRIPT. In addition to the student's name, a transcript should include the Social Security number (SSN) and date of birth, to protect against identity theft. Computerized transcript printing routines may be designed to omit this information when requested by the student. If the birth year and SSN are not printed on the transcript, it is important to include other personal information, such as the student's place of birth, birth date, or mother's maiden name to identify the student clearly.

FAMILY EDUCATION RIGHTS AND PRIVACY ACT AND STUDENT RECORD POLICIES. The federal Family Education Rights and Privacy Act (FERPA) gives students the right to inspect their education records and to challenge the content if they feel it is incorrect or misleading. Academic grades are exempted from this challenge process, however, and such disagreements are mitigated through institutional procedures.

FERPA also prescribes confidentiality standards for student records and describes in detail the process for defining "directory information" that may be released to the public, if not restricted by the student. Student records may be shared with certain agencies and individuals for financial aid and research purposes without student consent, but a record must be kept of any such release so that the student can be aware of how the information has been used.

Institutions are required to include in their course catalogues and on their Web sites information about their student record policies. FERPA is a federal statute that must be closely followed, and readers are directed to *AACRAO's 2001 FERPA Guide* (http://www.aacrao.org/ferpa_guide /enhanced/main_frameset.html) for detailed information, application examples, and sample forms.

INTERNAL RECORD SECURITY AND CONFIDENTIALITY. Student data stored in centralized data systems are vulnerable to tampering, and every precaution must be taken to prevent unauthorized access. Authorization systems controlled by passwords should include different security levels that limit access based on the user's need to know. The ability to update or change records should be carefully controlled, and access to critical information should be limited to personnel in the office of the registrar. Grade change programs and screens should generate an audit record whenever a grade is changed or a completed course is either added or deleted from the academic record, identifying the user that made the change and the date the change was made. These audit records should be compared daily against source documents to ensure that unauthorized changes have not occurred. Similar audit records should be generated for changes made to degrees awarded and for changes in residency status when residency determines fee-paying status. Institutions should carefully examine their records and determine if additional items should be included as part of the regular audit process.

PHYSICAL RECORD SECURITY. The academic record is the only official record of a student's enrollment and degrees, and information contained therein is irreplaceable. All precautions must be taken to ensure the permanent retention of these records. Copies of student database files should be made daily, or weekly with daily transaction files, and stored at off-site locations to protect against fire and other cataclysmic events.

Each semester, a computer tape containing copies of critical databases may be stored at a neighboring institution's data center for security backup. It is also strongly encouraged that selected pieces of information be made available on another medium, such as a compact disc (CD) or computer floppy disk, to be used in case of an emergency. The data might include current students only (showing current enrollment, address, phone number, and so on). In the event of a catastrophe on campus, such as fire, earthquake, or power failure, information stored on other media could be retrieved easily by campus officials who "need to know."

Degree Requirements

It is critically important for a university or college to have clearly described degree requirements and a process to review and communicate changes made to existing degree programs. As new knowledge and understanding emerge, courses and degree requirements are changed to keep programs current. Without an organized curriculum approval process, these never-ending program changes will quickly bring chaos to any campus. These degree requirements can, and should, be stored in the campus database, so that a student's record can be matched against the approved requirements.

General and Specific Degree Requirements

Undergraduate degree requirements typically fall into three categories: general education, proficiencies, and major requirements. For general education requirements, students most often must complete a minimum number of credits from a set of courses in the humanities, natural sciences, and social sciences. Institutions may have proficiency requirements for writing, mathematics, quantitative reasoning, and foreign languages. Beyond these curriculum requirements, institutions often require a minimum number of credits at the upper-division level and a minimum number of courses taken "in-residence" at the degree-granting institution.

Residence study. The terms *residence study* and *study in-residence* have not necessarily meant that the student lived on campus, but that classes were attended on campus with the student interacting with other students and faculty members, using library resources, and being involved in the general campus life of the institution. As universities extend learning opportunities through distance education to students living away from campus, a new understanding of the residence study requirement is needed. What were the educational and student development outcomes that universities and colleges expected from the residential experience? Are these outcomes essential to an undergraduate degree, and can they be replicated through degree programs offered entirely through distance learning? If outcomes of residence learning are substantive and cannot be replicated through distance learning programs, perhaps distance learning degrees should be uniquely identified on the diploma and transcript to show that the educational experiences were different.

Clearly, in many cases, course content can be transmitted and learned through distance education as effectively as through face-to-face instruction, but what are the intangibles that occur through personal interaction and working in groups? These and other questions will be answered as universities and colleges explore and analyze new opportunities offered by distance education. For now, many universities are reluctant to discard the required undergraduate resident experience until more is learned through pilot studies about distance learning degrees. Distance learning graduate programs, however, have been fully embraced and are widely available.

Managing Changing Degree Requirements

Some educational institutions do not modify degree requirements during the academic year but instead change requirements only at the beginning of each year, in concert with the publication of a new catalogue. In such cases, students must meet the degree requirements printed in the catalogue that is current when they enter the program or the university. Because catalogues may not be printed annually, however, and because the Web is increasingly used to communicate academic requirements, colleges may elect to change degree requirements during the academic year. In these cases, students are not held to published catalogue requirements but are instead held to the degree requirements listed on the Web or in departmental publications when students are admitted to their major.

Similarly, general education and proficiency requirements should be based on the policy existing when the student enters the university or college. Many campuses are beginning to use an electronic process to review and approve course and program changes at the department, college, and campus levels. The electronic process makes changes easier and more convenient. But changes have a great impact on students, as mentioned previously. Once a student is admitted to a degree program, the degree requirements generally should not change for that student. New students can and should be held to the new requirements in effect at the time they are admitted to the university or the program.

For examples of guidelines and forms used to manage the review of new degree programs and changes to existing programs, visit these Web sites: http://ar.byu.edu/catalog/curriculum and http://www.washington.edu/faculty/facsenate/councils/fcas/1503/index.htm.

Tracking Progress to Degree

Comprehensive universities have found it helpful to employ computerized degree audit systems to help students and advisers monitor degree progress. These systems are particularly helpful as they provide an organized way to catalogue changing degree requirements. They also obviate the need for faculty and staff advisers to be knowledgeable about detailed requirements of every degree program. Degree audit programs are also helpful to premajors as they investigate how courses already completed may apply to various campus programs. An option could be included in university databases that allows students to match their transcript against the requirements of any program major—a practice referred to as "major shopping." It gives students a clear, indisputable, and fast summation of where they would stand if they were to complete any major offered on campus, thus freeing advisers from a lengthy hands-on process.

Successful degree audit systems are typically administered from a central campus office. The systems are fairly complex, and a well-trained staff is necessary to understand the complexity of the software and the specific requirements of each degree program. A central degree audit office will typically employ more than one person, thereby allowing for staffing redundancy and an opportunity to train new employees. Campuses considering degree audit systems should plan on a careful and deliberate implementation. Staff members at the central office will need adequate time to meet with departmental faculty and advisers to ensure that degree requirements are properly encoded. Academic departmental personnel must develop a confidence in the system, and implementing a system before it has been well tested can undermine the success of the program. Because encoding degree programs can occur over an extensive period of time, it is advisable to begin encoding degree programs with substantial enrollments first to realize the greatest benefits most quickly.

Discontinuing Degree Programs

Universities have an ethical responsibility to allow students the opportunity to complete degree programs within a reasonable period of time. Students who have made substantial progress in academic programs that are eliminated through restructuring should be provided with the opportunity to substitute courses for those no longer offered or to transfer courses from other institutions to fulfill degree requirements. Universities that require students to complete degrees within a certain number of years, as well as those that place time limits on course applicability, should include their policies in their catalogue and on the Web.

Time-to-Degree Considerations

State legislatures, education boards, and boards of trustees have grown increasingly interested in the amount of time it takes students to complete their degree programs, and the federal government and the National Collegiate Athletic Association require universities to report first-year retention and six-year graduation rates. Students' families have also become increasingly interested in time-to-degree as the rise of education costs has outpaced that of family incomes. University advisers play a particularly important role in helping students identify their academic interests and assess their readiness to enroll in courses and programs. To be effective, advising staff members need timely and strategic information.

The student academic record provides information critical to monitoring degree progress and academic success. Names of students falling behind in their work can be provided to advisers who are responsible for student intervention strategies. Students can be monitored to ensure that they declare majors by the time they have earned a certain number of credits, and students not making adequate progress may be required to see an adviser to develop an individual education plan before they are permitted to register for the next term. The academic records of graduated students can be reviewed to identify majors that graduate students with more than the minimum number of credits required for the degree can declare.

One particularly interesting approach calculates a Graduation Efficiency Index (GEI) for each academic degree program (Gillmore and Hoffman, 1996). To determine a program's GEI, calculate the average number of credits earned by students graduating in the major and divide this number into the number of credits required for the degree—typically 120 semester or 180 quarter credits, and then multiply the result by 100. Students completing an average of 120 credits for a 120-credit major will have a perfect score of 100. Programs with lower GEIs may have structural impediments or may require earlier student advising to improve degree efficiency. For more details about the GEI, visit the GEI Web site: http://www.washington.edu/oea/asesgei.htm.

Academic Transfer Issues

Community college advising offices have perhaps the most difficult advising assignment in postsecondary education. Students enroll in community colleges for a variety of reasons, only one of which is to transfer to a four-year institution. High school completion, vocational/technical, continuing education, and academic transfer programs are all options for community college students. To make matters more difficult, students often do not know their final intentions when they initially enroll. Because community college students frequently change their plans from vocational to academic transfer programs, it is particularly important for advisers and counselors to continuously assess the student's educational intentions. Many courses offered by community colleges are not designed for academic transfer, and students need to be redirected into academic programs as soon as they begin considering a baccalaureate degree.

Planning for Efficient Transfer from a Community College

Ideally, before they apply for admission, transfer students will determine how their community college courses apply to an intended baccalaureate major. Because degree requirements vary among higher education institutions, it may be better for a student to attend one institution instead of another if there is to be a better match between courses taken and degree requirements. Miami University of Ohio has developed a Web-based program called the Course Applicability System (CAS) to help community college students select their lower-division courses in preparation for transfer to a baccalaureate program. The CAS Web site allows community college students to enter completed or planned community college courses on a screen that is sent to one of the CAS-participating institutions for electronic evaluation. The four-year institution's Degree Audit Reporting System (DARS) then assigns the appropriate course equivalencies, matches the courses against baccalaureate degree requirements, and sends a degree planning report back to the student. Miami University describes the system on its Web site: http://www.dars.muohio.edu/Handout_CAS.html. Although still in the early stages of development in the states of Ohio, Arizona, and Washington, CAS holds great promise for providing accurate transfer information to students investigating transfer alternatives.

Transfer Credit Evaluation and Recording Considerations

Gone are the days when registrars could expect that nearly all students would enroll only at their university to complete a bachelor's degree.

Increased geographic mobility and extensive development of community colleges ensures that a significant number of students will have earned credit from more than one educational institution by the time they graduate. Although transfer between educational institutions has become commonplace, transfer credit issues remain difficult to manage. Both the determination of transfer course content and the physical tasks associated with entering transfer courses into a data system are extremely time-consuming.

TRANSFER CREDIT RECORDING PRACTICE. A student's academic record should include the name of each transfer institution attended, followed by a list of the accepted transfer courses and the associated credits and grades. The courses may be arranged chronologically or grouped by discipline—such as mathematics or English. Printed alongside each transferred course should be an entry showing the receiving institution's equivalent course and credit. Courses that may be used to satisfy general education requirements should be so indicated. Degrees and dates awarded by the transfer institution should also be listed—for example, A.A., 1999.

Most baccalaureate institutions limit transfer credit from community colleges to sixty semester or ninety quarter credits. If the number of credits a student attempts to transfer exceeds these limits, the academic record should list each of the courses transferred, followed by a notation limiting the total number of credits transferred. Although only sixty or ninety credits transfer, typically, any of the courses may be used to satisfy specific degree requirements.

TECHNOLOGY AND TRANSFER CREDIT. Entering transfer courses from other institutions' transcripts into the receiving institution's academic record system is a labor-intensive job unless the transfer record is received in an electronic format that can be uploaded to a computer. If electronic records are not available, some universities scan transcripts to transform them into digital data. Because there is no such thing as a common paper transcript format, templates must be made for each college sending transcripts so that the data can be correctly scanned. For this reason, scanning is only effective when many students are transferring from a few colleges. Transcripts from colleges sending a few students must be individually evaluated and key-entered.

Electronic transcript record formats have been developed for sending transcripts between institutions, and they are available in the 1998

AACRAO SPEEDE Implementation Guide, Version 4, but these protocols are still not widely used. It is more common for colleges that share students to develop their own unique electronic transcript formats. Once transcripts are electronically uploaded or key-entered, course data can be computer analyzed against a transfer matrix to assign resident course equivalencies. Some courses will undoubtedly remain for manual evaluation, but most courses received from a set of well-defined trading partners can be easily evaluated and recorded. However, transfer credits are evaluated and the equivalency results need to be communicated to the student and to the advising office before the student arrives for advising and orientation.

Institutional Policies

Although universities and colleges are similar in many respects, institutional academic policies must be clearly stated in catalogues and on Web sites so that students and faculty and staff members may be fully informed.

Academic Record Policies

Information contained in the academic record comes from many different sources, and policies are required to control when the academic record may be modified and by whom. Actions and decisions based on information in the academic record may also affect a student's enrollment eligibility, and registrars must ensure that these policies are well understood by both students and faculty.

ACADEMIC FORGIVENESS AND REPEATED COURSES. As mentioned previously, the student academic record should be a permanent record of all courses attempted and completed. Institutions with forgiveness policies that permit the exclusion of certain courses and grades from the cumulative GPA should continue to show the original grades, with an indication that the courses, grades, and credits have been excluded from the GPA and credits earned. Similarly, if courses may be repeated for a better grade, the original grade should continue to show on the transcript with an indication that it has been repeated.

STUDENT NAME CHANGES. Academic records should include the current legal name of the student and all the former names. A referenced index system connecting current and former names will allow access to the record under either the former name or the current name; however, transcripts should show only the current name. Students and former students should be permitted to change their legal name when the change conforms to the institution's name change policy. Registrars typically require a court order, marriage license, or divorce decree to change a name on the permanent record. The driver's license, passport, or other acceptable identification should be obtained from the person requesting the change. Some institutions allow a nickname or alias to be printed on diplomas in addition to the legal name.

SEPARATION OF ACADEMIC AND DISCIPLINARY RECORDS. The transcript is a record of academic accomplishments and should not contain information about disciplinary actions. "Only academic statuses which interrupt a student's continued enrollment should be reflected on the transcript. These usually include *Withdrawal* [from course], *Suspension, Dismissal, Suspension* or *Dismissal for Academic Misconduct.* Interruptions resulting from disciplinary actions (except for academic dismissals) should not be reflected on the transcript. However, the transcript key should contain the name and address of the authority to contact at the institution sending the transcript in order to inquire about disciplinary matters" (American Association of Collegiate Registrars and Admissions Officers, 1996, p. 10).

LOW SCHOLARSHIP AND SATISFACTORY PROGRESS POLICIES. Students should be made aware of academic requirements during orientation and advising to inform them of the consequences of falling below specified minimums. Publications, such as the catalogue and class schedule, should include complete information about scholastic progress requirements. Most colleges require a 2.0 minimum GPA for good academic standing, but some also require that students complete a minimum number of credits each semester or year to make satisfactory progress. In such cases, it matters not that the student has maintained a satisfactory GPA if the minimum number of credits has not been completed.

Academic Grievance Policy

Colleges and universities should develop a policy outlining the procedures to follow when a student disagrees with a final grade. The academic grievance policy, used when the student believes that a final grade has been awarded in error or that the instructor was incompetent, might include the following regulations:

○ The student must initiate the grievance process within a reasonable amount of time after the end of the grading period—perhaps within one year.

○ Ideally, the student should first bring the grievance to the attention of the instructor, who is better acquainted with the situation than any other member of the faculty. Most instructors are willing to work through differences with students in a sensitive and fair-minded manner. A specific amount of time should be allowed for this process to be completed.

○ If the instructor is not available, if the student feels strongly that the instructor will not deal with the grievance in a fair manner, or if bringing it to the attention of the instructor does not resolve the problem to the student's satisfaction, then the student may appeal to the chair of the academic department offering the course. The chair should consider the grievance within a specified amount of time and notify the student, the instructor, and the college dean of the decision. The decision may include a recommended grade change.

○ If the student is not satisfied with the department chair's decision, the student may submit an appeal in writing to the dean of the college within which the department is housed. A specific amount of time should be allowed for the student to appeal. The written appeal should include details of the grievance and an outline of the student's efforts to resolve it prior to making this appeal to the dean. The dean should be given a specified amount of time to review the appeal and to consult with the instructor to determine whether the evaluation of the student's performance was fair and reasonable or whether the instructor's conduct in assigning the grade was arbitrary or capricious. Should the dean believe the instructor's conduct to be arbitrary or capricious and should the instructor decline to revise the grade, the dean should appoint an appropriate member, or members, of the full-time faculty of that department or college to evaluate the student's performance and assign a grade.

○ Both the student and the faculty member may call witnesses. The number of witnesses and the conduct of the hearing would be determined by the dean.

○ The dean's decision would be final and not subject to appeal. The decision might include a grade change. The student should be notified in writing of the decision within a specified amount of time of the hearing date.

o The department chair, dean, and academic vice president or provost should be informed of all academic grievance appeals.

o Once a student submits a written appeal, all documents relating to the appeal and all subsequent actions should be recorded in written form for deposit in a department (or college) file and become part of the student's academic record.

Transfer Credit Policies

The American Council on Education (1999) urges all institutions, "for reasons of social equity and educational effectiveness," to develop "reasonable and definitive" policies that govern acceptance of transfer credit and notes that such policies "should provide maximum consideration for the individual student who has changed institutions or objectives" (p. 680). Realistically, few admissions or registrar's offices have the resources to investigate the content and quality of each transfer course. Institutions are accredited by many different agencies, and thoughtful consideration should be given to the identification of those agencies that will ensure that the receiving institution's educational objectives are realized. The American Council on Education (1999, p. 680) lists three items to consider when developing transfer credit policies:

1. The educational quality of the institution from which the student transfers

2. The comparability of the nature, content, and level of credit earned with that offered by the receiving institution

3. The appropriateness and applicability of the credit earned to the programs offered by the receiving institution in light of the student's educational goals

General transfer credit policies will not only determine how to award credit for courses transferring from institutions accredited by certain agencies; they may also address certification of remaining credit by other methods such as credit by examination.

Awarding credit for study at unaccredited institutions or for life experiences. Many universities and colleges have developed programs to award credit to students with applicable work and life experiences. Credit awarded for work and life experience should be clearly identified as such on the transcript and in the academic record. Institutions should also develop policies and procedures that allow students to challenge courses and validate credit earned at unaccredited institutions. Special fees are generally charged for validating independent study or for certifying credit earned at unaccredited institutions.

The Academic Record in the Twenty-First Century

In the last century, the academic record was kept in a filing cabinet, but this century it is networked to servers and desktop computers to play a central role in campus decision making. Containing far more than student data, the student record has become the nexus for teaching/learning data systems. In addition to serving such traditional areas as enrollment management and student advising, today's student record supports studies of such things as admissions selection criteria, retention, graduation rates, academic standards, educational outcomes, faculty workload, cost of instruction, and the use of classroom space. As distributed access to the permanent student record continues to expand through the development of Web applications, services once centrally provided by the registrar's office have become more decentralized. Students are no longer required to come to the registrar's office to conduct business but may instead use the Web anytime, anywhere, to change their address, view their grades and transcripts, or add and drop courses. Soon, most instructors will submit grades on the Web for direct entry into the academic record, a very different scenario from that of the last century, when clerks in registrar's offices manually recorded or typed grades on a ledger card.

Authentication, Authorization, and Access

Relational databases have integrated information silos, making information in academic records readily available to a broad campus community. Previously, record keepers could physically restrict access to unauthorized users because information was stored on paper or in sequential data files rather than on distributed computer networks. Now that data can be easily accessed, sophisticated and robust data authentication, authorization, and access systems must be designed to provide access only to persons with a "need to know."

Distributive Access

Along with the demand for network security comes the demand to provide access to academic record information to those who genuinely need the information to perform their duties. And this access will allow the person or office responsible for initiating the data to enter and maintain the data.

Interactive, Real-Time Databases

Now that the Web makes displaying the catalogue, class schedule, and other useful information possible, institutions are no longer restricted by fixed publication schedules. Changes to courses or programs can be reflected immediately in the database. Because of these exciting developments, new questions must be answered. Decisions must now be made by each institution about when course, program, and policy changes will be posted to Web sites, when the changes become effective, and how historical records will be preserved to show changes that have occurred during the year.

Campuswide Integration of Databases

There is now more potential than ever before for integrating campus databases, and institutions must work to eliminate data duplication. It is no longer acceptable to require students to visit several different offices to update their name, address, telephone number, or other commonly shared information. To avoid redundancies, universities should develop campuswide relational databases to assist the student from admission to graduation. In the process of designing these databases, campuses will need to establish a data dictionary and protocol for storing and updating shared data. If a college continues to use multiple databases containing common information, each data element should be maintained in a single database with the information subsequently passed on to the other databases needing the information.

Who Is a "Data Steward"?

As the academic record database grows, many important questions need to be answered, such as, Who is responsible for the stored data? Who is authorized to make decisions that affect that data? Is the steward authorized to grant access to information? Who monitors changes to this data? Who is authorized to make changes or updates to the data? It must be clearly understood who is responsible and accountable for the data being stored.

Nontraditional Students

For years, campuses have offered educational services beyond the campus to local communities. Today, campuses are looking to deliver educational services to the world through the Internet. Students served through distance education need comprehensive information about degree programs and courses, as well as clear and concise procedural guidance. Many of these students will never set foot on a campus. Because these students live in many different time zones, personal assistance and information on the Web must be available twenty-four hours a day, seven days a week. Circumstances need to adapt to meet the demand of these students, including the times courses are offered, types of courses needed to refresh and retool skills, and courses that use different delivery methods and nontraditional beginning and ending times.

Emergency Access to Critical Data

Tragedies, such as fires, earthquakes, bombs, and computer failures, do happen, and we, as record keepers, must ensure that backup copies of critical records are stored at secure off-site locations. Immediate access to this information is important to meet the needs of students and the institution's administration. Secure data might include nothing more than a printed list of enrolled students, their addresses and phone numbers, and the names and phone numbers of emergency contacts. More sophisticated emergency data might use a compact disc to store the aforementioned data plus the classes each student is taking. In addition, institutions should consider a list of the classes that meet in each building by time of day and a class roster for each class section, so that they will know who might be trapped in a damaged building. Each institution should identify the critical information it will need and establish a routine to keep the data refreshed and available.

Not all universities have developed their data systems to take full advantage of information found in the permanent record, and even in advanced universities, not all offices have access to central data resources. As this new century progresses, so, too, will the ability to access ever increasing amounts of information from the permanent record. Data and information will flow more easily to and from central systems without human assistance, and issues of privacy and data security will become of even greater concern. Classroom instruction will be supplemented with rich Web content, and student examinations will undoubtedly be taken and scored on the Web, with little direct instructor involvement. Just as electronic switching systems have eliminated the long-distance operator, computing systems will continue to eliminate people from the intersection of information flows. And, strangely enough, higher education will become even more personal as communication barriers disappear and students interact more directly with their teachers and mentors.

REFERENCES

American Association of Collegiate Registrars and Admissions Officers. *Academic Record and Transcript Guide.* Washington, D.C.: American Association of Collegiate Registrars and Admissions Officers, 1996.

American Council on Education. "Appendix C: Joint Statement on Transfer and Award of Academic Credit." *Accredited Institutions of Postsecondary Education, 1998–99.* Washington, D.C.: American Council on Education, 1999.

Gillmore, G., and Hoffman, P. "Average Graduate Efficiency Indexes for University of Washington Undergraduate Degree Programs." *OEA Research Notes, N-96–8.* Seattle: University of Washington Office of Educational Assessment, 1996.

Quann, C. J., and others. *Admissions, Academic Records, and Registrar Services: A Handbook of Policies and Procedures.* San Francisco: Jossey-Bass, 1979.

STUDENT FINANCIAL SERVICES

Rita R. Owens, Bernard A. Pekala

OF THE MANY ACADEMIC SERVICES delivered in higher education in the United States, there is likely none more critical to a student's success than effectively delivered financial aid services. Whether in the public or private sector, a college degree remains one of the most significant expenditures an individual incurs over his or her lifetime and it is rarely financed without outside assistance. Help is available from grants, loans, and scholarships—from both private and state agencies—but it can be difficult for a student or a family to wade through myriad agents and agencies to actually find this help. Fortunately, however, many colleges and the industry that supports the financial aid endeavor are now taking advantage of technologies and new organizational models that simplify the financial aid process and better integrate it with other student academic services.

Delivering financial aid services is particularly challenging because there are two discrete and often conflicting views of the processes involved. A student or parent has one view of how he or she understands financial aid and what he or she needs to do in order to be successfully financed. The institution has the opposite but not always complementary view of how to successfully manage all the processes needed to run a financial aid department. The challenge is to strike the right balance between the two, with the ultimate goal of providing gold standard service to students and families while running a smooth, high-quality operation. Before designing support services, then, understanding specifically what the families and students need and want is imperative.

As students first interact with colleges in the admissions cycle, they usually encounter exceptional service. It's clear why. These departments are responsible for bringing into the college the best students possible. Admissions departments have learned to streamline their service delivery, representing the whole college and all its programs and services. Prospective students and their parents never question who or what department will answer their questions, guide them, or foster their needs. But once the student is enrolled, things change. Students must interact independently with each of the departments providing academic services. And these departments take care of students only in regard to the services for which they are responsible. Students expect that their academic responsibilities are the priority. They don't expect to spend inordinate amounts of time maneuvering their way around academic services. And they certainly don't want to take time out of class or spend their study time waiting in lines to get a question answered. Finally, they expect all of the college personnel they interact with to know about all the other interactions they have had on campus. These expectations sound reasonable, but implementing them in higher education is a challenge.

While the students are focused on their needs, the institution is focused on its own. In particular, financial aid offices face unique challenges in administering their responsibilities. Managing institutional requirements and policies regarding financial aid is critical. Interaction with state and federal agencies is mandatory. Training and retraining staff to be not only financial experts but also customer service experts is ongoing. Technological dependencies are tremendous. There's little time left to focus on the student, but there's little option not to.

In this chapter we focus on a variety of ways to go beyond these challenges and to create a methodology for providing gold standard service to students and parents. We'll look at innovations in financial aid service delivery as well as administrative innovations that ultimately support the student.

The Gold Standard

Before launching into the details of the services and processes of financial aid, it is worth spending time on the philosophy we refer to as the gold standard. This standard should apply to the delivery of all academic services, but the focus here, of course, is on the financial aid services and processes.

The gold standard assumes that all processes and services are designed to provide maximum support for the student, the family, or the agent supporting the student or family. While this sounds logical—and many colleges might think that their academic services departments already do this, it is more difficult and rarer than one might think. Typically, most functions are organized with the process, not the student, as the priority. Take, for example, the way most student information systems are designed. Each module is designed and presented independent of the other. This may make sense to a systems developer who wants to focus on one operation at a time, but it makes little sense to a staff member who needs to toggle between functions in order to answer students' complex questions. Employing the gold standard, a system is actually designed with the student, parent, or service provider in mind. A student's financial picture is displayed in total, regardless of whether its origin resides in the financial aid office or the bursar's. Of course, creating this view is easier said than done.

Most colleges prefer to organize their academic services departments traditionally—that is, by area of expertise. So, they separate registration and records from financial aid and advising from student accounts. Granted, this separation has made it easier for staff members in an area to understand, in depth, the specific service they deliver. And an entire generation of directors, expert in a particular discipline, has emerged. But who is focusing on the student? Where are the service experts? Where is the organization that values service first, with all supporting processes designed to meet that end? Thankfully, these types of service organizations, designed around the student, are becoming more common in American higher education. They epitomize the gold standard.

Student Gold-Standard Service

There are two major elements that must be considered when providing financial aid and scholarship services to students and parents: in-person and electronic services. In each case the services must be as personalized and user-friendly as possible.

In-Person Service—Facilities

Any academic services department—and certainly a financial aid office—must have space that is welcoming and open, as well as quiet and private. Unfortunately, like many other administrative departments, financial aid offices have often been housed in leftover space available in any building on campus. Typically, the office is next door to another academic department that has had the same fortune—not by design but by luck. Because these offices have been considered large processing areas (they certainly have their share of paper processing), quantity rather than quality has defined the space strategy. But when thinking about service as a priority, quality space must be considered.

College-age students are often intimidated by interactions with adults, especially when those involve finances. If financial aid service providers want students to freely approach them, they must create a welcoming environment. When students ask questions, especially about a confidential matter like grades or finances, they must be able to do that somewhat privately. And the more confidential the conversation, the more private the space should be. Many colleges and universities have begun using cubicle partitions in their academic services offices. And while that is a fiscally sound way to give staff members their own space, it's not a good alternative for a confidential conversation between, for example, a financial aid counselor and a student discussing parental income issues.

Proximity to other academic services areas is also important. Up until four years ago, students at our university had to walk one-quarter mile and up or down a hill between the bursar and the financial aid office. There's no question that bringing these areas together physically has improved student service. We know we have a better chance of totally solving a student's financial problem when we deal with all the elements of that problem at the same time.

So if offices are closer together, why can't the organizations be closer together? Even though we are focusing on financial aid services in this chapter, we should spend some time entertaining a broader, more innovative way of organizing all student academic services.

In-Person Service Organization

Typically, we think of a financial aid service organization as an entity unto itself. There are usually clerks who staff a counter and answer the phone, financial aid counselors who focus on awarding aid, and a few other specialists who support the operation. Many universities are now evaluating this model and creating new ways of working with other academic services areas to better serve students.

In the 1970s and 1980s, on-line systems proliferated higher education's administrative departments. Clerical functions that had been performed in the back of the office moved to the front. Clerks were now dependent on computer screens to research information and so less and less paper was kept. Then the phones began to ring. Support staff members found themselves answering phones and facing students at the office counter, and still having to run back to find information that was left in a paper folder. This situation was not exactly conducive to providing great customer service. Staff members had to make the decision of whether to answer the constantly ringing phone, file, do data entry, or talk to the student standing in front of them. Today, however, we have more technology to help support our efforts, and new organization models have emerged to complement that technology. With the volume of phone calls and e-mail correspondence, departments must consider separating their front-end service processes from their back-end paper and data entry processes. And while this is important to do in all academic service areas, it's critical in financial aid, where much paper still exists.

It's important for academic service providers to begin thinking of joining forces to serve students better. The IBM Best Practice Partners in Higher Education represent a collection of schools that have redesigned their student services by changing their organizations and by adopting new technologies. Some have created service centers where cross-trained staff members in all academic services departments join together to answer as many general questions as possible. They rely on specialists, such as academic advisers or financial aid counselors, to handle the more complex issues. Of course, organizational change is difficult and can be chaotic, but it's critical to support students in the best way. Others in this group have used Web portals and Web transactions to present one set of services to the student rather than many sets representing many departments within one college. All academic services department directors consider these possibilities.

In-Person Service Information

As more options for getting financial aid have become available, so, too, have the complexity of the processes associated with obtaining it increased. Later in this chapter we discuss the various agencies that have a piece of the financial pie, but it's important to state up front that these many agencies and rules and protocols should be transparent to a student. To a student and to his or her parents, the college is the agent that represents all academic and financial services. As we have just discussed, a college has the challenge of presenting one set of services to a student. Likewise, the financial aid office should present one set of financial services, whether or not those are directly under that office's control.

Take, for example, a student who wishes to obtain a Stafford Loan. In a college not using the federal direct lending program, banks and other lenders are involved in the process. It's difficult for the students to know at any time exactly where in the process their loan request is located. Is it still in the college's financial aid office? Is the lender reviewing it? Is it in the guarantee agency's processing center? Wherever it is, students should know. And they should know not by calling each of these agencies but by talking to someone at their college who has access to the information, or they should use an on-line system where they can directly access the information. Gone are the days when students and parents could be transferred from one office to another. Now it's critical, and possible, to access data and to present it with one face.

E-Services

As in all academic service areas, financial aid departments are taking advantage of electronic tools to present information to students. For example, students can now apply for financial aid, view and accept financial aid awards, and apply for payment plans—all on-line. Without stepping into an office, they can find the information they need and take the appropriate action. Beyond being convenient, however, providing services electronically is improving the quality of the services in many ways, both for the student and for the financial aid office.

E-services can transcend many of our in-person services. When delivering services over a secure Web site, students can be authenticated and matched up against a profile. This profile represents a repository of all vital data about students. Knowing this, information can be pushed out to students at the appropriate time. Here is where all academic services begin to merge. Regardless of organizational boundaries, students can access a suite of services matched, for example, to their profile or perhaps to the calendar. Look at the activities that take place in academic service areas between January and April. Students are expected to reapply for financial aid, register for fall courses, reapply for housing, and perhaps renew parking stickers and maybe even meal plans. When we deliver these services in person, each department responsible for the service decides where and when the activity will take place. There's little thought about how many of these transactions a student might be involved in and how the timing of these activities might conflict with actually going to spring classes. In an electronic environment, students would be presented with the suite of services at the appropriate time—day or night—regardless of which department coordinates the services or when their doors are open. Within each area, another suite of services would be presented. In financial aid during the spring semester, the application for aid, a history of indebtedness, payment plan options, and an actual estimated fall bill might be offered.

Just like in-person services, however, e-services must be designed in a comprehensive manner that will enhance the transaction and not just replace a poor in-person transaction.

From the students' perspective, any service should be conclusive. That is, when the service transaction is complete, students walk away knowing exactly what to do—or not to do—next. Unfortunately, some e-services begin a process but don't complete it. Take that student applying for a Stafford Loan. The financial aid office might accept the application for the loan on-line, but does it acknowledge by e-mail that the application is complete and in the process of being reviewed? If we don't provide an e-service that is thorough, all we have done is shift data entry from a clerk to a student. That is not gold standard e-service.

Financial Planning

Financial planning services are at the heart of contemporary financial aid services. Whether in person or electronic, this formerly optional type of advisement is critical today. As we mentioned earlier, a college education is typically the second largest investment for an individual and a family, after a house. The challenge for financial aid professionals is to provide counseling and electronic tools that will help a student plan successfully. And here is where in-person and e-services can merge into gold standard delivery.

Financial aid professionals can take a lesson from academic advisers when developing good financial planning models. When students need academic advising, they typically look to a degree audit to give them some information and to a professional or faculty adviser to fill in the blanks. Similarly, financial planning requires a good data tool and an equally good financial counselor.

Students need the ability, first of all, to understand how much debt they have accrued and how much more they might accrue. Fortunately, the federal government has now made this information available to colleges, and with some massaging, colleges can pass it on to their students. Any good electronic financial planning tool also allows the student and a counselor to project the implications of taking various financial paths. But to do this well, a repository of financial data on the student as well as on the college must exist. Projections can be made of cost of attendance for a student's career against an estimated family contribution. But this cannot be done in a vacuum. This is where the financial planner comes into play. Just as good academic advisers take their knowledge of students into account, so, too, should good financial counselors. Data doesn't tell all, but they can provide a powerful tool to students, their families, and the counselors.

The challenge for any financial aid director is to find staff members that can play the financial planner role. Most financial aid counselors are trained to award aid and to ensure that that award complies with federal and state regulations. They are not trained to support a student's financial planning issues. In the next section of this chapter we address complications in gold standard delivery of financial services.

Delivering Gold Standard Financial Services

Although financial aid offices always strive to improve the delivery of financial services, there are major obstacles that complicate these intentions. Academic adviser roles are very complex, but the delivery of these services is significantly controlled and complicated by internal factors. Degree requirements, course availability, classroom size, and many other factors needed for proper academic advisement are determined within the institution or are established with sufficient lead time. Unfortunately, the same is not true for financial planning and advisement. External factors have a considerable role in the delivery of most financial services.

The evolution of financial aid is part of the issue. For most of their history, the majority of institutions have awarded financial aid through the admissions or dean's office in a haphazard manner, without a great deal of forethought. During the last five decades, a great deal has changed. The awarding of financial aid based on need was formalized, separation of duties was implemented, legislative statutes and regulations were passed, and enrollment management was created. Unfortunately, most, if not all, of these changes were not student-centric. Today, financial and student services are designed to involve the student's perspective. A brief summary of the functions and processes within a financial aid office might be helpful in understanding this complexity and the complications that are part of financial aid delivery.

Need-Based Financial Aid

Whereas merit-based institutional financial aid has very few, if any, external factors, most financial aid programs are based on need-based concepts. This is especially true for undergraduate education. Need-based aid is predicated on the belief that a student's (or parent's, for dependent students) financial limitations should not limit the student's access to higher education. The best qualified students should be able to attend the schools of their choice regardless of financial means. Need-based aid policies support the academic mission of any higher education institution.

One of the major challenges in delivering the best gold standard financial services at an educational institution is the need to build bridges. A main focus is to bridge the gap of affordability. To accomplish this goal, many additional bridges—external and internal—need to be built.

Mapping the Resources

To best support students and their families, bridges to many external entities must be built. Some of these include high school counselors, elected officials (federal and state), federal departments (Department of Education, Department of Health and Human Services, Department of Internal Revenue Services, Department of Immigration and Naturalization Services, Department of Selective Service, Department of Social Security Administration, Department of Labor, Department of Justice, and others), state departments and agencies (departments of education and welfare and state scholarship agencies), national or regional Federal Family Educational Loan Program (FFELP) guarantee agencies, off-campus federal work-study agencies, professional organizations (National Association of Financial Aid Administrators, National Association of College and University Business Officers, National Association of Student Employment Administrators, the College Board, the College Scholarship Service, and related organizations), FFELP lenders, alternative loan providers, and auditors.

Internally, bridges should extend to all areas of financial services (financial aid, student employment, student loans, student account billing, student collection [account and loan] processes), academic services, undergraduate admissions, various professional and graduate admissions departments, academic deans, career services, information technology, athletics, human resources (benefits and compensation), housing, AHANA minority student programs, international student programs, foreign study programs, finance, payroll, and development departments, and various on-campus departments.

As one can imagine, the task of continually building new bridges, reinforcing old bridges, and demolishing obsolete bridges never ends. Financial aid services are in a constant state of change and challenge. How financial aid officers handle change and provide seamless transition from one bridge to another determines the level of service. The recipients of these services include students, parents, staff members, and business associates. However, it must not be forgotten that the primary focuses of these services are on the students.

The financial status of independent students, or of the parents of dependent students, is paramount to their need or desire for need-based financial services. Very few families neither require nor desire some delivery of appropriate levels of financial services. These services can be as basic as the presentation of the semester's bill and as complex as is needed to determine eligibility for financial aid awards and the delivery requirements of these awards. And the financial status of these students and their families can dramatically change during the students' tenure at the institution. And the quality and duration of students' academic experiences can be negatively affected when comprehensive services are not provided to the families.

Complicating an institution's desire to deliver gold standard financial services to families are the coordinated efforts required among the institution, students, parents, private organizations, and federal and state agencies to determine students' eligibility for various financial programs. A very large and critical effort is required to assimilate external processes into institutional service delivery.

THE NEED-BASED FINANCIAL AID PROCESS. The federal government provides the largest variety and amount of financial aid programs nationally. Most families begin their purchase of an education by applying for financial aid. To be eligible for the majority of federal programs, students must file the Free Application for Federal Student Aid (FAFSA) form. This initiates a multifaceted examination of students' eligibility to receive federal (and most state) aid as well as the amount indicated on the Estimated Family Contribution (EFC) form. The EFC is critical in determining students' financial need. Many private institutions require supplemental information for the determination of financial need for institutional funds. This supplemental information may include the College Board's PROFILE form, noncustodial parent's information, and business or farm information.

The eligibility process possibly includes resolutions of federal edits and rejects of student applications. These resolutions range in complexity from the simple collection of a signature to interpretation of Immigration and Naturalization Service (INS) statuses for federal aid-eligible noncitizens.

The determination of student eligibility requires a clear understanding by financial aid experts of eligibility laws and regulations. The dissemination of concise and clear information regarding the eligibility process to students and families is essential in providing quality financial services, since it is the starting point for most discussions with these families. Financial services employees often forget that the complicated regulations and processes we enforce as administrators mean little to a student or family trying to finance an education.

FINANCIAL AID PACKAGES. Once a student has been determined eligible for need-based financial aid, a financial package is awarded. These packages include awards from various financial aid programs. There are two types of financial aid programs: free money and self-help. Free money consists of scholarships, grants, and similar offerings that require no service or repayment. Self-help programs require repayment or service and consist of loans and work programs. Federal, state, and private agencies and the educational institution are sources of these programs. All of the programs are divided into two categories: campus-based and agency-indexed.

These financial aid packages can vary from institution to institution for the same student because of institutions' varying costs, policies, and endowments, as well as the allocation of federal and state programs. Also, similar students at the same institution may have dissimilar packages because of institutional policy, the timing of the application, or the institution's perception of the students' merit.

Because of the complexity of the financial aid process, it is critical to communicate in a clear and concise manner with the student and the family. In order to provide gold standard service, relationships must be built on trust and must benefit all. Since there are so many possible paths for the student to take, it is financial services' responsibility to provide the proper direction without being intrusive. At all times, it is important for financial services providers to remember their supporting role in students' ultimate goal—to attain an education.

Once the aid eligibility and a financial aid package have been determined for financial aid applicants, the next phase of financial planning begins. This next phase includes payment options for financing the education and is inclusive of students and their families.

Since there are many options available to finance educational plans in order to provide proper advice on the various options, it is critical to understand students' educational plans. Is a student planning on a traditional undergraduate plan (four years, or eight semesters, of full-time enrollment), part-time plan, cooperative work plan, a double major, a five-year combined program (undergraduate and graduate together), summer school, foreign studies, transfer credits, housing arrangements, or other options? Professional and graduate study students may have even more options regarding educational paths.

The rigidity of the planned educational paths varies widely from student to student. One student may have a passing interest in his future path, whereas another student may feel that her education evolves around her path. Six months later, both students may change their minds. The best financial plans are based on students' educational plans, with strong consideration given to flexibility and choice.

PAYMENT OPTIONS. There are three general sources that students (and their families) have in financing their portion of the educational costs: past earnings, current earnings, and future earnings.

Past earnings are made up of savings and assets. Some past savings are considered more accessible than others. These savings may represent the student's, a parent's, or another family member's earnings. Including savings from a summer job is a traditional way for a student to contribute from past earnings. Also, veteran's educational benefits can be considered savings from past earnings. Although most savings plans are considered very accessible, the perceived liquidity of home equity can vary greatly. Whereas some homeowners view their home equity as a sacred cow, others look at their home equity as a liquid asset that may be used to cover educational costs.

Current earnings may also include those of the student, the parents, and other family members. The work-study term-time program is a traditional part of a need-based financial aid package that requires students to be responsible for a portion of their educational costs through current earnings. These programs are financed through federal, state, or institutional funding. Similar off-campus part- or full-time student employment is usually considered a vital part of financing an education. Many institutions have monthly payment plans that extend the educational costs over a period of time. Students and their parents can use these payment plans but only if they receive appropriate guidance from the financial aid office.

Future earnings used to pay for educational costs are traditionally considered loans. Like the work-study program, student loans have been a traditional part of a need-based aid package. These funds come from federal, state, institutional, and private sources. Family educational loans are another means of converting future earnings to pay current educational costs. The Federal Parent's Loan for Undergraduate Students (PLUS) is a major source of funds for dependent undergraduates. Independent students (undergraduate and graduate) can take out an Unsubsidized Stafford Loan from the federal government to assist in the financing of educational costs. There are also various state, institutional, and private sources of family educational loans. Credit card payments are considered a loan on future earnings.

A future earnings option that has become increasingly more popular with students is the conversion of future employment into a scholarship or loan forgiveness. Traditionally, the Reserve Officer Training Corps (ROTC) and the Service Academies have provided scholarships for future military employment. The Peace Corps and AmeriCorps have stipend and loan forgiveness benefits. Several states have "futures"—programs that award scholarships or loans that are forgiven, based on specified future employment. Even private industry uses futures scholarships in the recruitment of top students as employees. Many employers provide tuition benefits to their staff based on continued employment; others have loan forgiveness as a benefit to recruit and retain prized staff members.

Student Employment—A Redesign

Successfully providing a gold standard of service requires significant research, planning, design, and flexibility. Let us review one component of financial services—the student employment process. This process at Boston College has undergone significant revision and is an example of using technology and process redesign to support student services.

The basic premise behind the student employment process is relatively simple: job openings are posted, student employees are hired, and payment is made to students for services rendered. Complications arise from federal and state employment laws and regulations and Federal Work-Study (FWS) regulations. It is a classic paper, people, and data dilemma. The old process was paper-intensive, time-consuming, and quickly outdated, and it did not support the educational experience. The goal of the redesign was to focus on the process from the perspective of the student and the employer, to improve efficiency, and to use technology.

Once the process was redesigned to provide service at the gold standard, many bridges needed to be built and rebuilt. Accounting, payroll, the budget office, career services, financial aid, human resources, information technology, student employment—all of the departments that hired student employees—needed to be incorporated into the process.

The old process started with an allocation of funds for student employees. Departments that hired FWS students were charged 30 percent (institutional share) of the student-earned wages. This process encouraged the hiring of FWS students but caused other outcomes that were not wanted. Student and employer continuity often suffered because many employers terminated FWS students, once their annual FWS funds were exhausted, or they required that the student appeal for additional FWS funds. In addition, trained FWS students were not rehired the following year if they were not eligible for a new FWS award.

To post a job opening, the department was required to complete paper job description and posting forms. Multiple copies of these forms were posted into three-ring binders, and two weeks before the opening of the fall semester, all job postings were typed into a newspaper format by the student employment staff. These newspapers were distributed around the campus the weekend before the first day of classes. The postings were removed from the binders, once the department requested removal or when the student employment staff called the hiring department to update the binders. There were obvious limitations to this process.

Any student seeking work would request a hire form. FWS amounts (if applicable) were manually noted. Also, students completed I-9 and W-4 requirements at this time. Students would then search for an employer. Once they were hired, the employer would complete the form and return it to the student employment office for approval of the wage rate. The approved form would then be forwarded to the budget office for approval and would finally go to payroll for input. Weekly, timesheets were printed and mailed, payroll checks were produced and distributed, and FWS earnings were monitored for each student. The paper, not the student, was the focus of the process.

The redesigned employment process changed everything. To improve continuity and the educational experience, departments are now funded at 100 percent for student employment. This change in budgeting has required no additional funds, just the inclusion of FWS funds. Behind the scene, FWS student hours and annual limits are electronically tracked and increased, if appropriate. Departments are required to hire FWS students during the first four weeks of school, unless they are hiring a previous student employee with trained skills. FWS use has improved each year since the implementation of this new process.

Job postings were converted to an electronic process. Departments input their openings into a system that automatically checks for budget and wage rate compliance. If compliant, the postings are electronically converted into html for daily Web posting. The student employment office controls the display and timing of the Web postings. Previous electronic postings are saved and can then be used for future requests.

Student hire forms are also electronic. Using a student's ID or Social Security number, the employer matches the job posting with the student file to create the hire form. Standard information is provided along with FWS authorization amounts. An edit requires the completion of an I-9 and a W-4 form before the electronic hire form can be approved. Also, at this time, the employer can decide whether to close or continue to list the posting (multiple positions).

Electronic timesheets have reduced redundancy and input errors. In addition, students are strongly encouraged to use direct deposit; currently, more than 99 percent of students are using it. And all students have their payroll records available to them electronically.

A great deal of coordination, cooperation, and communication was required to accomplish this improved process, though even more still needs to be done. Students and faculty and staff members are very satisfied with this new process because student job postings are accurate and timely, the budget is easier to plan, information is accessible and secure, and the retention of trained student employees has improved.

Still, strategies to improve the seamless incorporation of career services, academic internships, and research are evolving. These concepts are student-centric and enhance the academic experience. They include Web-based personalized student portfolios (similar to a curriculum vitae, with entering admission information) that detail employment and internship history as well as searchable databases (of employment, internship, and volunteer opportunities and applicants) for students and faculty and staff members.

Enablers

Today, providing quality service requires a combination of technology, partnerships, and staffs that are flexible, adaptive, and creative. It is an extremely difficult task that requires a never-ending evolution.

Technology

Especially with technology, the need to evolve is critical. The list of technologies that need frequent updating is huge: telephone (traditional and wireless), VRU (voice response units), computers (mainframes, terminals, client server, desktops, and laptops), networks (wired and wireless), personal digital assistants (PDAs), modems (telephone, DSL, cable, satellite), voice mail, e-mail, Web sites, portals, imaging, electronic document management, e-signatures, and so on. Technology is best used when it seamlessly integrates information for consumption or advice. Evolving this technology needs to be balanced with the appropriate allocation of resources. Sometimes, it is prudent to wait for technological improvements; at other times, waiting will cause you to fall behind.

Whereas the use of paper records and documentation is the answer for one institution, the reduction of paperwork through imaging (the conversion of paper documents into electronic images) may be the answer for a second institution; a third institution may use electronic document management.

After reviewing the documentation-intensive requirements associated with financial aid, our university has opted for the document management option. This option provides us with the flexibility to use current technologies such as imaging, indexing, document storage (audio, video, and data), remote processing, and XML (near real-time Web-based transaction processing). The improved processing of documents has led to improvement in delivery times and in the determination of financial aid eligibility. Imagine the improvement in services when an e-file tax file can be used to verify income instead of the paper tax return.

Without technology, a variety of simulations would be next to impossible to deliver. Currently, most simulation models are very basic, but as system integration and database access improve, these models will advance. Like a degree audit, financial modeling will support gold standard service. Financial service simulators can be used in the advisement of such topics as debt management, financing, budgeting, financial aid awarding, and academic planning. Current debt management models can advise the student (borrower) on loan history, repayment schedules, expected starting salary (based on career choice), and limited consolidation models. In the future, through the integration of information provided from current and future national databases, the financial counseling information for students can be comprehensive and cumulative. But there are limitations. Some noneducational loans and loan forgiveness options are usually not automatically included; nor is parent or spouse information accessible in all cases.

To properly support the academic planning process, financial service simulation models need to be integrated in a sensible way. Students, parents, and faculty and staff members should be able to easily simulate financial ramifications based on various educational options.

Partnerships

For many years, partnerships between educational institutions and third-party providers have provided services to students and their families. Traditionally, most institutions have purchased third-party campus administration software, contracted the administration or collection of the federal campus-based loan programs, evaluated and recommended Federal Stafford Loan lenders or federal direct loan programs, and employed various services offered by payment plan providers.

More recently, institutions have contracted outside providers of expanded financial aid services. Some such providers include the development and maintenance of administrative software systems, Web sites, financial aid application processing and awarding, student account billing, counseling on financing options, and more. Depending on the service provider, such partnerships can enhance or detract from the overall delivery of gold standard service. The appropriate selection, implementation, and integration of these services are critical.

Our university has instituted a pilot call center with a third-party provider of payment plans for the following reasons: the low unemployment rate and the scarcity of highly trained staff, the need to enhance the financial counseling on financing options, and the desire to provide additional debt management services to students (and parents). Initially, the focus of the pilot program has been to provide counseling to entering first-year undergraduate students—who had made a deposit—and their parents. The determination of eligibility and financial aid and related advisement has remained with the institutional staff.

A short description of the service with a toll-free telephone number is published in the financing pamphlet provided to all accepted undergraduate students. Inbound and outbound telephone call scripts were designed and approved. These scripts encourage the use of payment plans over loan options. Once the students or parents make a deposit, they receive a letter of introduction. This letter explains the service and notifies them of the coming outbound call. Financing counselors trained on the institution's process and using the approved script then call all of these families.

Initial results are extremely encouraging. Based on anecdotal information and discussions during orientation, families are pleased with the financing options and information provided by the financing counselors. More important, student account resolution improved dramatically while payment plan enrollment increased and borrowing from the Federal PLUS Loan program decreased.

Staff

A critical element in the delivery of gold standard financial services is the staff that delivers the information and advice. The integration of the financial services with academic services is essential. The organizational structure of the staff must not only support the delivery of services but must also include the evaluation, planning, design, and management of all the services that influence students' institutional experience.

Financial services staff members are required, more than most, to be extremely flexible. They must be able to focus on financial matters and be compassionate in their service to students and families. It should be the goal of every financial aid office to ensure that the administration of finances is so efficient that staff members can focus on the service aspect of their jobs.

Training alongside other academic services staff members is critical. It's the only way the financial staff can truly appreciate all the elements that make up a student's successful academic career. But to do this, academic services directors must cooperate and understand the interdependencies their departments have.

Considering the importance of their role in promoting student success, financial staff members must be well compensated for their services and for their efforts to continually improve. If they are not, financial aid offices will never attract and retain staff members who can absorb all the information they need to know and serve students by the gold standard.

Building for Success

Throughout this chapter, we have discussed a variety of options that can be used to create effective student financial services. It is worth highlighting a few of the most critical success factors involved in the delivery of these services:

- *Web services.* It is important to provide students and families with financial services over the Web. Web services give students access to critical, personalized information about their financial status. Without this knowledge being easily accessible, it is difficult for them to focus on their priority: academic activities.

- *Collaboration.* Financial services departments must strive to work closely with such departments as the registrar's office, career services, counseling, and academic advising. Staff cross-training programs, collaborative communications, targeted joint messages, and one-stop service delivery help focus services on students rather than processes.

- *Staff training and development.* As we've already mentioned, hiring the right staff and developing them to be collaborators who care deeply about providing exceptional customer service is very important. Students and parents are in day-to-day contact with the staff. Whether a student is properly advised or referred to an appropriate academic service depends entirely on a willing staff member.

- *Executive sponsorship.* At most colleges and universities, change in organizations and related processes does not happen easily. Often, financial services report to a leader different from the one academic services departments report to. This can make it challenging for the areas to collaborate. It becomes important, then, to find executives who are willing to look beyond their own organizational boundaries and support seamless, gold standard service.

Conclusion

As the Internet and intranet develop and software and hardware mature and become readily available to students and faculty and staff members, demands for speedy self-service increases. To provide gold standard service, communication must be accurate and consistent. Today's offices must be able to resolve issues and advise students and families instantaneously. The challenge is to build a flexible system and retain staff members who can adapt to future developments. What many managers face is the problem of how to balance appropriate services with limited institutional resources.

The proper combination of services and processes at one institution may not well serve another institution. However, it is critical for all institutions to continue to evolve and improve. Without that, gold standard service will never be delivered.

PART THREE

NEW DIRECTIONS
FOR PRACTICE

IN PART ONE, we examined student development and college success within the context of interrelated student academic services. Several models of institutional best practices were presented, all of which illustrated the student-centered approach through institutional programs of technology, with the all-important accompaniment of the human interface. In Part Two, the features and functions of each of the student academic services—from enrollment to graduation—were systematically discussed, with an emphasis on delivering interconnected services. Part Three builds on these previous and foundational sections by showing how student academic services, programs, and staffs, under effective management and leadership, can come together as a collaborative enterprise that ensures student success and development. Chapters Thirteen through Twenty, in this section, apply the managing theme to the promotion of student success. Finally, this section emphasizes why managers of student academic services must work together with other campus leaders to unify and develop a staff that is connected in the delivery of services to a diverse student body.

This section begins with discussions of the challenges and opportunities of student academic services in helping a diverse body of students achieve success in their educational journey. To begin, Joseph Cuseo, in Chapter Thirteen, describes methods, programs, and services to manage a successful first-year experience, which he argues is contingent upon timely, customized, and purposeful assistance. Recognizing that the curriculum is a fundamental obstacle to college success, Carmy Carranza and Steven Ender present, in Chapter Fourteen, services, programs, and strategies that can be implemented by the academy to address an array of academic deficiencies or enhance classroom learning. In Chapter Fifteen, Vasti Torres discusses offering the right amount of help and the right student services at the right time to an increasingly diverse and demanding student population. This chapter focuses on meaningfully meeting the needs of international students, distance learners, students with disabilities, multicultural students, and others with the same degree of consistency, accuracy, and personalization as any other student on the campus. Sally Johnstone and Patricia Shea, in Chapter Sixteen, feature the pros and cons of putting academic services on-line. They effectively point out that a clear and functioning alliance between electronic student information systems and service providers is tantamount to providing students with accessible, reliable, consistent, and timely information.

The final four chapters in Part Three focus on managing and leading student academic services from the student's point of view. In particular, managing change and continuous improvement in the organization through qualitative and quantitative program assessment and evaluation are the central themes in Earl Potter's Chapter Seventeen, as well as in Chapter Eighteen, authored by George Kuh, Anthony English, and Sara Hinkle. Potter sets the stage for change by placing emphasis on building a culture of evidence. He uses measurement tools such as Kaplan and Norton's Balanced Scorecard or Baldrige's National Quality Standards and other benchmarking measures as frameworks for change management and sustainable change in student academic services. Further application of change management is presented by Kuh, English, and Hinkle through an effectiveness model based on adaptation to change.

Perhaps the beginning and the end (or strength or weakness) of effective and coordinated student academic services delivery are determined by its providers. Put another way, high-quality, timely, comprehensive, and accurate services to students result from a connected and motivated staff, as Diane Foucar-Szocki, Rick Larson, and Randy Mitchell point out in Chapter Nineteen. Moreover, these authors assert that developing and empowering the staff is key to effective teamwork in a learning organization.

As pointed out earlier, the central theme of this book is to take the reader systematically through primary student academic services and then show how these can come together under effective management and leadership as interconnected services that support student development and success. In the concluding chapter of Part Three—and of the book, Gary Kramer, in summarizing the preceding chapters, dovetails and applies Peter Senge's concepts (1990) of "creative tension" and a "generative learning community" to student academic services. In this context, Kramer (1) summarizes institutional best practices and (2) applies principles to practice by looking at several perspectives on improving and leading student academic services in the twenty-first century.

13

COMPREHENSIVE ACADEMIC SUPPORT FOR STUDENTS DURING THE FIRST YEAR OF COLLEGE

Joseph B. Cuseo

THE MAJORITY OF NEW STUDENTS entering higher education leave their initial college or university without completing a degree (Tinto, 1993), and retention rates have been declining since the early 1980s at two-year and four-year institutions, both public and private (Postsecondary Education Opportunity, 2002). The first year of college continues to be the most critical or vulnerable period for student attrition at all types of higher education institutions, including highly selective colleges and universities ("Learning Slope," 1991). More than half of all students who withdraw from college do so during their first year (Consortium for Student Retention Data Exchange, 1999), resulting in a national attrition rate for first-year students of more than 25 percent at four-year institutions, and almost 50 percent at two-year institutions (ACT, 2001). Summarizing three years of campus visitation findings and extensive survey data gathered under the auspices of the Carnegie Foundation, Boyer (1987) categorically concludes that "Students find the transition from (high) school to college haphazard and confusing" (p. 21).

To address the problem of early attrition, the National Institute of Education's (1984) panel of scholars offers as their first recommendation for improving the quality of undergraduate education, the principle of "front loading"—reallocation and redistribution of the institution's best educational resources to serve the critical needs of first year students. Lee Noel, nationally recognized researcher and consultant on student retention also contends that "in retention, a minimal investment can put into place some practical approaches and interventions, frequently labeled 'front loading.' Our experience shows that even a modest investment in these critical entry-level services and programs can have a high payoff in terms of student retention" (1994, p. 6).

In addition to being a critical year for student retention, there is accumulating evidence that the first year of college may also be a critical period for student learning and cognitive development. Two independent studies conducted by the Washington Center for Improving the Quality of Undergraduate Education have revealed that more cognitive growth occurs during the first year than during any other year in the college experience (MacGregor, 1991). More recently, Light (2001) reported the results of extensive research conducted by two Harvard researchers on how undergraduates and alumni recall and describe "critical incidents" in their college experience. Working independently, these two researchers discovered the same pattern of results: "Memories of critical moments and events cluster heavily in the first few weeks of college" (p. 204). Such findings suggest that the first-year experience may represent a "window of opportunity" for promoting student learning that would be missed if colleges and universities do not front load their best learning resources and educational interventions during this pivotal period of college development.

Other research suggests that the cognitive and behavioral habits students develop during their first year of college may become their modus operandi for the entire college experience. For example, Karl Schilling (2001) reported a time-use study in which first-year students were equipped with beepers that were activated periodically by the investigators. When their students' beepers were activated, students were to write down what they were doing at the time. This study revealed that the amount of time which first-year students spent on academics predicted the amount of time they spent on academics during their senior year. One possible interpretation of this finding is that academic habits established during the first year may have long-term impact on students' level of academic involvement throughout their remaining years in college. Thus, it may be reasonable to expect that proactively delivered interventions, such as first-year academic support programs that increase students' academic involvement during their initial year of college, may continue to exert the same salutary effect beyond the first year.

The Case for Providing Comprehensive Academic Support During the First Year of College

National surveys conducted during the 1990s reveal that 73 percent of student support professionals claim the proportion of entering students requiring remedial or developmental education on their campus is increasing. These findings are consistent with surveys of students which reveal a 30 percent increase between 1976 and 1996 in the number of students reporting that they took at least one basic skills or remedial course in reading, writing, or math (Levine, 1998). National surveys of students also reveal that "fear of academic failure" and obtaining "help with academic skills" are among the most frequently cited concerns of beginning college students (Astin, Parrott, Korn, and Sax, 1997).

These quantitative findings are reinforced by qualitative research on the retrospections of college seniors, which also reveal that students must make significant academic adjustments during their first year of college. This is well illustrated by the following comments made by one senior during a personal interview.

> *Interviewer:* What have you learned about your approach to learning [in college]?
> *Student:* I had to learn how to study. I went through high school with a 4.0 average. I didn't have to study. It was a breeze. I got to the university and there was no structure. No one checked my homework. No one took attendance to make sure I was in class. No one told me I had to do something. There were no quizzes on the readings. I did not work well with this lack of structure. It took my first year and a half to learn to deal with it. But I had to teach myself to manage my time. I had to teach myself how to study. I had to teach myself how to learn in a different environment. (Chickering and Schlossberg, 1998)

The importance of addressing the academic adjustment difficulties of new students proactively during the first term of college, rather than waiting for students to make these adjustments on their own—via random trial-and-error, is underscored by research indicating that students who earn good grades during their first term are far more likely to persist to graduation than are first-term students who do not experience initial academic success (Pantages and Creedan, 1978; Seymour, 1993). It has also been found that decisions to stay or leave college correlate more strongly with first-year students' academic performance than with their preenrollment characteristics (Pascarella and Chapman, 1983). Furthermore, research findings suggest that there is an association between higher first-term GPA and shorter time to graduation (Goldman and Gillis, 1989; Young, 1982).

Students are more likely to withdraw from college not only when they receive poor or failing grades, but also when they perceive a sharp decline in their academic performance relative to grades previously attained (Getzlaf, Sedlacek, Kearney, and Blackwell, 1984). Thus, academically high-achieving students who perceive a significant drop in college grades relative to their high school performance may also be at-risk for withdrawal. For instance, it has been found that academically well prepared students who expect A's, but receive C's, are at risk for attrition (Widmar, 1994).

When first-year students improve their academic performance, their retention rate tends to improve as well (Roueche, Baker, and Roueche, 1984). One way in which colleges can improve both the academic performance and retention of first-year students is by increasing their use of campus support services, because research clearly suggests that there is a strong relationship between support service use and persistence to program or degree completion (Churchill and Iwai, 1981). In particular, students who seek and receive academic support have been found to improve both their academic performance and their academic self-efficacy—that is, they develop a greater sense of self-perceived control of academic outcomes, and develop higher self-expectations for future academic success (Smith, Walter, and Hoey, 1992). Higher levels of self-efficacy, in turn, have been found to correlate positively with college students' academic performance and persistence; this is particularly true for Hispanic students (Solberg, O'Brien, Villareal, and Davis, 1993) and underprepared students (Lent, Brown, and Larkin, 1987). Such findings dovetail with research on returning adult students, which suggests that reentry students who experience early success in college are more likely to overcome personal attributions of low ability (Cross, 1981).

Unfortunately, however, it has been found that college students underutilize academic support services (Friedlander, 1980; Walter and Smith, 1990), particularly those students who are in most need of support (Knapp and Karabenick, 1988; Abrams and Jernigan, 1984). At-risk students, in particular, have trouble recognizing that they are experiencing academic difficulty and are often reluctant to seek help even if they do recognize their difficulty (Levin and Levin, 1991). These findings are also particularly disturbing when viewed in light of meta-analysis research, which reveals that academic support programs designed for underprepared students exert a statistically significant effect on their retention and grades when they are utilized, particularly if these programs are experienced by students during their freshman year (Kulik, Kulik, and Shwalb, 1983).

Taken together, this collection of findings strongly suggests that (a) institutions should deliver academic support intrusively—by initiating contact with students and aggressively bringing support services to them, rather than offering services passively and hoping that students will come and take advantage of them on their own accord; and (b) institutional support should be delivered proactively—early in the first year of college in order to intercept potential first-year attrition, rather than responding reactively to student difficulties after they occur. As Levitz and Noel (1989) report, "It has been our experience that fostering student success in the freshman year is the most significant intervention an institution can make in the name of student persistence" (p. 65).

It may also be reasonable to argue that provision of early academic support during the first year of college will result in cumulative gains in learning and development during subsequent years of the college experience, culminating in higher levels of academic achievement at college completion. Student development in college is likely to follow a cumulative or hierarchical path that involves immediate, intermediate, and ultimate outcomes (Patton, 1978). Any educational intervention that serves to increase the achievement of immediate outcome goals, such as first-year academic performance and retention, also has the potential for promoting the realization of intermediate and ultimate outcomes because learning is an "iterative process with current outcomes influencing future achievement" (Alexander and Stark, 1986, p. 24). Thus, provision of timely academic support for first-year students may not only serve to increase student success during the first year of college, it may also increase the likelihood that new students will persist to degree completion and elevate the ultimate level of academic achievement they display at college graduation.

Collaboration: The Key to Comprehensive and Effective Academic Support for First-Year Students

To effectively address the full range of issues that affect students' academic success during the first year of college, collaboration among different organizational units and members of the college community is critical. In particular, the following four forms of collaboration appear to be indispensable elements of a comprehensive academic support program for first-year students, and they will serve as the nexus for the remainder of this chapter.

Collaboration Between Students (Peer Collaboration)

Effective academic support programs for first-year students capitalize on the power of peers. Interaction between students has long been known to have a positive impact on student retention (Feldman and Newcomb, 1969), and intentionally fostering collaboration among students represents an effective strategy for promoting retention because it fosters students' social integration into the college community (Tinto, 1993; Braxton, Sullivan, and Johnson, 1997). Peer collaboration has also been found to advance students' cognitive development, as evidenced by an extensive review of research on critical thinking conducted by Kurfiss (1988), who concluded that use of peers as resources is a powerful strategy for promoting the development of students' higher-level thinking skills. More recently, Astin (1993) conducted a longitudinal study of over 24,000 students, spanning a nine-year period, and discovered "a pervasive pattern of positive benefits associated with frequent student-student interaction" (p. 385).

In this chapter, the following forms of peer collaboration will be showcased because they are supported by a substantial body of empirical evidence: (a) peer tutoring, (b) peer mentoring, and (c) supplemental instruction.

Collaboration Between Classroom Instructors and Academic Support Services

Students' academic success depends not only on the quality of the curriculum and classroom instruction, but also on the effectiveness of two key out-of-class services that colleges have created to support students' academic success: learning assistance and academic advisement. Support programs that connect students with learning specialists and academic advisers can provide timely and seamless support for first-year students whose academic achievement may be hampered by ineffective learning strategies or a lack of educational goals and sense of direction. Furthermore, when instructional faculty interact and collaborate with academic support-service professionals, combinatorial or synergistic effects are likely to be exerted on student learning and development, thereby magnifying the educational impact of the college experience.

Perhaps most importantly, through collaboration with faculty and connection to the curriculum, academic support professionals and their programs assume a more central (rather than a peripheral or marginal) place in the college's organizational and functional structure. National evaluations of special service programs indicate that their success hinges upon the degree to which those involved in the program perceive themselves as central to institutional life (Tinto, 1993). Unfortunately, this sense of centrality has been missing from first-year student support programs, as noted in a national report issued by the Education Commission of the States (1995): "A consensus is emerging that the first years of undergraduate study—particularly the freshman year are critical for student success. Yet, comprehensive efforts to integrate first-year students into the mainstream of collegiate experience are treated as auxiliary experiences, just the reverse of what a growing body of research indicates as 'best practice'" (p. 6). Similarly, research indicates that the effectiveness of academic support programs designed for disadvantaged minority students are compromised by the fact that they are not well integrated with mainstream institutional activities (Richardson and Bender, 1987). Collaboration between faculty and academic support specialists can enable support programs to become more "mainstreamed," thus increasing the likelihood that they are not viewed as "supplemental" but as integral to the college's day-to-day operations and essential to the college mission.

Two specific forms of collaboration between instructional faculty and academic support services will be showcased in this chapter because of their promising potential for integrating in-class learning with out-of-class academic support: (a) early warning (early alert) systems, and (b) course-integrated support programs.

Collaboration Between the Divisions of Academic and Student Affairs

Academic success depends not only on cognitive factors, but also on students' social adjustment, emotional stability, and personal wellness. Comprehensive academic support for first-year students needs to focus on the student as a "whole person" and address the full range of academic and nonacademic factors that affect student success. Research repeatedly demonstrates that academic support programs which include different program features, targeting different student needs, are more effective than single-focus programs that are restricted solely to the academic or cognitive domain (Boylan, Bliss, and Bonham, 1992; Roueche and Roueche, 1993). Research has also shown that student retention is more effectively promoted at institutions whose campus culture is characterized by collaboration between academic and student affairs (Kuh, Schuh, Whitt, and Associates, 1991; Stodt and Klepper, 1987).

Student Affairs professionals have long argued that the success of a college's student development program is contingent upon collaborative relations between Student Life staff and faculty (American College Personnel Association, 1975). More recently, the Joint Task Force on Student Learning—a collaborative initiative created by the American Association for

Higher Education (AAHE), the American College Personnel Association (ACPA), and the National Association of Student Personnel Administrators (NASPA)—has been created to promote approaches to student learning that forge connection or integration between educational experiences occurring inside and outside the classroom. As two members of the joint task force argue, "It takes a whole college to educate a whole student. Administrative leaders can rethink the conventional organization of colleges and universities to create more inventive structures and processes that integrate academic and student affairs; [and] offer professional-development opportunities for people to cooperate across institutional boundaries" (Engelkemeyer and Brown, 1998, p. 12).

In this chapter, the following forms of collaboration between academic and student affairs are showcased because of their strong base of empirical support or their capacity for implementing powerful student learning and retention principles: (a) living-learning centers, (b) residential learning communities, and (c) extended orientation courses (also known as, first-year experience seminars).

Collaboration Between Colleges and Schools (Secondary and Elementary)

Academic success during the first year of college hinges critically on students' academic preparedness at college entry. Collaboration between higher education and the school systems that prepare future college students represents a potentially fruitful partnership because it can serve to clarify, in advance, what colleges expect of their first-year students, and to better equip these students with the preparatory knowledge, basic skills, and academic competencies needed to successfully navigate the first-year experience.

Three specific forms of school-college collaboration will be highlighted in this chapter that have received the most empirical support and scholarly attention in the higher education literature: (a) summer bridge programs, (b) high school outreach programs, and (c) academic alliances.

Peer Support Programs That Promote Academic Collaboration Among Students

The power of peers for promoting student learning is highlighted by the work of McKeachie, Pintrich, Lin, and Smith (1986), who reached the following conclusion after completing an extensive review of higher education research on teaching and learning: "The best answer to the question of what is the most effective method of teaching is that it depends on the goal, the student, the content and the teachers. But the next best answer is students teaching other students" (p. 63).

In addition to its strictly cognitive benefits, peer collaboration also serves to develop the key social skills that are essential for success in life after college (Cross, 1985). Arthur Chickering eloquently expresses the need for higher education to more consciously develop students' ability to collaborate and their capacity for interdependence: "To the extent that we emphasize isolated, individual, competitive work and products, we both mislead students about the nature of work and construct obstacles to their interpersonal development. It is in the area of interdependence of all work that higher education has a largely uncharted world to explore. And in such exploration we will also find ways to help our students move toward increased capacity for intimacy" (1969, p. 210).

The following practices illustrate how peer collaboration can be intentionally fostered among first-year students—inside the classroom, outside the classroom, and across the curriculum.

Peer Tutoring

This academic support program involves utilization of academically successful students, advanced in their understanding of subject matter or in their development of academic skills, who provide learning assistance to less advanced students. Peer tutors typically receive special training for their teaching role that is usually conducted under the aegis of the college's Center for Learning Assistance or Academic Enrichment.

Higher education research on peer teaching and learning consistently indicates that both the peer learner and the peer teacher (tutor) experience significant gains in learning as a result of their collaborative interaction (Whitman, 1988). For example, college students display deeper levels of understanding for concepts they teach to other students (Bargh and Schul, 1980; Benware and Deci, 1984) and achieve greater mastery of course content (Johnson, Sulzer-Azaroff, and Mass, 1977). Also, research reported by a variety of institutions points to the positive impact of peer tutoring on student retention, especially the retention of underrepresented and disadvantaged students with underdeveloped basic academic skills (National Academy of Sciences—National Research Council, 1977).

Peer tutoring is more cost effective than tutoring provided by faculty or staff, and may also be more educationally effective because (a) it allows the learner to seek academic assistance from a similar-age peer, which is often less threatening to the learner's self-esteem than seeking help from an authority figure (Gross and McMullen, 1983), and (b) the peer teacher and learner have more similar amounts of prior experience with the concept being learned and are at a more proximal stage of cognitive development, both of which serve to facilitate learning (Vygotsky, 1978).

Peer Mentoring

This peer support strategy has a more holistic focus than peer tutoring, whereby the peer mentor provides social and emotional support to the protégé in addition to academic assistance. Also, mentor-protégé contacts tend to occur in a wider range of contexts than tutor-tutee contacts—which are commonly confined to the classroom or Learning Center. Typically, peer mentoring programs involve more experienced students (juniors or seniors) serving as mentors for less-experienced students (freshmen or sophomores), for the dual purpose of promoting the educational success of the protégé and fostering the leadership development or counseling skills of the peer mentor.

The effectiveness of peer mentoring is supported by cross-institutional research which indicates that students who participate in such programs display higher rates of retention and academic achievement (grade point average) than nonparticipating students with comparable college entry characteristics (Guon, 1988).

Peer Study Groups

This academic support strategy may be succinctly defined as students meeting in small groups outside of class to help each other study and master course material. These collaborative groups can develop spontaneously among students, or they may be intentionally promoted by instructors and academic support professionals. Traditionally, the term *study group* has been used to refer to a group of students who come together for review sessions in preparation for exams. However, student groups may also be formed to accomplish additional learning tasks that include the following: (a) note-taking groups—students convene immediately after class to compare and share notes; (b) reading groups—students collaborate after completing reading assignments to compare their highlighting and margin notes; (c) library research groups—students join together to conduct library research and combat "library anxiety"; and (d) test results review groups—after receiving test results, students review their individual tests together to help members identify the source of their errors and to observe "model" answers that received maximum credit.

The positive impact of collaborative study groups on the retention and achievement of underrepresented students, in particular, is supported by research on African American students majoring in math and science at the University of California-Berkeley. Five-year retention rates for African American students who participated in collaborative learning workshops was 65 percent, while the retention rate for black nonparticipants was 41 percent (Treisman, 1986 1992).

These findings were replicated in a five-year longitudinal study of underrepresented Latino students enrolled in mathematics, science or engineering programs at California Polytechnic State University, Pomona. This study revealed that fewer than 4 percent of Latino students who participated in out-of-class collaborative learning sessions withdrew or were academically dismissed, compared to 40 percent of Latino students who did not participate in the program (Bonsangue, 1993).

Curriculum-Integrated Peer Collaboration Programs

The peer collaboration practices described in this section are distinguished by the fact that they have been incorporated into the formal curriculum, thus moving them from the auxiliary position of an academic support service to the more central position of a course-integrated program.

SUPPLEMENTAL INSTRUCTION (SI). This academic support program was developed in the 1970s at the University of Missouri-Kansas City, which now serves as an international model for SI programming (Martin and Arendale, 1994). In SI programs, a student who has done exceptionally well in a particular course is paid to reattend the same class along with novice learners, and helps the novices both individually and in group sessions that are regularly scheduled outside of class time. The student leader functions as a model learner, who takes notes, completes assignments, and takes tests along with the novice students.

The "supplemental" (out-of-class) sessions are typically conducted as informal seminars in which students compare notes, discuss reading assignments, predict test questions, and study collaboratively. The extra sessions may or may not be credit-bearing; if they do carry credit, one unit of college credit is the amount usually awarded. Historically difficult courses (also known as "high risk" or "killer" courses) with high dropout or failure rates are typically targeted for this peer teaching-learning strategy. Often, these are introductory "gateway" or "gatekeeper" courses taken by first- or second-year students who must successfully complete them in order to progress to more advanced courses required for general education or their major field of study.

More recently, video-based supplemental instruction (VSI) has also been adopted as an alternative course delivery system, whereby faculty lectures are presented on videotape and the student facilitator provides guided review of the lecture tapes, stopping and replaying the tapes at key points to allow for personal reflection and group discussion (Martin and Blanc, 1994).

More than 350 colleges in the United States and abroad have adopted SI programs, and their positive impact on student retention has been reported for both entry-level and advanced courses across different institutional types, as well as for students at different levels of academic preparedness (Martin and Arendale, 1994). Research also indicates that students who participate in SI earn higher average course grades compared to students of equal ability who do not participate in the program, and SI programs have been found to be more cost effective than tutoring services or learning skills courses (Kochenour and others, 1997).

The effectiveness of SI may be attributed to its following qualities: (a) It integrates academic skills instruction into a meaningful credit-earning, content-specific course; (b) it removes the remedial stigma often associated with "developmental" or "remedial" programs; and (c) it enables initially less prepared students to gain access to and receive supplemental support in academically demanding courses, without lowering course instructors' academic standards (Arendale, 1994; Levitz, 1990; McGrath and Townsend, 1997; Peters, 1990).

EMERGING SCHOLARS PROGRAM. Based on Uri Treisman's (1992) collaborative workshops that promoted the academic success of African American students' in mathematics courses, this academic support program involves groups of seven to twelve students who enroll in the same course and participate in group problem-solving workshops that are facilitated by advanced undergraduates.

The program typically focuses on students in math, engineering, or introductory-level science courses, and although originally targeted for underrepresented minorities and women, many campuses now intentionally create heterogeneous collaborative learning groups comprised of white students and students of color (MacGregor, 2000).

Writing Fellows Program

This academic support strategy functions as a "writing across the curriculum" program whereby upper-division students with strong writing skills are recruited, receive extensive peer-teaching training, and are deployed to an undergraduate class (particularly large introductory courses in their major) where they read and respond to students' written work.

Collaboration Between Instructional Faculty and Academic Support Services

Academic support is more effectively delivered and received if it is not isolated from, but integrated with, the content of college course and classroom learning. Effective learning strategies tend not to be permanently adopted and routinely applied by students in different subject areas if they are developed within isolated and insulated "learning skills" workshops or "study skills" courses (Gamson, 1993; Weinstein and Underwood, 1985). Educational research indicates that basic academic skills are most effectively learned in a meaningful context, as when they are applied to the learning of specific subject matter (Levin and Levin, 1991; Means, Chelemer, and Knapp, 1991). For effective learning skills to "take hold" in students, that is, to become fully incorporated into their habitual approach to learning, students need to have a sense of purpose for using these skills in relation to a specific subject area or particular course content. The importance of integrating learning skill development with classroom-based learning is reinforced further by research on the human brain, which indicates that there is a clear difference between "declarative" knowledge—knowing *what* to do, as opposed to "procedural" knowledge—knowing *how, when, and where* to implement or apply that knowledge (Squire, 1986).

Described in this section are programs and practices that effectively connect or integrate academic support services with students' coursework and classroom performance.

Early Alert (Early Warning) System

This academic support strategy involves a formal feedback system though which course instructors alert learning assistance professionals or academic advisers about students in their classes who are in academic jeopardy at or before midterm. A recent national survey reveals that more than 60 percent of postsecondary institutions report midterm grades to first year students for the purpose of providing them with early feedback on their academic performance; 10 percent of these institutions obtain student right-to-privacy waivers that enable them to report midterm grades to both first-year students and their parents (Barefoot, 2001). Students with dangerously low midterm grade reports are typically notified by letter to speak with their academic adviser who, in turn, refers the notified student to the appropriate support service. At some institutions, such as New York University, advisers make follow-up phone calls to students who fail to respond to their letter of notification (Early Intervention Programs, 1992). At Brooklyn College (New York), faculty notify peer tutors when students are having academic difficulties, and their tutors initiate contact with the student (Levitz, 1991).

While issuing midterm grade reports to struggling students is a laudable practice, Tinto (1993) warns that, by the time midterm grades are recorded and disseminated, feedback may come too late in the term to be optimally useful. Consequently, some institutions are resorting to an earlier feedback mechanism, based on student attendance during the first four to six weeks of class. For example, at New Mexico State University, attendance problem requests are sent to instructors during the second week and sixth week of the term. Students demonstrating attendance irregularities who fall into any of the following categories receive a phone call from the Office of Advisement Services: (a) first-semester students, (b) students on academic probation, and (c) students with multiple early alert reports (Thompson, 2001).

Another potential limitation of using midterm grade reports as an early alert mechanism is that the grade itself does not specify the source(s) of the poor performance. Thus, rather than merely reporting a letter grade, some colleges issue early alert forms that request additional information from the instructor, which is used to help diagnose the specific nature of the problem and facilitate targeted intervention. For instance, at Adelphi University (New York), early warning rosters are released during the fourth week of class and faculty report students who are experiencing academic difficulty, using an efficient abbreviation code to identify the specific area(s) of weak performance: AS = assignment performance, C = class participation, EX = examination performance, IA = intermittent attendance, NA = never attended, NC = noncompleted assignments, and WE = weak expository skills (Carlson, 2000).

Empirical evidence for the effectiveness of an early alert system is provided by campus-specific research conducted at Vincennes University Junior College (Indiana). When a student begins to miss class at this institution, course instructors tear off one part of a computer-generated ticket whose keystroke input generates two postcards indicating concern about nonattendance, one of which is addressed to the student's local residence and one to the student's permanent address. Additional absences generate a second, more strongly worded postcard indicating that the student is in danger of being dropped from the course. The system also generates lists for academic advisers, alerting them of students majoring in their academic field who have received attendance notifications. Following institutional implementation of this early alert system, the number of students receiving grades of D, F, or W was substantially reduced. The beneficial effect of the early alert system was particularly pronounced in developmental mathematics classes, for which there was a 17 percent drop in D and F grades an' ~oncomitant 14 percent increase in A, B, and C grades (Budig, Koenig, and Weaver, 1991).

Evidence for the positive impact of an early alert system on student retention is provided by local research conducted at the University of Wisconsin–Oshkosh. After the third of week of the semester, early alert forms are sent to instructors teaching preparatory and basic skill courses that are populated by previously identified "high risk" students. Forms are sent to the Office of Academic Development Services, which initiates intrusive intervention by contacting and meeting with each student to provide academic counseling, referral to a peer tutor program, and suggestions for other forms of assistance. Since the program was initiated, retention rates for at-risk students have risen steadily, reaching a level over 70 percent (Green, 1989).

In addition to formal early alert or early warning systems, the following course integration strategies represent noteworthy approaches to collaboration between classroom faculty and academic support service professionals that serve the needs of first-year students.

○ *Course-integrated library instruction* that incorporates information literacy (information search, retrieval, and evaluation skills) is integrated into the content of courses taken by first-year students. For example, librarians and professors may team teach or codesign courses, course components, and out-of-class assignments that integrate library-research skills with course content (for example, via research papers or group projects).

○ *Faculty* provide specific information about the academic requirements of their courses to learning assistance professionals in order to enhance the relevance and effectiveness of academic support and tutorial services. For example, instructors may provide a sample of reading assignments or lecture videotapes for tutorial use in the college Learning Center.

○ Academic support professionals provide instructional faculty with diagnostic feedback (via newsletters, presentations or workshops) about the types of academic assistance that first-year students typically need or seek with respect to their courses, and alert faculty to the common errors in new students' approaches to learning course material that are witnessed in academic support settings.

○ *Learning assistance professionals visit "at-risk courses"* (courses with high rates of student withdrawal and low grades) to describe how their services can contribute to student success in the course, and explicitly encourage students to capitalize on these services.

○ Instructors intentionally design class assignments that connect students with learning assistance professionals. For instance, students can be given an assignment that requires them to visit the Learning Center to complete a self-assessment inventory on learning styles or learning habits, the results of which may then be reviewed to determine their implications for improving students' course performance.

Educational Partnerships Between Academic and Student Affairs

For approximately twenty-five years, the higher education literature has pointed to a "persistent gap" or "schism" between the formal (academic) curriculum and the cocurriculum (student development programming outside the classroom) (American College Personnel Association, 1994; Miller and Prince, 1976). Some disturbing consequences of this schism have been (a) rigid bifurcation, compartmentalization, and isolation of student services into either "academic" or "student" affairs, (b) divisive territorial politics and dysfunctional competition for resources between these two major units of the college (Kuh and Banta, 2000), and (c) splintering of students' liberal education and holistic development into disjointed parts (Barr and Upcraft, 1990).

Collaborative partnerships between academic and student development professionals can help close the persistent gap between the formal curriculum and the cocurriculum, serving to unite members of the college community who have been historically separated by artificial organizational or functional boundaries. One specific way in which this unification may be forged is through joint planning and execution of educational programs that serve to integrate academic and student life, such as those described below.

Living-Learning Centers

Living-learning centers are residentially based educational programs combining academic and student affairs programming, which are typically designed for first-year students. For example, academic advising and learning assistance services may be provided in student residences, or seminar-style classes may be taught in residence lounges. At large universities, living-learning centers typically are designed to provide a more intimate "small college" atmosphere, while at small colleges these centers are organized around different learning themes, such as wellness or diversity (Schein and Bowers, 1992).

Residential Learning Communities

These are programs that involve implementation of the learning community model, which involves coregistration of a cohort of students, who take the same block of courses together during the same academic term. What defines a residential learning community is the addition of a residential life component to the model, whereby students who are enrolled in the same courses also share the same living space on campus. For example, at the University of Missouri-Columbia, Freshman Interest Groups (FIGs) of twenty students who live on the same floor of a residence hall also enroll in the same four courses (Levine and Tompkins, 1996).

Extended Orientation Courses (or First-Year Experience Seminars)

Student affairs professionals have played a key role in the adoption and proliferation of first-year experience seminars, which are intentionally designed to facilitate the college adjustment and success of first-year students by "extending" new-student orientation into a credit-earning, first-term course. The course represents a collaborative venture with the academic sector to ensure that beginning students receive the holistic support they need to survive and thrive during their critical first year of college. The content of first-year experience seminars (hereafter, referred to as first-year seminars) typically includes any or all of the following topics: (a) understanding the purpose, values, and expectation of higher education, (b) learning how to learn (for example, academic skill development, learning strategies, and critical thinking), (c) self-management (for example, time and stress management, self-discipline and self-motivation), (d) self-assessment and self-awareness (for example, assessment of learning styles and career interests), (e) life planning—connecting the present academic experience to future personal and vocational goals, and (f) holistic development (social, emotional, and physical wellness),

First-year seminars are rapidly becoming familiar additions to the college curriculum, as evidenced by the following findings: (a) Almost 70 percent of American colleges and universities surveyed have implemented an extended orientation course (National Resource Center, 1998); (b) approximately 80 percent of first-year seminars were initiated during the 1980s and nearly 25 percent during the 1990s (Barefoot and Fidler, 1996); (c) 88 percent of first-year seminars carry academic credit toward graduation; and (d) approximately 47 percent of first-year seminars are required for all first-year students (National Resource Center, 1998).

In their meticulous synthesis of more than 2500 postsecondary studies relating to how college programs and experience affect student development, Pascarella and Terenzini (1991) reached the following conclusion about first-year seminars: "The weight of the evidence suggests that a first-semester freshman seminar is positively linked with both freshman-year persistence and degree completion. This positive link persists even when academic aptitude and secondary school achievement are taken into account" (pp. 419–420).

The most frequently assessed outcome of the first-year seminar has been its impact on student retention (persistence). Using virtually all major types of research methods (quantitative and qualitative, experimental and correlational), the positive impact of the course on this student outcome has been reported for all types of students (for example, at-risk and well-prepared, minority and majority, residential and commuter), at all institutional types (two- and four-year, public and private), institutional sizes (small, mid-sized, large), and institutional locations (urban, suburban, rural). As Barefoot and Gardner note, "First-year/student success seminars are remarkably creative courses that are adaptable to a great variety of institutional settings, structures, and students" (1998, p. xiv).

Evidence for the positive impact of first-year seminars on students' academic performance is not as extensive as it is for student retention (Barefoot, 2000). Nevertheless, there are many campus-specific studies indicating that student participation in the seminar is associated with improved academic performance—as measured by different academic achievement indicators, such as the following: (a) cumulative grade point average (GPA) attained at the end of the first term or first year of college (House, in Barefoot and others, 1998), (b) cumulative GPA attained beyond the first year of college (Wilkie and Kuckuck, 1989), (c) GPA attained versus GPA predicted (Wilkie and Kuckuck, 1989), (d) total number of first-year students in good academic standing, that is, students neither placed on academic probation nor academically dismissed (Soldner, in Barefoot and others, 1998), (e) total number of first-year courses passed (Garret, in Barefoot, 1993), (f) total number of first-year courses completed with a grade of "C" or higher (Stupka, in Barefoot, 1993), and

(g) percentage of students who qualify for the Dean's List and Honors Program (Thomson, in Barefoot and others, 1998).

Advantages of First-Year Seminars

The success of first-year seminars in promoting student retention and academic performance may be attributed to a number of course characteristics. Among the most powerful educational advantages of offering the first-year seminar as an academic support strategy stem from the following course qualities and potentialities.

By "extending" new-student orientation into a full-semester course, the first-year seminar assures that there is sufficient time for coverage of a wide range of topics pertinent to effective college adjustment and student success. Moreover, the course allows for timely discussion of college adjustment issues when they arise during the critical first semester. As Upcraft and Farnsworth (1984) point out that "Too often, orientation planners overwhelm students with anything and everything they might need to know. Orientation planners must not only decide on what entering students need to know but when they need to know it" (p. 30). For example, the topics of note-taking and reading strategies may be covered in the seminar at the very start of students' first term because these skills will be immediately required of new students in all their courses. Coverage of test-taking strategies could be intentionally scheduled to take place later in the term, perhaps prior to midterm exam week, when students could immediately apply these strategies to midterm exams, and discuss their effectiveness after receiving midterm test results. Timely class discussion of adjustment problems and solution strategies, at or around the time students experience them during their first term of college, should highlight for students the immediate relevance and usefulness of course information, thereby increasing their motivation to attend to it and put it into practice.

By explicitly emphasizing the development of highly adaptable and transferable skills, the first-year seminar fills a curricular void left by traditional, content-driven college courses which tend to focus largely on the acquisition of circumscribed and prescribed bodies of knowledge. (Any transferable skill development that happens to take place in content-driven courses usually remains tacit and incidental to discipline-specific content coverage.) In contrast, the seminar has the capacity to function in a "meta-curricular" manner—transcending specialized content and traversing disciplinary boundaries by focusing on the development of portable strategies and skills that have cross-disciplinary applicability.

Extending new-student orientation into a full-semester course allows for continuity of contact between the seminar instructor and new students throughout their first term of college enrollment. This continuous contact enables the instructor to closely monitor the progress of new students during their critical first semester, and allows sufficient time for bonding to take place between students and teacher. Moreover, if it can be arranged for academic support professionals to be involved as course instructors (for example, students' academic advisers), then the seminar may serve as a vehicle for providing close and continuous student contact with a key academic support agent during the critical first term of college life. Research conducted at North Dakota State University indicates that, if new students' academic adviser also serves as their first-year seminar instructor, then these students make significantly more out-of-class contact with their academic adviser during their first term than students whose advisers do not coserve as their first-year seminar instructor (Soldner, in Barefoot and others, 1998)

Extending orientation into a full-length course provides ample opportunity for peer bonding to develop among classmates because they interact regularly in a social context that is devoted to the student-centered topic of college adjustment and success. This arrangement can provide students with an ongoing, intentionally structured forum or social support group within which they may discuss relevant personal issues that arise during the often stressful first semester of college. Boyer (1987) succinctly captures the gist of this advantage of first-year seminars: "After the flush of newness fades, all new students soon discover that there are term papers to be written, course requirements to be met, and conflicts between the academic and social life on campus. Students need to talk about these tensions" (p. 51).

Course assignments in the first-year seminar can be intentionally designed to connect new students with key academic support professionals and campus services. Among the most frequently reported objectives of first-year seminars offered by institutions across the country is to promote student awareness or knowledge of key campus programs and out-of-class support agents, and to increase student use of college resources and services (Barefoot and Fidler, 1996). Local research conducted at various types of postsecondary institutions indicates that the seminar is effective for achieving these objectives. For instance, at Champlain College (Vermont), student utilization of the learning resource center and tutoring services has remained consistently and substantially higher among first-year seminar participants than nonparticipants (Goldsweig, in Barefoot and others, 1998). At the University of Wyoming, library circulation and use of student services increased significantly following institutional adoption of the first-year seminar as a required course (Reeve, in Barefoot, 1993).

Connecting students with support-service professionals via the first-year seminar is usually accomplished by either or both of the following course practices: (a) inviting support professionals to class as guest speakers or as members of a presentation panel, and (b) having students interview or complete course assignments that involve interaction with support-service professionals outside the classroom (for example, professionals in learning assistance, library science, or computer technology; academic advisers, college faculty, peer tutors, or upper-division students in the first-year students' intended major).

Course assignments can also be intentionally constructed that require students to immediately apply success strategies learned in the seminar. For example, students may be given an assignment that requires them to implement a time management plan for the first term, such as constructing a semester schedule that includes due dates for tests and assignments in all courses, as well as designated times for study, recreation, and employment. Or, students may be asked to apply effective learning strategies to current courses, such as keeping a "learning log" of academic success strategies discussed in the seminar that they are attempting to use in other first-semester courses.

Students may be given course assignments in the first-year seminar that require them to engage in long-term educational and career planning, which serve to connect their present college experience with their future goals and aspirations. For instance, the following types of assignments serve to promote first-year students' long-term planning: (a) an undergraduate plan that includes courses in general education and the student's intended academic specialization (major field of study), (b) a tentative postbaccalaureate educational plan for graduate or professional school, and (c) a tentative career plan that encourages first-year students to identify potential positions, construct a model resume that would prepare them for entry into such positions, and initiate a professional portfolio—a collection of materials that illustrates student competencies or achievements, and demonstrates educational or personal development (for example, best written work, art work, research projects, letters of recommendation, cocurricular accomplishments, personal awards, and certificates of achievement).

Norwich University (Vermont) uses its first-year seminar in this fashion to engage students in long-range educational planning and promote student dialogue with their academic advisers about their educational plans. The first-year seminar syllabus at Norwich calls for students to meet with their adviser on three occasions during the first semester, in addition to their meeting for course scheduling. The second meeting occurs at about the midpoint in the semester, at which time students bring a self-assessment report that they have completed as a first-year seminar assignment. Advisers use this report to focus discussion with students about their present academic progress and future educational plans (Catone, 1996).

Marymount College (California), a two-year institution devoted exclusively to preparing students for successful transfer to baccalaureate degree-granting colleges and universities, requires a first-year seminar for all its incoming students. The Director of the Advisement and Transfer Center visits each class and outlines for students the course requirements of different four-year institutions for general education and different academic majors. Following the classroom visitation by the Director of Advisement and Transfer, first-year seminar students are given an assignment carrying significant point value that requires them to meet with their academic adviser during the first four to six weeks of their first term to develop a general education plan that includes what courses they are planning to take and when they are planning to take them—fall, spring, or summer. (Students and advisers receive a three-year institutional plan of projected fall, spring, and summer course offerings to assist them in this long-range planning and scheduling process.) Students are also supplied with a form or grid with blank lines for courses to be taken during the next two to three years. Students work with their advisers to complete a tentative, personal two- to three-year plan that includes general education requirements for the associate degree (A.A. or A.S.) and premajor requirements for their intended field of specialization. (For students still undecided about their intended major, they are advised to identify elective courses in academic fields which they might consider as a possible major, or minor, in order to test their interest and aptitude for that academic field.)

The student's educational plan is completed on a triplicate form, one copy of which is kept by the adviser, one copy is kept by the student, and the third copy is returned by the student (along with a written reflection on the plan) to the first-year seminar instructor who accepts it as a completed course assignment and credits it toward the student's course grade.

Students typically report in their written evaluations of this long-range planning assignment that it had a motivating effect on them, often claiming that the plan made their academic goals more concrete and provided them with a visible "road map" of their educational future. Students also frequently comment that the assignment enabled them to either confirm their plans or modify them while there was still time to do so. For example, students frequently report that they did not have a clear idea about what specific courses were required for their intended major and the assignment made them realize that these course were not compatible with their personal interests, abilities, or values (Cuseo, 2001).

The first-year seminar can serve as a vehicle for early identification of first-term students who may be academically "at-risk." Evidence gathered at the University of South Carolina suggests that a failing grade in the first-year seminar may be a "red flag" that calls attention to students who will later experience academic problems or attrition (Fidler and Shanley, 1993). This finding reinforces research conducted on four consecutive cohorts of first-year students at the Massachusetts College of Liberal Arts, where it was found that students' first-year seminar grade is a better predictor of their overall first-year academic performance than either high school grades or college entry SAT/ACT scores (Hyers and Joslin, in Barefoot and others, 1998). These findings strongly suggest that students' academic performance in the first-year seminar can serve as an accurate diagnostic sign for identifying first-term students who may be academically at-risk and in need of academic assistance or psychosocial intervention.

This diagnostic and prognostic capability of the first-year seminar may be tapped more proactively if seminar instructors issue midterm grades or midterm progress reports to students experiencing these problems, and if these grades are also sent to academic advisers or academic support professionals (for example, via the academic dean's office or the learning assistance center). First-term students receiving grades below a certain threshold or cutoff point in the seminar could then be contacted for consultation and possible intervention. To determine this cutoff point, research might be conducted on grade distributions in the first-year seminar to identify the grade below which a relationship begins to emerge between poor performance in the course and poor overall first-year academic performance or first-year attrition. Such research has been conducted at the Massachusetts College of Liberal Arts, where it was discovered that students who earned a grade of C+ or lower in the seminar had a significantly higher rate of first-year attrition ($p<.001$) than students who earned a grade of B- or higher in the course (Hyers and Joslin, in Barefoot, and others, 1998).

Use of midterm grades as an "early alert" or "early warning" system is nothing new to higher education. However, a perennial problem with successful implementation of this procedure is lack of compliance because faculty may have neither the time for, nor the interest in, calculating and reporting midterm grades for all their students. However, if the first-year seminar grade is a good proxy for first-year academic performance in general, then the midterm grade in this single course may serve as an effective and efficient early warning signal. Moreover, given that first-year seminar instructors often self-select into the program because of their personal interest in and concern for promoting the success of first-year students, they should display a high rate of compliance or reliability with respect to submitting students' midterm grades in an accurate and timely manner.

The first-year seminar can provide a convenient classroom context for gathering assessment data on students at college entry. Diagnostic assessment of beginning college students' support-service needs is now possible with the availability of instruments intentionally designed to identify freshmen who are academically "at risk," such as the (a) Learning and Study Skills Inventory (LASSI)(Weinstein, Schulte, and Palmer, 1987), (b) Motivation, Study, and Learning Questionnaire (MSLQ)(Pintrich, McKeachie, and Smith, 1989), (c) Study Behavior Inventory (SBI) (Kerstiens, 2000) and (d) Behavioral and Attitudinal Predictors of Academic Success Scale (Wilkie and Redondo, 1996).

In addition to these instruments designed for identifying students who are at-risk academically, there are also instruments available that are designed specifically to identify students who are at-risk for attrition, such as the (a) College Success Factors Index (CSFI) (Hallberg and Davis, 2001), (b) Noel/Levitz College Student Inventory (Striatal, 1988), (c) Anticipated Student Adaptation to College Questionnaire (Baker and Schultz, 1992), and (d) Student Adaptation to College Questionnaire (Baker and Siryk, 1986). The prospects for college success of at-risk students identified by any of the foregoing assessment instruments could be greatly enhanced if these students experience proactively delivered support services or early interventions that are personally tailored to meet their identified needs. However, institutions interested in using these instruments to identify at-risk students must find the time and place to conduct these assessments. The first-year seminar can serve this function, providing a relevant curricular structure and a comfortable classroom context within which to conduct comprehensive and proactive assessment of new students' needs during their first term in college. If the seminar is a required course, then these instruments may be administered to the entire entering class at the onset of the semester, and the results analyzed to identify patterns of potential adjustment difficulties among the cohort of new students on campus. This information could be used by the college to help design broad-based, data-driven support programs that may serve to proactively combat or "short-circuit" identified sources of potential academic threat and early attrition among its newly admitted students.

School-College Partnerships

Probably the most proactive and preventative approach to increasing students' academic success is through collaboration with the schools that prepare future college students. During the 1990s, the American Association for Higher Education (AAHE) made school-college collaboration a key focal point of its national reform agenda (American Association for Higher Education, 1993). This national reform effort fueled a proliferation of school-college partnerships that focused primarily on the following objectives: (a) early identification and intervention programs which bring K–12 students to college campuses for educational enrichment and academic skill building, (b) school-college course articulation and curriculum development programs, and (c) professional development opportunities for college faculty and academic support professionals to engage in K–12 service and scholarship (Wilbur and Lambert, 1995). Listed below are the major forms of school-college partnerships that have been designed to implement these specific objectives, and to achieve the more overarching goal of facilitating the academic transition of students from school to college.

Summer Bridge Programs

This form of school-college partnership unites high school faculty with college faculty and learning-assistance professionals to teach in a summer program (ranging from one to six weeks). The program is delivered to students during the summer intervening between their last term in high school and their first term in college, thus serving as a "bridge" between high school and higher education. Summer bridge programs typically target academically "at-risk" students (for example, low-income, first-generation, or underrepresented students) and typically include the following program components (a) academic skills assessment and instruction, and (b) orientation to higher education, and (c) a residential experience whereby participants take courses together and reside on campus in the same college residence.

Probably the most extensively employed and systematically evaluated summer bridge program is the one conducted by the California State University system, which enrolls over 2,000 freshmen and 300 first-year transfer students annually in its four- to six-week program (Garcia, 1991). Statewide policy mandates that all campus-specific summer bridge programs conclude with two exit exams: The California State University's English and Mathematics placement tests for university-level instruction.

Students who do not pass these tests are enrolled in the university's year-long freshman basic skills program, thus ensuring that entering students who need additional preparatory instruction in basic skills will receive this instruction proactively—during the first year of college experience.

Research conducted by external evaluators demonstrates that students who participate in the Summer Bridge program (a) are more likely to enroll in college in the fall semester, (b) make more frequent use of campus services, (c) interact more frequently with faculty and students outside of class, (d) report greater satisfaction with their campus friend-ships, and (e) display significantly higher first- and second-year retention rates, relative to students who have not experienced the program (Garcia, 1991).

Additional evidence supporting summer bridge programs has been gathered at the Indiana University at Kokomo, where matriculation and graduation rates for cohorts of underprepared students who participate in the college's summer bridge program have remained significantly higher than for cohorts who entered the college prior to program implementation (Green, 1994).

High School Outreach Programs

These programs involve collaboration between secondary schools and colleges to facilitate high school students' college access, transition, and retention. Typically, underrepresented high school students are targeted for program participation. However, outreach programs have also been designed for younger students (junior high or elementary school), which are commonly referred to as "Early Identification Programs."

Academic Alliances

These are partnership programs between high school and college educators who teach in the same academic discipline. They come together for the purpose of identifying critical subject matter knowledge, core concepts, and pedagogical strategies that promote cumulative learning in their shared subject area. For example, high school and college educators may collaborate to develop subject-specific capstone courses for high school seniors.

Listed below are other promising school-college partnership strategies that have yet to evolve into formal programs but, nevertheless, warrant mention as promising practices.

○ Academic support professionals teach advanced college-credit courses to high school seniors for the purpose of stimulating their interest in and attendance at college. High school students may take these courses on the college campus, where they may also be allowed free access to the university's educational and recreational facilities, thereby further promoting student identification with and involvement in the college community.

○ Academic support professionals from colleges meet with teachers and counselors at feeder high schools—where they review the academic performance of the school's graduates during their first year at the college—for the purpose of identifying strengths and voids in the college preparatory program.

○ College students tutor high school students in subject matter relating to the college students' academic major—for purposes of promoting high school students' (a) knowledge of the subject matter, (b) preparation for college, and (c) interest in attending college.

○ Colleges provide a teaching-learning "hotline" for use by local high school students and high school instructors (for example, math education hotline).

○ College academic support professionals administer Math and English placement tests to students during their sophomore or junior year in high school, thereby enabling high school teachers to more proactively diagnose and cultivate college-relevant academic skills prior to high school graduation.

○ Colleges offer summer programming for high school juniors to prepare them for their senior year experience, their upcoming college application process, and their eventual first-year experience in college.

Summary and Conclusion

A retrospective look at the most successful academic support programs cited in this chapter suggests that there are recurrent features that traverse successful programs which may be abstracted and highlighted as core principles of effective or exemplary program delivery of academic support services to first-year students. These key principles of powerful program delivery are identified in this section and will serve as the conclusion to this chapter.

Effective First-Year Support Programs Are Intentionally *Student-Centered*

Powerful first-year programs are oriented toward, focused on, and driven by the intentional goal of promoting student success. This defining feature of effective first-year support programs is articulated by John Gardner, founding father of the freshman year experience movement: "The freshman year experience efforts are manifested by their deliberateness, their effort to make things happen by design, not by accident or spontaneity, i.e., those things that must happen if students are more likely to be successful" (1986, p. 267).

Rather than being hampered or hamstrung by the force of preexisting procedural habits, organizational convenience or institutional inertia, the effective programs showcased in this chapter often involve creative and intentional restructuring or reorganization of traditional delivery systems to center them squarely on the goal of promoting students' academic success and retention. These student support programs reflect the type of shift to "learning-centered management" called for by Astin (1979) and reiterated by Pascarella and Terenzini (1991), that is, they take an approach to programmatic decision making which "consistently and systematically takes into account the potential of alternative courses of administrative action for student learning" (p. 656).

For example, learning community programs cited in this chapter serve to radically restructure the college curriculum to promote student learning by capitalizing on the proven power of peer collaboration. The cooperative learning structures cited in this chapter work to achieve the same objective by reorganizing the college classroom—transforming it from its traditional format of one large group of individuals working independently—into small teams of peer learners who work interdependently and collaboratively. Interestingly, when learning community programming is combined with cooperative learning pedagogy, the positive impact of peer collaboration is further magnified, as evidenced by research conducted at Seattle Central Community College—where students in learning communities who also experience cooperative learning methods in their classes, report greater intellectual gains than do learning-community students who are not exposed to cooperative learning methods in the classroom (Tinto, 2000).

Effective First-Year Support Programs Are Intrusive

Powerful programs initiate supportive action by reaching out to students and bringing or delivering support to them, rather than passively waiting and hoping that first-year students will seek it out on their own. Ender, Winston, and Miller (1984) captured the gist of this principle almost twenty years ago when they forcefully stated that: "It is totally unrealistic to expect students to take full advantage of the intellectual and personal development opportunities [on campus] without some assistance from the institution" (p. 12). Their words are equally or perhaps more relevant today because of the growing number of underprepared, underrepresented, and first-generation students on college campuses. Recent research indicates that the retention and academic success of underrepresented and first-generation students, in particular, is seriously undercut by institutional overreliance on student-initiated involvement in campus-support programs (Rendon, 1994; Terenzini and others, 1994).

Both student effort and institutional effort are required to promote students' success, but very short shrift has been paid to the latter form of effort in the higher education literature (Kuh, Schuh, Whitt, and Associates, 1991). It is patently clear that effective programming for first-year students is characterized by a high degree of institutional initiative and expenditure of substantial institutional effort to ensure that programmatic support reaches all students who are likely to profit from it.

Effective support programs cited in this chapter implement the principle of intrusiveness by engaging in such practices as (a) delivering support services to students on their "turf" (for example, via living learning centers and residential learning communities), (b) infusing support services directly into the classroom (for example, through supplemental instruction and course-integrated library instruction), and (c) requiring students to use support programs (for example, as course assignments in the first-year seminar).

Effective First-Year Support Programs Are Proactive

Powerful program delivery is characterized by early, preventative action designed to addresses students' needs and adjustment issues in an anticipatory fashion—before they eventuate in full-blown problems that require reactive intervention. As Tinto (1993) categorically states, "One of the clearest aspects of effective programs for academically at-risk students is their proactive orientation toward intervention. However constructed, the principle of effective programs for at-risk students is that one does not wait until a problem arises, but intervenes proactively beforehand or at least as soon as possible" (p. 182).

Proactive program delivery is the sine qua non of effective first-year support programs because it ensures that support reaches students at the time they need it the most—when they are most vulnerable to academic failure and attrition—and when support is most likely to have its greatest long-term impact on students. "Front loading" has become an almost axiomatic principle of effective undergraduate education, and many of the successful programs described in this chapter successfully implement this principle, such as (a) summer bridge programs, (b) early alert systems, and (c) first-year experience courses.

Effective First-Year Support Programs Are Collaborative

Powerful student support programs typically involve cooperative alliances or partnerships between different members and organizational units of the college, which work together in an integrated, interdependent, and symbiotic fashion to provide comprehensive, holistic (whole person) support for first-year students. Recent scholarly support for the importance of collaboration as a program delivery principle is provided by Braxton and Mundy (2001–2002), who reviewed a special series of contemporary articles that focused on merging retention theory with retention practice. After synthesizing the recommendations cited in these articles, the reviewers reached the following conclusion about programs and practices designed to promote student retention: "The most meaningful and far-reaching institutional efforts call for collaboration within university divisions and departments. These relationships are imperative to effective retention programs and efforts" (p. 94).

Successful support programs cited in this chapter are distinguished by the presence of cross-functional collaborative relationships, such as those between (a) faculty and academic support specialists—to implement effective early alert systems and course-integrated learning assistance programs, and (b) colleges and schools—to coordinate summer bridge and school outreach programs.

Perhaps one of the most important benefits of collaborative programs is that they serve to foster the development of a "culture" of collaboration on campus. Higher education research reveals that campus cultures which are identified as collaborative, rather than competitive or individualistic, are characterized by a higher level of faculty and staff morale and a greater sense of perceived "community" among its members (Austin, Rice, Splete, and Associates, 1991). This positive byproduct of collaborative programming on faculty and staff may, in itself, serve to promote the retention and success of first-year students on campus.

REFERENCES

Abrams, H., and Jernigan, L. "Academic Support Services and the Success of High-Risk Students." *American Educational Research Journal,* 1984, *21,* 261–274.

ACT. "National College Dropout and Graduation Rates, 1999." [http://www.act.org/news], Feb. 2001.

Alexander, J. M., and Stark, J. S. *Focusing on Student Outcomes.* Ann Arbor: University of Michigan, National Center for Research to Improve Postsecondary Teaching and Learning, 1986.

American Association for Higher Education. "AAHE's New Agenda on School/College Collaboration." *AAHE Bulletin,* 1993, *45*(9), 10–13.

American College Personnel Association. "A Student Development Model for Student Affairs in Tomorrow's Higher Education." *Journal of College Student Personnel,* 1975, *16,* 334–341.

American College Personnel Association. *The Student Learning Imperative: Implications for Student Affairs.* Washington, D.C.: American College Personnel Association, 1994.

Arendale, D. R. "Understanding the Supplemental Instruction Model." In D. C. Martin and D. R. Arendale (eds.), *Supplemental Instruction: Increasing Achievement and Retention.* New Directions for Teaching and Learning, no. 60. San Francisco: Jossey-Bass, 1994.

Aronson, E., and others. *The Jigsaw Classroom.* Thousand Oaks, Calif.: Sage, 1978.

Astin, A. W. "Student-Oriented Management: A Proposal for Change." In *Evaluating Educational Quality.* Washington, D.C.: Council on Postsecondary Accreditation, 1979.

Astin, A. W. *What Matters in College?* San Francisco: Jossey-Bass, 1993.

Astin, A. W., Parrott, S., Korn, W., and Sax, L. *The American Freshman— Thirty Year Trends.* Los Angeles: University of California, Los Angeles, Higher Education Research Institute, 1997.

Austin, A. E., Rice, E. R., Splete, A. P., and Associates. *A Good Place to Work: Sourcebook for the Academic Workplace.* Washington, D.C.: The Council of Independent Colleges, 1991.

Baker, R. W., and Schultz, K. L. "Measuring Expectations About College Adjustment." *NACADA Journal,* 1992, *12*(2), 23–32.

Baker, R. W., and Siryk, B. "Exploratory Intervention with a Scale Measuring Adjustment to College." *Journal of Counseling Psychology,* 1986, *33,* 31–38.

Barefoot, B. O. (ed.). *Exploring the Evidence: Reporting Outcomes of Freshman Seminars.* (Monograph no. 11). Columbia, S.C.: National Resource Center for The Freshman Year Experience, University of South Carolina, 1993.

Barefoot, B. O. "Evaluating the First-Year Seminar." [http://www.Brevard.edu /fyc/BarefootRemarks.html]. Sept. 2000.

Barefoot, B. O. "Summary of Curricular Findings." [Survey/CurrentPractices /SummaryofFindings.html]. July 2001.

Barefoot, B. O., and Fidler, P. P. *The 1994 Survey of Freshman Seminar Programs: Continuing Innovations in the Collegiate Curriculum.* (Monograph no. 20). Columbia, S.C.: National Resource Center for the Freshman-Year Experience and Students in Transition, University of South Carolina, 1996.

Barefoot, B. O., and Gardner, J. N. "Introduction." In B. O. Barefoot, C. L. Warnock, M. P. Dickinson, S. E. Richardson, and M. R. Roberts (eds.), *Exploring the Evidence, Volume II: Reporting Outcomes of First-Year Seminars.* (Monograph no. 29). Columbia, S.C.: National Resource Center for the First-Year Experience and Students in Transition, University of South Carolina, 1998.

Barefoot, B. O., and others. (eds.). *Exploring the Evidence, Volume II: Reporting Outcomes of First-Year Seminars.* (Monograph no. 29). Columbia, S.C.: National Resource Center for the First-Year Experience and Students in Transition, University of South Carolina, 1998.

Bargh, J., and Schul, Y. "On the Cognitive Benefits of Teaching." *Journal of Educational Psychology,* 1980, *72*(5), 593–604.

Barr, M. J., and Upcraft, M. L. (eds.). *New Futures for Student Affairs: Building a Vision for Professional Leadership and Practice.* San Francisco: Jossey-Bass, 1990.

Benware, C. A., and Deci, E. L. "Quality of Learning with an Active Versus Passive Motivational Set." *American Educational Research Journal,* 1984, *21*(4), 755–765.

Bonsangue, M. V. "The Effects of Calculus Workshop Groups on Minority Achievement in Mathematics, Science, and Engineering." *Cooperative Learning and College Teaching,* 1993, *3*(3), 8–9.

Boyer, E. L. *College: The Undergraduate Experience in America.* New York: Harper and Row, 1987.

Boylan, H. R., Bliss, L., and Bonham, B. S. "The Impact of Developmental Programs." *Research in Developmental Education,* 1992, *10*(2), 1–4.

Braxton, J. M., and Mundy, M. E. "Powerful Institutional Levers to Reduce College Student Departure." *Journal of College Student Retention,* 2001–2002, *3*(1), 91–118.

Braxton, J. M., Sullivan, A. S., and Johnson, R. M. "Appraising Tinto's Theory of College Student Departure." In J. C. Smart (ed.), *Higher Education: Handbook of Theory and Research.* Vol. 12. New York: Agathon, 1997.

Budig, J., Koenig, A., and Weaver, T. "Postcards for Student Success." *Innovation Abstracts,* 1991, *12*(28), 4.

Carlson, L. [carlson@adelphi.edu]. "Early Alert Programs." Message to fye-list [fye- list@vm.sc.edu]. Oct. 2, 2000.

Catone, J. E. "'Triad' Program Gives Entering Students Three Kinds of Support." *The First-Year Experience Newsletter,* 1996, *9*(2), 7.

Chickering, A. W. *Education and Identity.* San Francisco: Jossey-Bass, 1969.

Chickering, A. W., and Schlossberg, N. K. "Moving On: Seniors as People in Transition." In J. N. Gardner, G. Van der Veer, and Associates, *The Senior Year Experience.* San Francisco: Jossey-Bass, 1998.

Churchill, W. D., and Iwai, S. I. "College Attrition, Student Use of Campus Facilities, and a Consideration of Self-Reported Personal Problems. *Research in Higher Education,* 1981, *14*(4), 353–365.

Consortium for Student Retention Data Exchange. *Executive Summary 1998–1999 CSRDE Report: The Retention and Graduation Rates in 269 Colleges and Universities.* Norman, Okla.: Center for Institutional Data Exchange and Analysis, University of Oklahoma, 1999.

Cooper, J. L. "New Evidence of the Power of Cooperative Learning." *Cooperative Learning and College Teaching,* 1997, *7*(3), 1–2.

Cross, J. P. *Adults as Learners.* San Francisco: Jossey-Bass, 1981.

Cross, K. P. "Education for the 21st Century." *NASPA Journal,* 1985, *23*(1), 7–18.

Cuseo, J. B. "The Transfer Transition." Preconference workshop presented at the Eighth National Conference on Students in Transition, Oak Brook, Illinois, Oct. 2001.

Cuseo, J. B. *Igniting Student Involvement, Peer Interaction, and Teamwork: A Taxonomy of Specific Cooperative Learning Structures and Collaborative Learning Strategies.* Stillwater, Okla.: New Forums Press, 2002.

"Early Intervention Programs Help Keep New Students on Course." *Recruitment and Retention in Higher Education,* 1992, *6*(3), 9.

Education Commission of the States. *Making Quality Count in Undergraduate Education.* Denver, Colo.: ECS Distribution Center, 1995.

Ender, S. C., Winston, R. B., Jr., and Miller, T. K. "Academic Advising Reconsidered." In R. B. Winston Jr., T. K. Miller, S. C. Ender, T. J. Grites, and Associates, *Developmental Academic Advising.* San Francisco: Jossey-Bass, 1984.

Engelkemeyer, S. W., and Brown, S. C. "Powerful Partnerships: A Shared Responsibility for Learning." *AAHE Bulletin,* 1998, *51*(2), 10–12.

Feldman, K. A., and Newcomb, T. M. (eds.). *The Impact of College on Students.* San Francisco: Jossey-Bass, 1969.

Fidler, P. P., and Shanley, M. G. "Evaluation Results of University 101." Presentation made at the annual conference of The Freshman Year Experience, Columbia, S.C., Feb. 1993.

Friedlander, J. "Are College Support Programs and Services Reaching High-Risk Students?" *Journal of College Student Personnel,* 1980, *21*(1), 23–28.

Gamson, Z. "Deep Learning, Surface Learning." *AAHE Bulletin,* 1993, *45*(8), 11–13.

Garcia, G. "Summer Bridge: Improving Retention Rates for Underprepared Students. *Journal of The Freshman Year Experience,* 1991, *3*(2), 91–105.

Gardner, J. N. "The Freshman Year Experience." *College and University,* 1986, *61*(4), 261–274.

Getzlaf, S. B., Sedlacek, G. M., Kearney, K. A., and Blackwell, J. M. "Two Types of Voluntary Undergraduate Attrition: An Application of Tinto's Model." *Research in Higher Education,* 1984, *20*(3), 257–268.

Goldman, B. A., and Gillis, J. H. "Graduation and Attrition Rates: A Closer Look at Influences." *Journal of The Freshman Year Experience,* 1989, *1*(1), 56–77.

Green, M. G. (ed.). *Minorities on Campus: A Handbook for Enhancing Diversity.* Washington, D.C.: American Council on Education, 1989.

Green, S. "Graduation Rates Double for Underprepared Students at Indiana University at Kokomo." *The Freshman Year Experience Newsletter,* 1994, *7*(2), 4.

Gross, A. E., and McMullen, P. A. "Models of Help-Seeking Process." In F. D. Fisher, A. Naples, and B. M. DePaul (eds.), *New Directions in Helping and Help-Seeking.* Vol. 2. New York: Academic Press, 1983.

Guon, D. G. "Minority Access and Retention: An Evaluation of a Multi-University Peer Counseling Program." Paper presented at the annual meeting of the Midwestern Psychological Association, Chicago, Apr. 1988.

Hallberg, E., and Davis, G. "The College Success Factors Index." [http://www.Brevard.edu/fyc/FYA_contributions/Resources.htm]. Nov. 2001.

Johnson, D. W., and others. "Effects of Cooperative, Competitive, and Individualistic Goal Structures on Achievement: A Meta-Analysis." *Psychological Bulletin,* 1981, *89*(1), 47–62.

Johnson, K., Sulzer-Azaroff, B., and Mass, C. "The Effects of Internal Proctoring upon Examination Performance in a Personalized Instruction Course." *Journal of Personalized Instruction,* 1977, *1,* 113–117.

Kagan, S. *Cooperative Learning.* San Juan Capistrano, Calif.: Resources for Teachers, Inc., 1992.

Kerstiens, G. "Study Behavior Inventory." [http://www.sbi4windows.com]. Nov. 2000.

Knapp, J. R., and Karabenick, S. A. "Incidence of Formal and Informal Academic Help-Seeking in Higher Education." *Journal of College Student Development,* 1988, 29(3), 223–227.

Kochenour, E. O., and others. "Supplemental Instruction: An Effective Component of Student Affairs Programming." *Journal of College Student Development,* 1997, (Nov. /Dec.), 577–585.

Kramer, M. "Lengthening of Time to Degree." *Change,* 1993, 25(3), 5–7.

Kuh, G. D., and Banta, T. W. "Faculty-Student Affairs Collaboration on Assessment: Lessons from the Field." *About Campus,* 2000, 4(6), 4–11.

Kuh, G. D., Schuh, J., Whitt, E., and Associates. *Involving Colleges: Encouraging Student Learning and Personal Development Through Out-of-Class Experiences.* San Francisco: Jossey-Bass, 1991.

Kulik, C., Kulik, J., and Shwalb, B. "College Programs for High-Risk and Disadvantaged Students: A Meta-Analysis of Findings." *Review of Educational Research,* 1983, 53, 397–414.

Kurfiss, J. G. *Critical Thinking: Theory, Research, Practice, and Possibilities.* ASHE-ERIC, Report no. 2. Washington, D.C.: Association for the Study of Higher Education, 1988.

"Learning Slope." (1991). *Policy Perspectives,* 1991, 4(1), 1A-8A. Pew Higher Education Research Program.

Lent, R. W., Brown, S. D., and Larkin, K. C. "Comparison of Three Theoretically Derived Variables in Predicting Career and Academic Behavior: Self-efficacy, Interest Congruence, and Consequence Thinking." *Journal of Counseling Psychology,* 1987, 34, 293–298.

Levin, M., and Levin, J. "A Critical Examination of Academic Retention Programs for At-Risk Minority College Students." *Journal of College Student Development,* 1991, 32, 323–334.

Levine, J. H. *When Hope and Fear Collide: A Portrait of Today's College Student.* San Francisco: Jossey-Bass, 1998.

Levine, J. H., and Tompkins, D. P. "Making Learning Communities Work: Seven Lessons from Temple University." *AAHE Bulletin,* 1996, 48(1), 3–6.

Levitz, R. "Supplemental Instruction Takes Off." *Recruitment and Retention Newsletter,* 1990 (Nov.), 7.

Levitz, R. "Adding Peer Tutors to Your Retention Program." *Recruitment and Retention in Higher Education,* 1991, *5*(10), 5–7.

Levitz, R., and Noel, L. "Connecting Students to Institutions: Keys to Retention and Success." In M. L. Upcraft, J. N. Gardner, and Associates, *The Freshman Year Experience.* San Francisco: Jossey-Bass, 1989.

Light, R. J. *Making the Most of College: Students Speak Their Minds.* Cambridge, Mass.: Harvard University Press, 2001.

MacGregor, J. "What Differences Do Learning Communities Make?" *Washington Center News,* 1991, *6*(1), 4–9.

MacGregor, J. "Restructuring Large Classes to Create Communities of Learners." In J. MacGregor, J. L. Cooper, K. A. Smith, and P. Robinson (eds.), *Strategies for Energizing Large Classes: From Small Groups to Learning Communities.* New Directions for Teaching and Learning, no. 81. San Francisco: Jossey-Bass, 2000.

Martin, D. C., and Arendale, D. R. (eds.). *Supplemental Instruction: Increasing Achievement and Retention.* New Directions for Teaching and Learning, no. 60. San Francisco: Jossey-Bass, 1994.

Martin, D. C., and Blanc, R. A. "VSI: A Pathway to Mastery and Persistence." In D. C. Martin and D. R. Arendale (eds.), *Supplemental Instruction: Increasing Achievement and Retention.* New Directions for Teaching and Learning, no. 60. San Francisco: Jossey-Bass, 1994.

McGrath, D., and Townsend, B. T. "Strengthening Preparedness of At-Risk Students." In J. G. Gaff, J. L. Ratcliff, and Associates, *Handbook of the Undergraduate Curriculum: A Comprehensive Guide to Purposes, Structures, Practices, and Change.* San Francisco: Jossey-Bass, 1997.

McKeachie, W. J., Pintrich, P., Lin, Y., and Smith, D. *Teaching and Learning in the College Classroom: A Review of the Research Literature.* Ann Arbor: University of Michigan, National Center for Research to Improve Postsecondary Teaching and Learning, 1986.

Means, B., Chelemer, C., and Knapp, M. (eds.). *Teaching Advanced Skills to At-Risk Students.* San Francisco: Jossey-Bass, 1991.

Miller, T. K., and Prince, J. S. *The Future of Student Affairs.* San Francisco: Jossey-Bass, 1976.

Millis, B. J., and Cottell, P. G., Jr. *Cooperative Learning for Higher Education Faculty.* Phoenix: American Council on Education and Oryx Press, 1998.

National Academy of Sciences—National Research Council "Retention of Minority Students in Engineering." Washington, D.C.: National Academy of Sciences, 1977. (ED 152 467).

National Institute of Education. *Involvement in Learning: Realizing the Potential of American Higher Education* (Report of the NIE Study Group on the Condition of Excellence in American Higher Education). Washington, D.C.: U.S. Government Printing Office, 1984.

National Resource Center for the First-Year Experience and Students in Transition. *1997 National Survey of First-Year Seminar Programming.* Columbia: University of South Carolina, National Resource Center for the First-Year Experience and Students in Transition, 1998.

Noel, L. "Defending Against Budget Cuts." *Recruitment and Retention in Higher Education,* 1994 (Jan.), 6.

Pantages, T. J., and Creedan, C. F. "Studies of College Attrition: 1950–1975." *Review of Educational Research,* 1978, *48,* 49–101.

Pascarella, E. T., and Chapman, D. W. "Validation of a Theoretical Model of College Withdrawal: Interaction Effects in a Multi-Institutional Sample." *Research in Higher Education,* 1983, *19,* 25–48.

Pascarella, E. T., and Terenzini, P. T. *How College Affects Students: Findings and Insights from Twenty Years of Research.* San Francisco: Jossey-Bass, 1991.

Patton, M. Q. *Utilization-Focused Evaluation.* Thousand Oaks, Calif.: Sage, 1978.

Peters, C. B. "Rescue the Perishing: A New Approach to Supplemental Instruction." In M. D. Svinicki (ed.), *The Changing Face of College Teaching.* New Directions for Teaching and Learning, no. 42. San Francisco: Jossey-Bass, 1990.

Pintrich, P. R., McKeachie, W. J., and Smith, D. *The Motivated Strategies for Learning Questionnaire.* Ann Arbor: University of Michigan, National Center for Research to Improve Postsecondary Teaching and Learning, 1989.

Postsecondary Education Opportunity. "Institutional Graduation Rates by Control, Academic Selectivity and Degree Level, 1983–2002." *The Environmental Scanning Research Letter of Opportunity for Postsecondary Education,* 2002, (Mar.), 1–16.

Rendon, L. I. "Validating Culturally Diverse Students: Toward a New Model of Learning and Student Development." *Innovative Higher Education,* 1994, *19*(1), 23–32.

Richardson, R. C., Jr., and Bender, L. W. *Fostering Minority Access and Achievement in Higher Education.* San Francisco: Jossey-Bass, 1987.

Roueche, J. E., Baker, G. A., and Roueche, S. D. *College Responses to Low-Achieving Students: A National Study.* New York: HBJ Media Systems, 1984.

Roueche, J., and Roueche, S. *Between a Rock and a Hard Place: The At-Risk Student in the Open-Door College.* Washington, D.C.: American Association of Community Colleges, 1993.

Schein, H. K., and Bowers, P. M. "Using Living/Learning Centers to Provide Integrated Campus Services for Freshmen." *Journal of The Freshman Year Experience,* 1992, *4*(1), 59–77.

Schilling, K. "Plenary Address." Presented at the Summer Institute on First-Year Assessment, Asheville, North Carolina, Aug. 2001.

Seymour, D. "Quality on Campus: Three Institutions, Three Beginnings."
Change, 1993, *25*(3), 14–27.

Slavin, R. E. *Cooperative Learning: Theory, Research, and Practice.* Englewood
Cliffs, N.J.: Prentice Hall, 1990.

Smith, J. B., Walter, T. L., and Hoey G. "Support Programs and Student Self-
Efficacy: Do First-Year Students Know When They Need Help?" *Journal
of The Freshman Year Experience,* 1992, *4*(2), 41–67.

Solberg, V. S., O'Brien, P., Villareal, R., and Davis, B. "Self-Efficacy and Hispanic College Students: Validation of the College Self-Efficacy Instrument." *Hispanic Journal of Behavioral Sciences,* 1993, *15*(1), 80–95.

Squire, L. "Mechanism of Memory." *Science,* 1986, *232,* 1612–1619.

Stodt, M. M., and Klepper, W. M. (eds.). *Increasing Retention: Academic and
Student Affairs Administrators in Partnership.* New Directions for Higher
Education. San Francisco: Jossey-Bass, 1987.

Striatal, M. L. *College Student Inventory.* Coralville, Iowa: Noel/Levitz
Centers, 1988.

Terenzini, P. T., and others. "The Transition to College: Diverse Students,
Diverse Stories." *Research in Higher Education,* 1994, *35*(1), 57–73.

Thompson, Karla [kthompso@cavern.nmsu.edu]. "Early Warning Systems."
Message to fye-list [fye-list@vm.sc.edu]. Apr. 4, 2001.

Tinto, V. *Leaving College: Rethinking the Causes and Cures of Student
Attrition.* (2nd ed.) Chicago: University of Chicago Press, 1993.

Tinto, V. "Linking Learning and Leaving: Exploring the Role of the College
Classroom in Student Departure." In J. M. Braxton (ed.), *Reworking the
Student Departure Puzzle.* Nashville: Vanderbilt University Press, 2000.

Treisman, P. U. "A Study of the Mathematics Performance of Black Students at
the University of California, Berkeley." Unpublished doctoral dissertation,
University of California, Berkeley, 1986.

Treisman, U. "Studying Students Studying Calculus: A Look at the Lives of
Minority Mathematics Students in College." *College Mathematics Journal,* 1992, *23*(5), 362–372.

Upcraft, M. L., and Farnsworth, W. M. "Orientation Programs and Activities."
In M. L. Upcraft (ed.), *Orienting Students to College.* New Directions for
Student Services, no. 5. San Francisco: Jossey-Bass, 1984.

U.S. Bureau of the Census. *Statistical Abstract of the United States: 1994.*
(114th ed.) Washington, D.C.: U.S. Government Printing Office, 1994.

Vygotsky, L. S. "Internalization of Higher Cognitive Functions." In M. Cole,
V. John-Steiner, S. Scribner, and E. Souberman (eds. and trans.), *Mind in
Society: The Development of Higher Psychological Processes.* Cambridge:
Harvard University Press, 1978.

Walter, T. L., and Smith, J. "Self-Assessment and Academic Support: Do Students Know They Need Help?" Paper presented at the annual Freshman Year Experience Conference, Austin, Texas, Apr. 1990.

Weinstein, C. E., Schulte, A. C., and Palmer, D. R. *Learning and Study Strategies Inventory (LASSI).* Clearwater, Fla.: H&H Publishing, 1987.

Weinstein, C. E., and Underwood, V. L. "Learning Strategies: The How of Learning." In J. W. Segal, S. F. Chapman, and R. Glaser (eds.), *Thinking and Learning Skills.* Hillsdale, N.J.: Lawrence Erlbaum, 1985.

"What We Know About First-Year Students." In J. N. Gardner and A. J. Jewler, *Your College Experience* (Instructor's Manual). Belmont, Calif.: Wadsworth, 1996.

Whitman, N. A. *Peer Teaching: To Teach Is to Learn Twice.* ASHE-ERIC Higher Education Report no. 4. Washington, D.C.: Association for the Study of Higher Education, 1988.

Widmar, G. E. "Supplemental Instruction: From Small Beginnings to a National Program." In D. C. Martin and D. R. Arendale (eds.), *Supplemental Instruction: Increasing Achievement and Retention.* New Directions for Teaching and Learning, no. 60. San Francisco: Jossey-Bass, 1994.

Wilbur, F. P., and Lambert, L. M. (eds.). *Linking America's Schools and Colleges.* (2nd ed.) Washington, D.C.: American Association for Higher Education, 1995.

Wilkie, C., and Kuckuck, S. "A Longitudinal Study of the Effects of a Freshman Seminar." *Journal of The Freshman Year Experience,* 1989, *1*(1), 7–16.

Wilkie, C., and Redondo, B. "Predictors of Academic Success and Failure of First-Year College Students." *Journal of The Freshman Year Experience,* 1996, *8*(2), 17–32.

Young, R. W. "Seventeen Year Graduation Study of 1963 Freshmen at the University of New Mexico." *College and University,* 1982, *57*(3), 279–288.

14

RESPONDING TO STUDENTS' NEEDS

Carmy Carranza, Steven C. Ender

THE CONTEMPORARY SYSTEM of American higher education is unique in the world. One quick glance at the 2001–02 almanac issue of the *Chronicle of Higher Education* (Weidlein, 2001) reveals the complexity of the American system with regard to learners, types of institutions, and opportunities to pursue postsecondary education. This complexity creates enormous challenges for the academy as it creates appropriate learning opportunities for students at different levels of academic readiness, sequences the curriculum, and designs support services to meet the vast array of students' academic and psychological needs.

Student Demographics

If the academy is to successfully respond to the learning needs of today's students, institutions of higher education must have a thorough understanding of the types of students enrolled on their campuses and their corresponding learning needs. Only with this understanding can appropriate systems, programs, and interventions of academic support be implemented.

When we examine today's undergraduate higher education environment, we discover a broad and diverse student clientele. According to the 2001–02 almanac of the *Chronicle of Higher Education,* 62.7 percent of today's learners are traditional with respect to age (younger than twenty-five years old) and 37.3 percent are considered nontraditional. Women make up 56.1 percent of the total population, and 59.4 percent of all students study full-time. Minority students make up 28.1 percent of the student population, and 3.5 percent of students are from foreign countries.

Students are enrolled at public and private four-year institutions (62.2 percent) as well as community colleges (37.8 percent). Approximately 60 percent will matriculate immediately following high school graduation. Others may be absent from formal learning environments for several years prior to returning to school. Students attend these colleges to earn degrees and certificates, enhance existing skills, and find personal fulfillment.

Preparation for College Study

The publication *A Nation at Risk* (U.S. Department of Education, 1983) set off a national debate on the readiness of high school graduates for college or university study. Among its findings, the report exclaims, "If an unfriendly foreign power had attempted to impose on America the mediocre educational performance that exists today, we might well have viewed it as an act of war" (p. 1).

The report (U.S. Department of Education, 1983) made several recommendations to improve the quality of high school education in America. One was that "State and local high school graduation requirements be strengthened and that, at a minimum, all students seeking a diploma be required to lay the foundation in the Five New Basics by taking the following curriculum during their 4 years of high school: (a) 4 years of English; (b) 3 years of mathematics; (c) 3 years of science; (d) 3 years of social science; and (e) one-half year of computer science. . . . For the college-bound, 2 years of foreign language in high school are strongly recommended in addition to those taken earlier" (p. 24).

It is interesting that students graduating from high school today are among the first group of learners in the United States to benefit from this warning and appeal for policy and curriculum change in secondary education. Are they better prepared than their 1983 counterparts for postsecondary success? The results are mixed and have implications for higher education. We know, for instance, that between 1987 and 1997 the proportion of ACT-tested college-bound high school seniors who had completed the College Core Curriculum—which is similar to the commission's curriculum—increased from 37.9 to 61 percent (Mortenson, 1997). While encouraging, a closer review of the data suggests that family income continues to play a key factor with regard to preparation. Mortenson reports that the proportion of college-bound high school seniors who have completed the College Core Curriculum has increased directly with family income. "For those from families with incomes below $18,000 per year, 51 percent completed the College Core. . . . For those from families with incomes of more than $100,000 per year, the percentage was 72.5 percent. . . . Between these extremes, the relationship was nearly linear" (p. 8).

In summarizing the impact of the results of *A Nation at Risk,* Mortenson (1997) concludes that although high school students have greatly improved their high school course selection in preparation for college, some groups of students, particularly those from low-income households and some minorities, are not entering college well prepared to meet the academic challenges of college. Also, gains are uneven, with women showing more progress than men, and the gains in academic preparation appear to be slowing.

Freshman-to-Sophomore Persistence

With the improvements in student preparation that have been made since 1983, one might logically expect today's students to perform better than their 1983 counterparts. Unfortunately, this is not the case. At four-year colleges and universities, the persistence rate from the freshman-to-sophomore year has declined slightly from 75.5 percent in 1983 to 73.9 percent in 2001. At two-year colleges the persistence rate declined from a high of 56.8 percent in 1983 to 54.1 percent in 2001 (Mortenson, 2001).

Private two- and four-year colleges have higher persistence rates than their public counterparts, and there is a clear relationship between admissions selectivity and persistence. In 2001, the average persistence rates at four-year colleges and universities ranged from 91.6 percent in highly selective institutions to 60.6 percent in open admissions institutions (Mortenson, 2001).

Students with Disabilities

In 1996, approximately 6 percent of all undergraduates reported having a disability, with approximately 29 percent reporting a learning disability (U.S. Department of Education, 1999). These learning disabilities included dyslexia and other reading, writing, or math disabilities. The Center for Education Statistics also reports that those with disabilities were less likely to attend a public four-year institution. About 53 percent of students with disabilities had persisted in their postsecondary program, contrasted with 64 percent of students without disabilities. Persistence in this instance was defined as having graduated or as still being enrolled five years after matriculation.

Emotional Concerns

Many students enter higher education with significant personal issues. Newton (1998) reports that the chief concern among today's college students is stress. This strain comes from a variety of sources—social, academic, and financial. In the *Chronicle*'s 2001–02 almanac issue, 28.1 percent of entering freshmen indicated that they had felt overwhelmed by all that they had to do, and 8.1 percent had felt depressed during the past year. Coping behaviors were evident. Of the students responding to the survey concerning the past year, 53.9 percent had drunk beer or wine, 35.3 percent had overslept and missed classes or appointments, and 64.5 percent had come late to class.

A more recent report, summarized in the *Chronicle* (Bartlett, 2002), points to the often troubling transition of first-year students. This report is based on the responses of 3,680 freshmen at fifty four-year institutions. These students were surveyed in Fall 2000 and again in Fall 2001. Several findings point to troubled freshman-year transitions: (1) only 44.9 percent of freshmen rated their emotional health "above average" at the end of their first year of college, compared with 52.4 percent at the beginning of the academic year, (2) 16.3 percent reported feeling depressed at some point during the year, compared with 8.2 percent, who felt depressed in the year before college, and (3) 44.3 percent had felt overwhelmed by all that they had to do, compared with 31.6 percent in the preceding year.

This profile shows that institutes of higher education are enrolling a diverse student body with a wide range of academic and personal needs. The institution has an ethical responsibility to offer an academic curriculum and support system that ensures each admitted student the opportunity to compete. This requires systematic and seamless academic interventions on the part of the university community.

The Role of Academic Services

Given the complexity of the range of learning characteristics students possess, higher education is challenged to implement appropriate interventions to respond to students' academic needs. The cooperation and collaboration of many academic departments and academic services is critical if a seamless approach is to be implemented. These departments and services will be defined within the context of enrollment management and matriculation services.

Enrollment Management

Enrolled students do not worry about their institutional classification. They may be honors, remedial, returning, full-time, or part-time students, but the intention of almost all students is to accomplish educational goals and enjoy an enhanced quality of life as a result of their efforts. It is the institution's responsibility to ensure that the curriculum and support services available match the learning needs of students.

To do this, an institution must first assess its learners and their needs. This requires collaboration from specific areas of the institution, including institutional research, admissions, and the registrar.

INSTITUTIONAL RESEARCH. Planning for the present and future involves some looking back at entering students' learning preparedness and subsequent academic progress and success. Such student profiles are critical and will be different, depending on the institution. For instance, a remedial student at an elite institution might not be labeled as such at a community college. The academic programs of the institutions will be different, as will the support systems necessary to promote academic success.

Through the area of institutional research, colleges can develop these student profiles and track persistence and graduation rates. A thorough review would include an analysis of major fields of study. For example, institutional, longitudinal records may show that students with certain types of profiles rarely succeed in particular fields of study, having high attrition rates and low graduation rates. This type of analysis can also point to particular courses within programs or majors that have high student failure or withdrawal rates and can lead to an array of academic interventions designed to promote student success.

Many of these data are captured through admissions trends, retention and graduation rates, and students' academic readiness rates as profiled through institutional testing programs, formal SAT and ACT scores, and students' ranks in high school classes. An analysis of recruitment areas and the growth and decline of student populations in these areas provides evidence of the numbers and quality of students who may attend the institution in subsequent years. This type of "global" analysis and profiling sets the stage for the institutional response to and curriculum readiness for later cohorts of students.

ADMISSIONS OFFICE. Armed with the data provided by institutional research and its own data and records, the admissions office can make the first response to individual student needs. Establishing college success predictions, using students' entering academic profiles, the admissions office identifies students in need of certain types of programs before admitting them (Tinto, 1986).

Prior to the admissions cycle of recruitment and admission for any given year, decisions must be made regarding entering student cohorts. For example, the admissions office must decide how many students will be admitted into certain categories of selectivity and programs of study. These decisions are based on the college's ability to offer appropriate courses and services to promote student success. Making such decisions requires strong channels of communication between the office of admissions and programs and support services across campus.

Students may demonstrate a need for a program that offers remedial courses, intrusive advisement, close monitoring of progress, and even a precollege summer program. Part-time students, adult returning students, associate degree-seeking students, or honors students may each have access to a separate category of admissions, a particular program of study, or a special learning community arrangement. The admissions program begins the important process of identifying the nature and needs of its entering students and matching them with the appropriate service or program of services.

REGISTRAR OFFICE. In close collaboration and cooperation with deans, department chairs, and academic support services, the registrar prepares the college's curriculum to correspond with the academic needs of each entering class by ensuring the availability of appropriate courses. To accomplish this task, the registrar's office must consult historical patterns of entering student cohorts and their academic profiles, be knowledgeable about enrollment goals with respect to categories of admissions, and be aware of curriculum requirements and subsequent learning interventions.

Examples of special learning interventions include learning communities, supplemental instruction, linked courses, clustered courses, freshman interest groups, and coordinated studies. Each is described later in this chapter. Suffice it to say, if these types of academic strategies are to occur in a seamless environment, significant cooperation, collaboration, and planning must occur across campus.

Significant campus players in this collaborative process include the registrar, the admissions office, the provost, college deans, and department chairs. Informed academic advisers will perform a critical role, linking students to appropriate programs, courses, and special curriculum offerings (Braxton, 2000). Significant communication and information sharing are critical to link students at various ability levels to support services and special interventions planned to assist them in their quest for a successful academic experience.

Matriculation Services

Through significant analysis, communication, and collaboration among the offices of institutional research, admissions, the registrar, and other academic and student services, an institution's curriculum can be planned to successfully host each new entering group of students. To this point in the admissions and matriculation process, the institution has relied on historical data, past student profiles, admissions goals, and carefully planned student interventions to foster student academic success.

There comes the time, however, when real students must be matched with real academic schedules—schedules and course offerings that have been planned through a careful analysis of the entering students' learning characteristics, background, and potential need for additional curriculum support. This matching process takes place through the various matriculation services offered by the college. These include testing and placement programs, orientation, and the special role of first-year seminars—or "University 101."

TESTING AND PLACEMENT. Understanding students' academic curriculum needs often requires more information than can be provided by the typical college application, high school transcript, or ACT or SAT test scores (Astin, 1971, 1984). A well-rounded testing program can add meaningful data for placing students into the appropriate level of introductory courses, for identifying students who need remedial work in reading, math, or writing, for determining the first level of foreign language study, and for identifying students with learning disabilities or those for whom English is a second language.

Placement tests can be institutionally developed or standardized. Collaboration with each relevant academic department is essential for determining the appropriate testing instrument and for setting the criteria that will establish specific placement standards and benchmarks for course registration purposes. The cooperation of academic departments is also important where tests must be hand-scored, as is the case with essays, writing portfolios, and foreign language tests.

Linking placement testing with academic advising, course selection, and registration helps create a seamless system of student academic support.

ORIENTATION. New student orientation is an ideal time to administer placement tests. In one effective model, the institution invites students and their parents prior to matriculation (Forbes, 2001; Lowery, 2001). Depending on the size of the incoming student cohort, this may be done in groups or with the entire incoming class. Ideally, students stay in residence halls with access to dining facilities. Parents may do likewise, giving both the students and their parents a flavor of the actual university experience.

With testing completed, students receive general advisement about the meaning of the test results, information related to distributive, general, or liberal studies requirements, and an individual or small group session with a faculty adviser to develop a specific schedule. After this session, students can register for the selected courses and receive a printed schedule to take home in anticipation of the first term.

It is not difficult to see that, to work well, such an endeavor requires the coordinated effort of many offices, faculty and staff members, and even students serving as peer advisers and peer educators. Admissions staff members must be in constant contact with advising and testing personnel. Faculty advisers must be trained and well informed about course offerings and special offerings. The registrar and advisers must know about linked, clustered, honors, freshman seminar courses, as well as any special populations for whom these courses are to be reserved. Someone, such as a student development specialist, should coordinate presentations from the staff of such offices as financial aid, career services, and residence life, as well as the counseling center, the health center, the learning center, and internship and study abroad programs. Student orientation and advising leaders need to be trained and supervised. And the test checkers and the computer center must be efficient if test scores are to be delivered essentially overnight.

FIRST-YEAR SEMINARS. The freshman year is fraught with multiple hurdles to success as students make the transition from home, family, and structure to separation, strangers, and freedom—not to speak of the challenges of a different academic environment and a new set of systems, policies, and procedures to learn (Pickering, Calliotte, and McAuliffe, 1992; Pascarella, 1991). Many students require the guidance, knowledge, and skills found in courses specifically designed for the first-year student, and all students can benefit from the connections to persons, places, and concepts that such courses provide. Studies show that when students are given a formal introduction to college, they are more likely to experience satisfaction and graduate (Bean and Metzner, 1985).

The implementation of first-year seminars to augment the initial orientation experience is now commonplace in higher education. These formal experiences are commonly offered in the form of courses or seminars (Upcraft and Gardner, 1989; National Resource Center for the First-Year Experience and Students in Transition, 2001), and they usually incorporate three fairly discrete topic areas: (1) an orientation to the systems, resources, facilities, policies, and procedures of the institution, with some emphasis on time management, educational planning, goal setting, and decision making, (2) a focus on the theory and application of various learning strategies, and (3) career exploration—an examination of the student's strengths, weaknesses, interests, and abilities in relation to the world of work, to help students choose a major and career direction. According to the 2000 *National Survey of First-Year Seminar Programming,* conducted by the National Center for the First-Year Experience and Students in Transition, approximately 74 percent of colleges and universities offer an extended orientation or college survival seminar. Nearly 89 percent of these offer the experience for credit toward graduation, and 50 percent require the seminar for all first-year students.

To provide flexibility in serving the needs of all students, one suggested model is to offer the seminar in three one-credit modules. For example, all three modules might be required for students who need developmental or remedial education. For other students, whose entering profiles suggest a need for study skills development, as well as for students who simply want to improve those skills, a course that covers time management, reading comprehension, test taking, concentration, motivation, and note taking can make the difference between academic good standing and probation. And students struggling to choose a major or wanting to take an informed approach to career planning are prime candidates for the module in career exploration. These courses may be combined into one three-credit course, one or two may be taken at a time, or the courses may be started in the summer, with the first "orientation" module being offered as an early start program. This gives students an opportunity to move in early and adjust to the college experience prior to the fall term (Carranza, 2000).

Studies show that students make a decision to stay or drop out of college during the first part of their freshman year and that whether they have made an academic or social integration into the institution is important to that decision (Tinto, 1993). The connections made with students, faculty members, and other institutional personnel during first-year experience programs and early start programs help with this essential integration, thereby reducing attrition (Barefoot and others, 1998). Given the complexity of today's entering students, all institutions of higher education should offer a structured freshman year experience for all students.

Academic Strategies

Within the literature are numerous illustrations of programs that support the learning and the emotional needs of students. These can be complex comprehensive learning centers, tutorials, or learning communities.

These services and learning strategies may vary from comprehensive, centralized learning centers to a combination of academic support services and library resources (for example, the learning resource center), or they may vary from independent tutorial centers, writing centers, or supplemental instruction centers to college- or department-based services.

Comprehensive Learning Centers

Many colleges and universities have created comprehensive learning centers to house various components of academic assistance or learning enhancement. Depending on the nature and needs of the institution's entering students, these centers may contain programming to serve students at both ends of the learning continuum—those who require remediation, academic support, and intrusive advisement in order to make a successful transition into college and those who desire academic and learning enhancement services in order to excel academically (Commander, Stratton, Callahan, and Smith, 1996). Core features of these centers include both remedial and developmental coursework, tutorial interventions, supplemental instruction, and advising services.

The terms *remedial* and *developmental* are often confused or misunderstood in higher education (Boylan and Bonham, 1994a). In remedial coursework, students are repeating concepts and basic skills that should have been mastered prior to matriculation (Higbee, 1993). Developmental education, however, refers to "a field of practice and research within higher education with a theoretical foundation in developmental psychology and learning theory. It promotes the cognitive and affective growth of *all* postsecondary learners, at *all levels* of the learning continuum" (National Association for the Development of Education, 2002, p. 1). By this definition, remedial education is but one part of the developmental continuum and is only one aspect of developmental education. In other words, developmental education seeks to "help the under-prepared student prepare, the prepared student advance, and the advanced student excel" (National Association for the Development of Education, 2002, p. 1). Therefore, all students can benefit from courses and programs that address a particular learning need or learning enhancement.

REMEDIAL CURRICULUM. Students who enter higher education with poor academic backgrounds and with low SAT or ACT scores are usually in need of some measure of remediation. An effective testing, orientation, and advising program will seamlessly place students into these courses when appropriate. The focus of remedial work is usually in the basic skills areas of mathematics, reading, and writing.

The typical remedial math curriculum reviews arithmetic skills and basic and intermediate algebra skills, which will prepare students to be successful in the standard math curriculum required by their major course of study. The goal of reading remediation is to raise students' comprehension and reading skills to the desired level of an entering college freshman. Writing ability is a bit more subjective to judge, but, generally, a student who requires work in reading will also benefit from work on basic writing skills. A typical remedial curriculum will include two or three courses in math, one or two in reading, and one or two in writing (Maxwell, 1979, 1994a). These courses often carry nongraduating credit.

Remedial courses have proven to be effective. Studies show that 70 percent of students who complete a remedial course are successful at the C level or better in the follow-up course in the standard curriculum (Boylan and Bonham, 1994b).

DEVELOPMENTAL CURRICULUM. The freshman seminar courses discussed earlier are an example of a developmental curriculum. They can be of benefit to all new students; but for the underprepared, "at-risk" student, they are essential. Such a course or series of courses focuses on orientation, goal setting, decision making, learning strategies, and career topics. These not only prepare students to deal with the college experience more effectively but also offer an opportunity for students to develop relationships with people and become aware of resources that can make the difference between early success and untimely failure (Carranza, 1998).

One way to increase the effectiveness of such courses is to link instruction with advisement. In this model, the instructors also act as educational counselors or academic advisers to students enrolled in their individual seminars, monitoring students' academic progress as they move through the first year and adding outside conferencing and application requirements, depending on the students' individual needs.

Tutorials and Other Academic Interventions

Many types of interventions beyond formal coursework are found in most comprehensive learning centers or as stand-alone services offered by academic departments and student services (Maxwell, 1979, 1994a). These include one-on-one or group tutorials, homework-helper and supplemental instruction sessions, and workshops (Maxwell, 1994b; Martin and Arendale, 1993; Commander, Stratton, Callahan, and Smith, 1996).

ONE-ON-ONE AND GROUPS SESSIONS. Tutorial services can be delivered in one-on-one or small group sessions, arranged by appointment or on a walk-in basis. Some tutoring can take place in the classroom. This is especially true, for example, in the remedial classes, where doing is more important than listening. The service may be limited to those courses in which students experience the most failure—usually introductory, liberal studies or general studies requirements. The increasing need for help with mathematics and writing has led many centers to develop independent math or writing centers or labs (Maxwell, 1994b; Roueche and Roueche, 1993).

HOMEWORK HELPERS. Homework helper sessions are effective for promoting a proactive approach to studies. Here, students attend regularly scheduled sessions to do their daily homework, where tutors circulate to provide assistance, students work together, and problems can be solved before they becoming major barriers to success.

SUPPLEMENTAL INSTRUCTION. Because of its proven effectiveness, supplemental instruction (SI) is a growing academic support program, used in more than eight hundred higher education institutions. SI has certain advantages over other support activities because its emphasis is on the high-risk nature of a course rather than on the high-risk academic profile of students.

Courses that have high rates of D, F, and withdrawal grades are targeted to receive SI support, which is provided in out-of-class sessions by SI leaders—students who have previously done well in the class. These leaders are trained to lead students to identify their own problems, work collaboratively to find solutions, and develop learning strategies while mastering the course content. According to studies conducted by the University of Missouri-Kansas City (1996), "research suggests that the learning strategies and critical thinking skills students develop through SI are transferred to future academic work" (p. 109). Furthermore, studies show that SI can be an effective programming strategy for both academically at-risk and minority students (Maxwell, 1997). Also, the mean grade point averages for students who participate in SI are significantly higher than those of students who do not, student satisfaction and retention are increased (Arendale, 1996; Kluepfel, Parelius, and Roberts, 1994; Simmons, 1994).

STUDY SKILLS WORKSHOPS. An efficient way to address the learning needs of students is to offer a variety of study skills workshops where students may select from an array of topics to meet their individual interests or needs. These small group workshops may deal with the traditional study strategies found in a formal semester-long course (for example, note and test taking and listening skills), but in separate, one-hour sessions. The workshop format also allows for the delivery of special interest topics, to help students manage stress, midterm exams, slumping motivation, math anxiety, or self-monitoring and self-evaluation efforts.

Campuswide Retention Efforts

Services, supports, and interventions that work for underprepared students have benefits for better-prepared students as well. In fact, often, the better student is often the first to access services such as tutoring, homework helpers, and SI to excel (Maxwell, 1994b). In addition to these standard academic support services, educational designs that form students into a learning community can be incorporated into the curriculum for students at all levels of the learning continuum and are now widespread in many colleges and universities.

Learning communities may be formed through the creation of linked courses, clustered courses, coordinated studies, or residence hall arrangements (Terenzini, 1984; Tinto, 1994a, 1994b; Zeller, Fidler, and Barefoot, 1996). Learning communities may be formed using simple arrangements (such as two linked courses) or complex arrangements (such as a cohort of developmental students who move together through the entire freshman year), or they may be developed in an individual classroom through the efforts of a faculty member who involves students together in the activity of learning (Wilcox and others, 1997; Tinto, 1999).

Learning communities promote collaborative learning among the participants, engaging students in learning experiences that promote shared knowledge, learning, and responsibility (Tinto, 1999).

Linked courses. This form of a learning community is created when courses are "linked." In linked courses, the same students are enrolled together in two courses for which the instructors work together to coordinate content areas and develop assignments and activities that complement and reinforce the skills or knowledge of each other. For example, an effective combination for underprepared students might link a reading course with a social studies or history course—a course that requires the student to accomplish many and varied kinds of reading tasks. Studies show that students who are enrolled in linked courses have higher gain scores in reading and higher average grades in the content course, compared with students who are not enrolled in linked courses (Lipsky, 2001).

Cluster courses. In cluster courses, students are enrolled together in three or more courses that often are delivered around a common theme, promoting the students' ability to draw associations between different content areas. For example, students may be enrolled in a cluster of courses in writing, art, and history—a cluster connected by the theme A Cultural Perspective of the Human Body. Students in cluster courses may be asked to live in the same residence hall, be encouraged to study together, and be assigned projects as groups.

Freshman interest groups. Another model links a studies skills course with the content of another course, such as a history, science, or language course, adding SI as an out-of-class option. Freshmen who are members of a freshman interest group would attend a large group lecture class but would be divided into small groups for discussion sessions led by a graduate student or student leader (Tinto, 1994b).

Coordinated study groups. In this arrangement, students are enrolled together in the same two or three introductory courses, such as biology, sociology, and psychology (Wilcox and others, 1997; Tinto, 1999). Any of these arrangements offers many opportunities to incorporate other collaborative activities into the learning experience, such as SI, study groups, or common residence hall arrangements for the participants.

Residence life/specialty floors. Colleges and universities with residential facilities can promote student success through the use of various living arrangements. Students sharing the same residential facility are, after all, members of a common community. It is a natural step to arrange students to create a living/learning environment.

Specialty floors are one such example. Here, students are encouraged to select a housing assignment based on their major course of study or some other shared goal, such as the decision to avoid the use of tobacco, alcohol, and drugs or a desire to inhabit an intensive study environment. With the living arrangement as a basis, shared learning can easily be built into the design. For example, when students in the same major occupy a common space, tutorial services, SI sessions, and visits from faculty members can be easily arranged. Students may form study groups, simultaneously immersing themselves in their academics and building social connections.

Students in developmental education programs may begin with a summer program that builds from a living/learning arrangement. And honors college students may inhabit the same floor or building as they move through an honors curriculum.

Linking of Services to Students

As explained at the outset, much of the work of linking students to the various systems, resources, and services of the institution will take place automatically and seamlessly if the institution has identified the nature and needs of its entering students prior to their matriculation and has engaged in coordinated behind-the-scenes planning. Coordination is best accomplished through an approach that includes global leadership, team effort, and individual responsibility. This approach must be supplemented by both traditional and new methods of communication. In addition, such communication must be formative and summative, culminating in followup efforts to identify strengths and weaknesses and make recommendations for the future.

Global Interactions and Connecting Bodies

Every institution needs to have a global, campuswide committee for communicating and collaborating. Formal, ongoing communication among relevant constituents of the campus community is essential for both planning and troubleshooting on all matters relevant to the smooth operation of the institution. Such a committee creates and sustains connections to identify and solve problems, generate operational calendars, examine policy, and establish procedures. Membership should include representatives from every system, office, resource, and constituent. This kind of campuswide "troubleshooting group" can reinforce ongoing processes and policies and tackle the challenges of change. For example, if a new group of students is arriving for an early entrance program, financial aid will need to determine if the program qualifies for aid, accounts receivable will need to know how to bill the students, residence life will need to know where to house them, scheduling needs to know when to register them, the registrar needs to know when to record grades, and so on. This kind of mechanism promotes communication and collaboration in student services.

Governing Bodies

Each institution has its own methods of governing. In addition to provosts, vice presidents, deans, and chairs, there are faculty or university senates, faculty and staff unions, student congresses, departments, councils, and committees. All of these groups meet, discuss, argue, and make decisions. All of these groups have the responsibility for communicating their deliberations and decisions to the campuswide community through open meetings, published agendas, minutes, and other public forms of communication. It goes without saying that representatives on the global communicating body and the governing bodies have a responsibility to inform their respective constituents regarding the discussions and decisions of these larger networks; senate representatives must report to their departments, union representatives must report to their membership, chairs must report to their faculty, and so on.

Teams

Like a good committee, a team can bring together the best ideas of the individual, combined with the powerful efforts of the whole group. Unlike the typical committee, however, a team comes from a particular office, system, or resource, and each member has a stake in the image and operation of that unit. Having a stake in the outcome leads to responsibility and engenders satisfaction when a job is well done. Leaders who create a team approach to planning and implementation can and do contribute to the satisfaction of both students and staff members.

Communication Mechanisms

The challenges to effective communication and collaboration are as varied as the types of institutions themselves. Certainly, the larger the academy, the more challenging the task of coordinating and informing its members becomes. Technology has given us many ways to communicate. E-mail has many advantages over the former, slower ways of communicating. E-mail is great for attaching minutes, sending flyers, making mass announcements, or replacing the phone call. Campus newspapers, magazines, and newsletters should not be overlooked as forms of information distribution. And, of course, there is the campus Web site for posting all manner of information. Whether or not the material is accessed is always a question, and maintaining an accurate and up-to-date Web site can be time-consuming and costly. Also, with so much information to peruse, important information could become lost on the site. Face-to-face and telephone communication still work best for many purposes. In the end, no method should be overlooked. The more approaches used, the better the chances for success.

Directors, Heads, and Leaders

In addition, every system, office, service, and resource must have strong, responsible leadership—someone who assumes full and ultimate responsibility not only for the operation, its efforts, and outcomes but also for providing accurate and timely information concerning its functions. Even with global mechanisms and high-profile governing bodies, someone still needs to be in charge to delegate roles and responsibilities, organize additional informational meetings, generate memorandums, make phone calls, write e-mails, and double-check everything. In the end, someone has to count the donuts.

Staffing Considerations

As has been described, many programs can be designed and implemented to support student learning and academic success. Most require additional human resources to augment the traditional faculty. In addition, faculty members will need to offer additional services beyond course scheduling during their academic advising sessions with students if the interventions designed are to reach those students who need them. These human resources and advising requirements can be enhanced through the use of undergraduate peer educators and programs that promote developmental advising.

Peer Educators

At many points of the academic support effort, institutions can take advantage of student peer educators. The literature is rich with examples of successful undergraduate peer educators offering academic services to their peers (Hamid, 2001). As a human resource, student helpers can provide an inexpensive means for supporting many of the activities to serve students. Because they are positive role models, their presence can have a powerful public relations component and a positive influence on both students and parents (Ender and Keaghan, 2001).

Student undergraduates may function as ambassadors, tour leaders, orientation leaders, student panelists, peer advisers, peer tutors, SI leaders, workshops leaders, or in-class tutors. Selection and training are critical to the success of this type of staffing intervention. (Ender and Newton, 2000; Hamid, 2001). With appropriate training, undergraduate students may have a more powerful influence on their peers than do professional educators (Ender and Winston, 1984; Ender and Newton, 2000).

Developmental Advising

Developmental advising is not new to higher education. Several authors have suggested, over the years, that this more holistic approach to academic advising enhances the overall well-being of undergraduates (Gordon and Habley, 2000). As mentioned earlier, one model connects the faculty adviser to the student, both formally and informally, by giving the faculty member a dual role: academic adviser plus instructor for the student's freshmen seminar or orientation course. In this way, student and adviser will meet many more times than in the more common model where students and advisers meet infrequently, often only for course advisement for scheduling purposes.

Whether formal or informal or department-, college-, or center-based, the most effective approach to advising is for the faculty member to be able to take an educational counseling approach to advising, where monitoring the student's progress becomes a key component in the interaction. As with the other academic services, advising of this type requires communication and interaction among many parties (other faculty members, peer helpers, academic support coordinators, and so on) to achieve the best result for the individual student. Appropriate developmental advising continually assesses student needs and links students to appropriate campus services and interventions (Ender and Wilkie, 2000).

Evaluation

For any system to work efficiently and effectively, it is necessary to have a plan of evaluation on which responsible decision making and ongoing refinement may be based. A realistic plan must include a comprehensive system of data collection and analysis. It is the responsibility of every office, agent, or system in the campus community to collect data that relate to its area or to see that the institution has a system for providing the required information. Without this essential information, it is impossible to know the value and effectiveness of its activities or to communicate its needs or ideas to others.

Outcomes will be based on an analysis of the various data. It is important not to miss important sources of information such as the kind that can be collected from students and parents on satisfaction surveys or from personnel involved in the processes. With comprehensive data to draw upon, research models at any level of sophistication may be employed in an attempt to determine the value or effectiveness of a particular service (Schuh and Upcraft, 1996). At the same time, simple forms of information such as an ongoing list of things that misfired or didn't measure up (change lists) can be essential in maintaining a continuous improvement stance.

Refining student services requires evaluation, data, and outcomes assessment. In addition, the process of refinement or continuous improvement calls upon the same teamwork that is required to provide seamless service in the first place. Each agency must work within its own area to perfect its efforts and must also be engaged in contributing to the team approach of determining the nature and needs of students, developing the academic and other support services to meet those needs, and evaluating the outcomes.

Conclusion

Successful learning interventions mandate cooperation and collaboration across campus. From institutional research to the delivery of the intervention, the process requires the tremendous combined efforts of many campus departments and services, as the outcomes for students are well worth the effort and attention. Students admitted to higher education deserve the opportunity to experience success. Many do not arrive with the prerequisite academic or emotional tools to compete successfully. Higher education has the responsibility to ensure that this opportunity to compete is provided.

REFERENCES

Arendale, T. (ed.). "Key Elements of Supplementary Instruction." *Learning & Study Skills SPIN Newsletter,* 1996, *19*(4), 2, 8.

Astin, A. W. *Predicting Academic Performance in College: Selectivity Data for 2300 American Colleges.* New York: Free Press, 1971.

Astin, A. W. "A Look at Pluralism in the Contemporary Student Population." *NASPA Journal,* 1984, *21*(3), 2–11.

Barefoot, B. O., and others. *Exploring the Evidence: Reporting Outcomes of Freshman Seminars.* The Freshman Year Experience, Vol. II, no. 25. Columbia, S.C.: University of South Carolina, National Resource Center for the Freshman Year Experience, 1998.

Bartlett, T. "Freshman Pay, Mentally and Physically, as They Adjust to Life in College." *Chronicle of Higher Education,* Feb. 1, 2002, p. 35.

Bean, J. G., and Metzner, B. S. "A Conceptual Model of Nontraditional Undergraduate Student Attrition." *Review of Educational Research,* 1985, *55,* 485–540.

Boylan, H. R., and Bonham, B. S. "Seven Myths About Developmental Education." *Research and Training in Development Education,* 1994a, 10(2), 5–11.

Boylan, H. R., and Bonham, B. S. "The Impact of Development Education Programs." In M. Maxwell (ed.), *From Access to Success.* Clearwater, Fla.: H&H Publishing, 1994b.

Braxton, J. M. *Reworking the Student Departure Puzzle.* Nashville, Tenn.: Vanderbilt University Press, 2000.

Carranza, C. "Developmental Students' Perceptions of the Factors That Contribute to Academic Success." Published doctoral dissertation, Department of Educational Leadership, Grambling State University. Ann Arbor, Mich.: UMI Dissertation Services, 1998.

Carranza, C. "CUSP: The College Undergraduate Success Program." *FYE,* 2000, *13*(2), 3, 10.

Commander, N., Stratton, C., Callahan, C., and Smith, B. "A Learning Assistance Model for Expanding Academic Support." *Journal of Developmental Education,* 1996, 20(2), 8–14.

Ender, S. C., and Keaghan, K. "Peer Leadership Programs: A Rationale and Review of the Literature." In S. H. Hamid (ed.), *Peer Leadership: A Primer on Program Essentials.* Monograph, no. 32. Columbia, S.C.: University of South Carolina, National Resource Center for the First-Year Experience and Students in Transition 2001.

Ender, S. C., and Newton, F. B. *Students Helping Students: A Guide for Peer Educators on College Campuses.* San Francisco: Jossey-Bass, 2000.

Ender, S. C., and Wilkie, C. J. "Advising Students with Special Needs." In V. N. Gordon and W. R. Habley (eds.), *Academic Advising: A Comprehensive Handbook.* San Francisco: Jossey Bass, 2000.

Ender, S. C., and Winston, R. B., Jr. (eds). *Students as Paraprofessional Staff.* New Directions for Student Services,, no. 17. San Francisco: Jossey-Bass, 1984.

Forbes, K. J. "Students and Their Parents: Where Do Campuses Fit In?" *About Campus,* 2001, Sept.–Oct., 11–17.

Gordon, V., Habley, W., and Associates. *Academic Advising: A Comprehensive Handbook.* San Francisco: Jossey-Bass, 2000.

Hamid, S. H. (ed.). *Peer Leadership, a Primer on Program Essentials.* Monograph no. 32. Columbia, S.C.: University of South Carolina, National Resource Center for the First-Year Experience & Students in Transition, 2001.

Higbee, J. "Developmental Versus Remedial: More Than Semantics." *Research and Teaching in Developmental Educational,* 1993, *9*(2), 99–105.

Kluepfel, G., Parelius, R., and Roberts, G. "Involving Faculty in Retention." *Journal of Developmental Education,* 1994, *17*(3), 16–26.

Lipsky, S. "Enhancing Students' Academic Performance via Supplemental Instruction and Linked Courses." *The Act 101 Journal,* 2001, *17*(1), 3–6.

Lowery, J. "The Millennials Come to Campus." *About Campus,* 2001, July–Aug., 6–12.

Martin, D. C., and Arendale, D. R. *Supplemental Instruction: Improving First-Year Student Success in High-Risk Courses.* The Freshman Year Experience, no. 7. Columbia, S.C.: University of South Carolina, National Resource Center for the Freshman Year Experience, 1993.

Maxwell, M. *Improving Student Learning Skills.* San Francisco: Jossey-Bass, 1979.

Maxwell, M. "Does Tutoring Help? A Look at the Literature." In M. Maxwell (ed.), *From Access to Success.* Clearwater, Fla.: H&H Publishing, 1994a.

Maxwell, M. *From Access to Success: A Book of Readings on College Developmental Education and Learning Assistance Programs.* Clearwater, Fla.: H&H Publishing, 1994b.

Maxwell, M. "Successful Programs and Strategies for Teaching High-Risk College Students." In M. Maxwell (ed.), *Improving Student Learning Skills.* (2nd ed.) Clearwater, Fla.: H&H Publishing, 1997.

Mortenson, T. *Postsecondary Education Opportunity,* no. 66. Oskaloosa, Iowa: The Mortenson Research Seminar on Public Policy Analysis of Opportunity for Postsecondary Education, 1997.

Mortenson, T. *Postsecondary Education Opportunity,* no. 110. Oskaloosa, Iowa: The Mortenson Research Seminar on Public Policy Analysis of Opportunity for Postsecondary Education, 2001.

National Association for the Development of Education. "NADE Developmental Education Definition and Goals." Presented at the National Association for Developmental Education Conference, Orlando, Fla., Mar. 2002.

National Resource Center for the First-Year Experience and Students in Transition. 2000 *National Survey of First-Year Seminar Programming.* [http://www.sc.edu/fye/research/surveys/survey00.htm]. Apr. 2001.

Newton, F. "The Stressed Student." *About Campus,* 1998, *3*(2), 4–10.

Pascarella, E. T. "The Impact of College on Students: The Nature of the Evidence." *Review of Higher Education,* 1991, *14*(4), 53–66.

Pickering, J. W., Calliotte, J. A., and McAuliffe, G. J. "The Effect of Noncognitive Factors on Freshman Academic Performance and Retention." *Journal of the Freshman Year Experience,* 1992, *4*(2), 7–30.

Roueche, J., and Roueche, S. *Between a Rock and a Hard Place: The At-Risk Student in the Open-Door College.* Washington, D.C.: Community College Press, 1993.

Schuh, J., and Upcraft, M. *Assessment in Student Affairs.* San Francisco: Jossey-Bass, 1996.

Simmons, R. "Precollege Programs: A Contributing Factor to University Student Retention." *Journal of Developmental Education,* 1994, *17*(3), 42–45.

Terenzini, P. T. "Freshman Attrition and the Residential Context." *The Review of Higher Education,* 1984, *7*(2), 111–124.

Tinto, V. "Retention: An Admission Concern." *College and University,* 1986, *61,* 290–293.

Tinto, V. *Leaving College: Rethinking the Causes and Cures of Student Attrition.* (4th ed.) Chicago, Ill.: University of Chicago Press, 1993.

Tinto, V. "Coordinated Studies Programs: Their Effect on Student Involvement at a Community College." *Community College Review,* 1994a, *22*(2), 16–25.

Tinto, V. "Freshman Interest Groups and the First-Year Experience: Constructing Student Communities in Large University." *Journal of the Freshman Year Experience,* 1994b, *6*(1), 7–28.

Tinto, V. "Taking Retention Seriously: Rethinking the First Year of College." *NACADA Journal,* 1999, *19*(2), 5–9.

University of Missouri-Kansas City. *Supplemental Instruction Supervisor Manual.* Kansas City: University of Missouri-Kansas City, 1996.

Upcraft, M. L., and Gardner, J. N. *The Freshman Year Experience: Helping Students Survive and Succeed in College.* San Francisco: Jossey-Bass, 1989.

U.S. Department of Education. *A Nation at Risk: The Imperative for Educational Reform.* Superintendent of Documents. Washington D.C.: Government Printing Office, 1983.

U.S. Department of Education. *Students with Disabilities in Postsecondary Education: A Profile of Preparation, Participation, and Outcomes.* Statistical Analysis Report. Washington, D.C.: Government Printing Office, 1999.

Weidlein, E. (ed.). *Chronicle of Higher Education: Almanac Issue 2001–02.* Vol. XLVIII. Washington, D.C.: Chronicle of Higher Education, 2001.

Wilcox, K., and others. "The 'Package Course' Experience and Developmental Education." *Journal of Developmental Education,* 1997, *20*(3), 18–27.

Zeller, W. J., Fidler, D. S., and Barefoot, B. O. *Residence Life Programs and the First-Year Experience.* The Freshman Year Experience, no. 5. Columbia, S.C.: University of South Carolina, National Resource Center for the Freshman Year Experience and Students in Transition, 1996.

15

STUDENT DIVERSITY AND ACADEMIC SERVICES

BALANCING THE NEEDS OF ALL STUDENTS

Vasti Torres

IF ALL COLLEGE STUDENTS were homogenous, high-achieving, and high-income, and had parents with a high level of education, most colleges would not have to deal with retention issues. Diversity in our student body makes higher education in the United States unique and also presents many challenges for academic services practitioners. From 1990 to 2000, the number of people from diverse races and ethnicity in the United States increased by more than twenty-four million people (U.S. Census Bureau, 2000). This is further highlighted when viewed through percentage increases for each group. Whereas non-Latino whites increased by 5.9 percent, Latinos increased by 57.9 percent, Asian Americans increased by 48.3 percent, American Indians increased by 26.4 percent, and African Americans increased by 15.6 percent (U.S. Census Bureau, 2000). It is clear that the U.S. population is racially and ethnically more diverse and that diversity is likely to increase during the twenty-first century.

In addition to racial and ethnic diversity, higher education must serve groups of students, such as nontraditional, disabled, and international students, which are not highlighted in the census. Murdock and Hoque (1999) have written that early in the twenty-first century, "31.2% of the net increase in [higher education] enrollment [would] be due to students 30 years of age or older" (p. 10). This mixture of diversity continues with the growing number of disabled and international students. In 1994, it was estimated that 10.3 percent of the students in higher education would report having at least one disability (Paul, 2000). From 1990 to 2000, the international student population increased by over 140,000. This is a 1 percent increase in ten years (Institute of International Education, 2001). With this influx of diversity into higher education, it is difficult for any college to effectively serve *all* students, yet colleges have the responsibility of promoting the educational success these diverse students need in today's society. For this reason, colleges must face the changing nature of diversity and prepare to meet the demands of the growing diverse population.

The goal of this chapter is to get practitioners to think through how their academic services support and integrate the needs of diverse students. In order to fulfill this goal, research conducted specifically with diverse populations is presented within each of the following sections. The first section focuses on defining diversity and ways to assess if a college has a campuswide approach to serving diverse students. The second section reviews the research on diverse student populations and discusses what we know about academic success for such groups. And the final section provides a summary of recommendations that are extracted from proven approaches to create an inclusive and supportive environment for all students. Because diversity is an issue of great magnitude for higher education, it is impossible to address every need in one chapter. For this reason, this chapter should be seen as a starting point for exploring how the institution can approach issues of diversity.

Defining Diversity

Federal mandates, regional accreditation, national associations, state policymakers, the court system, and institutional leaders use various definitions when discussing the concepts involved in diversity. This confusion has created an additional hurdle for diversity efforts on many campuses. Visual diversity is the easiest and most commonly used definition. This would include those who can be identified as being from a minority culture, either visually or by their surnames. This type of diversity is also referred to as a structural diversity, which is the numerical demonstration of racial and ethnic groups (Hurtado, Milem, Clayton-Pedersen, and Allen, 1999). A predominantly white institution with little visual diversity on campus or in the surrounding community may decide that there is no need to consider diversity in the delivery of services, yet it would be ignoring entire segments of diverse students, such as adult, learning-disabled (especially undiagnosed), or first-generation college students. Relying solely on federal definitions or visual diversity may not result in an environment supportive of all students.

The first step in creating a supportive environment for all is to assess the needs of current and potential students at the institution. This process should be seen as identifying a community-based definition of diversity. Community-based definitions incorporate local, state, and regional needs with those of current students, resulting in a campus that can serve all constituents in the community. By incorporating community needs—be they college, town, state, regional, or national, diversity efforts can be more accurately tailored to the institution's community-based definition of diversity, rather than to broad state or federal goals. For the most part, campus dialogues on diversity are focused on national or state goals related to visual diversity. Although those goals are critical to advancing education and democracy, it is critical that each institution define how it will contribute to this goal within its own context.

The second step in creating a supportive environment for all students is to have the institution's definition of diversity infused into the campus community as a whole, rather than just into one office. The mission of an institution identifies what is and is *not* valued by the campus community (Smith, 1999). An important aspect in helping diverse students succeed is for all student support offices to understand how the institution's diversity goals are integrated into the campus values—and also into their daily practice. Student retention programs are more likely to work when they are seen as a vital part of the college mission (Nettles, Wagener, Millett, and Killenbeck, 1999). Diverse students can perceive institutional values in both positive and negative ways (Smith, 1999). For this reason it is critical that an institution understand the impact of its values on diverse populations. Rather than assuming that only the offices concerned with minority students, or disabled students, or international students, or commuter students will take care of special populations, it should be remembered that every office on campus must assess how its services and policies affect all students. This does not mean that the special population offices should be dissolved; rather, it places the responsibility for student success on the entire campus and not just on those directly involved with the diverse student experience. This collaboration throughout the college is critical to creating a seamless learning environment for all students (Joint Task Force on Student Learning, 1998). How to create this type of collaboration is contextual, and every college may take a different approach to making such a collaboration appropriate to the campus culture.

The key question to ask in order to evaluate whether your institution maintains a supportive environment that emphasizes collaboration between offices and administrators is, how well do those new to the institution recognize these efforts? Most practitioners think they are providing a collaborative environment for students and that they understand the importance of collaboration. Yet few assess whether diverse students perceive that collaborative environment when they interact with various campus offices. Research has found that certain ethnic groups of students (black, Latino, and white) perceived less racial tension on campuses that were perceived to be student-centered (Hurtado, 1992). Student-centered campuses are those that convey a supportive environment for both the academic and the personal development of students (Hurtado, Milem, Clayton-Pedersen, and Allen, 1999). Colleges where a new student or staff member can clearly respond to the questions that follow are likely to be perceived as successful in creating a supportive, student-centered environment for all students.

o Are students clear about how to proceed through the academic maze? How is this information disseminated?

o Is there intentional outreach to first-year students who may not understand processes? Is the information free of academic lingo that a first-generation or international college student may not understand?

o Can all faculty members and academic advisers articulate what services (with locations and phone numbers) are available for students with special needs?

o How is the communication and collaboration between faculty members and academic services offices maintained?

o How often do you assess how your campus environment is perceived by new students?

These questions can help academic services professionals begin to determine if the environment on their campus truly supports all students. This type of internal audit can help a campus strengthen its collaborative endeavors and in turn create a supportive environment for diverse students. Without collaboration between the faculty and the administration, the student experience is fragmented. This fragmentation is even harder on diverse students who are not familiar with the academic culture or the unstated values of higher education. Once the audit is complete, the next step is to think about what diverse students need in order to transform the institution so that it meets those needs.

Promoting Success for Diverse Students

Much of what we know about student success and retention uses statistical variables to predict college performance. What many of us do not realize is that many researchers feel that the suggested correlation of variables does not tell us enough about the choice to depart from college or about what is actually learned in college (Tinto, 1993; Astin, 1993, 1994). Retention models and theories have been tested on some diverse populations, yet many questions remain unanswered. In order to learn how these accepted models for explaining student attrition can be applied to diverse populations, one must look to research done specifically on diverse groups. It should be understood that the majority of research done on diverse populations advocates that institutions consider the interplay between the person, the institution, and external factors when developing programs for diverse students (Cabrera, Castaneda, Nora, and Hengstler, 1992). Therefore, institutions that truly wish to address diversity issues must see this as a complex process that involves the entire institution. This section presents the research on predicting academic achievement, social integration, and academic integration as it applies to diverse populations.

Predicting Academic Achievement

There is little question that, when entering college, diverse student populations, as a subgroup, tend to have lower prior academic achievement measures than their majority counterparts. Yet research indicates that these types of measures are likely to be the result of other background variables such as social economic status or parents' educational level (Hossler and Stage, 1999). These studies illustrate that academic success or educational aspirations are not a matter of race or ethnicity; rather, they are heavily influenced by many variables. The notion that better-prepared students will do better in college is not a complete picture. Several studies provide insight into factors other than academic preparation, and these should be considered when looking at academic achievement and persistence.

○ While testing a model to explain high school students' predisposition to college, Hossler and Stage (1999) found that "parents of minority students had higher educational expectations despite the fact that minority students had lower GPAs" (p. 81). This could indicate that first-generation college students, especially minority students, have parental encouragement. But those parents may not have the information or skills to help their children maneuver the maze of college life.

○ A study on Latino students in community colleges found that motivation to persist and commitment to attend college play a significant role and are directly related to persistence (Solis, 1995).

○ In a longitudinal study, Tracey and Sedlacek (1985) found that noncognitive variables, such as self-concept and understanding of and ability to cope with racism, were critical influences on the academic success of minority students. Using the same instrument, Boyer and Sedlacek (1988) found that the noncognitive variables were also effective in predicting international student grades and retention.

These findings indicate that colleges should consider variables other than those measuring prior academic achievement. These other variables also provide insight into how to help these students succeed. Though much emphasis is placed on the variables prior to entering college, there is sufficient evidence to illustrate that with academic, social, and financial support, diverse students can succeed.

For international students, the most commonly used representation for predicting academic achievement is the Test of English as a Foreign Language (TOEFL). Depending on the admissions requirements for the college, students may be determined to be either proficient or deficient in English. At times, the numerical requirement for this exam may be seen as unwelcoming and nonreflective of the institutional mission (Ewing, 1992). Regardless of the numerical scores, many of these students will still need further help with acculturation, writing, and classroom expectations. Though TOEFL scores are worth considering, it certainly is not the only admissions variable that should be considered.

For disabled students, a college education can be seen as a way to improve their value to society. For this reason, disabled students are three times as likely to enroll in higher education programs (Paul, 2000). Though not all of these students will be degree-seeking, they will still become part of the college community and thereby affect the nature and level of the services provided.

The common thread in all of these studies is the need to look beyond the numbers in order to gain a broader understanding of how to help diverse students succeed. This closer examination requires that practitioners consider the research on social and academic integration as well as the openness of the campus culture.

Social Integration

Most practitioners assume that a supportive social community prevents or reduces the stress of college life and therefore benefits the retention of students. Yet many studies show that social community support comes primarily from formal involvement in extracurricular activities. Though this type of involvement should be encouraged and seems to promote greater attachment to the institution (Astin, 1993), it should not be seen as the only form of social integration for diverse students.

One of the significant issues in the social integration of diverse students is the possibility of having to deal with discrimination and prejudice. In a single institution study conducted on racially and ethnically diverse students, Nora and Cabrera (1996) found that minority students "were more likely to perceive a discriminatory campus climate, sensed more prejudices on the part of faculty and staff, and were more prone to report negative in-class experiences than were whites" (p. 130). Further analysis confirmed that discrimination and prejudice negatively affect minority students' adjustment to college. It should also be noted that these and other researchers found that other factors (performance in college, parental encouragement, and positive experiences with academic and social realms) are much more influential in predicting academic success, indicating that discrimination and prejudice do not have the "overwhelming effect" (p. 141) many might presume (Nora and Cabrera, 1996; Eimers and Pike, 1996). These two studies also found that parental support and encouragement were important in helping students adjust to college and in assisting with their commitment to complete a college degree. This finding was found to be true for both minority and white students, which conflicts with some traditional notions of the benefit of disengagement from parental influences during the developmental process (Chickering and Reisser, 1993).

In the community college setting, Nora and Rendon (1996) found that social integration was not as crucial for Latinos. This finding may be a result of the nonresidential nature of the campus or the fact that many community college students are more likely to be nontraditional students. Older students seem to attend college for specific reasons and are less likely to look for social support within the college (Cross, 1991). For the most part, their support system is already established, and many do not recognize the need to establish a support network for their academic endeavors.

Though there is wide diversity among international students. Studies on specific populations provide insight into their experiences. In a study comparing American students with Japanese students at several institutions in a metropolitan area, Kinoshita and Bowman (1998) found that Japanese students demonstrated and expressed greater anxiety and difficulty in social and personal settings. These findings could indicate that international students are likely to experience anxiety as they adjust to differences in teaching styles in the United States, as well as differences in social expectations, finances, and language (Parr, Bradley, and Bingi, 1992; Selvadurai, 1991).

Issues surrounding the social integration of disabled students can cover many different realms. Disabled students can experience an internal conflict between their desire to be independent and their desire to use services and accommodations available to them (Paul, 2000). This conflict can also influence the availability of research on this type of student. Recently, several unpublished dissertations have focused on disabled students, and from those studies, we know that disabled students encounter barriers, such as lack of understanding and cooperation from administrators, faculty members, and other students, as well as physical barriers within school buildings and the lack of adaptive aids. These conflicts, as well as the fact that disability services tend to focus mainly on accommodations and not on social interactions, can be seen as some of the reasons why disabled students have reported lower social integration scores (Paul, 2000). Though these students may report less social integration, in a study using a small sample of hearing-impaired college students, the lower social integration scores did not influence their intention to stay in college (English, cited in Paul, 2000).

Academic Integration

Most of the research conducted with diverse populations indicates that the most influential issues in academic integration concern the role of the faculty members, the campus climate, and the creation of cognitive maps that help students navigate the college experience. From previous research studies, we recognize that minority students tend to have lower academic integration scores (Nettles, Thoeny, and Gosman, 1986; Stage, 1989) and that "academic integration was more important than entering ability in predicting first-year achievement" (Eimers and Pike, 1996, p. 17). This latter study, though, conducted at a single institution, also found that academic performance did not assist in predicting the intentions of minority students to remain or leave college, whereas academic performance did predict nonminority students' intention to stay in college. Though single institution studies can inform practice, it is important to also look at larger studies, to complete the picture of academic integration and diverse population in higher education.

In a multi-institutional study comparing black students' and white students' college achievement and experiences, Nettles, Thoeny, and Gosman (1986) found that there were significant racial differences in several predictors of college performance: type of high school attended and preparation, majority/minority status in college, where students live while in college, academic integration, feelings of discrimination, satisfaction with college, and study habits. In addition, the issue of minority status has also been investigated, showing that minority students may feel additional stress. Smedley, Myers, and Harrell (1993) found that minority status presents additional stress and is associated with increased risk for negative behavior. These findings suggest that "conflicts between academic expectations and questions about readiness to compete academically are an important additional source of academic vulnerability for these [minority] students" (p. 446). This stress is the result of minority students feeling that the college community questions their legitimacy as students. These studies illustrate the interplay between the academic integration, the campus culture, and personal concerns.

For international students, most of the academic integration issues revolve around language and the differences in educational structures in the United States. In their study of Japanese students, Kinoshita and Bowman (1998) point to students' discomfort with initiating interactions in the classroom and making classroom presentations, as well as their expectations in the teacher-student relationship, as reasons for their higher anxiety scores in academic settings.

In a single institution study on disabled students in the Southwest, Keim, McWhirter, and Bernstein (1996) found that university support programs are effective in helping students with learning disabilities. This study also advocates the use of special computer support labs and has found that students who use such services are likely to have a significantly higher academic performance.

Interestingly, the degree of autonomy that faculty members possess under academic freedom has been found to be related to disabled students' academic performance. Using qualitative methods, it has been concluded that there is a potential relationship between accommodations received, how the student approaches a faculty member, and the willingness of a faculty member to modifying his or her teaching style to meet the needs of the disabled student (Paul, 2000). This study indicates the need to educate the faculty as well as improve disabled students' communication and negotiation skills.

From the studies noted in this section, it is clear that diverse populations experience additional stressors that can influence their academic integration. In order to make a difference, academic support services must do more to address the multiple needs of diverse students.

Recommendations for Helping Diverse Populations

The main theme that runs throughout the research on diverse populations is the need to create a positive campus culture for diverse students. Significant research has been conducted on the benefits of diversity in the educational environment (Hurtado, Milem, Clayton-Pedersen, and Allen, 1999). What continues to need more review is the question of how to create a culture in which students are open to diversity and respectful of differences. Changing the campus culture is difficult and takes many years. For this reason, most colleges focus on quick hits and create programs to address the immediate needs rather than consider long-term programs to address the concerns. The following sections provide information and suggestions to assist institutions in understanding how the process of creating a supportive diverse environment can benefit both students and the faculty. Research shows that the more students interact with diverse peers through conversations on controversial issues and the more they attend cultural programs, the more likely they are to develop openness to diversity and challenge (Pascarella and others, 1996). There are three ways in which this type of interaction can be fostered: through (1) collaborative learning opportunities, (2) a developmental approach to academic advising, and (3) intentional change in the campus culture.

Collaborative Learning Opportunities

In a recent study, it was found that minorities "were more predisposed to collaborative learning than were Whites" (Cabrera and others, 2002, p. 25). This study also found that collaborative learning was the single best predictor for cognitive and affective outcomes. If a college wants to change or improve the campus climate, creating collaborative learning environments needs to be strongly considered. As a way to influence the campus culture, these learning opportunities should include multicultural educational materials to further the openness to diversity in students and faculty and staff members.

At Portland State University (PSU), the general education requirements were transformed in 1994 into the University Studies Program, which emphasizes the "abilities, knowledge and skills that would be needed for educated people to function in a modern society as life-long learners" (Portland State University, 2000, p. 3). This multidisciplinary, theme-based approach to general education has four primary goals: (1) inquiry and critical thinking, (2) communication, (3) understanding the variety of human experience, and (4) learning about ethical issues and social responsibility

(p. 4). The freshman inquiry courses are constructed to address the primary goals and are team-taught in an interdisciplinary format. In order to make this program work, the university culture had to transcend disciplinary boundaries and promote collaboration and interdisciplinary learning. Because the inquiry courses are supported by student mentors, additional classroom instruction can be conducted in a collaborative manner that is respectful of diverse learning styles. The end of freshman year course evaluations found that 84 percent of responding students agreed—or strongly agreed—that they had the opportunity to work with other students in a cooperative manner (Portland State University, 2000). This program engages the faculty in collaborative situations and encourages more student-faculty interaction through its interdisciplinary approach to general education.

The PSU example is one that has prompted a change in the culture and promoted more collaboration among faculty members and students. This kind of change in the academic culture helps diverse students by approaching learning from a more personally meaningful perspective and by creating a learning environment that fosters the success of diverse learners.

Developmental Approach to Academic Advising

It is critical that colleges understand the link between diverse student programs and the campus culture. If the entire college community does not understand this connection, then the link between formal programs and minority enrollment and retention is nebulous (Gordon, 1997). The interplay among academic, social, personal, and cultural issues is critical to diverse student success. For this reason, the concept of a developmental approach to advising (Ender, Winston, and Miller, 1984) is critical to recognizing the multiple interactions that influence the diverse student experience. Faculty members and academic advisers who understand how quality of life issues can influence the college experience are more likely to be successful with diverse students. The research presented earlier illustrates the additional stressors that diverse students experience and provides reasons for creating an advising system that looks at the *whole student* in order to promote academic success.

Northeastern Illinois University (NEIU) is a good example of how mentoring and special programs can help diverse students. In 1972, NEIU established a program that considers the whole student. Proyecto Pa'Lante (Project Moving Ahead) develops leadership in the Latino student community from the Chicago Public Schools. The program accomplishes its goal by providing personal and academic support services that promote academic achievement and persistence to graduation (Northeastern Illinois University, 2002). Students can choose to enter the program or be referred if they do not meet the general admissions requirements. Though this program works with at-risk students, the freshmen cohort in 1999 that participated in Proyecto Pa'Lante had a 4 percent higher one-year persistence rate than the general freshman cohort.

For minority students who do not qualify for Proyecto Pa'Lante, the dean of students office offers a mentoring program. Students are asked during summer orientation if they would like to sign up for a mentor. If they say yes, a staff member will assign a mentor from one of the student's areas of interest. Latino students interviewed on the campus mention either Proyecto Pa'Lante or the mentoring program as being important to their success in college (interviews with students at Northeastern Illinois University, April 9–10, 2002).

The key to the success of this program is making sure that academic advising is coordinated with orientation, tutoring, career assistance, personal counseling, and academic seminars. The advertising brochure illustrates the integration of all the issues that contribute to academic success. In addition to sections on admission requirements, the brochure includes information on financial aid, Latino involvement on campus, and academic areas of study.

It should be noted that this program is funded with institutional funds rather than soft money. This illustrates the commitment the university has toward diverse students.

Intentional Change in the Campus Culture

In order to purposely make a difference for diverse populations, colleges should consider three major strategies. The first strategy emerges from evidence that early intervention makes a difference. The second strategy focuses on the need for institutions to understand that retention is contextual and that context can best be understood through a campuswide self-study of retention efforts. The third strategy emphasizes the transition to college for first-year students.

EARLY INTERVENTION PROGRAMS. Early intervention programs come in many shapes and sizes, but their overall goal is to inform, prepare, and assist underrepresented students in higher education. Most institutions look to the federally funded TRIO or GEAR UP programs to provide this type of intervention. Locally based evaluations of these programs indicate that they make a difference (Fenske, Geranios, Keller, and Moore, 1997). Future evaluations of the GEAR UP programs will provide more information on the influence of early intervention. Other larger studies continue to indicate that the greatest influences on college attendance for many underrepresented students are social economic status (SES), student aspirations, college reputation, and college expenses (Somers, Cofer, and VanderPutten, 2002). Though colleges have little control over SES, these findings continue to advocate the need for early interventions to provide information on financial assistance, admissions processes, and realistic expectations in order to meet educational aspirations. Students born outside the United States have a greater need to receive more information at an earlier point. These students can feel alienated from the mainstream educational environment because they do not understand things that are taken for granted by those in the majority culture (Torres, 2002). The type of early intervention needed by students is dependant on the institution's community-based definition of diversity. For this reason, there is a critical need for campuswide self-assessments of retention efforts and how programs for diverse students are integrated into the campus culture.

CAMPUS SELF-STUDY OF RETENTION EFFORTS. Though there is no clear recipe for doing a self-study that purposely considers diverse populations, colleges can be intentional about including many voices by including appropriate structural representations of the diverse constituents in retention work groups. The self-study process requires a college to realistically assess its success with diverse populations, as compared with the majority population, and to honestly ask what can be done to make a difference. This approach is drastically different from saying that diverse students do not succeed here because of variables the institution cannot control. This is the easy and most commonly used response to differential retention and graduation rates. Poor, unprepared students, from any background, can succeed if an institution is genuinely willing to assist them.

In reviewing the literature, two different types of frameworks have emerged that illustrate how institutions can approach this campuswide self-assessment process. One focuses on assessing the local minority student experience and how success can be facilitated (Padilla, Trevino, Gonzalez, and Trevino, 1997); the other focuses on understanding the "dynamic interaction that occurs between students and institutional culture" (Woodard, Mallory, and DeLuca, 2001, p. 54). Each of these frameworks is based on different philosophies, yet each one offers valuable lessons for institutions wanting to understand this complex issue.

The Padilla, Trevino, Gonzalez, and Trevino model (1997) focuses on the philosophy that successful minority students can tell institutions what knowledge and actions are needed to overcome barriers. Thus the students become "experts" at being successful as students. This expertise model helps to develop a local model that specifies the knowledge and actions that successful ethnic minority students employ to overcome the barriers on their campus. The model recommends that, through qualitative methods, institutions assess compiled knowledge, which includes both theoretical (book) knowledge and heuristic (experiential) knowledge. In the validating study for this model, the authors found that there were four categories of barriers for minority students. The first were *discontinuity barriers,* which hindered students' transition from high school to college. For example the students in this study had developed an "expectational stance," meaning they expected to receive less emotional support than they had been accustomed to in their home environments (p. 130). The second category was *lack-of-nurturing barriers,* which dealt with the absence of resources on the campus to support and facilitate students' adjustment. The third category was *lack-of-presence barriers,* which were associated with the lack of minorities in university programs and curricula. The fourth category was *resource barriers,* which related to the difficulties connected to the financial aid system and other financial resources.

The goal of this local expertise model is to balance the challenges diverse populations face with sufficient support to help them develop successfully. The accurate assessment of barriers and what causes them would help an institution develop intentional programs to assist in the transition, adjustment, and retention of diverse students.

The retention self-study framework developed by Woodard, Mallory, and DeLuca (2001) focuses on the question "How can institutions better understand the interaction impacting on graduation performance?" (p. 54). This framework was developed using large, land grant research universities and is not solely for use with diverse populations. However, this framework does include student characteristics that would highlight a broad definition of diversity and can assist an institution in developing effective campuswide retention programs. The framework identifies student and institutional characteristics, as well as academic and student affairs good practices. In sharing the lessons learned from this process, the authors found several important lessons, two of which are especially pertinent. The first is that retention is locally constructed and that each institution must determine what factors and outcomes they would like to consider. The second lesson is that students do leave—and what is important to understand is whether they are leaving for the right reasons or for the wrong reasons. This requires that institutions promote better assessment and data-gathering techniques.

Which framework works for a college depends on the context and culture of the institution. What is important is that colleges assess the knowledge, experiences, and skills necessary to make sure all students succeed at their college. If a college is sincere about addressing the needs of all students, it must come to recognize how its own culture and policies can actually hurt some students while helping others.

TRANSITION TO COLLEGE. The most often used method to help students make the transition to the college environment is orientation. The goal of transition programs should be to acculturate the students to the environment and norms of the college (Jakobsen, 1991). This acculturation process is critical for diverse populations because they may not know what to expect or how to manage the academic environment. Special first-year experience programs that span beyond the initial orientation are helpful for students who are unaware of what college life is like. Though another chapter in this book covers the first-year experience, it is important to ensure that the goals of these programs are consistent with the needs of diverse populations (Zeller, Fidler, and Barefoot, 1991).

Making the College Experience Better for All Students

The myth that colleges treat all students the same, and that all students are therefore treated fairly, is inaccurate. This chapter has provided a framework to think through the issues. The hard part is getting the institution to make the necessary commitments to help all students succeed. It is important that those involved in academic services understand the need to clarify their own values regarding diverse groups and retool their thinking to serve the success of diverse populations. The need for additional training to serve diverse populations is not new (Saunders and Ervin, 1984). Academic services professionals represent one of the most important resources diverse students have on a college campus. If academic service professionals cannot have an honest dialogue about the needs of diverse students, then the college should admit that they are only paying lip service to diversity and not meeting the needs of all students.

REFERENCES

Astin, A.W. *What Matters in College.* San Francisco: Jossey-Bass, 1993.

Astin, A. "Educational Equity and the Problem of Assessment." In M. J. Justiz, R. Wilson, and L. G. Bjork (eds.), *Minorities in Higher Education.* Washington, D.C.: American Council on Education and Oryx Press, 1994.

Boyer, S. P., and Sedlacek, W. E. "Noncognitive Predictors of Academic Success for International Students: A Longitudinal Study." *Journal of College Student Development,* 1988, *29*(3), 218–223.

Cabrera, A. F., Castaneda, M. B., Nora, A., and Hengstler, D. "The Convergence Between Two Theories of College Persistence." *Journal of Higher Education,* 1992, *63*(2), 143–164.

Cabrera, A. F., and others. "Collaborative Learning: Its Impact on College Students' Development and Diversity." *Journal of College Student Development,* 2002, *43*(1), 20–31.

Chickering, A., and Reisser, L. *Education and Identity.* San Francisco: Jossey-Bass, 1993.

Cross, K. P. *Adults as Learners: Increasing Participation and Facilitating Learning.* (2nd ed.) San Francisco: Jossey-Bass, 1991.

Ender, S. C., Winston, R. B., Jr., and Miller, T. K. "Academic Advising Reconsidered." In R. B. Winston Jr., T. K. Miller, S. C. Ender, and T. J. Grites (eds.), *Developmental Academic Advising.* San Francisco: Jossey Bass, 1984.

Eimers, M. T., and Pike, G. R. "Minority and Non-Minority Adjustment to College: Differences or Similarities?" Paper presented at AIR Annual Forum, May 5–8, 1996.

Ewing, R. V. "A Supportive Environment for International Students." In R. W. Franco and J. N. Shimabukuro (eds.), *Beyond the Classroom: International Education and the Community College. Volume II: Internationalizing the Campus Environment.* Honolulu: Hawaii University and Kapiolani Community College, 1992. (ED 372 777)

Fenske, R. H., Geranios, C. A., Keller, J. E., and Moore, D. E. *Early Interventions Programs: Opening the Door to Higher Education.* ASHE-ERIC Higher Education Report, vol. 25, no. 6. Washington, D.C.: The George Washington University, 1997.

Gordon, J. A. "A Critical Interpretation of Policies for Minority Students in Washington State." *NACDA Journal,* 1997, *17*(1), 15–21.

Hossler, D., and Stage, F. K. "Family and High School Experience Influences on the Postsecondary Educational Plans of Ninth-Grade Students." In A. Kezar (ed.), *Advances in Educational Research.* Washington, D.C.: U.S. Department of Education, 1999.

Hurtado, S. "The Campus Racial Climate: Contexts for Conflict." *Journal of Higher Education,* 1992, *63*(5), 539–569.

Hurtado, S., Milem, J., Clayton-Pedersen, A., and Allen, W. *Enacting Diverse Learning Environments Improving the Climate for Racial/Ethnic Diversity in Higher Education.* ASHE-ERIC Higher Education Report, vol. 26, no. 8. Washington, D.C.: The George Washington University, 1999.

Institute of International Education. 2001. [www.opendoorsweb.org/2001%20Files/layout_1htm]. Sept. 2001.

Jakobsen, L. "Promoting Diversity Among New Students in Predominantly White Residence Halls." In W. J. Zeller, D. S. Fidler, and B. O. Barefoot (eds.), *Residence Life Programs and the First-Year Experience.* Columbia, S.C.: University of South Carolina, The First-Year Experience, 1991.

Joint Task Force on Student Learning. *Powerful Partnerships: A Shared Responsibility for Learning.* Washington, D.C.: The American Association for Higher Education, the American College Personnel Association, and the National Association of Student Personnel Administrators, 1998.

Keim, J., McWhirter, J. J., and Bernstein, B. L. "Academic Success and University Accommodations for Learning Disabilities: Is There a Relationship?" *Journal of College Student,* 1996, *37*(5), 502–509.

Kinoshita, A., and Bowman, R. L. "Anxiety Levels Among Japanese Students on American Campuses: Implications for Academic Advisors." *NACADA Journal,* 1998, *18*(1), 27–34.

Murdock, S. H., and Hoque, M. N. "Demographic Factors Affecting Higher Education in the United States in the Twenty-First Century." In G. H. Gaither (ed.), *Promising Practices in Recruitment, Remediation, and Retention.* New Directions for Higher Education, no. 108. San Francisco: Jossey-Bass, 1999.

Nettles, M. T., Thoeny, A. R., and Gosman, E. J. "Comparative and Predictive Analyses of Black and White Students' College Achievement and Experiences." *Journal of Higher Education,* 1986, *57*(3), 289–318.

Nettles, M. T., Wagener, U., Millett, C. M., and Killenbeck, A. M. "Student Retention and Progression: A Special Challenge for Private Historically Black Colleges and Universities." In G. H. Gaither (ed.), *Promising Practices in Recruitment, Remediation, and Retention.* New Directions for Higher Education, no. 108. San Francisco: Jossey-Bass, 1999.

Nora, A., and Cabrera, A. F. "The Role of Perceptions of Prejudice and Discrimination on the Adjustment of Minority Students to College." *Journal of Higher Education,* 1996, *67*(2), 119–148.

Nora, A., and Rendon, L. "Hispanic Student Retention in Community Colleges: Reconciling Access with Outcomes." In C. Turner, M. Garcia, A. Nora, and L. I. Rendon (eds.), *Racial and Ethnic Diversity in Higher Education.* Boston: Pearson Custom Publishing, 1996.

Northeastern Illinois University. "Proyecto Pa'Lante." [www.neiu.edu/~ppalante]. Apr. 2002.

Padilla, R. V., Trevino, J., Gonzalez, K., and Trevino, J. "Developing Local Models of Minority Student Success in College." *Journal of College Student Development,* 1997, *38*(2), 125–135.

Parr, G., Bradley, L., and Bingi, R. "Concerns and Feelings of International Students." *Journal of College Student Development,* 1992, *33*(1), 20–25.

Pascarella, E. T., and others. "Influences on Students' Openness to Diversity and Challenge in the First Year of College." *Journal of Higher Education,* 1996, *67*(2), 174–195.

Paul, S. "Students with Disabilities in Higher Education: A Review of the Literature." *College Student Journal,* 2000. [www.findarticles.com/cf_0/m0FCR/2_34/63365/]. Sept. 2001.

Portland State University. "Progress Report University Studies 2000." [www.ous.pdx.edu/assess/title.html]. Apr. 2002.

Saunders, S. A., and Ervin, L. "Meeting the Special Advising Needs of Students." In R. B. Winston Jr., T. K. Miller, S. C. Enders, and T. J. Grites (eds.), *Developmental Academic Advising.* San Francisco: Jossey-Bass, 1984.

Selvadurai, R. H. "Adequacy of Selected Services to International Students in an Urban Technical College." *Urban Review,* 1991, *23*(4), 271–285.

Smedley, B. D., Myers, H. F., and Harrell, S. P. "Minority-Status Stresses and the College Adjustment of Ethnic Minority Freshmen." *Journal of Higher Education,* 1993, *64*(4), 434–452.

Smith, D. G. "Organizing for Diversity: Fundamental Issues." In C. Turner, M. Garcia, A. Nora, and L. I. Rendon (eds.), *Racial and Ethnic Diversity in Higher Education.* Boston: Pearson Custom Publishing, 1999.

Solis, E. Jr. "Regression and Path Analysis Models of Hispanic Community College Students' Intent to Persist." *Community College Review,* 1995, *23*(3), 3–15.

Somers, P., Cofer, J., and VanderPutten, J. "The Early Bird Goes to College: The Link Between Early College Aspirations and Postsecondary Matriculation." *Journal of College Student Development,* 2002, *43*(1), 93–107.

Stage, F. K. "Reciprocal Effects Between the Academic and Social Integration of College Students." *Research in Higher Education,* 1989, *30*(5), 517–530.

Tinto, V. *Leaving College: Rethinking the Causes and Cures of Student Attrition.* Chicago: University of Chicago Press, 1993.

Torres, V. "Factors Influencing Ethnic Identity Development of Latino College Students in the First Two Years of College." Paper presented at the American College Personnel Association Conference in Long Beach, Calif., Mar. 18, 2002.

Tracey, T. J., and Sedlacek, W. E. "The Relationship of Noncognitive Variables to Academic Success: A Longitudinal Comparison by Race." *Journal of College Student Personnel,* 1985, *26*(5), 405–410.

U.S. Census Bureau 2000. [http://www.census.gov/population/cen2000/phc-t1 /tab04.pdf]. Sept. 2001.

Woodard, D. B., Jr., Mallory, S. L., and DeLuca, A. M. "Retention and Institutional Effort: A Self-Study Framework." *NASPA Journal,* 2001, *39*(1), 53–83.

Zeller, W. J., Fidler, D. S., and Barefoot, B. O. *Residence Life Programs and the First-Year Experience.* Columbia, S.C.: University of South Carolina: The First Year Experience, 1991.

16

PUTTING ACADEMIC
SERVICES ON-LINE

Sally M. Johnstone, Patricia A. Shea

ALL OF US HAVE done a good job of selling higher education to the pub-lic. Earning a college degree, or at least taking classes, is seen as the ticket to promotion and better-paying jobs. Consequently, people of all ages are enrolling in colleges and universities. Today's student population is more diverse than ever, and colleges are changing their curricula, activities, and services to better meet those needs. The average undergraduate is older, not necessarily upper middle class, may come from any one of a number of different ethnic and racial backgrounds, and may have a wide range of learning and physical abilities. On campuses, the "Web generation" has arrived. Many of them are working part-time and, like older students, they expect their classes and services to be available to fit into their schedules.

To add to this complexity, today's new students are not as loyal to a single institution as students were a generation ago. We have encouraged this shift from the single-institution tradition by developing deliberate pol-icy initiatives such as the "2 plus 2" articulation systems between public two-year and four-year institutions (Ewell, 2002). Students have learned to shop for colleges and universities that will meet their needs with learn-ing options available at a time and location convenient to them and at a cost they can afford. Even a decade ago, about half of higher education students did not take all their classes from a single institution. By 1994, almost half of those students who had begun college in 1989 had enrolled in more than one institution (National Center for Educational Statistics, 1997). Examining national transcript data only a few years later, Adelman (1999) found that 54 percent of those ultimately earning baccalaureate degrees had attended two or more institutions, whereas 19 percent had attended three or more. He also found many instances of simultaneous enrollment at multiple institutions and of "reverse transfer" from four-year to two-year institutions. This tendency has been called "swirling," and the institutions through which such students swirl may not even be aware of one another. The phenomenon is hard to track because most of the data we have about student enrollment behavior in higher education come from institutions, not students. But it seems highly unlikely that it has slowed in recent years.

Swirling is even easier in the fast-growing electronic education environment, where students can move from one school to another with the click of a mouse or the press of a button. The latest year for which we have national data regarding the incidence of distance learning is 1998 (National Center for Educational Statistics, 1999). In 1998, 78 percent of public four-year institutions and 62 percent of public two-year institutions were offering some form of electronic distance learning, and 97 percent of all institutions in the United States, serving more than ten thousand students, being offered electronic distance learning in some form. Compared with a survey conducted by the same organization in 1995 (National Center for Educational Statistics, 1999), the 1998 numbers represent a 33 percent increase in the number of institutions offering electronic distance learning. The survey is scheduled to be repeated in 2002. If another one-third increase occurs, nearly all U.S. higher education institutions will be involved in some type of electronic distance learning.

Just as the current growth in distance learning corresponds with the increasing availability of the Internet, in the early 1980s there were three distribution technologies whose availability grew rapidly. This rapid growth in distribution capabilities made it possible for institutions to export their campus-based classes to students who were not coming to a campus. These enabling technologies were (1) televised classes via local and national broadcast networks, (2) public service satellite systems, and (3) educational cable television channels. As this growth occurred, the number of students using these technologies increased and colleges began to address the need to support them. Looking at this set of events in more detail seems useful to understanding how colleges and universities have evolved in different ways to reach the state of academic student support services we see today.

Technology and Distance Education

In the 1980s, colleges and universities took advantage of support from the U.S. Department of Commerce's National Telecommunications and Information Agency (NTIA). The NTIA made grants through their Telecommunications and Information Infrastructure Assistance Program to colleges and universities to enable them to develop Instructional Television Fixed Service (ITFS) systems and the studio classrooms that could feed them. These ITFS signals could reach a limited area in the immediate vicinity of their origination point. Many of the early adopters of these ITFS systems used them for engineering classes. The on-campus classes would be televised from the studio classrooms to companies that employed engineers, so that the employees could receive continuing education or take classes that would lead to a degree. Because the studio classrooms could serve any technology, some were also used to feed satellite distribution systems that extended the institution's reach to the entire nation and world.

It soon became obvious that many engineering students working in large companies wanted to complete their studies, but they moved around frequently. It was also obvious that few single institutions could offer all the classes these students needed. To serve this need, the National Technological University (NTU) was formed by a group of deans of various colleges of engineering under the leadership of Lionel Baldwin at Colorado State University. Participating universities contributed televised classes that were distributed throughout the country to students at their places of work. The students could earn their master's degree from NTU by taking classes from multiple institutions. NTU provided technical and administrative services. The students' academic services were left up to the institution providing the course. There was a local facilitator on site at the business location where the students were employed to assist with nonacademic services. As NTU developed its own degree programs, it also developed student academic support services for this unique group of engineering graduate students.

Prior to the development of cable television systems, public television broadcast stations offered educational programming in early-morning and late-night time slots. As cable television expanded across the country, there was a requirement that some channels be set aside for educational and community use. Because of this, many colleges and universities acquired such channels and funding that allowed them to build broadcasting systems and studio classrooms, which provided an excellent vehicle for reaching potential students in the surrounding communities at any time of the day or night. Community colleges took the lead in offering telecourses through this medium. Degree programs were developed around these telecourses, but students were expected to come to the campus for their support services.

During this same period of time, the Public Service Satellite Consortium (PSSC) took the lead in offering educational institutions access to satellite distribution at a reasonable price. The PSSC acted as a broker for limited amounts of time on satellite transponders so that a single institution did not have to lease an entire transponder for just the few classes it would be uploading. The Public Broadcasting Service began a similar program in the early 1990s.

All of this activity put more and more higher education institutions into the business of serving students farther and farther from their campuses. Most of these institutions used their departments of engineering or their continuing education programs as the vehicles for these off-campus academic programs. The groups running these systems within the institutions were linked to the academic departments with which the instructors who "starred" in these programs were affiliated, and the programs were expected to support themselves economically. The distance learning programs were rarely in a direct reporting line to the academic officers of an institution. This gave rise to these institutions' first set of concerns: that academic and broadcast quality be ensured. And it quickly became obvious that students had concerns of their own. To be successful, they needed special attention and services from the faculty members and from the institutions.

The Educational Network of Maine, developed by George Connick in the early 1990s, was a statewide higher education system that served both graduate and undergraduate students, an entirely different set of students from those using the NTU. These students were more similar to those served by community college telecourses, but the Maine students, scattered across the state (and on several islands), could not come to a campus to receive services. The network's small central staff developed systems to serve the non-class-related needs of these students. The staff developed ways for these students to have remote access to library resources, electronic registration systems, phone-based academic advising systems, and even degree programs from universities from other states when the programs were not available from Maine campuses. Their work became a model for multi-institutional collaborative student support systems around the country.

Many of the colleges and universities that began their distance learning activities using either ITFS, cable television, or satellite channels are now migrating to the Web. The newcomer institutions that start with the Web have to catch up with the support services offered by these more experienced institutions.

This increase in accessible technological distribution systems in the last two decades has given rise to a rapid increase in the number of institutions serving off-campus students. Since the mid-1990s, the increases in the number and types of students being served have given rise to consortia models at the state level. In addition to offering combined listings of courses available electronically from the member institutions, some of these consortia have focused on combining student support services. The trend began with Maine and has spread to projects in Kentucky, Connecticut, South Dakota, Georgia, Oregon, and other states.

Distance learning and the Web. As Web use has proliferated among the public, it has also increased among academicians. According to Casey Green's "Campus Computing Survey" (2002), in 2001, more than 45 percent of all classes at public and private universities had Web pages. The percentage was slightly lower for four-year colleges and dropped to about a quarter of the classes at community colleges.

Students with access to the Web are pushing institutions to provide access to courseware—as well as access to teachers—from the comfort of their desktops. Right now it is estimated that more than 2.25 million people study on-line at U.S. colleges and universities (Eaton, 2001). But it is more than student demand that is promoting the on-line learning movement. Some colleges, such as Brigham Young University in Idaho and Fairleigh Dickinson University in New Jersey, believe that it is important for students to learn in an on-line environment as preparation for the future. Both of these institutions require students to complete on-line courses in order to graduate.

The Web has made it easier for institutions to provide distance learning, but the institutional leaders cannot assume that as soon as classes have Web pages, they will be accessible as distance learning courses to noncampus students. Without the student academic support services, they are not useful learning tools. Just as in the early days of distance learning, Web-based distance learning managers are responding to these student demands by moving their student services, or certain components of them, to the Web. This is an enormous task for institutions, in that it requires reexamining all aspects of their current operating structures and helping their staff members develop new skills. This is typically done in stages on a continuum of increasing functionality. Frequently, the stages look something like this:

- The first stage is an information-only set of static Web pages for most of the services. These allow a visitor to the Web site to read about services available and it provides some directions for finding help.

- The next stage is to add interactive forms, self-assessment tools, and e-mail capability. This allows the student to use the Web site as a communication tool for getting assistance from the staff.

- Some institutions have moved to the next stage, in which some personalized services are offered. A one-on-one relationship with the student is established. He or she can access his or her own records and customize the display of this information on his or her personal home page.

- A few institutions have gone on to the next step, which is to use Web portals to establish communities of interest and to build an ongoing relationship between the student and the institution.

- A select few are really harnessing the power of the Web, by integrating their services and using artificial intelligence to provide students with better service than ever before.

- This last level is optimum, but hard to obtain. It results in much more rewarding experiences for both the students and the staff as some of the examples that follow make clear. But it requires a new vision, changes in campus staff structures, and a strategic plan to get there.

Strategic Planning for Developing Electronic Student Services

Traditionally, most campuses have supported their campus-based students with a full array of services developed over time in an ad hoc fashion as the need for them arose. In most cases, these services have been, and continue to be, operated by separate offices with different and sometimes conflicting policies and procedures. This has led to much confusion for students and, in some cases, only a moderately satisfactory level of support. For example, a student might get permission from her academic adviser to drop a class, based on her ability to do well in the class. Afterward, she might learn from the financial aid office that she is now no longer eligible for financial aid because she has dropped below the course load minimum.

Even less satisfactory has been the support offered to institutions' distance learning students. Many campus student services offices have had their hands full with on-campus students and have had little time, support, or administrative encouragement to serve the more time-consuming distance learning students. As a result, staff in the various campus divisions or in the units offering the distance learning courses have usually provided all the support such students receive from the campus. This usually falls far short of the full array of services available to students on campus. In too many cases, the faculty members providing the instruction serve as the *only* contact with the institution. In the early years of on-line learning, we found that 36 percent of institutions offering distance learning programs relied on the teaching faculty to provide even the technical support for students (Dirr, 1999). This is neither the best approach to helping students be successful nor the best use of institutional resources.

The Web offers the opportunity to address these issues. By its nature, the Web makes it possible to integrate support services in a seamless fashion so that the student perceives a single institutional voice on administrative and academic policies and procedures. It is also possible to design Web-accessible services that use a common interface to address the needs of both on- and off-campus populations. This last point is critical. It no longer makes sense to maintain separate support systems, as these populations increasingly blend together.

Today's distance learning students serve as a good model for what the traditional student body of tomorrow will progressively look like. Thus, it is important to be guided by the needs of the remote learner in developing on-line services. Two simple examples of considering the remote learner are (1) including area codes with telephone numbers listed on an institution's Web site and (2) noting the applicable time zone for deadlines. On a more complex level, institutions should plan services that support rolling enrollments and open-ended courses, which are common in electronic offerings. Focusing on the needs of today's distance learning students will raise many policy and procedural issues, but to ignore them as a growing influence on tomorrow's student body is to bury one's head in the sand.

Defining goals for electronic student support services. The Web provides the opportunity for campuses to rethink the missions of their services for students and to reengineer them as an integrated "Web of services" versus a "crazy quilt" collection with conflicting and missing parts. The academic services, as defined in this book, are an ideal place to start because many of them are offered centrally and more of their practices are codified in established practices and campus policy. In addition, they can serve as the foundation upon which to build other personalized electronic services. A sweeping campuswide initiative such as this, however, requires the strong support or mandate of the campus leadership. A good example of this kind of leadership is Eduardo Padron, president of Miami Dade Community College, who has set aside funds for each of the last three years for the development of on-line student services. He calls the money a "vision budget," clearly sending the message that the new on-line services will represent new ways of doing things. On other campuses, the provost has provided the critical initiative. For example, John Morton at Kapi'olani Community College (KCC) in Hawaii reorganized the campus in 1999 so that all distance learning and noncredit courses are now offered through their respective academic units. He also charged these academic units with providing those student services that are not available centrally—that is, admissions, registration, library services, and tech support—to their respective students. The result has been the creation of a one-stop enrollment center and individual unit initiatives to provide program-specific services on-line.

In campuses with which we have worked, one useful starting point is the formation of a cross-functional vision team. It should include key representatives from the various campus offices and constituencies, such as marketing, admissions, the registrar, financial aid, academic advising, counseling, disabilities, and continuing education—plus student and faculty leadership. One good way to get the ball rolling is to hold a kickoff meeting to build awareness and support for electronic services. For members of the vision team to understand what is possible, it is helpful to show them what other campuses have accomplished. These best practices may even come from industry if they demonstrate methods of better serving constituents that could be translated to the educational sphere.

The campus vision team needs to determine what institutional goals can be achieved by making its services accessible via the Web. Is the intention to attract more students, or is it to attract students who are different from the institution's current student body? Are the expectations for quality service similar to those currently provided, or are they higher? To what extent should the services be personalized and interactive? Can the services be provided twenty-four hours a day, seven days a week, or is that unrealistic? What additional services could be provided that are not possible with the use of the current infrastructure? Can the new electronic services be designed to reduce the staff workload on routine tasks so that more time can be spent on specialized services for individual students?

Once the goals are articulated, several brainstorming sessions usually follow. These sessions focus on the creation of a holistic vision of what electronic services could be like, and they concentrate on the human operations side, not on what technical solutions might be used. The discussion of technical solutions can come later. For now, it is important that technologies enable the vision, not define it.

At KCC, the vision team devised an unusual approach to create this vision for electronic services. After an initial meeting, the team attended a two-day retreat. Rather than coming to the table to represent their respective campus affiliations, each team member was assigned a student alias with the profile of a current student—often a distance learning student. A facilitator then walked the group through the various stages of a student's relationship with the campus—from being a prospective student to being one who is ready to graduate. This approach allowed everyone to participate at the same level and focus on services from the student's point of view. And it resulted in a greater understanding of what students might need or want at various points and, perhaps more important, how various offices could work together to respond via integrated electronic services.

Visioning meetings require high energy and concentration. They are best accomplished in a retreat-like setting where individuals can get away from their daily responsibilities. A strong facilitator—preferably from outside the campus—can help speed the process along by avoiding political issues that frequently arise in a reengineering project such as this.

Once an institution has its new "big picture" vision for serving students, it can compare it with its existing practices. Where there is overlap, less time will be needed in the design phase to determine the requirements for technical solutions. Where there are strong differences, campuses should allow more time to hammer out the details of the operational aspects before moving on to technical requirements.

Designing and Developing Technical Solutions

After the team has articulated the general vision, the campus leadership can select an area of concentration for initial development. This can be used to generate more widespread acceptance and serve as a model for future work. It is important to have a skilled project director in charge and responsible for this initial project. A development team of subject matter experts in student services and IT staff members should be given appropriate release time to work on the project. This group should define the operations of this service in more detail and should carefully think about the new policies and procedures needed to provide this service in its new Web format.

The usual tendency for this group is to rush to a solution by "Web-enizing" current practices. That is, they may try to put their current policies, procedures, and materials on the Web and consider their job done. Instead, they need to think creatively about what these services could be like. By focusing in part on distance learning students, this will be easier to achieve, as many more factors enter the equation. For example, many distance learning courses have open enrollment, so registration services need to be available on a rolling basis to accommodate multiple start and end times. This introduces more complexity to the requirements for a technical solution, but it ensures flexibility in the system to accommodate the full gamut of campus offerings.

When the development team has fully examined the proposed operations and has defined the details of this initial electronic service, the technical specifications can then be determined by the IT staff or outside consultants. It is important to consider a number of factors at this stage, including time line, scalability, budget, staff skill sets, compatibility with existing software systems, and campus acceptance issues. Of these, the last two are probably the most complex.

Understanding the Capability of the Existing Technical Infrastructure

Some new student information systems (SIS) and on-line course management systems provide limited student service functionality. None of them does the complete job, however, and many campuses are not in the financial position to replace their current systems, even if new systems did have built-in support services. To provide many personalized student services, the technical solutions supporting these services must be integrated into the campus student information system, which can be very complex. In some cases, old records systems have limited storage and functionality. For example, in 2000, KCC's student information system could not store e-mail addresses. Although the University of Hawaii system was investing in a new SIS system to serve all Hawaii institutions, its implementation schedule is still up in the air one year later. For a temporary solution, the staff at KCC built a shadow registration database to provide Web-based tutoring to their medical assisting students. This worked because the problem was a small one involving a limited number of students. This solution would not have served as a long-term or campuswide solution.

Other campuses may have the functionality to support personalized electronic services in their existing system, but the necessary student data may be scattered among multiple databases without a common interface.

For example, in 2000, when planners at Kansas State University began to design a Web-based academic advising system, they found that student data were stored in seventeen different databases. In order to proceed, the campus leadership mandated that all databases would come under the oversight of the registrar. The registrar's staff worked to eliminate the redundancy of records, increase the reliability of the data, and create the infrastructure that would be needed to develop a full array of personalized electronic student services in the future.

Developing a Prototype

In some cases, student services personnel fear that by making services available on-line, they will lose their personal connection with students or, even worse, their jobs. Others are simply resistant to change. Thus, it may be necessary to start with a pilot program, especially for the initial project, to demonstrate how technology can be used to assist the staff in better serving students. In 1997, at Pennsylvania State University, developers created a Web-based academic advising system called eLion, named after their campus mascot. The system gives students and advisers access to most of the information they would need for the academic advising process. This includes the ability to see students' current class schedule, run degree audits, and print unofficial transcripts. Students can also use the system to drop classes without talking with their advisers.

For this last function, developers of the system interviewed advisers to learn the most common reasons students gave for wanting to drop a class. The developers put together a series of Web pages that students had to work through before they could actually drop a class. These pages gave students advice as they contemplated dropping a course. The system went beyond this, however, and provided students with the information necessary to understand what repercussions their decision would have in relation to various degree requirements. For example, the system allowed students to receive advice based on their current major or other majors. It notified students when dropping a class would cause them to fall below the minimum load requirement, jeopardizing their financial aid. It advised students of classes that could be used as a prerequisite for other courses in their major and pointed students to other resources they should check. It also pointed out courses that might not to be offered in the upcoming semester, thus delaying students' progress toward a degree.

Academic advisers, fearing they would lose contact with their advisees, were reticent about this last capability of the system—until the developers demonstrated how the system would automate routine tasks to save time for more specialized interactions and services. Although an adviser could gather all this information for a student without eLion, it would take hours. At the click of a mouse nearly around the clock, students could access eLion and go through the process of dropping a class. Academic advisers were impressed with the pilot program, and developers have now built a system with this functionality that serves all undergraduate students.

Selecting a Solution: Buy, Build, Partner, or Outsource

Once the technical requirements are drafted, based on the in-depth description of the new service, they can be evaluated against a matrix of options. These may include using existing campus-owned software, buying software available in the marketplace, or partnering in the development of solutions with other campuses or corporate partners. Another option for certain services is to outsource the tasks to a service provider.

All of these options have advantages and disadvantages. Critical questions to consider in evaluating these options, in addition to price, scalability, and their accessibility to students with disabilities, include

- Buying software: How well does the product fit your needs? Can it be customized to support the nuances of your vision? How easily can it be integrated into your existing technical systems?

- Building software solutions: Does your staff have the skills and time to develop, upgrade, and maintain the solution over time?

- Partnering in the development of solutions: Are the goals of the partners complementary? How strong is the commitment to the partnership? Can the ownership issues for intellectual property be satisfactory to all?

- Outsourcing: Can the provider of the service be transparent to the student? What quality controls will the campus have? How reliable is the provider? What exit strategy makes the most sense?

The last option, outsourcing, may be the fastest one to implement, but it carries the greatest risk. For example, although service providers may agree to keep student data private, the institution must rigorously assess the provider's ability to ensure the security of its technology as well as the reliability of its staff. It is the institution that is ultimately responsible for ensuring compliance with Family Educational Rights and Privacy Act regulations. In addition, the institution should insist that the service provider deliver services that reflect the campus philosophy and attitudes. Generic service may be acceptable in some areas, but to maintain a student's loyalty for the long run, the campus needs its own brand of service. Finally, the campus must define the quality of service considered acceptable. There must also be an appropriate metric for assessing the service provider's performance. Although campuses may have performance measures for their face-to-face services, many must define them anew for the electronic environment.

Integrating Technology Solutions and Developing a New Campus Culture

Before a campus initiates a new electronic service, the technology solutions should be tested with small groups of students. These groups should represent the array of users likely to need the service. These would include both on- and off-campus students and students with disabilities who would test the solution to make sure the service operates as planned. These users may also identify additional features they would like to have available, to enhance the service in a later version.

The staff should also test the new service. Campus staff members supporting the service are likely to be the secondary users, after the students. In fact, the new service may automate many of the staff's former routine tasks. This may, in turn, allow staff members to shift the types of activities they perform. If the staff members' responsibilities change, it is critical that they receive adequate training for the new activities.

On campus after campus, the story is the same. However complex and difficult it is to design these integrated technical systems supporting student services, it is harder still to convince staff members that using the technology can improve their service to students. Ongoing campaigns to build awareness about the benefits of proposed new services should be in place from the earliest planning stages to make the transition easier. For some staff members, these new electronic services will provide opportunities to learn new skills or the time to focus on the aspects of the service they prefer.

At Regis University in Colorado, for example, the staff in the School for Professional Studies is developing a Web-based module to provide orientation services to the approximately three thousand students enrolled in their distance learning programs. This module will perform a series of steps that are critical to supporting adult learners through the entire admissions and enrollment process. The Web module, which will be integrated into the campus's student information system, will monitor a student's application for admission, notify him or her when the application is missing components and when it is complete, issue the student an account to access RegisNet, where he or she can find more specific information about the school's programs, set up his or her access to the library, and notify the student when it is time to make his or her first appointment with an adviser. This module will also let the adviser know where the student is in this process. Currently, the first ten minutes of an adviser's initial meeting with a student are devoted to these routine tasks. In the future, the advisers will have more time to spend discussing educational goals with students. The new technology will allow the advisers to spend their time on the most interesting and rewarding part of their job.

It is important to note that automating student services may not result in reduced staff or reduced workload. The convenience of accessing a student service on-line may actually increase the number of students using the service. For example, most colleges report receiving an increased number of applications, once they make them accessible via the Web. And for many institutions, while the student side is electronic, the staff side is not. Indeed, the National Association for College Admission Counseling's Admission Trends Survey for 2001 reports that in the 421 institutions responding to the survey, only 24 percent were capable of uploading the applications directly to a database, whereas 76 percent said that the staff must key application information into a database (National Association for College Admission Counseling, 2001). So although the public perception is that the application process is automated for all these schools, most schools are still using the same old manual process on the staff side, which results in a higher volume of work for the staff. To remain competitive, these institutions had no choice but to make their application available on the Web. Now, to make real progress, they must tackle the more complex task of integrating the Web front end with a database back end.

As campuses automate the staff side of service operations, they are likely to need staff members with more advanced technical and analytical skills. Data entry and paper copies of admissions materials will fall by the wayside. Staff members with the skills to create and analyze electronic reports from the admissions data will help ensure that service is fast and efficient for the students the campus seeks to serve.

Indeed, many new professional categories in student services are likely to be created in the next few years. Most are likely to offer opportunities to work more closely with students. For example, at Brigham Young University, much of the financial aid service has been automated and is now accessible on-line. The financial aid staff members, some of whom did routine clerical tasks previously, have been retrained as certified financial planners. These new counselors assist students in creating their financial paths to graduation—a much more beneficial service.

A key word here is *retrained*. Those institutions moving services into the on-line environment must recognize that most staff members will need training opportunities and support. This will be especially true for the newly integrated services that require staff members to understand policies and procedures for a wide array of service areas.

Flattening Organizational Barriers and Empowering Students

For years, students have been held captive by institutional policies and practices that have not been designed holistically and consequently do not serve them well. As we mentioned earlier, most services have developed as the need has arisen on the campus. For example, prior to the GI Bill, there were no offices of veterans affairs on campuses. As each service developed, people were hired to specialize in that area. The decentralized groups of people staffing each service area developed individual policies and practices. They made sense within their own context, but students moving through the whole system had to deal with the inconsistencies and conflicts. KCC's vision team wanted to end this experience on their campus. To do so, they are currently testing a new approach in an on-line pilot program. New "learning support services" will be available to pre-health and medical assisting students through a portal developed specifically for them. The concept is to build a community of people with an interest in the medical field—from prospective students to alumni—who will help one another learn. Several services are integrated, including orientation, admissions, academic advising, and tutoring. For example, a prospective student can find out about the eight medical programs available at KCC, receive advice on how to decide among them, and then apply to a selected program. Admitted students can customize their personal page, share documents with other program students via their projects page, and receive and share information through bulletin boards and news groups. The calendar section features several calendars—for the institution, program, and student activities, along with the dining calendar to entice students to meet socially for lunch. Through the portal, students can find financial aid designed specifically for learners in these medical programs, or they can link to the generic aid available through the campus financial aid office. They can also link to library learning resources specifically supporting their required courses. In addition, they can participate in assessments of their skills, using on-line tutoring modules designed to address their weaknesses.

Some of the tutoring modules are particularly interesting. These modules address skills that are implicitly required by the programs but not specifically addressed by them. For example, listening and observation skills are very important in all of the medical programs. So are applied math skills. Although KCC students have traditionally done well in the required math course, they have had difficulty in their practicum applying math concepts to calculate drug dosages. As a result, the retention rate has suffered in the second year of the program. KCC hopes that these new on-line tutoring modules in calculating drug dosages and in improving listening and observation skills will advance students' understanding and increase retention.

Academic advisers are available by both e-mail and in a chat room during hours published in the portal. Future plans call for making portions of this portal environment public and encouraging medical personnel and consumers of medical services in the state of Hawaii to use it to seek and supply information pertinent to the medical programs. In this way, the KCC staff hopes to ensure that the program stays current with the needs of those whom KCC intends to serve through its graduates—broadening both the definition of KCC's support service and its constituent learners.

Thus, through a single log-on, health science students receive just-in-time services that melt into one another as "learning support services"—from first encounter to graduation and beyond. If this integrated approach proves successful, KCC will develop other on-line learning communities for its campus.

By designing services for on-line access from the student's point of view, and especially by using the holistic and integrated approach we have advocated, it is necessary to address many policy and procedural issues. Just as integrating technological tools into the teaching and learning process has forced a reexamination of policies and practices in the classroom, so do these technological tools become an excuse to rethink how the whole institution provides services to students. For example, Regis University is now considering several policy issues related to its new orientation modules. Considering that its operation is primarily based on the use of e-mail, should students be required to have an e-mail account and use it in official correspondence with the institution? Should the institution set up a review process to limit the amount of e-mail a student receives from various offices? What print communications are no longer necessary or need to be altered to support e-mail as the primary process?

Automation, too, forces institutions to look for commonalities of practice among colleges and departments and to establish consistency in operations. To be effective, it puts the students' needs in the driver's seat for all decisions about how the organization should be structured. This drive for consistency may even change the way some institutions are structured and how they do business. For example, during the spring 2001 semester at Kansas State University, 85 percent of the on-line students were campus-based full-time students. These students had to register for their on-campus classes with the campus registrar and pay full tuition. Then they had to register in the Division of Continuing Education for their on-line courses and pay a separate tuition. To add to the confusion, the Division of Continuing Education provided the support services for the on-line classes, while the campus student services staff supported the traditional classes. When the enrollments in on-line classes were small, this was not a significant problem—which is no longer the case. The university, as noted earlier, is in the process of integrating its data systems. Will this drive a change in policy to allow on-line courses to be counted in the regular load? How will this affect the institution's budget and its staffing structure?

Providing student services on-line allows institutions to increase student access and provide consistency in the type of services offered. In some instances, it also provides the opportunity for institutions to offer a better quality of service. Two examples of this are the eLion academic advising system at Penn State and the Financial Path to Graduation at Brigham Young University. Both of these are examples of integrated services, where the student is made aware of multiple factors to consider in making a decision.

At Penn State University, the number of late dropped classes decreased after the campus instituted eLion. Before that, students were rushing into academic advisers' offices at the last minute, when it was impossible for advisers to meet with all of them or provide the type of in-depth advice desired. Now, students use eLion to learn about options that could prevent their needing to drop the class. Many opt to stay enrolled, whereas those who have difficult situations seek out their academic adviser earlier to discuss the options in more depth.

At Brigham Young University, the staff developed an on-line service to teach freshmen to avoid the high debt that was common to many students graduating in the 1990s. This service, called the Financial Path to Graduation, helps students determine how much money they really need, what the cost of loans will be upon graduation, what their income level is likely to be for their prospective career choices, and how long it will take for them to pay back their loans at that level. In the four years since the program's inception, the amount of money borrowed by students has dropped by 30 percent, and the school's default rate has dropped to 0.5 percent at a time when the national average was 6 percent.

Conclusion

Integrating technology into the delivery of a service is not a simple process for any complex organization. Doing so means rethinking the needs of the consumers of the service, redefining the goals of the service, reexamining the skills of the people involved in delivering the service, and reengineering relationships throughout the organization. It means looking for commonalities of practice and driving toward consistency in the quality of operations. It means supplying adequate funds for designing and implementing technical solutions supporting electronic services. And it means training staff members to assume new responsibilities. The resulting services can more effectively and efficiently support students in their quest to be successful learners, making this well worth the effort.

REFERENCES

Adelman, C. *Answers in the Toolbox: Academic Intensity, Attendance Patterns, and Bachelor's Degree Attainment.* Washington, D.C.: U.S. Department of Education, Office of Educational Research and Improvement, 1999.

Dirr, P. "Putting Principles into Practice: Promoting Effective Support Services for Students in Distance Learning Programs: A Report on the Findings of a Survey." 1999. [http://www.wiche.edu/wcet/Resources/publications/index.htm.] 2002.

Eaton, J. S. *Distance Learning: Academic and Political Challenges for Higher Education Accreditation.* Washington, D.C.: Council on Higher Education Accreditation, 2001.

Ewell, P. "Three 'Dialectics' in Higher Education's Future." Paper prepared for Allan Gaskin's Project on the Future of Higher Education, 2002.

Green, K. C. "Campus Computing Survey." 1999. [www.campuscomputing.org]. 2002.

National Association for College Admission Counseling. "2001 Survey Examines Trends in College Admission. Part I." 2001. [http://www.nacac.com/trends_2001.pdf]. 2002.

National Center for Educational Statistics. *Transfer Behavior Among Beginning Postsecondary Students: 1989–94.* Publication no. NCES 97–266. Washington D.C.: U.S. Department of Education, Office of Educational Research and Improvement, 1997.

National Center for Educational Statistics. *Distance Education at Postsecondary Education Institutions.* OERI Publication no. NCES 2000–013. Washington, D.C.: U.S. Department of Education, 1999.

17

PROMOTING AND SUSTAINING CHANGE

Earl H. Potter III

CONFERENCE SPEAKERS HAVE LONG OPENED their commentary on change in higher education with variations on the theme that *it is easier to move a graveyard than change an institution of higher education.* Such an observation always gets a laugh, but it is not strictly true. No one who knows the history of higher education since the end of World War II could agree with the notion that higher education has not changed. But, still, there are enduring characteristics of the culture of higher education that have remained the same even as institutions have grown, changed missions, and entered a competitive new environment.

The ability to survive change is both the strength and the challenge inherent in the nature of the university. Some aspects of academic culture are essential to the creation of a successful learning environment—academic freedom, for example. However, other aspects of academic cultures are side effects of higher education's history. Many of these aspects are not essential to the mission of the university and may even interfere with the institution's pursuit of its mission. For example, the role of the university in creating and disseminating knowledge imbues the institution with great authority. In such a culture, the faculty members lead and the students follow. Students are not customers but, as one Ivy League business school professor calls them, "work in progress inventory" (Joe Thomas, personal communication to the author, 1995). When this relationship is transferred to the world of student academic services, however, progress toward the achievement of an institution's mission may falter.

This can happen when the world calls for change but institutional leaders don't hear the call or when leaders are confused about what aspects of the culture to protect from change and what aspects of the culture must be changed. The first and greatest challenge of leadership in higher education is to recognize an opportunity for change. The second greatest challenge is to bring about change while protecting those things that should not change. This chapter examines processes and tools for managing change in today's world of higher education and, in particular, student services. More important, however, this chapter looks at processes and tools for creating change in ways that protect the essential core of what is most valuable about our institutions.

Setting the Stage for Change

Since World War II, the total enrollment in American institutions of higher education has grown from 1.5 million to more than eighteen million. In 1946, the largest academic institution in the United States had a total enrollment of fewer than ten thousand. Today, the University of Phoenix boasts 110,000 students. Size has brought change. At one time, it might have been possible to offer the equivalent of today's one-stop service center just because our institutions were not large. However, as they grew larger, institutions borrowed the model of industrial production from business and created specialized offices to deal with the various steps involved in providing services to students. This change was paralleled by increases in government regulations, in the costs of higher education, in the socio-economic diversity of our student bodies, in the numbers of international students on our campuses, and in the complexity of how students paid for their educations. For the most part, however, these changes happened gradually. Faculty and staff members across our campuses adjusted to changes that happened to them, in part because the basic nature of work in student services did not change during this time.

At the same time, American businesses were going through their own changes. The United States emerged from a period of rapid post-war growth into a time when competitive pressures began to drive innovations in the way that success was courted and measured. In the early 1960s the first of these innovations was Management by Objectives. The Ford Company's Robert McNamara led the move to evaluate performance with objective measures and to manage effort through an elaborate hierarchy of goals or objectives. The system collapsed when leaders discovered that more effort was spent on manipulating the measures than on meeting the objectives. Most significantly, however, customer satisfaction was seldom one of the measures included among the objectives.

It took the Japanese success in automobile manufacturing—being at the time superior to that of the United States—to bring the customer into the picture. In the 1970s, America rediscovered Edward Deming, the American management expert who laid the foundations for the rebirth of Japanese industry. Deming created what came to be known as Total Quality Management (TQM) in the United States. TQM taught business leaders that frontline employees are the ones with the knowledge it takes to improve performance in manufacturing and service operations. TQM also made the customer the party with the right to define quality. But TQM failed to remain a powerful force in business because it was cumbersome and lacked excitement.

Excitement about quality erupted in American business circles with the publishing of Tom Peters's book *In Search of Excellence* (1982). With the persuasive power of a carnival barker, Peters told the stories of America's best companies in a way that captured the imagination of business leaders. Peters's work began the search for best practices, which drives today's continuous improvement efforts. More important, however, Peters focused on the creation of a self-sustaining culture in which the pursuit of quality was fundamental to the day-to-day experience of every employee.

While these changes were taking place in American business, the world of higher education began to change. Astronomic increases in tuition during the 1970s and early 1980s had caught the attention of legislators and taxpayers. New competitors—for-profit providers of higher education— entered the marketplace. But, most important, the changes in the ways customers were treated by businesses began to have an impact on higher education. Far from the world of the 1960s, when American manufacturers produced what they wanted, convinced that Americans would buy what they produced, manufacturers and service providers in the 1980s discovered that consumers have choices. If the customer could find a better product or service elsewhere, he or she would do so. Thus, the drive for quality, *the search for excellence,* elevated the role of the customer. It should have been no surprise that our students and their parents would eventually bring these expectations to the services that were provided by colleges and universities.

Whether or not universities saw what was going on around them and began their own pursuit of quality was largely a matter of leadership. In 1985, the University of Delaware initiated a project to improve services to students that has resulted in Delaware becoming one of the most widely recognize. *best practice sites* in the nation. This effort is noteworthy for the length of time over which a commitment to change has been sustained. Over the same period of time, countless campuses across the country have initiated TQM projects, engaged in reengineering efforts, and targeted initiatives to create, for example, one-stop service centers. The best of these projects have succeeded. Many others have not succeeded. This situation might have continued, with the best universities and colleges taking lessons from best practices in business and the rest trying to follow a trend but abandoning it when they could not overcome the barriers to change— but for one thing: during the 1990s the World Wide Web transformed the playing field.

The Web opened the door to ways of working with students that had been unimaginable five years earlier. This is true despite the temporary setbacks of a crash in the value of speculative dot.com enterprises and an economy recovering from recession.

Sir John Daniel (2001), writing in the *Chronicle of Higher Education,* describes the ways in which students in Great Britain's Open University are using the Web. Student numbers are up, and expectations for the quality of service are ever increasing. Location is becoming less significant, and services must be available 24/7. The impact of the Web on the pace of change has been even more important than its impact on the ways in which students can be served. It took forty years for the telephone to reach 25 percent of the American population; it took fifteen years for television to reach the same percentage. The Web reached that same percentage of Americans in four years. It is evident that one way to secure a place in the market is through the quality of service provided to customers— but just for the time being. The pace of change expected by our customers—our students and their families, as well as those who will employ our graduates—has increased. The number of choices they have has also increased. Quality may give an advantage for now, but soon, quality will be expected of all. Those institutions that do not provide quality services will fail.

It is only recently, however, that increasing customer expectations, calls for accountability, and the continuing battle to contain costs have met the means to address these challenges—tools for assessing and improving quality, strategies for actively managing change, and use of the World Wide Web. Every institution must use new tools to address the forces that drive change. But right now, new tools pose a great opportunity for institutions that are ready to lead. These institutions will have a clear view of what they intend to accomplish and a systematic approach to evaluating where they are and where they want to go. This journey begins by creating a *culture of evidence.*

Building a Culture of Evidence

It is often said that organizations *measure what they care about.* On a personal level, it is said that if you want to know what someone values, look at that person's checkbook and his calendar. That is where you will find out how he spends his most important assets—his money and his time. All American academic institutions measure and track student credit hours. These data are a primary means of evaluating the success of enrollment management initiatives and justifying the allocation of resources. Most American institutions of higher education also claim a commitment to student success, but many of these institutions cannot provide data that document the success of different subgroups of students or even success beyond first-year retention rates. Fewer institutions regularly gather data concerning student satisfaction with services provided on campus. Even fewer institutions make the data that are gathered available to decision makers in time and in a shape that supports decision making. Those institutions without data would likely defend their commitment to their stated values, but the evidence suggests that such commitments have not been fully realized.

It is also said that *the most important things are the hardest to measure.* We might add that *the important things are the most expensive to measure.* This is perhaps why, after more than two decades of debate, substantive learning outcome measures are not used pervasively in higher education (see Astin, 1991). Every institution has a mission statement that could, at least theoretically, be evaluated by a set of concrete measures. Moreover, it should be possible to compare institutions in terms of how effectively they address similar commitments.

A culture of evidence exists when all members of the university community expect that evidence should be provided to demonstrate that the university is meeting the objectives defined by its mission. Furthermore, the members of the community carry this expectation to every activity of the university for which objectives can be set. Members in such a community are willing to do the hard work required to identify measures for important objectives, and the university is willing to invest in gathering and managing the resulting data. Finally, the community uses the data to guide practice and support the case for change.

Change comes to higher education most easily when faculty and staff members who care deeply about their work discover two things: (1) they could be doing a better job and (2) there is a way to do better and survive. The foremost challenge is to give people a vision of what might be. At the University of North Carolina at Greensboro (UNCG), leaders understood that they would need to change the university's culture in order to achieve objectives in enrollment management (see Black, 2002). UNCG's vision for change was grounded on the evidence that in key performance areas, it lagged behind competitors. The university created a leadership team that built a "compelling case for change" and sold this case to the campus community. The team then spent three months building a vision statement that, in turn, provided the foundation for identifying *key performance indicators:* student enrollments, student quality, student diversity, retention rates, graduation rates, student satisfaction, staff satisfaction, professional growth, and institutional image.

Choosing What to Measure: The Balanced Scorecard

UNCG's choice of measures was determined by its vision statement. A different institution with a different mission and vision might have addressed the definition of measures differently. For example, all of the top fifty business schools in the country use GMAT averages as an indication of student quality. A primary goal for all is to increase the average GMAT scores. A public institution committed to maximizing access to higher education for the citizens of its region might set a very different objective—for example, improvement in basic skills, as measured by standardized tests or employer evaluations of the quality of graduates. Furthermore, an institution will have a wider set of measures than will a single unit, even one with a mission as broad as student services.

Business organizations have also faced the challenge of establishing a set of comprehensive measures that can guide action in areas of key importance to the organization. For businesses, the challenge has been to move beyond financial measures to a balanced set of measures that assess current performance and predict future performance. For higher education, the challenge is to move beyond student credit hours and activity measures to outcome measures related to the institution's mission and leading indicators that predict the development and future health of the institution.

The Balanced Scorecard (BSC) is a framework developed by Harvard professor Robert Kaplan and consultant David Norton (1996). The BSC calls for measures in four areas: financial performance, customer perspective, internal business process perspective, and learning and growth perspective. The first two of these reflect the results of past performance. The last two are *process measures,* which predict future performance. For example, student satisfaction with student services is clearly a result of all that students have experienced up to the point of the survey. Time spent in lines waiting for service and trends evident in successive samples are predictors of future satisfaction. The astute reader will quickly note that an absolute value has little meaning. It is the comparison of time spent in line with what the student expects that is important, and, furthermore, this is a moving target. Comparison data are important and covered later in this chapter.

Financial Measures

In UNCG's case, student enrollments are the sole financial measures. On a broader institutional scale, productivity ratios (number of students per faculty member) are often tracked. These measures are more than simple budget figures. They are institutional performance indicators that track conditions and factors that are essential to bottom-line financial performance. They are the kinds of things that reflect institutional practices that affect budget outcomes. As such, they guide action, whereas the size of the budget deficit or surplus gives little information that could guide corrective action.

Customer Perspective

In Kaplan and Norton's system, customer measures include market share, customer acquisition, customer retention, customer satisfaction, and customer profitability. At UNCG retention rates, graduation rates, student satisfaction, and institutional image all fall into this category. One might argue that student quality and student diversity belong in this arena as well. One might also note that the BSC was developed for application to any business. In essence, the model doesn't know or care what business you are in. For higher education, it would be appropriate to define a complementary set of measures that are mission-driven, such as measures of educational effectiveness. The risk, however, is that institutions sometimes create goals that have little value for stakeholders. Diversity may have value in contributing to the quality of the educational environment or it may be a question of access for all peoples served by the university. The challenge is to know why the institution is doing what it is doing and how a measure supports the accomplishment of mission.

Internal Business Process Perspective

There are no internal business process measures in UNCG's set of measures. A business process is a description of all the steps involved in achieving an outcome. One such process might be student registration; another might describe international student admissions. The obvious measures are the time and money it takes to complete a process. These measures are useful at the operating level but are seldom included at the BSC level. At the level of the BSC, an institution needs to track the overall effectiveness of its business processes. In this regard, a measure of internal customer satisfaction might be useful (for example, how satisfied are the participants in the international admissions process with the way it works?). Of course, such measures require that the institution identify its key processes and know who all of the participants are. This activity nearly always takes place as institutions move toward improved student services that include new data management and Web-based delivery systems (for example, see Foucar-Szocki, Larson, and Mitchell, Chapter Nineteen, in this book).

The institution should also track its effectiveness in improving its processes. Taking the broader view, for example, program review exists for the purpose of improving programs. What measures would indicate that the program review is working? Traditionally, most universities would track the number of program reviews completed in a given year, as well as, perhaps, the number of recommendations for change. Yet the institution is really most concerned about increasing enrollments in declining programs and improving the reputation of weak programs. Surely, there are measures that could track the effectiveness of program review. This would be a good example of a case in which bringing business practices into the university might find favor with the faculty.

It is not necessary to track all business processes at the BSC level. A culture of evidence would imply that process effectiveness is of concern throughout the institution. The tools needed for process improvement would be an important element of the university's staff education program. The requirement for these skills would be included in appropriate job descriptions, and evidence of efforts to improve processes would be presented in annual performance reviews. The BSC measures might include a tally of savings or the numbers of processes that had undergone revision in a year. This area of the BSC supports continuous improvements in the way business is done. The results are evident in immediate improvements and long-term gains in financial performance and customer satisfaction.

Learning and Growth Perspective

UNCG's staff satisfaction measure clearly falls within the learning and growth perspective. Staff satisfaction should reflect the quality of support for the staff, including training and education, leadership, and work systems, as well as compensation and recognition. Many universities use satisfaction measures to track staff morale, but few have developed a strategic approach to human resources management. For example, most institutions evaluate training by counting the numbers of employees who attend and how they respond to the event. Few institutions track improvements in performance that result from training.

Success in improving student services requires a more systemic approach to changing culture and "reskilling" the workforce for new roles and requirements. With a clear vision and specific indicators of success in place, UNCG then defined the character of the culture that would be necessary to meet the university's goals. The culture was defined in terms of a set of ten behaviors and attitudes that all employees must exemplify. These included such things as *exemplify the service standards adopted by enrollment services and your department* and *pursue professional development as well as knowledge of enrollment issues and the university.* When such behaviors are linked to an effective performance appraisal system, the university can profile the degree to which the workforce has developed the skills needed for the new culture. This measurement allows the university to assess the degree to which a learning agenda is supporting the advancement of quality in service to students. The key is to link skill requirements with goals for change and align training and education systems with those goals.

Designing a *balanced scorecard* will help an institution in a number of ways. In fact, the process may be more important than actually using the scorecard. First, the institution must define its mission, and then it must ask how anyone would know if the institution were successful in achieving its mission. Second, the institution must give attention to the "leading indicators" that predict future performance and not just to measures that reflect past behavior. This step forces leaders to examine the connections between a wide array of initiatives and their value in fulfilling the mission of the organization. Finally, the measures actually yield data that can support evaluation and action planning. These data in and of themselves, however, have no meaning unless they can be viewed against a set of objectives—and it is impossible to develop meaningful objectives without some scale of value. That's the role that *benchmarking* plays.

Benchmarking

Benchmarking is the process of finding comparison data for a given set of measures. The term is often used as a synonym for *best practice research* but is actually a more general term. Best practice research is a discovery process through which the very best performer in any category is identified. The category can be broad or very narrow. For example, when the Ford Motor Company created the Taurus, designers identified four hundred automobile features that were important to their customers. Ford then identified the manufacturer that was "best in class" for each of the four hundred features. These examples were then used in the design of the Taurus, one of Ford's most successful models in its history.

Universities that have identified key measures can use benchmarking and best practices research to evaluate current performance and to set goals. The first step in this direction should probably be to identify a set of schools that are similar to one's own institution at the present time. This sounds obvious, but it is not uncommon for universities and colleges to use athletic conferences as a comparison set. It is doubtful that this is a legitimate foundation for the comparative measurement of key performance data for an institution. At Eastern Michigan University (EMU), strategic planners have identified nineteen universities comparable in mission and character. Data from these universities is used to assess resource allocation and key performance measures, such as retention and graduation rates.

In order to create this set, institutional research staff members relied upon data from the IPEDS Peer Analysis System, the AAUP Faculty Salary Survey, the College Board Annual Survey of Colleges, and nine other publicly available data sets. From a set of fifteen hundred colleges and universities, researchers then eliminated institutions that were not a match on nine dichotomous variables, such as private versus public institutions— with hospitals or not, and tribal versus nontribal institutions. Next, researchers drew upon a set of six strategic directions in the university's strategic plan to create proxy variables representing strategic commitments. For example, institutions with less than or equal to a 5 percent non-Asian minority enrollment were eliminated. Finally, researches created an index consisting of values representing expenditures, revenue, financial aid, and discipline match. A matrix was developed for the correlation between EMU's index score and the scores of the 149 remaining institutions. The nineteen most similar institutions were selected as the comparison set.

Purdue University-Calumet (PUC) took a very different approach to define its comparison set of institutions. At PUC, planners had identified retention and graduate rates as key strategic challenges for the university.

With this in mind, researchers sought out metropolitan universities of similar size and mission with established retention programs in place. This strategy differs significantly from EMU's strategy, in that almost all of the institutions chosen had better first-year retention and graduation rates than PUC. In fact, a key strategic objective for PUC was to increase its own retention and graduation rates to rank in the middle of the comparison group within three to five years. The comparison group chosen by PUC is probably what most would call an "aspirational set"—that is, a set of institutions whose performance on key measures is both above the institution's current performance and reasonably attainable within a normal planning time frame. The process for choosing such a set is value-driven and therefore more subjective. Nonetheless, for such a comparison set to be most useful, institutions need to pay attention to the same kind of comparability tests used by EMU in its selection of a comparison group. Neither of these efforts will necessarily result in the identification of best practices in areas of interest. The identification of best practices is a much more difficult exercise. Thankfully, there is a lot of help available.

Beginning in 1996, IBM has identified universities and colleges whose innovations and commitment to quality in student academic services qualifies them as Best Practice Partners. Through 2001, twenty institutions had been so identified. Each institution cited by Burnett and Oblinger in this book (Chapter Two) is an IBM Best Practice Partner. The lessons from these examples include the need for a shared vision, the importance of technical competence, the centrality of a commitment to customer service in building a foundation for success, and the need for active change management in creating new approaches to student academic services. In each of these institutions, success is defined as achieving goals on time, within budget, and with resources intact to address the next change. Not all "partners" have had equal success, but each helps us understand what it takes to transform institutions.

Other helpful resources are widely available. The National Association of College and University Business Officers supports the National Consortium for Continuous Improvement. The members of the consortium freely share performance data for the purpose of building a culture of quality improvement in higher education as well as for the individual improvement of each member. Specialized accrediting bodies are increasingly supportive of best practices information sharing. For example, the Association for the Advancement of Collegiate Schools of Business International has partnered with a for-profit benchmarking firm to provide support for self-analysis, comparative analysis, and longitudinal analysis of its member institutions. These practices differ significantly from past practice in higher education.

National conferences in every discipline and "mega-conferences," such as the American Association for Higher Education's annual conference and the annual conference of the American Council on Education, have long offered examples of best practices. The difference now is in the focus on measurement data. In the past, attendees would hear about innovative new programs and go home to implement a new program on their own campuses. Today we are much more focused on results and more sensitive to the transferability of programs from one environment to another. Furthermore, best practice comparisons are more focused on strategic initiatives. The search is focused and investments in new programs are prioritized to yield the greatest impact on key program objectives.

Those at institutions that have not yet begun to collect comparison data may wonder if peer institutions will be willing to share information. As noted earlier, much information is available via public sources, and benchmarking services can provide more sensitive data in anonymous formats. More significantly, however, all institutions are increasingly under pressure to provide comparative data as part of their own self-analysis for accreditation, grant reporting, and budget preparation. It is, therefore, increasingly in the best interest of institutions to develop consortia of peer schools willing to share data. For EMU this would mean developing a partnership with institutions that it has identified as optimal matches for its own profile. Ideally, institutions would open the door to partnership in the early stages of creating the comparison group. In short, it is possible to get good comparison data that can support planning and change, but it is very hard to do in a two-year self-study just before the accreditation team makes its visit.

Process improvement, or reengineering tools, offers the means to make change, but without a vision of what is possible, it is difficult to engage a campus community in these processes. Benchmarking and best practice studies create the motivation for change by providing a vision of what could be. Even with a vision, however, it is difficult to sustain change in student services if the rest of the university is not also committed to change. Thankfully, there are ready-made approaches to institution-wide continuous improvement that can guide campuswide efforts or help individual units assess their approaches to continuous improvement (see Creamer, Creamer, and Brown, Chapter Ten, in this book).

The Malcolm Baldrige National Quality Award

The Malcolm Baldrige National Quality Award was created by an act of Congress in 1987. Named for Malcolm Baldrige, who served as U.S. secretary of commerce from 1981 until his death in 1987, the Baldrige

National Quality Program is a public-private partnership established for the purpose of improving national competitiveness in industry. In the years following its establishment, there were increasing calls for the creation of standards that could be more easily applied to different kinds of organizations. The Education Criteria for Performance Excellence Award was first offered in 2000. The University of Wisconsin-Stout was the first higher education winner of the award in 2001.

The Baldrige Program offers a model that institutions can use to assess the systems, processes, and practices they have in place to support continuous improvement. The selection process is rigorous, and many organizations apply for several years before winning the award. Even more organizations use the Baldrige criteria as a guide for development. The program is founded on a set of eleven core values:

1. Visionary leadership
2. Learning-centered education
3. Organizational and personal learning
4. Valuing faculty and staff members and partners
5. Agility
6. A focus on the future
7. Managing for innovation
8. Managing by fact
9. Public responsibility and citizenship
10. A focus on results and creating value
11. A systems perspective

The criteria are divided into seven categories:

1. Leadership
2. Strategic planning
3. Student, stakeholder, and market focus
4. Information and analysis
5. Faculty and staff focus
6. Process management
7. Organization performance results

Institutions that apply for the award complete a self-evaluation using the criteria. The Baldrige Program then assigns a team of eight to twelve evaluators to read and score the fifty-page application. Approximately one-third of the applications will move onto the second round of the evaluation. In this round, the individual members of the evaluation team participate in an exercise that leads to a consensus-based evaluation. A team of Baldrige judges uses this document to determine which applicants will receive a site-visit, usually 25 to 30 percent of those applicants reviewed in the consensus process. Three to five awards are typically given each year.

Although the criteria are designed for institutions, major units can use elements of the criteria or the complete criteria to guide self-improvement. Apart from the values stated earlier, the criteria are "values free," to allow for differences in institutional mission. They are particularly powerful because they begin by asking for a statement of purpose and move on to results that demonstrate the accomplishment of purpose. An institution may score well because of a well-defined purpose and clear plans (its approach) but fall short in the implementation (deployment) of its plan. At PUC, the Business Services Office made a commitment to use the Baldrige criteria as the framework for assessing its own performance. At the same time, the Student Services organization undertook to redesign student services but did not choose to use the Baldrige criteria. PUC's accomplishments in student services led to its designation as an IBM Best Practice Partner. Now that the university is engaged in a campuswide commitment to quality improvement, the experiences of both business services and student services are important assets. In fact, the different perspectives developed by the two functional offices have helped PUC take a discerning approach to quality improvement, in contrast to a rigid adherence to the only system they know.

A student services organization might begin its exploration of the Baldrige criteria by addressing the criteria for student services (criterion 6.2 under the Process Management). In this section, institutions address the following questions:

1. What are your key student services?

2. How do you determine key student service requirements, incorporating input from students, faculty and staff members, other stakeholders, and suppliers/partners, as appropriate? What are the key requirements for these services?

3. How do you design and deliver these services to meet all the key requirements?

4. What are your key performance measures/indicators used for the control and improvement of these services? Include how in-process measures and feedback from students, faculty and staff members,

stakeholders, and suppliers are used in managing your student services, as appropriate.

5. How do you improve your student services to keep them current with educational service needs and directions, to achieve better performance, and to control overall costs? How are improvements shared with other organizational units and processes, as appropriate? (National Institute of Standards and Technology, 2002)

Having described its approach to providing student services, the organization might then address the questions under Organizational Performance Results (criterion 7.2—Student- and Stakeholder-Focused Results) (National Institute of Standards and Technology, 2002). In this section, institutions are asked to "summarize . . . results, including student and stakeholder satisfaction" (p. 31), segmenting results by student and stakeholder groups and market segments, as appropriate and including comparative data. The questions are:

1. What are your current levels and trends in key measures/indicators of current and past student and key stakeholder satisfaction and dissatisfaction, including comparisons with competitors and/or comparable organizations' levels of student and stakeholder satisfaction?

2. What are your current levels and trends in key measures/indicators of student- and stakeholder-perceived value, persistence, positive referral, and/or other aspects of building relationships with students and stakeholders, as appropriate? (National Institute of Standards and Technology, 2002)

In addressing these questions, respondents are asked to include a brief description of how the appropriateness of each comparison is ensured. For example, many organizations state goals in terms of being the best at some aspect of service, yet they provide national averages for comparison. Other institutions use the athletic conference as the comparison group. It is true that at EMU three members of its athletic conference did end up in the final comparison group of nineteen—but only three.

The preceding questions are only two of nineteen sets of criteria in the Baldrige evaluation process. The process is rigorous and stimulating and the chase for the award has captured the imaginations of many organizations. However, even institutions with limited energy for self-improvement might consider using the criteria for an initial assessment. Increasingly, regional accrediting agencies are moving toward evaluation frameworks that are in sympathy with the spirit of the Baldrige Award (see Eaton, 2001). The region that is probably farthest down this path is the Higher Learning Commission of the North Central Association of Colleges and Schools (NCA).

The NCA's Academic Quality Improvement Project

As Eaton (2001) notes, prescriptive accreditation processes do not serve mature academic institutions very well. As a result, most American accrediting agencies are moving toward mission-based evaluations that support quality improvement. This shift will constitute a radical transformation in accreditation culture. The NCA Academic Quality Improvement Project (AQIP) is a prime example. It is a developmental program that requires improvement and change but does not specify a specific level of accomplishment that must be achieved. In this respect, it differs from the Baldrige Program.

The AQIP process begins with extensive self-evaluation that supports application for admission to the program. There are nine evaluation criteria that are based on the Baldrige criteria: helping students learn, accomplishing other distinct objectives, understanding students' and other stakeholders' needs, valuing people, leading and communicating, supporting institutional operations, measuring effectiveness, planning continuous improvement, and building collaborative relationships.

Like the Baldrige system, the AQIP requires that participants describe the context for analysis, processes, results, and strategies for improvement in each area of interest. For example, in the area of student and stakeholder needs, respondents are asked to address these questions (a sample of the twenty-two questions in this area):

- ○ *Context:* Into what key groups do you break down your student and key stakeholder base? How do you define and differentiate these students and other stakeholder groups?

- ○ *Processes:* How do you identify the changing needs of your student groups? How do you analyze and select a course of action regarding these needs?

- ○ *Results:* What are your results regarding student satisfaction with your performance? How do your results compare with the results of other higher education institutions and, if appropriate, organizations outside of the education community?

- ○ *Improvement:* How do you improve your current processes and systems for understanding the needs of your key student and stakeholder groups?

It is important to note that the AQIP process is flexible enough to accommodate institutions with a commitment to improvement that cannot answer all of the questions in the self-assessment. This flexibility results from the design of the program. Participants enter the program after application through participation in a "strategy forum." In this forum, new participants bring forward three to four "action projects" designed to help the organization improve both its performance and its approach to performance improvement. Thus, an institution in the early stages of a commitment to continuous improvement could define a project focused on establishing key measures and creating the information management systems necessary to support improvement in a key program area.

Participants in the strategy forum are grouped into clusters of peer institutions that serve as partners in strengthening the design of each other's action projects. Once projects are finalized, participants report annually on their action projects. At the same time, the institutions maintain systems portfolios organized around the nine AQIP quality criteria and describing the processes that the institutions use to achieve institutional goals and present performance results. Participants work with the AQIP to conduct a systems appraisal every four years that evaluates institutional strengths, identifies opportunities for improvement, and provides concrete actionable feedback for improving processes and performance (North Central Association of Colleges and Schools, 2000). Accreditation is reaffirmed every seven years, based on successful participation in the AQIP process.

Both the Baldrige and AQIP criteria offer colleges and universities a framework for self-appraisal based on the fundamental commitments they make in their mission statements. The questions ask for clear definitions of objectives, unambiguous descriptions of how institutions intend to meet those objectives, and evidence that objectives have been met. Results are evaluated against the results that peer institutions obtain on sets of comparable measures driven by similar missions. The process is deceptively simple. What drives change is, first, the realization that an institution can't answer all of the questions and, second, that the results achieved to date are seldom what institutional leaders would like to have achieved. Any institution or unit can use the criteria to create a case for change, as several mentioned in this book have.

Change Management

It takes a compelling vision of a possible future to build support for change in an organization. The understanding that emerges when institutions use a rigorous system for self-analysis can help shape a picture of that possible future. A possible future that differs from the present reality is most often the reason for successful change. Yet even when leaders and organization members know that change must take place, the work of change management is not easy. Whenever people's control over their environment is threatened by change, they will resist it. This is true, whether change is positive or not. Change management deals with the human side of change. Project management deals with the tasks that must be accomplished to bring about change. Both perspectives on change must be taken into account to ensure successful change. But management of the human side of change is often overlooked. It is therefore no accident that nineteen of the twenty IBM Best Practice Partners have employed active change management strategies to create service environments that support excellence in student services.

The key to active change management is understanding resistance to change. The most potent force underlying resistance is an employee's inability to see him- or herself in the future organization. Very often, leaders do a good job of describing what the "brave new world" will look like. They see themselves playing a leading role in creating that future. But organization members know that they have been successful under the existing order. They have had the skills and the tools to succeed in the present environment. It is not at all clear that they will have the tools or skills to be successful in the future. This creates a period of great uncertainty between *now* and the future order.

The management of the reasonable fears of employees requires little more than providing a path from now to the future. To do this, leaders first need to know what skills will be required for employees to succeed in this future. Second, they need to be able to assess the gap between where employees are now and where they will need to be. Third, leaders need to develop a strategy for closing this gap. Finally, leaders need to create a strategy that both safeguards the loyalty of essential personnel and deals with the eventuality that some current employees will not be able to make the transition to the skill set required in the organization following change. Organizations deal with this last challenge differently. Some promise job security; others create systems to help employees who cannot go forward move out of the organization. In either case, humane, employee-centered policies are essential to foster the loyalty of those who will remain.

A key element of helping people move forward is information concerning what will be required of them in the future. A second key element is an effective evaluation and training system that allows employees to do a self-assessment concerning their skill development needs. The most effective systems create supports and incentives that encourage employees to take responsibility for their own development. Such an approach deals with the current skill development needs and fosters the capacity for continuing development that will be needed in the future. The human capacity that is developed in this way is supportive of the culture of continuous improvement that is created when institutions use either the Baldrige or AQIP processes to guide development. Assessment creates a vision of what might be; active change management enables employees to reach that vision.

Sustainable Change

As long as we continue to look outward from our own institutions, we will see a compelling case for change in the progress of our peers and competitors. If we look far, we will even see ideas in very different "industries" that can fuel the vision of our imaginations. If we add to this vision a system that organizes our energies toward a common agenda and tools that enable us to chart our direction, movement and change will happen. If we remember to take care of our most precious assets—our people—along the way, we will be able to sustain a culture that changes and grows indefinitely.

References

Astin, A. W. *Assessment for Excellence: The Philosophy and Practice of Assessment and Evaluation in Higher Education.* New York: American Council on Education and McMillan, 1991.

Black, J. "Creating a Student Centered Culture." In D. J. Burnett and D. G. Oblinger (eds.), *Innovation in Student Services: Planning for Models Blending High Touch/High Tech.* Ann Arbor, Mich.: Society for College and University Planning, 2002.

Daniel, J. "Lessons from the Open University: Low-Tech Learning Often Works Best." *Chronicle of Higher Education.* Sept. 7, 2001, B24.

Eaton, J. S. "Regional Accreditation Reform: Who Is Served?" *Change,* 2001, 33(Mar.-Apr.), 38–45.

Kaplan, R. S., and Norton, D. P. *Translating Strategy into Action: The Balanced Scorecard.* Boston: Harvard Business School Press, 1996.

National Institute of Standards and Technology. *Baldrige National Quality Program: 2002 Education Criteria for Performance Excellence.* Gaithersburg, Md.: National Institute of Standards and Technology, 2002.

North Central Association of Colleges and Schools. Academic Quality Improvement Project. Chicago: Commission on Institutions of Higher Education, North Central Associations of Colleges and Schools, 2000.

Peters, T. J., and Waterman, R. H. *In Search of Excellence: Lessons from America's Best-Run Companies.* New York: HarperCollins, 1982.

18

STUDENT-CENTERED
ACADEMIC SERVICES

George D. Kuh, Anthony M. English, Sara E. Hinkle

With a sense of anticipation and a bounce in her step, Amy Rogers is off to register for her first-semester classes. Upon entering the student services building lobby, she's surprised to see a very long line snaking down the hall and around a corner.

After making her way to the end of the line, she asks the man ahead of her, "How long have you been here?"

"About two minutes," he replies. "But my roommate got here an hour ago, and he just got in the door. We're in for a wait." Shifting restlessly, he moves forward another few inches. "This is really bogus. For what we're paying, you'd think the university could speed up this operation."

Amy is dismayed but resigns herself to the wait.

Forty-five minutes later, when she finally reaches the service counter, she gets a perfunctory glance from the service agent and a tired request for her identification number. The agent enters the number into his computer and then frowns. Amy silently hopes that everything is in order.

"Ms. Rogers," the service agent says, "I can't let you register yet. Your SAT scores aren't on file."

"But that's impossible," Amy replies. "I turned those in months ago with my application for admission."

"Well, I'm sorry," the agent replies, "but they don't show up on my screen. I have to put a hold on your registration until this gets cleared up."

"When will that happen?" Amy asks.

"I can't really say. It might be a computer foul-up. Maybe the tech support folks over in admissions are working on it. We'll let you know."

Amy is close to tears. "But I'm supposed to register for classes now. Can't you do anything?"

"I'm afraid not."

"Is there anyone else here I can talk to—a manager or somebody like that?" Amy asks.

The service agent hesitates and then with a sigh glances over his shoulder. The other staff members look like they'd rather walk across hot coals than take on another problem. "I'm sorry, but it doesn't look like anyone is available at the moment. The best I can do is have you fill out this 'lost records' form and go to the admissions office." Staring at the two-page form, Amy moves away from the counter. The line is even longer. There's no bounce in her step as she tries to remember where the admissions office is located.

---

o

AMY'S FIRST COLLEGE REGISTRATION was a frustrating experience. Though we don't know all the causes of the poor service she received, some things are obvious. Communication with other academic units on campus seems to be hobbled by data problems, perhaps exacerbated by student overload. Staff morale could also use a boost. The lackluster response that Amy received is perhaps symptomatic of a rigid, bureaucratic office culture that discourages cooperation.

No student should ever experience what Amy went through. And no college or university has to function like this. In this chapter, we offer a dramatically different vision of what academic student services can and should be—a responsive, student-centric unit staffed by motivated professionals who understand that their mission is to support student learning and success. We explain why high-performing, student-centric academic services are needed and we describe what such organizations look like. We also suggest practical steps institutions can take to deal effectively with the challenges that academic services organizations are likely to face in the future. When appropriate, we use examples from colleges and universities to illustrate key points.

Assumptions

Our vision of student-centric academic services is based on several assumptions about how conditions in the external environment are shaping and will continue to shape colleges and universities in the future, the changing nature of students and their expectations, and the relevant features of academic service units in institutions of higher education.

The External Environment

The escalating pace of change in virtually every aspect of contemporary life requires that colleges and universities respond more quickly to shifting economic, social, and political realities. Economic cycles are shorter and more volatile. The demand for higher education will continue to increase, fueled by a spike in the number of high school graduates (Zusman, 1999), the steadily growing number of older students taking courses to advance in their careers (Munitz, 2000), and an insatiable need for continuous learning. According to the University Continuing Education Association, the percentage of adults pursuing some form of postsecondary education jumped about 25 percent between 1991 and 1995 (*Lifelong Learning Trends,* 1998). Traditional institutions and proprietary entities alike are trying to attract their share of this booming market, both with on-campus and distance education offerings. The University of Phoenix, for example, enrolls more than forty thousand students at more than fifty for-profit learning centers in twelve states (Marchese, 1998). Other entities, such as the DeVry Institute of Technology and ITT Educational Services, serve thousands more (Marchese, 1998). Overall, more than six hundred for-profit organizations grant degrees, and nearly a thousand institutions give students the opportunity to take courses electronically (Newman, 2000). Students expect to be able to choose from an array of academic services options (such as registration and advising), whether they accomplish their learning on campus or on-line.

Institutions will have to deal with changing external conditions by continually adjusting their structures and processes without the benefit of added resources. In addition, pressing social issues besides those facing higher education often compel legislators to direct funds elsewhere (Zusman, 1999).

The Twenty-First Century Student

The large wave of post-1965 immigration is changing the complexion of college classrooms (Keller, 2001), as nearly one-quarter of all students today are ethnic minorities (Zusman, 1999). "New majority" students, aged twenty-five or older, attending classes part-time, now make up more than 40 percent of undergraduates (Kuh, 2001). In addition, many more learners—especially computer-savvy students right out of high school— prefer doing business with their institutions asynchronously. Colleges and universities must be sensitive to their student consumers, who expect convenient, "one-stop shopping" services that are available around the clock, much like those offered by banks and convenience stores (Levine and Cureton, 1998).

Academic Services Units

Efficiency, client satisfaction, and quality are the watchwords of service units at colleges and universities that want to meet students' academic support needs. In addition to a steady or decreasing share of state appropriations (Zusman, 1999), colleges and universities also face unprecedented demands to more effectively document their value and achievements (Banta and Borden, 1994; Heller, 2001). If anything, these demands for accountability and assessment will intensify. As a result, units will probably have to provide more services with fewer resources.

As we note later in this chapter, technology, if used wisely, may yield some efficiencies in registration and advising services (Ehrman, 1999; Slaughter, Kittay, and Duguid, 2001; Turoff, 2000). At the same time, technology is not an elixir. Moreover, the "silo mentality" (Marchese, 1994; Schroeder, 1999), exacerbated by the continuing specialization of disciplines and support services, will make it increasingly difficult for staff members to stay abreast of the policies, procedures, and requirements of other offices (Godwin and Markham, 1996). The combination of these trends will force changes in the character and manner in which academic services are delivered. The key to delivering high-quality service may well rest on whether academic service units can become student-centric organizations.

Characteristics of High-Performing, Student-Centric Academic Services Units

Given the factors listed earlier, what does a student-centric academic services unit look like? The experience of Kari Rogers, Amy's twin sister, provides some clues. Kari is also starting college, but at another university, in a neighboring state.

○

Kari enters the lobby of the registrar's office and joins a line of students. Within a minute she's moved at least ten feet and is only a few yards from the door. "People seem to be getting their classes pretty fast," she says to the young man in line ahead of her.

"Looks like it," he replies.

"That's great," Kari remarks, as she notices the long tables that line the hallway. One pamphlet among the many informational brochures catches her eye: Answers to Frequently Asked Questions.

Kari barely has time to scan the brochure before she's at the front counter. The service agent greets her with a smile and introduces himself. "I'm Greg. How are you doin' today?" He asks Kari for her name and ID number, and then asks where she went to high school. As he pecks away at his computer, he asks if she knows John Wagner, who taught at Kari's high school.

"I do!" Kari exclaims. "How do you know Mr. Wagner?" Turns out that Wagner, Kari's former chemistry teacher, was a college classmate of Greg's uncle. Small world.

Out of the corner of her eye, Kari sees someone making the rounds of the room, occasionally stopping to answer a question. Her attention comes back to the counter, and Greg glances up at Kari with a mildly concerned look. She silently hopes that everything is in order.

"Have you been to the academic advising office yet?" Greg asks.

"Yes, I was there this morning," Kari replies. "They helped me figure out which classes to take first." She digs through her backpack to show the agent her notes.

"Well, whoever helped you over there didn't record it in your file. Technically, we're supposed to verify that before you can register. But you've obviously been there. I think I can fix this. Hang on a sec." Greg chats briefly with someone by phone. He hangs up with a smile. "Good news. They're updating your record. It won't show on my screen for a while, but I'm going to clear you here so you can get going."

Kari is relieved. "Thanks, I really appreciate it!" Greg walks her over to a row of computer terminals, orients her to the user-friendly registration interface, and tells her about the registration Web site that she can now use. After finalizing her class registration, Kari starts toward the student union to meet her roommate. It may be her imagination, but the registration line seems to be moving even more quickly than before.

○

Kari's experience is vastly different from that of her sister. The efficient, responsive, student-friendly office at Kari's school is a product of a deeply rooted, highly collaborative ethic that places student success and satisfaction foremost in everyone's minds. Such highly effective academic services units have these and several other features in common that characterize a student-centric organization. We'll now consider four of the more important features.

A Shared Vision and Philosophy for Student Success

The philosophy driving the work of a student-centric academic services unit is predicated on two operating principles. The first is that all students can succeed if they are given the opportunity and support to work through the inevitable challenges that college presents. The second is that academic services' raison d'être is to provide accurate, timely information to all students in the most helpful and efficient manner possible. These principles are articulated clearly and consistently by senior staff members in a way that creates a mindscape, or a way of visualizing these principles in action—how they are manifested in day-to-day activities, decisions, and interactions with students and other clients.

On an annual basis, staff members collectively review the formal statement of the unit's mission. Doing so ensures that newcomers are systematically introduced to the mission and that continuing staff members are reminded of the unit's values and goals as well as of their individual responsibilities for promoting student success. Through such public events, a common language is developed and expanded. This language allows people to easily communicate within the unit in a way that is consistent with its espoused values and operating philosophy and that facilitates cross-functional dialogue and cooperation. Being on the same page helps buoy and maintain morale.

The Office of Enrollment Services at the Harvard University School of Public Health exemplifies these principles. The first line of its mission statement declares that it will "support all activities related to students' admission, registration, progress to degree, and financial support" ("Welcome!" 2001). Another example is the Maricopa County Community College District in Phoenix, Arizona, which embarked on a "Quantum Quality" initiative several years ago. An executive council of faculty and staff members and high-ranking leaders fleshed out a vision statement that focuses on "educational excellence for the student through a superbly prepared faculty and staff, twenty-first century technology, and a striking level of innovation" (Assar, 1993, p. 33). This effort launched the district onto a course that emphasized widespread communication, quality training and education for each member of the organization, and continuous monitoring of progress (Assar, 1993).

A Pervasive Ethic of Collaboration

The importance of collaboration to a student-centric academic services unit cannot be overstated. Collaboration enhances virtually every aspect of organizational functioning. It simplifies and adds a measure of clarity to inter- and intraoffice communications and facilitates decision making. In addition, it enables the unit to be more responsive and nimble, especially when crises or challenges arise. Moreover, when an ethic of collaboration characterizes academic services, students' questions and needs are typically addressed directly and efficiently, because those with the knowledge are more easily consulted when decisions are needed or when problems arise (Kuh, Schuh, Whitt, and Associates, 1991).

Cultivating a collaborative ethic, however, can be a challenge. Academic service units often require something of a paradigm shift to move from a focus on functional responsibilities to a systems perspective (Kuh, 1996; Schroeder, forthcoming). That is, each unit must achieve an understanding of its role in relation to the entire scope of academic services. Johnson County Community College was successful in this regard by establishing its Student Success Center, which linked, aligned, and integrated formerly disparate functional units into a seamless system of services for first-year students. One staff member at the college used the analogy of a quilt to describe this new integrated student services model: "Individual pieces of a quilt are unique in size, color, and design and without real beauty or function until they are sewn together to make a beautiful, intricate, and strong covering" (Schroeder, forthcoming).

Student-Friendly, Accessible Technology

Believing in the value and worth of each student is necessary but not by itself sufficient to implement a student-centric vision. Another essential feature is a sound technology infrastructure functioning 24/7 to meet students' needs. Convenience is especially important. It's no longer acceptable to permit service queues to form (if it ever was). Indiana University, for example, offers its "RegWeb" on-line registration system, which allows students to register for classes from any Internet-ready terminal, on or off campus, in just a few minutes. Students can also use the university's secure "Insite"

(Indiana Student Information Transaction Environment) system to check the status of an undergraduate admissions application, review bursar account information, look at course offerings, print out transcripts, and verify course scheduling information—among other options ("What Is Insite?" 2001).

Competent, Well-Prepared, and Motivated Personnel

The heart of a student-centric academic services unit is its people. For this reason, leaders take great care to seek out, appoint, and develop personnel who have the requisite knowledge and experience and are comfortable working with students and colleagues from a variety of racial and ethnic backgrounds and sexual orientations. At the Community College of Denver (CCD), for example, where about 55 percent of the student population belongs to a minority group, leaders strive to instill in all faculty and staff members and students a conscious appreciation for and attention to diversity and multiculturalism (Roueche, Roueche, and Ely, 2001). Hiring and developing people who hold these values can eliminate barriers to educational achievement. At CCD in 1998, for instance, tracking results indicated that race, ethnicity, age, and gender had no significant impact on the success of student cohorts (Roueche, Roueche, and Ely, 2001).

Furthermore, institutional leaders and managers must place a high value on the development of generalist knowledge so that employees are prepared to adequately address inquiries that cross departmental boundaries. One of the defining characteristics of the newly developed Student Success Center at James Madison University, for instance, is the effort to enhance employees' current repertoire of skills with "general support" knowledge that allows them to better serve and support students (Foucar-Szocki, Harris, Larson, and Mitchell, 2002).

Summary

The student-centric academic services organization that we previously outlined is dedicated to helping students succeed—primarily in an academic sense but also socially. The culture of such units typically features an ethic of cooperation and collaboration. Competent, highly motivated personnel develop and sustain an organizational infrastructure that is efficient, effective, and continually improving as it adjusts to changing conditions and student characteristics.

Is the promise of student-centric academic services simply a fantasy— too good to be true? No. What is true is that to create, sustain, and grow such an organization requires both short- and long-term strategies that are challenging, personally and professionally rewarding, and renewing. In the next section, we discuss some concrete actions that can help transform an academic services unit into a student-centric organization.

Transforming Student Academic Services into Student-Centric Organizations

It's Karen Shalley's first month as director of the newly organized Student Success Center at Illiana State University, and it's clear that she's got a tiger by the tail. Not only is she charged with bringing under one organizational umbrella the previously independent offices of admissions, orientation, registrar, academic advising, and study skills, but the institution's core curriculum is being revised for the first time in forty years. These moves were prompted by a suggestion from the regional accrediting agency that urged the institution to become a leader in measuring learning outcomes and promoting an institution-wide commitment to student success. In the few spare moments that punctuate her busy workdays, Karen occasionally ruminates on the challenges that lie ahead:

○

I've got my work cut out for me, no question. As a part of the university's strategic plan to become more student-centered and to place a greater emphasis on student learning, we're taking the bold step of creating a set of general curriculum requirements that will directly address specific learning outcomes recommended by the Core Curriculum Committee and ratified by the Faculty Senate. Such sweeping changes are going to have a huge impact on how we conduct business in academic services. We've got to figure out how to make the transition from the old set of requirements to the new ones. These changes will undoubtedly affect a host of other policies and practices, including academic advising, transfer policies, transcript evaluations, and class scheduling.

It won't be easy, but fortunately, we've got a terrific staff. At the same time, we don't operate in a vacuum—we're just one small cog in the wheel of a very complex organization. Academic support services affect almost every facet of the university. We need to be able to see beyond what is directly in front of us and understand how what we do is intertwined with the activities of all the other campus offices. We're constantly learning how to better communicate with our partners elsewhere on campus—the academic departments, the library, the media center, the learning resources center, the computer center—to keep them informed of what we are doing and to understand from them what we can do to help smoothly implement the curricular revision.

○

The challenge facing Shalley and her colleagues is not uncommon. Increasingly, student success and institutional effectiveness depend on the extent to which meaningful, productive working relationships exist between offices, programs, and personnel that may well be scattered throughout the university and sometimes beyond the campus (Kuh, Schuh, Whitt, and Associates, 1991). This director seems to be on the right track by focusing on developing a shared vision of a collaborative, integrated unit with a student-centric mission. In the following sections, we suggest how academic services units can move even closer toward becoming student-centric.

Support of Senior Campus Leaders

It's possible to begin developing a student-centric vision for academic student services without the involvement of senior academic and student life administrators, but it's much more difficult. In the best of circumstances, the student-centric approach will be compatible with the philosophy and vision of key institutional leaders, including the president and provost or senior academic officer (Kuh and Hinkle, 2002). If this is not the case, a persuasive argument must be developed for why a student-centric vision and mission are not only desirable but also essential in light of changing student characteristics and the other factors mentioned earlier. At some point, to sustain the student-centric change strategy, institutional leaders must become vocal champions and advocates for the innovation. They must also make visible commitments to collaborative initiatives (Kuh and Hinkle, 2002; Schroeder, 1999).

In the early 1990s, Syracuse University set out to become just such a "student-centered research university" (Vincow, 1993). The strategy Syracuse followed illustrates how a firm commitment by senior leadership to a student-centric vision can make a difference (Wright, 2001). As a means of promoting a new academic plan, Chancellor Gershon Vincow initiated campuswide dialogues about future directions for the university. Through this series of ongoing communications, the chancellor was able to create not only a shared mission and vision for educational reform but also an infrastructure in which to carry it out. These efforts have resulted in rising retention and graduation rates, higher-quality students, and the gratitude of learners for the smaller class sizes, good teaching and advising, and personal attention that this student-centeredness has promoted.

Kennesaw State University in Atlanta is another institution that has realized the value of making students a priority at the highest levels of administration. "We felt it was extremely important to focus on student success," notes President Betty L. Siegel, "since facilitating our students' growth and development is at the heart of the University's mission." Toward this end, Kennesaw State formed a division led by the aptly named vice president for student success and enrollment services. "Grouping offices together that have as their primary purpose providing exemplary enrollment services, encouraging an appreciation of diversity, creating a sense of community, and fostering student learning," states Siegel, "is a way to acknowledge that we are intentionally creating a more student-centric environment" (personal communication, February 2002).

Cultivating a Shared Vision

In addition to the support of senior leaders, organizations need a core ideology and vision to guide and sustain them over time. An early step in developing a student-centric vision is to help academic services personnel think more concretely and clearly about the desired outcomes of their work. Certainly the ways in which work gets done—the day-to-day processes and practices—are important. That said, focusing more on outcomes has the potential to engage staff members in fruitful self-examination and organizational introspection. Thus, it's desirable to ask:

○ What is it we do?
○ Why do we do it this way?
○ What is our overriding purpose as a unit?

To illustrate, it would be extremely helpful if all the units now part of Shalley's Student Success Center agreed that their collective purpose is "to promote student success by providing needed information and removing obstacles to the academic process." This is a big step toward developing the type of student-centric vision that is needed to increase the productivity of academic services and promote higher levels of student satisfaction, achievement, and persistence.

Another tactic to encourage a shared vision is to involve staff members in establishing superordinate goals—organizational aims that are bigger and better than anything that has ever been accomplished before. In

Shalley's case, the large and important undertaking of curricular revision fits this bill. A goal of this magnitude cannot be achieved individually, but, by definition, it requires the collective efforts of everyone in the academic service unit. To induce commitment to this activity, it's essential that each stakeholder see how his or her work helps the organization move closer to attaining the superordinate goal. Indeed, it will be critical for Shalley to consistently articulate and reinforce to the staff members in the disparate offices that she manages how their various functions play a vital role in the development of the core curriculum and the promotion of student success. This type of approach is, as Senge (1994) puts it, a "commitment to the whole," whereby "individuals committed to a vision beyond their self-interest find they have energy not available when pursuing narrower goals, as will organizations that tap into this level of commitment" (p. 171).

Communication vehicles are also essential for involving key stakeholders (PriceWaterhouse Change Integration Team, 1995). For a shared vision of student success to take root, this goal and its underlying rationale must be repeatedly articulated over many months. Effective preachers follow the maxim, "'Tell them what you're going to say, say it, and then tell them what you've said.' . . . You need to stay fresh in front of the communication task, without overlooking the fact that repetition is the point" (PriceWaterhouse Change Integration Team, 1995, p. 39). Furthermore, going the extra mile to involve stakeholders in problem solving, knowledge sharing, and examination of the progress and problems of change will yield better results.

One way to achieve this is through large-scale events that engage substantial numbers of stakeholders in a collaborative task via dialogue, reflection, and action (Brigham, 1996). These events are based on Senge's "systems thinking" concept (1994), which emphasizes how various elements of an organization work together (as contrasted with their independent actions). Examples of large-scale events include

- o "Future Search"—participants come together in a retreat setting and format to focus on creating preferred alternative future scenarios for the organization
- o "Open Space Technology"—an organizing theme is identified from which any number of interested participants can become involved in planning or solving problems
- o "Interactive Design"—participants are involved in a continuing interactive process that requires several phases in order to develop alternative "ideal" design options

When conducted well, large-scale events can help build a sense of community and commitment to common goals and values. People throughout academic services units gain a better understanding and deeper appreciation of how their work contributes to the whole and influences each other. For example, at Belmont University, a group of eight faculty members held a ten-hour retreat over two days with sixty-seven other professors in order to collaboratively explore the issue of curricular reform (Brigham, 1996). During this retreat, related issues were passionately discussed, which resulted in a host of recommendations for changes to the university's general education program, which were supported by sixty-five of the participants. A similar approach could be used within academic services in order to promote the "systems thinking" that is so vital to instilling a shared vision.

Instilling an Ethic of Collaboration

Collaboration can be facilitated, but it can't be forced. That is, an administrative edict will not bring about the spirit of cooperation and the collaborative skills needed to work effectively and efficiently within and across organizational lines. Collaborative efforts will be most successful when focused on a specific purpose or problem that affects many or most clients and staff members. For example, a required 100-level English class consistently fills up before all the students can enroll, thus creating frustrated and dissatisfied students. Chances are good that staff members from academic advising, the registrar's office, the English department, and admissions will be motivated to find a solution to this problem because it plays into their own self-interests. When people are motivated to solve a problem, they often become personally invested, a quality critical to achieving the desired results.

Various forms of cross-functional team learning can be especially useful in this regard. For example, sending a team of people with representatives from advising, admissions, and orientation to a meeting or conference together is an effective way to build shared knowledge and begin to develop a common language. A core group of more than a dozen academic administrators, faculty members, and student affairs professionals from Indiana University Bloomington used this approach when visiting the University of Missouri-Columbia to see and hear firsthand from people like them about the promising educational practices being implemented at the sister school to enhance the first-year student experience. The trip introduced the participants to the vision and language of student success, convincing key people that embracing promising practices was not only doable but indeed preferable to the way the campus was currently operating (Hossler, Kuh, and Olsen, 2001).

Another way to facilitate collaboration is to model the desired behavior. According to William G. Tierney (1999), "when institutional participants incorporate in their own behavior the kind of work they desire from others they offer potent incentives for what they want" (p. 132). Certainly, it would be wise for Shalley to frequently bring together her staff from different departments in order to discuss common problems and provide feedback for important departmental decisions. In addition, she should demonstrate her own willingness to work with other areas of the campus. If done consistently, such actions can send a powerful message to Shalley's staff about the value of collaboration within the organization.

Improving Organizational Responsiveness

Ultimately, whether academic services units contribute to student success depends on whether students get what they need to achieve their educational objectives. Following are things that student-centric organizations do very well.

PROVIDE STUDENTS WITH FREQUENT, TIMELY FEEDBACK. In the absence of feedback, it's difficult to change behavior or improve performance. Early warning systems that link academic services personnel with colleagues elsewhere on campus are most helpful in this regard. For example, at Truman State University, academic advisers go over their advisees' results from the College Student Experiences Questionnaire. They then use this information to help students reflect on the way they spend their time as compared with how their peers spend their time. This gives students an empirically derived student success baseline against which to measure their own performance. A student might ask,

- Am I studying more or less than my friends?
- Am I writing a larger or smaller number of drafts of papers?
- Am I talking more or less frequently with faculty members about assignments?

At DePauw University, the Horizon Scholars Program serves a similar purpose through the collaborative efforts of admissions, financial aid, select faculty members, the writing center, and other student support services. At the time of admission, "at risk" students are identified in order to provide them with the structure and support that institutional research has indicated will increase their chances for academic success. These efforts include faculty assistance in plotting out assignment due dates on a calendar and working with students to develop a financial plan that will enable them to manage their resources appropriately. Overall, Horizon Scholars are well satisfied with their college experience, and 92 percent of the first Horizon Scholars cohort (class of 2001) graduated on time.

ENSURE THAT ACADEMIC SERVICES ARE ACCESSIBLE. One way to become more accessible is to deliver services from a point more conveniently located to students. Indiana University Bloomington did this by establishing academic support centers in two residence halls (Hossler, Kuh, and Olsen, 2001). The centers are accessible to students Sunday through Thursday from 7 to 11 P.M., hours during which students are most likely to take advantage of the services. Institutional research shows that students in high-risk courses are almost twice as likely to seek tutoring when it was available in their own residence hall, rather than being provided at other campus locations. Moreover, first-year students who used the services got better grades and were more likely to return for their sophomore year.

By the same token, Auburn University made its academic services more accessible by integrating into a centralized student success center the programs provided by academic support, career development, student counseling, and freshman year experience and students in transition (McDaniel, James, and Davis, 2000). Now, twenty-six retention-related initiatives are housed in three nearby buildings in the main part of campus to approximate a one-stop student services model. Though staff members are spread among different buildings, Auburn has made services convenient by using technology to enhance interoffice communication, developing an on-line student referral and database system, and cross-training personnel.

Another way to make services more accessible is to use off-campus venues. This is especially important for institutions in metropolitan areas that enroll large numbers of students who are taking courses in addition to working full-time or raising a family. Georgia State University, for example, located in downtown Atlanta, has several sites throughout the metro area near safe parking or public transportation that require only a short commute from a student's place of employment or home. Such ventures require coordination between a number of campus departments in order to ensure the smooth delivery of academic services.

Technology is another tool that student-centric academic services units use to improve student access to services. Western Iowa Tech Community College in Sioux City, for instance, infused technology into its instruction and student support functions (Stoik, 2001). Software upgrades permit more information to be included in the school's database, including a new student profile showing academic standing, class attendance, and grading capabilities; revised graduation and transcript processes; and expanded data-tracking and reporting functions. Faculty advisers and student service staff members developed course placement, early-alert, and referral systems and were subsequently cross-trained in course placement assessment, orientation, career services, counseling, financial aid, and registration. Key to the success of the effort was the collaboration between instructors and academic support staff members to modify the curriculum and instructional methods to address the special needs of particular students. This systematic approach to using technology resulted in improved student advising and learning assistance, as well as an increase in student retention—an important indicator of student success.

CONTINUALLY MONITOR AND IMPROVE ORGANIZATIONAL PERFORMANCE. Student-centric units are constantly striving to improve what they do (Kuh, Schuh, Whitt, and Associates, 1991). Ongoing formative evaluation and assessment activities are commonplace. Teams of staff and faculty members and students help the unit stay true to its mission by looking closely at the student experience through the eyes of students themselves. Thus, before deciding what or how aspects of a unit's performance should be improved, it must first be discovered and understood how what the unit does is actually experienced by students. That is, members of the unit must "see" through students' eyes.

Another way to efficiently gather feedback for performance refinement is through telephone or Web surveys that can be administered to the entire student population or to strategically identified subgroups. Penn State University's Pulse projects—short telephone surveys focused on current issues affecting students and the campus—are an example (Kuh, Gonyea, and Rodriguez, 2002). The advantages of this kind of approach are the reduced cost and the ease of summarizing responses—especially when the questions focus on what President Dean Hubbard of Northwest Missouri State University calls "actionable" data—issues the institution can do something about almost immediately.

Continuous improvement also applies to personnel. Ongoing staff development is essential in the form of on- and off-campus workshops, conferences, and targeted training sessions that help employees stay abreast of technology advances. Learning about the actions of peers at other institutions where innovations have been highly successful can provide employees with powerful experiences. For instance, members of Indiana University Bloomington's Office of Academic Affairs, College of

Arts and Sciences, Enrollment Services, Campus Life, and the Registrar's Office came together in the late 1990s to form "Frosh Up," a cross-functional team that took it upon itself to search for ways to elevate the academic and social performance of new students. The group adhered to a best practices approach, whereby members became familiar with what the research on college student development indicated were promising policies and practices for promoting student success. With this knowledge, they then proposed to their colleagues a number of improvements to student academic services on campus. One such activity was to develop and distribute to all first-year students and their families an academic expectations video, designed to help students more accurately anticipate and subsequently adjust to academic demands and other aspects of college life (Hossler, Kuh, and Olsen, 2001).

Finally, certain student-centric initiatives may best be addressed using a "soft project team" (Tierney, 1999) or a kind of "disappearing task force" common at Evergreen State College in Washington (Kuh, Schuh, Whitt, and Associates, 1991). These types of groups form to focus on a specific task but disband after solving the problem. Such highly focused, limited-duration efforts help "create an organization that is fluid enough to respond to the press of the environment and, at the same time, cohesive enough to maintain a sense of ideology and group identity" (Tierney, 1999, p. 37). The University of Wisconsin-Madison Graduate School is such an example. Consistent with Tierney's suggestion, several years ago the institution revamped its admissions process to better serve its more than fifteen thousand applicants. To reduce the amount of time to process applications, a team of staff members identified best practices from peer institutions and located internal structural barriers that prevented timely decision making. The office was able to shave its data entry backlog from six weeks one year to zero the next. Prospective students noticed the rapid response time. One wrote, "I applied to several schools, and UW-Madison was the most organized and human—surprising for a school of this size!" Another observed, "After applying to many of the nation's best graduate schools, I can easily rate UW-Madison's admissions process and responsiveness to inquiry as the most simple and most attentive to the students' needs!!" (Nagy and others, 1993, p. 40).

Conclusion

Academic student services compatible with the student-centric vision and philosophy have always been desirable. Today, however, changing circumstances on and off campus make highly collaborative, responsive, student-centered academic services essential. The type of organization we've described in this chapter emphasizes function and process over form and structure, though form and structure certainly cannot be ignored. The characteristics we've discussed exist in part on many campuses, but only a small fraction of institutions are systematically moving to develop student-centric units.

The knowledge and technology exist for almost any academic services operation to morph into a student-centric office. Occasionally, financial resources may limit how much a school can do over a short period of time. However, money is not the key element needed for the successful transformation of academic services into a student-centric organization. What matters more is developing a shared vision of student success that is compatible with the institution's educational mission, the needs of students, and the will and commitment to implement the vision campuswide.

Students should never have to encounter the frustration and poor customer service experienced by Amy Rogers. Rather, if institutions of higher education are serious about promoting a culture that is sensitive to student needs and dedicated to the promotion of student success, they will strive to offer services that more closely approximate the experience of Kari Rogers. Such a goal requires the efforts of all segments of the university. Indeed, individual functional units must cultivate a systems perspective to see how what they do contributes to the overriding goal of student success. An ethic of collaboration is essential to an organizational infrastructure that is efficient, effective, and continuously improving in response to changing conditions and student characteristics.

A student-centric culture takes time to cultivate. But the result is well worth the investment. When academic services are fashioned in the ways that we have described in this chapter, faculty and staff members at colleges and universities strengthen the ability of students to reach their highest potential.

REFERENCES

Assar, K. E. "TQM on Campus: Case Study Number Two: Phoenix: Quantum Quality at Maricopa." *Change,* 1993, 25(May–June), 32–35.

Banta, T. W., and Borden, V.M.H. (eds.). *Using Performance Indicators to Guide Strategic Decision Making,* New Directions for Institutional Research, no. 82. San Francisco: Jossey-Bass, 1994.

Brigham, S. E. "Large-Scale Events: New Ways of Working Across the Organization." *Change,* 1996, 28(Nov.–Dec.), 28–37.

Ehrman, S. C. "Technology's Grand Challenges." *Academe,* 1999, 85(5), 42–46.

Foucar-Szocki, D., Harris, L., Larson, R. D., and Mitchell, R. L. "Layers of Learning: Planning and Promoting Performance Improvement and Action

Learning." In D. Burnett and D. Oblinger (eds.), *Innovation in Student Services: Planning for Models Blending High Touch/High Tech.* Ann Arbor, Mich.: Society for College and University Planning, 2002.

Godwin, G. J., and Markham, W. T. "First Encounters of the Bureaucratic Kind." *Journal of Higher Education,* 1996, *67*(6), 660–689.

Heller, D. E. (ed.). The States and Public Higher Education Policy: Affordability, Access, and Accountability. Baltimore: Johns Hopkins University Press, 2001.

Hossler, D., Kuh, G. D., and Olsen, D. "Finding (More) Fruit on the Vines: Using Higher Education Research and Institutional Research to Guide Institutional Policies and Strategies." (Part II). *Research in Higher Education,* 2001, *42,* 223–235.

Keller, G. "The New Demographics of Higher Education." *The Review of Higher Education,* 2001, *24*(3), 219–235.

Kuh, G. D. "Guiding Principles for Creating Seamless Learning Environments for Undergraduates." *Journal of College Student Development* 1996, *37,* 135–148.

Kuh, G. D. "College Students Today: Why We Can't Leave Serendipity to Chance." In P. Altbach, P. Gumport, and B. Johnstone (eds.), *In Defense of the American University.* Baltimore: The Johns Hopkins University Press, 2001.

Kuh, G. D., Gonyea, R. M., and Rodriguez, D. P. "Assessing Student Development During the College Years." In T. W. Banta (ed.), *The Scholarship of Assessment.* San Francisco: Jossey-Bass, 2002.

Kuh, G. D., and Hinkle, S. E. "Enhancing Student Learning Through Collaboration Between Academic Affairs and Student Affairs." In. R. M. Diamond (ed.), *A Field Guide for Academic Leaders.* San Francisco: Jossey-Bass, 2002.

Kuh, G. D., Schuh, J. H., Whitt, E. J., and Associates. *Involving Colleges.* San Francisco: Jossey-Bass, 1991.

Levine, A., and Cureton, J. S. "Collegiate Life: An Obituary." *Change,* 1998, *30*(3), 12–18.

Lifelong Learning Trends: A Profile of Continuing Higher Education. (5th ed.) Washington, D.C.: University Continuing Education Association, 1998.

Marchese, T. "Assessment." Paper presented at the annual meeting of the American College Personnel Association, Indianapolis, Mar. 1994.

Marchese, T. "Not So Distant Competitors: How New Providers Are Remaking the Postsecondary Marketplace." *AAHE Bulletin,* 1998, *50*(9), 3–7.

McDaniel, N., James, J. B., and Davis, G. "The Student Success Center at Auburn University." *About Campus,* 2000, *5*(1), 25–28.

Munitz, B. "Changing Landscape." *Educause Review,* 2000, *35*(1), 12–18.

Nagy, J., and others. "TQM on Campus: Case Study Number Three: Madison: How TQM Helped Change an Admissions Process." *Change,* 1993, 25(May–June), 36–40.

Newman, F. "Saving Higher Education's Soul." *Change,* 2000, 32(Sept.–Oct.), 16–23.

PriceWaterhouse Change Integration Team. *Better Change: Best Practices for Transforming Your Organization.* Burr Ridge, Ill.: Irwin, 1995.

Roueche, J. E., Roueche, S. D., and Ely, E. E. "Pursuing Excellence: The Community College of Denver." *Community College Journal of Research and Practice,* 2001, 25, 517–537.

Schroeder, C. C. "Forging Educational Partnerships That Advance Student Learning." In G. S. Blimling and E. J. Whitt (eds.), *Good Practices in Student Affairs: Principles to Foster Student Learning.* San Francisco: Jossey-Bass, 1999.

Schroeder, C. C. "Collaborative Partnerships: Keys to Enhancing Student Learning and Success." In L. Upcraft, J. Gardner, and B. Barefoot (eds.), *Meeting Challenges and Building Support: Creating a Climate for First-Year Student Success.* San Francisco: Jossey-Bass, forthcoming.

Senge, P. M. *The Fifth Discipline: The Art and Practice of the Learning Organization.* New York: Doubleday/Currency, 1994.

Slaughter, S., Kittay, J., and Duguid, P. "Technology, Markets, and the New Political Economy of Higher Education." *Liberal Education,* 2001, 87(2) Spring, 6–17.

Stoik, J. H. "Technology's Role in Collaboration." *Community College Journal of Research and Practice,* 2001, 25(1), 37–47.

Tierney, W. G. *Building the Responsive Campus: Creating High-Performance Colleges and Universities.* Thousand Oaks, Calif.: Sage, 1999.

Turoff, M. "An End to Student Segregation: No More Separation Between Distance Learning and Regular Courses." *On the Horizon,* 2000, 8(1) 1–6.

Vincow, G. *Pursuing the Vision of a Student-Centered Research University: A Progress Report to the Faculty.* Syracuse, N.Y.: Syracuse University, Office of the Vice Chancellor for Academic Affairs, 1993.

"Welcome! Greetings from the Assistant Dean for Enrollment Services." [http://www.hsph.harvard.edu/enrollment/]. Nov. 2001.

"What Is Insite?" [http://insite.indiana.edu/about.html] Nov. 2001.

Wright, B. D. "The Syracuse Transformation: On Becoming a Student-Centered Research University." *Change,* 2001, 33(4), 38–45.

Zusman, A. "Issues Facing Higher Education in the Twenty-First Century." In P. Altbach, R. Berdahl, and P. Gumport (eds.), *American Higher Education in the Twenty-First Century: Social, Political, and Economic Challenges.* Baltimore: The Johns Hopkins University Press, 1999.

19

DEVELOPING PROVIDERS

Diane Foucar-Szocki, Rick Larson, Randy Mitchell

To adequately and appropriately provide student academic services, staff members must comprehend and transform institutional philosophy and values into programs and services that reflect the institution's mission and culture. Only then can they respond affirmatively to the question "Does what we are doing and how we are organized help advance the mission of the institution?" (Sandeen, 2001, p. 204). As professionals, student academic service providers strive to provide quality service related to the part of the institutional mission concerned with student success. Quality, in this context, refers to student academic services that are timely, comprehensive, collaborative, accurate, and based on outcomes. If these services are provided effectively, students will graduate, develop skills, and achieve because of their college experience. To provide quality service, academic service providers must be inspired and their work must be collaborative and learning-centered (Kuh, Siegel, and Auden, 2001). These notions reinforce the theme of this book: *student academic services are most effective when managers and practitioners take the student-centric view and work together to collaborate and seamlessly interconnect undergraduate academic services to support students from enrollment to graduation.*

A major premise of this chapter is that student academic service providers must be inspired to achieve individual and organizational objectives. Staff inspiration is distinguishable from staff empowerment in a significant manner. Whereas staff empowerment is based on the granting of power and permission, "inspiration is encouragement, revelation, exhilaration, and stimulation in thought and action. We draw on the principles, thoughts, ideas, people, and beliefs that inspire us so that we can find the meaning, courage, and energy to do our work" (Mitchell, 2001, p. 164). Managers cannot motivate others; they can only find out what motivates individuals and then create environments in which those individuals can achieve their motivations. If staff members can make the link between what they perceive as important and what they believe they can accomplish, they will be motivated to succeed (McMillan and Donelson, 1991).

Three ideas—collegiality, collaboration, and connection—are pervasive throughout this volume. This chapter expands on those ideas by focusing on developing and coordinating the work of student academic service providers in delivering quality, timely, comprehensive, collaborative, and accurate academic services to students within a student-centric context. The chapter also addresses quality customer support that employs teamwork and a balanced distribution of technology, generalists, and specialists. Overall, this chapter emphasizes the development of student academic services as learning-oriented organizations that encourage continuous individual and group improvement by inspiring staff members and by encouraging students to take responsibility for their educational success.

Creating a Learning-Oriented Student Academic Services Organization

Creating a learning-oriented student academic services organization requires a systems approach in which several key elements are intentionally identified, analyzed, and implemented. Without encountering each of the elements described in the paragraphs that follow, it is difficult to ensure a collaborative student academic services enterprise. The Learning-Oriented Organization Continuum (LOOC) is an approach for creating a learning-oriented organization, and it considers the principles outlined in the following paragraphs (see Figure 19.1).

First, expectations for improvement must come from the top. Someone at the senior level must identify a standard or ideal that is benchmarked beyond the current conditions to which student academic services contribute. Although the vision for improvement may be initiated at any level of the organization, improvement will be realized only if it has senior-level support (Creamer and Creamer, 1990).

Leadership to implement the improvement and create the change must be identified and empowered. According to Kotter (1996), "leadership defines what the future should look like, aligns people with that vision, and inspires them to make it happen despite the obstacles" (p. 25). Leadership for change indicates a distribution of responsibility to achieve improvement across the organization.

Figure 19.1. Learning-Oriented Organization Continuum

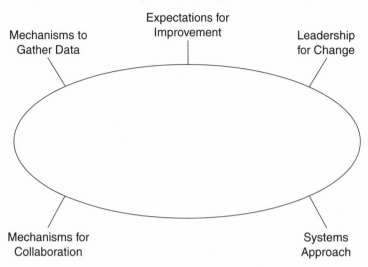

A systems approach "calls on leaders to help all members comprehend the organization's big picture and not just its parts" (Winston, Creamer, and Miller, 2001, p. 12). In a learning-oriented organization, leaders must understand and promote the development of effective working relationships among individuals so that those individuals will personally support improvements within the system. The systems approach implies integration and a deconstruction of the traditional silo mentality—or departments operating independently from one another. Departments that operate in this fashion are isolated and segregated.

As understanding of the organization shifts toward a systems view, individuals' increasing recognition of the need for relationships requires mechanisms for collaboration. "Collaboration is creating partnerships, across and within departments, based on trust, respect and commitment, for the purpose of achieving organizational and educational goals" (Mitchell, 1999, p. 27). Mechanisms for collaboration enhance communication, can be formal and informal, and might include retreats, workshops, meetings, teams, committees, neighborhood associations, and opportunities for social interaction and community involvement outside the organization.

When people begin to work together and focus on the big picture, information is needed to inform their efforts to change and improve the organization. Mechanisms to gather data should be established to ensure fact-based decision making. These mechanisms might include focus groups, surveys, interviews, observations, document reviews, site visits, and literature reviews. The gathered data are then analyzed and interpreted to inform decisions.

The LOOC model remains one-dimensional (isolated, segregated, and limited to independent efforts), unless expectations for improvement are shared, fully understood, and valued by all who are now part of a learning-oriented organization. Shared authority, shared accountability, and shared responsibility become the basis for a culture of continuous improvement. Shared expectations for improvement become the ethos of the organization as well as the mode of practice; the original expectations of leadership become the practice of all personnel. The depth of these shared relationships is represented in the Shared Learning-Oriented Organization Continuum (SLOOC). The SLOOC model is multidimensional (connected, integrated, and expanded to interdependent effort). (See Figure 19.2.)

Figure 19.2. Shared Learning-Oriented Organization Continuum

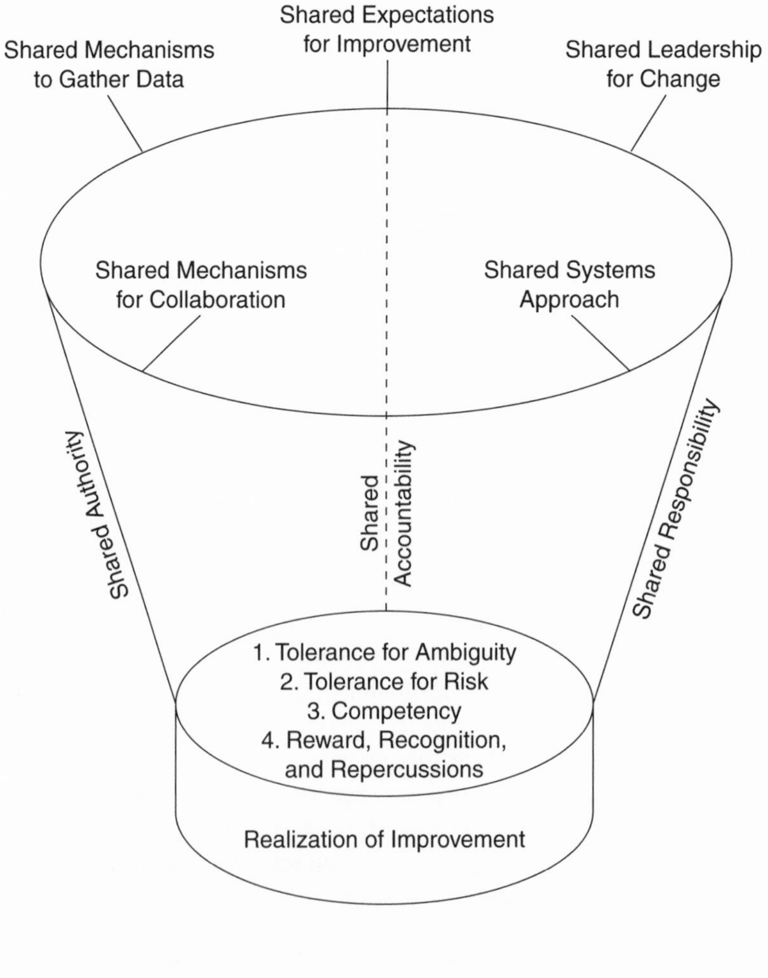

Creating Conditions for Improvement

Creating conducive conditions for improvement in a student academic services organization requires that staff members effectively use LOOC and SLOOC in three domains, collectively referred to as the 3 P's of ImPP-Provement (Foucar-Szocki, Harris, Larson, and Mitchell, 2002). *Performance improvement* enhances the capacity of service providers to assist students in making educational progress through action learning, student learning, training, development, and continuous improvement initiatives. *Place improvement* entails changing facilities to make them more accessible, flexible, and integrated in the delivery of student academic services. *Process improvement* involves studying, mapping, and changing student academic service processes to make them more efficient and effective for all constituents. Each of these domains will be examined in succeeding sections of this chapter.

Performance Improvement: Creating a Learning Organization

Although it could be said that the university was the first learning organization, many institutions of higher education are far from today's conception of a learning organization. Learning by students is the heart of the institutional enterprise, but organizational learning and change usually come at great cost, if they come at all. The modern university is in flux and must adjust to provide the best quality services to its many constituents. Student academic services personnel must continually learn new skills, acquire new knowledge, and become competent in providing service in a changing environment. The changing demographic mix of the campus requires greater attention to meeting the needs of diverse students and staff members. Changing labor markets require that staff members acquire new skills, particularly in information technology, and become more familiar with the skills students will need. Alternative forms of training and education require that institutions reexamine whether credentials are more important than competency. And accountability and productivity are increasingly prioritized, requiring the best attention and input of all involved in the higher education endeavor.

Responding effectively to these modern demands requires inspired personnel committed to the university and involved in its development through individual, team, and organizational learning. Inspiration is necessary but insufficient; inspired individuals must be able to work together to extend the impact of their learning to others at the university. Focusing on performance improvement recognizes the need for organizational change and uses learning to enhance individual value and excellence without subjecting individuals to the trauma of organizational restructuring.

A learning-oriented organization willingly scrutinizes all aspects of its operation and creates mechanisms and opportunities for all constituents to participate in this analysis. The learning-oriented organization uses the knowledge gained by analysis for improvement in all areas of the organization. Members of a learning-oriented organization are consistently attentive to what they are doing and cognizant of their contribution to the organization.

Performance is often a reflection of how processes are put into practice by the personnel who make up a part of the university. Performance improvement is integrating learning into the work to achieve enhanced results. Performance improvement incorporates workplace diagnosis, documentation, and data-driven decision making related to individual, team, process, and organizational improvement.

A standard performance improvement model consists of five phases: analysis, design, development, implementation, and evaluation (Rothwell and Kazanas, 1998). In the analysis phase, five performance variables of data are gathered. Four of these variables—mission/goals, systems, motivation, and capacity—are considered management elements, to be addressed internally. The fifth variable—expertise—requires external support (Swanson, 1996). In the design and development stages, collaboration and data-driven decision making must be maintained. Analysis, design, and development should lead to a proposal for improvement, informed by as many constituents as is feasible. The proposal brings all involved constituents into congruence and allows for clear, action-oriented management and human resource development. Suggested actions may take many forms and may include a process mapping group (described in detail later) involving employees, whereas building signage (for example, directories and office signs) might involve a contractor or specialist. Implementing a new quarterly newsletter or establishing a series of training programs could involve both internal and external expertise.

Facilitating high levels of involvement and commitment to performance improvement requires a combination of expositive, experiential, and action learning strategies for use by students and staff and faculty members. Expositive learning is *content-centered* and occurs when learners are exposed to material deemed necessary for their success and assumed to be beyond their knowledge and understanding. This is the primary approach for many college classrooms and is often the basis for training programs for university personnel. Experiential learning is *student- or learner-centered* and focuses on the active participation of the learner in making the material and the learning meaningful. Experiential learning recognizes learner differences and incorporates their understanding of content into the learning experience. Action learning is "working in small groups in order to take action on meaningful problems while seeking to learn from having taken this action" (Yorks, O'Neil, and Marsick, 1999, p. 3). Action learning integrates the *context*, or setting, in which learning takes place, the *individuals* who participate in learning, and the *purposes* for which learning is undertaken, recognizing that the individual, team, and organizational purposes will intersect and vary. Deliberate learning within the situation and acting on that learning require some explicit support and actions by the organization, as illustrated in Figures 19.1 and 19.2.

CREATING A LEARNING-CENTERED ORGANIZATION THROUGH PERFORMANCE IMPROVEMENT. Later in this chapter, we use an example from James Madison University (JMU) to demonstrate the application of the LOOC and SLOOC. To articulate expectations for improvement in customer service, student satisfaction, cost effectiveness, and "time on task" to staff members beyond those who had been serving as the leadership for change, a learning effort was undertaken through the Student Success Curriculum Development Steering Committee, which consisted of administrators, students, and faculty and staff members. The committee came together to learn about how best to support improved performance in their respective areas.

The committee was initially exposed to action learning and performance improvement through various scholarly articles. This literature served as the basis for a daylong learning event in which participants were asked to share their knowledge, understanding, and experience with action learning and performance improvement and explain how they thought these ideas related to their charge of advancing student success at JMU. The result was a yearlong learning project designed to clarify the nature of student success and what it means to promote that success while performing traditional work functions, such as being a cashier.

By working together as an integrated, cross-divisional team concentrating on learning at all levels (students, staff and faculty members, and administrators), JMU took a systems approach. As a central factor in performance improvement, a systems approach facilitates the creation of a learning-oriented organization and requires a commitment to institution-wide knowledge sharing (Senge, 1990). Students and faculty members from the Human Resource Development program served as consultants, data gatherers, analysts, and report writers. Administrators initially served as subject matter experts and coaches but came to be involved in data analysis, report writing, design, development, implementation, and evaluation, along with the students and faculty members. Membership of the committee evolved to include different students and administrators as the focus of the work shifted over time.

Mechanisms for collaboration were developed through both formal and informal means, perpetuating a collaborative learning spirit and ongoing opportunities for communication. We, the authors of this chapter, continue to meet as a "community of practice" (Wenger and Snyder, 2000), building on the insights of one another to further our effectiveness in this work—the larger student success project, and elsewhere in our professional lives. Assigned students meet weekly throughout the semester, and various staff and administrative groupings meet at least monthly. E-mail is used to extend and clarify communication. Members report on accomplishments and barriers in meetings and presentations. Cross-functional, multilevel teams, known as neighborhood associations, developed into central conduits for communication, ongoing development, and learning. This has led to a new level of shared responsibility for improvement that includes all levels of the organization, making change management a learning process, in which all constituents and stakeholders acknowledge and advocate the power of their own learning to make a difference, where tolerance for ambiguity and tolerance for risk (and acceptance of failure) are high, where competent performance is recognized, and rewards, recognition, and repercussions are made known throughout the university.

LEARNING ORGANIZATION CONSTITUENTS. The learning of each of the three constituent groups described in the following paragraphs varied and each had a different impact on the organization. However, all were critical in achieving the organizational change desired for student success.

1. *The students.* Employing an action learning process for performance improvement allows an institution to use a variety of learning techniques and interventions. In this learning environment, students develop new skills and acquire new knowledge as they work at the highest levels of cognitive functioning. Students engaged in these performance improvement projects at JMU reported an increased understanding and respect for the university and its employees. By working hand in hand with the institution to solve problems encountered daily by the staff, the students gained increased knowledge of university operations and experienced how their own contributions made a difference. Graduate students

appreciated an authentic environment for learning and applying human resource development tools that surpassed experiences traditionally found in a master's program. Ultimately, through the students' efforts to improve student success at the university, they personally experienced student success.

2. *The faculty.* In this model, faculty members are challenged to create meaningful, responsive learning interactions in which applicable knowledge, skills, and abilities are examined and analyzed (for example, what happened, why was what happened important, and what do we do next in response to what happened?). By participating in performance improvement activities and adopting a learning stance, faculty members gain insight about their own work, one another's work, and the work of the university. Faculty members approach the classroom differently when the impact of student learning is determined and assessed by a much larger audience than the professor alone.

3. *The staff.* Through engagement in performance improvement and the development of a learning orientation, staff members also gain insight about their own work, one another's work, and the work of the university. They learn during the process of analysis and in the development of interventions. With a heightened sense of community and neighborhood in their work settings, they develop a value-added context for their specialist and generalist contributions to the university. They come to understand that teamwork has less to do with sharing an office and more to do with sharing a vision. This learning has a direct impact on how staff members deal with customers and with each other in productive, respectful ways.

Learning cannot be left exclusively to students. By modeling and reinforcing shared roles and responsibilities as learners, regardless of status or role, all involved in a learning-oriented organization assume a learning perspective. This perspective mollifies the negative aspects of change, making change more plausible and palatable. Employees must allocate time to reflect on learning if the student academic service organization is to continue developing as an organic, learning-oriented organization responsive to internal and external demands.

A commitment to the development of an ethos of learning is required. Administrators must show respect and appreciation for the knowledge possessed and the knowledge needed by employees. Recognition should be provided for employees who have acquired new knowledge, skills, and abilities. Where possible, resources of people, materials, funding, and time should be allocated to facilitate learning. Administrators must be sensitive and responsive to the changing learning needs of employees and must recognize the valuable learning resources of students and faculty members. Continuous open discussion and the systematization of individual development and training plans for all employees help create the desired culture of learning. The increasingly important role of the generalist should be held in high esteem. The institution should care genuinely about its people and work tirelessly to inspire excellent performance by individuals, groups, and the organization. "Changing organizational structure alone does not improve performance; yet improving performance changes the organization" (Foucar-Szocki, Harris, Larson, and Mitchell, 2002, p. 79).

Place Improvement: Creating Environments for Positive Change

Campus ecology literature illustrates how college environments influence student development and behavior (see Baird, 1988; Huebner and Lawson, 1990; Kuh, 2000; Pascarella, 1985; Schroeder, 1981; Strange, 1996, 1991). Unfortunately, analysis of college environmental influences on staff development and behavior is rare, and efforts to make a campus environment more conducive to student development and success may face resistance from those who created the existing environment (Kleinman, 1999). Nonetheless, many campuses are recognizing the value of involving staff members at all levels in place improvement—the process of changing facilities to make them more accessible, flexible, and integrated in the delivery of academic programs and services.

Place improvement is the consequence of internal and external demands for redesigned services and increased requirements for the use of technology to improve services. A heightened sense of accountability, changing demographics, and increased expectations for higher education all contribute to a mandate for change (Wingspread, 1993). Emerging trends in student services include a greater focus on the student as a customer and learner, the establishment of one-stop service centers, the development of cross-functional teams, the establishment of Web-based services and other self-service options, and systemic changes regarding campus information technology. In addition, best practices in student services include choice in service delivery (Web-based or over the counter), an empowered and skilled frontline staff, a shift from transaction to relationship in customer service, and a perspective that sees academic student services as being strategic to the institution (Burnett, 2002). These trends suggest the need for significant changes in both the *manner* in which student academic services are delivered and the *places* where student academic services are provided (Beede, 1999).

Higher education institutions in diverse settings are creating environments for positive change by redesigning student academic services in the form of student success or service centers. The University of Delaware, using the metaphor of a branch bank and its increased reliance on self-service functions, designed one of the earliest one-stop service centers in higher education and pioneered the development of Web-based "no-stop" shopping for student services (Hollowell, 1999). Seton Hall University in New Jersey has combined four separate student academic service functions into one enrollment services organization, emphasized the value of generalist service support, created a one-stop service center, and developed Web-based self-service technology (Kleinman, 1999). Utah's Brigham Young University has developed a one-stop, student-centered academic services project based on guiding principles, such as increased customer satisfaction, cross-functional teams, self-service access, and appropriate uses of technology (Kramer and Peterson, 1999). Carnegie Mellon University set out to "create a climate and culture of change" (Anderson and Elliot, 1999, p. 48) in a project called Enrollment Process Reengineering. This project included creation of "The Hub," a one-stop shop for enrollment transactions and the use of technology as an enabling resource for enrollment functions. In an effort to provide one place where students could find answers to all of their questions, Johnson County Community College in Overland Park, Kansas, developed a "success lab" as the first stop for current or potential students (Day and Pitts, 2002).

In their respective place improvement projects, many of these institutions realized that student academic services required a shift from an institution-centered vision to a student-centered vision. This shift required viewing processes, performance, and places from the student's viewpoint. Students in focus groups and surveys at these institutions requested direct access to information, the capacity to do business with the university on their own schedules and terms, and the opportunity to meet with experts when necessary. The traditional model of service delivery contained a heavy emphasis on specialists providing time-consuming and costly individualized service, a modest role for generalists, and a minimal opportunity for self-initiated service. These institutions chose to invert this ingrained service triangle—that is, self-service opportunities would be expanded to give students the access and control they desired, the role and importance of generalists would be increased to give individuals broad knowledge and the capacity to provide service, and specialists would focus on specific, complex issues.

Emerging technology allows students twenty-four-hour, self-initiated, secure access to information and certain services via the Web. The Internet has become a significant, dynamic place in which transactions can occur when needed by the student. Such services include financial aid status reports, degree audits, reports of change in address and other student information, payment of fees, registration for classes, and career planning and placement. This change in service delivery creates opportunities for the redesign of the physical facilities where many of these transactions formerly took place.

At JMU, two metaphors effectively exemplified the need for place improvement and an increased generalist focus on the provision of student academic services. "The Bermuda Triangle" reflected students' perception of the relationship between registration, financial aid, and student accounting. All three services were located in separate buildings, distant from each other. With physical separation came philosophic and programmatic separation, and "things" got lost in translation between these offices. "Trekking Through Europe" demonstrated that each time students crossed the border from one office (country) into another, they were exposed to different language, currency, customs, laws, and norms. To overcome these perspectives, the decision was made to create a one-stop service center. These and other related departments were moved— physically, philosophically, and programmatically—into one location, where students could receive on-line and counter service for many of their academic support needs. In such centers, staff members are cross-trained and organized into teams, information is shared, resulting in more efficient and effective student academic services, and space is used more proficiently with the reduction of redundant waiting rooms, lobbies, and support facilities.

These changes allow specialists to provide quality attention to students requiring individualized service. Where possible, institutions engaging in place improvement have attempted to keep specialists as close as possible to generalists to minimize the time and distance potentially encountered by students whose needs exceed those that can be adequately addressed either by self-service or generalist service centers. In many locations, professional staff members fill both roles, spending part of their time providing generalist service and part of their time in the specialist setting.

Place improvement, under this new model of student academic services, parallels a set of principles identified by Babson College in Babson Park, Massachusetts (Lewis, 1999): academic business processes should focus on and meet the needs of students, locations of student services should be centralized, integrated and accessible, universities should be accountable for quality, and technology should be employed to improve service. In place improvement, the focus for reengineered facilities is on processes rather than functions. The silo mentality of the past must give way to an institutional, student-centered vision in which the students' needs are effectively met. Physical places must be designed to fulfill this vision.

Creating a learning-centered organization through place improvement. Place improvement begins with senior-level concern for a diverse set of expectations for improvement. Students insist that student academic services should be convenient, accessible, friendly, and integrated. Parents and all parties with a stake in the cost of higher education insist that funds be expended prudently, efficiently, and with all due stewardship. Governing boards and administrators insist that their facilities provide the highest levels of quality service at the most economical cost. Staff members insist that the work environment be functional, well organized, sociable, and responsive to their needs. These various motivations can best be synchronized through a collaborative planning process designed to involve all of the constituents.

Leadership for change of this magnitude requires vision, inspiration, and a distribution of responsibility. Although anyone can contribute to leadership in the place improvement process—and many will be required to contribute—the initial inspiration is likely to come from two sources, identified by Creamer and Creamer (1990). The first source of inspiration should come from the leadership of influential managers or project directors "who focus energy and resources within the organization toward the implementation or adoption of the idea on a continuing basis" (p. 183). The second source of inspiration should come from the championship of a group committed to planning and implementing a change project. Both sources of leadership bring about change and place improvement by helping others identify needs and motivations and subsequently create environments in which those needs can be effectively addressed.

Effective place improvement is only possible if employed within a systems approach that incorporates mechanisms for collaboration. Integrated systems and teams in integrated facilities must replace the segregated, functional silos found in traditional student academic service models. The silos must be dismantled; moving silos closer together and replacing physical silos with Web silos will not produce improvement (Hollowell, 1999). The emergent model for student academic services requires collaboration, a common vision, and systemic change (Beede, 1999). One-stop student service or student success centers, complemented by Web-based student information systems, effectively replace the departmentalism of the traditional student academic services organization.

Decision making related to place improvement must be driven by data. Mechanisms to gather data may include neighborhood associations (for example, organized groups of stakeholders in a physical facility), measurement (for example, student surveys, focus groups, and benchmarking), cross-functional teams, and action learning processes as described earlier in this chapter.

With all of these elements in place, a culture of continuous improvement develops, marked by shared expectations for improvement. Buildings and physical facilities of any type cannot remain dormant; they must continuously evolve to meet the changing needs of the campus and all of its constituencies. Shared responsibility, authority, and accountability become the driving forces behind ongoing expectations for place improvement, and they represent the realization of improvement. The providers of student academic services, through teamwork, common goals, and a sense of community, collaboratively develop tolerance for ambiguity and risk. They collectively identify and acquire the competencies pertinent to success in the new environment. They share in the rewards, recognition, and repercussions related to the results they cooperatively produce. They understand that behavior is indeed influenced by the student's interaction with the environment (Lewin, 1936; Banning, 1989) and work jointly and individually to guarantee that the interaction leads to student success.

Process Improvement: Creating Effective and Efficient Systems

Virtually all of the activity directed toward academic student service provision can be thought of as being part of a process—a sequence of steps, tasks, or activities that converts inputs (people, money, material, time, and data) into outputs (grade reports, class schedules, identification cards, college catalogues, and so on). A work process adds value to the inputs by changing them or using them to produce something new (Galloway, 1994). Numerous inputs and outputs are present in student academic services operations, and the output of one process may become the input for another. For example, a report identifying students who have withdrawn for the semester (output for process A) is provided to the faculty (input for process B) to ensure the appropriate assignment of grades (output for process B). Service providers must often think of colleagues as customers, just as their students are customers related to these inputs and outputs. Student academic services are holistic and systemic in nature; most processes operate in conjunction with many others.

Process improvement enables student academic service practitioners to improve the timeliness and accuracy of service while inspiring employees and helping them to sharpen their focus on established outcomes. A critical examination of processes helps stakeholders better understand what happens in the student academic service operation. Greater understanding increases the likelihood that appropriate decisions will be made regarding improved processes to benefit internal customers (such as fellow workers from different departments) and external customers (such as students and parents). Processes can only be improved when understood, analyzed, and measured against outcomes established prior to the analysis.

Process improvement is defined here as the studying, mapping, and changing of processes to make them more efficient and effective for all constituents of the university (Foucar-Szocki, Harris, Larson and Mitchell, 2002). Stakeholders must be involved in any process improvement effort, and the student academic service provider should be prepared to initiate change as a result of the effort. If the initiative is undertaken with an assumption that change is improbable or that those directly affected by change will have no input, the process improvement initiative is likely to fail.

The implementation methods of process improvement include studying and mapping; information gleaned through studying and mapping is used to make fact-based decisions on appropriate changes. Descriptions of both methods follow.

PROCESS STUDYING. Process studying is an informal approach to process improvement. Service providers generally know instinctively where the greatest opportunities for improvement exist within their operations; unfortunately, many managers of student academic service operations don't act on their instincts. To appropriately respond, the first task is to examine the various services by using a macro view and simple logic. If serving students quickly is an important cultural factor, then long lines in certain areas at certain times indicate an opportunity for process improvement. Universities want satisfied customers; when students complain about a process that is particularly difficult to negotiate, that process is a candidate for process improvement.

The second task in process studying is to record inputs, steps, outputs, and how well the process accomplishes predetermined outcomes. The primary method of collecting information should be through simple observation and interviews with customers and employees who are closely tied to the process.

Once the data are collected, the third task is to list possible changes in the process. Changes should be based on their likelihood of reducing steps, shortening the time it takes to implement the process, or making the process easier to complete.

An example of an improved process accomplished through a simple study would be the moving of a printer closer to a cashier who must repeatedly print documents and hand them to student customers. Placing the necessary equipment nearby means that fewer steps and less time are required to complete the process of generating the report. A few seconds saved during a transaction amounts to a few hours saved during a busy registration period.

PROCESS MAPPING. Process mapping is a sophisticated and thorough approach to process improvement. Total Quality Management (TQM) is an improvement model that was embraced by many corporations in the nineties. It uses a variety of techniques and is often referred to as TQM, Kaizen, or continuous improvement and focuses on constant change to improve quality (Abbott, 2000). Established in the TQM movement, process mapping evolved from flowcharting, in which specific symbols are used to indicate the various steps in a process (Damelio, 1996). The process map helps communicate the process but does not rely on specialized symbols. Process mapping provides a proven tool for understanding and changing processes to help improve a bottom-line and competitive position (Hunt, 1996).

Process mapping begins with a group interview led by a skilled facilitator who is somewhat familiar with the process. People selected for development of the process map should understand and be knowledgeable about the process. The team should include a supervisor who, though not directly involved in the process, has responsibility for it. The interview questions should result in an accurate, detailed description of the process (Damelio, 1996).

The team should have an investment in making the process better and should be willing to participate through completion of the map. As in brainstorming, each person's contribution should be valued. If a group interview is not possible, a map can be generated based on conversations with a few stakeholders and then routed to the various parties for enhancement and approval (Damelio, 1996).

Once the input, steps, and output are clearly articulated, the map should be drawn on a large surface (such as a flipchart, chalkboard, whiteboard, or poster board). A process map is a graphic representation of the process, displaying the input, steps, and output. Each step is represented by a written description surrounded by a square. Arrows between squares point to the subsequent steps. Inputs and outputs are clearly marked, and the name of the process depicted in the diagram should be listed. The time it takes to complete a step or other applicable factors may be listed beside the pertinent box that represents it. An example of a process map appears in Figure 19.3.

Figure 19.3. Generic Process

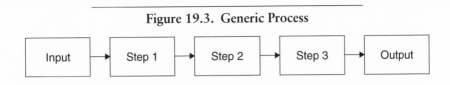

To increase the likelihood of success, the map should be completed in a comfortable location with minimal interruptions. For convenience, Post-It notes can be used (Damelio, 1996) to represent each step in the process. After creating and displaying the map, the group should work to reduce clutter in the diagram, since clutter generally represents opportunities for improvement.

Each step must be reviewed to determine its necessity. The map will usually reveal redundant steps. For example, is every required signature on a particular form really necessary? If many departments are involved with the process, they should be denoted on the map. The more departments involved in the process, the more opportunities for redundancies and subsequent improvements. The completion of process changes may require appropriate approvals from supervisors and pertinent legal or governmental agencies.

PROCESS MAPPING CASE STUDY. The director of the campus card center is concerned about long lines during the busy registration process, believing a reduction in the time it takes to issue identification cards would help eliminate lines and increase customer satisfaction.

The director calls together a group for a daylong meeting. This process mapping team includes her supervisor, three card center clerks, two students, and two other employees: one from the registrar's office (an office that provides a report listing registered students for the card-issuing process) and one from the campus police (an office concerned about the accuracy of information on student identification cards). An on-campus colleague with facilitation skills and a general understanding of the card center functions is requested to lead the process mapping.

Using the group interview approach, the team fully describes the process. The product of the meeting is a large piece of poster paper filled with Post-It notes, each containing phrases identifying a step in the process and connected by hand-drawn arrows. The inputs are clearly marked, as is the output—a completed and accurate identification card. The process *before* mapping is depicted in Figure 19.4.

Figure 19.4. Process Mapping Case Study—*Before* Process Mapping

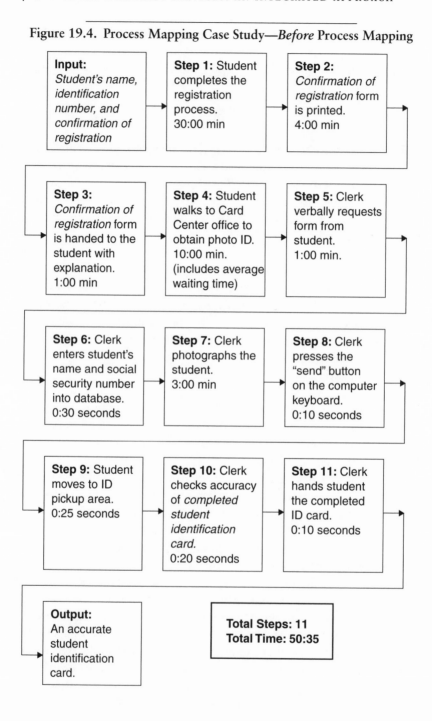

Input:
Student's name, identification number, and confirmation of registration

Step 1: Student completes the registration process.
30:00 min

Step 2: *Confirmation of registration form is printed.*
4:00 min

Step 3: *Confirmation of registration form is handed to the student with explanation.*
1:00 min

Step 4: Student walks to Card Center office to obtain photo ID.
10:00 min. (includes average waiting time)

Step 5: Clerk verbally requests form from student.
1:00 min.

Step 6: Clerk enters student's name and social security number into database.
0:30 seconds

Step 7: Clerk photographs the student.
3:00 min

Step 8: Clerk presses the "send" button on the computer keyboard.
0:10 seconds

Step 9: Student moves to ID pickup area.
0:25 seconds

Step 10: Clerk checks accuracy of *completed student identification card.*
0:20 seconds

Step 11: Clerk hands student the completed ID card.
0:10 seconds

Output:
An accurate student identification card.

Total Steps: 11
Total Time: 50:35

The team reviews their work for precision and generates a list of possible changes made evident by the graphic representation of the process they've created. Senior leadership accepts their list of recommendations.

As a result of the process mapping exercise, Social Security numbers are sent directly to a database accessible by the card center staff. Social Security numbers are entered with three mouse clicks, as opposed to the previous thirteen keystrokes; the *after* mapping is depicted in Figure 19.5. Student customers enter from a different direction, making the newly minted identification cards more accessible while speeding service. An activity report for the campus police is printed only once each week rather than five times a week. As a result of the group's work, service hours are expanded for students.

CREATING A LEARNING-CENTERED ORGANIZATION THROUGH PROCESS IMPROVEMENT. Whether an informal study is conducted or a complex process map is completed, change is most likely to occur if the organizational leadership communicates an expectation for improvement. By keeping initial efforts focused on simple processes with fewer steps, success can come early, leading to a greater likelihood that a culture of continuous improvement will evolve. Because change is a by-product of process improvement, employees using this technique can exhibit true leadership for change. A systems approach is essential to process improvement, since the outputs of many processes serve as the inputs for others. The mechanisms for collaboration inherent in the implementation of process improvement engage various stakeholders who are close to the process, especially across departmental lines. The mechanisms to gather data that facilitate decision making are vital to successful process mapping. The decisions made ultimately lead to shared expectations for improvement. Process improvement provides many opportunities to communicate via the description and joint analysis of processes, thus minimizing the impact of organizational silos.

Creating Measurement That Matters

In 1996, the American College Personnel Association and the National Association of Student Personnel Administrators, engaged in a joint project to identify principles of good practice related to student services (Blimling and Whitt, 1999). One of the seven principles identified by the group highlighted the need for systematic inquiry to improve student and institutional performance. Intentional, organized, and ongoing systematic inquiry leads to better decisions. The most common forms of systematic inquiry are the assessment of student outcomes, the evaluation of program effectiveness, and research to generate knowledge and theories.

Figure 19.5. Process Mapping Case Study—*After* Process Mapping

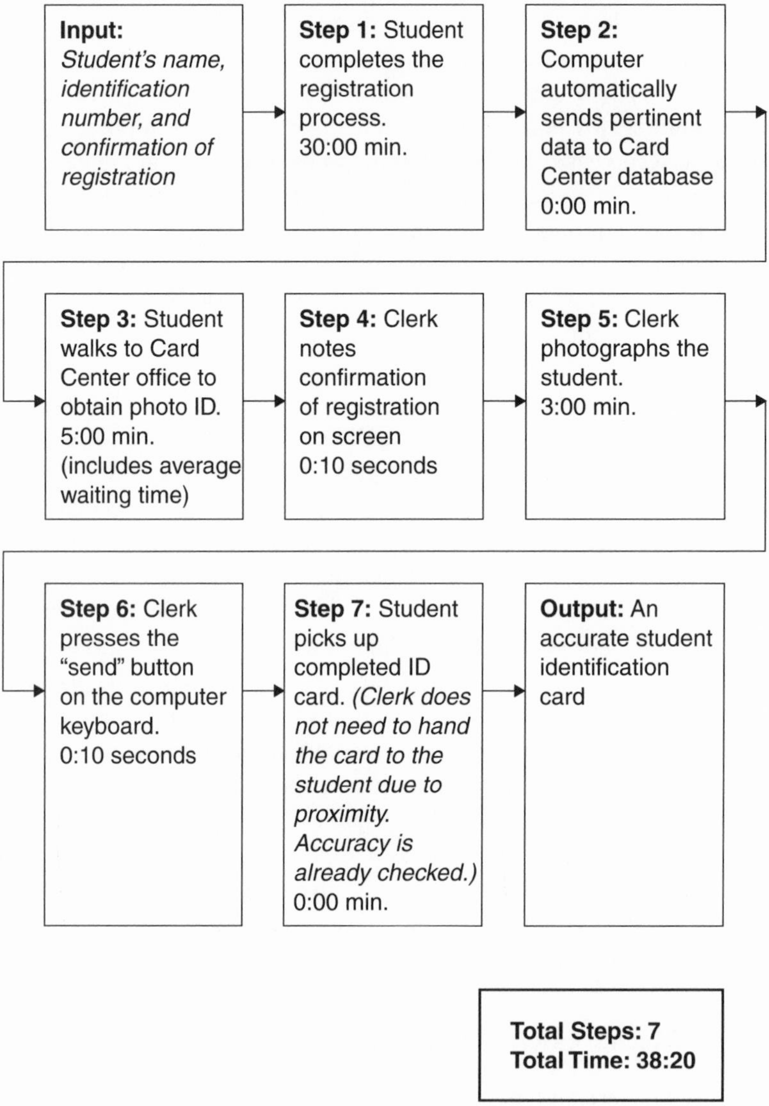

Input: *Student's name, identification number, and confirmation of registration*	**Step 1:** Student completes the registration process. 30:00 min.	**Step 2:** Computer automatically sends pertinent data to Card Center database 0:00 min.

Step 3: Student walks to Card Center office to obtain photo ID. 5:00 min. (includes average waiting time)	**Step 4:** Clerk notes confirmation of registration on screen 0:10 seconds	**Step 5:** Clerk photographs the student. 3:00 min.

Step 6: Clerk presses the "send" button on the computer keyboard. 0:10 seconds	**Step 7:** Student picks up completed ID card. *(Clerk does not need to hand the card to the student due to proximity. Accuracy is already checked.)* 0:00 min.	**Output:** An accurate student identification card

Total Steps: 7
Total Time: 38:20

The LOOC and the SLOOC provide numerous opportunities for data collection and analysis. Inherent in the continua are mechanisms to gather data. These mechanisms—focus groups, surveys, interviews, observations, document reviews, site visits, and literature reviews—create intentional, organized, ongoing opportunities to collect information from which better decisions can be made regarding programs, services, processes, performances, and places. A learning-oriented organization must "obtain, create and transfer knowledge and change [its] behavior on the basis of that knowledge and the insights it develops" (Pascarella and Whitt, 1999, p. 98).

Service providers must clearly identify desirable results and corresponding measures that indicate both current and future performance. If faster service is desired, then a corresponding measure may be elapsed transaction time from start to finish. If better customer relations are desired, then a corresponding measure may be the percentage of surveyed students who rank service levels as "excellent."

These critical statistics become key result indicators. When viewed collectively, they provide an accurate reflection of the overall performance of the organization. Caution should be taken to ensure that key result indicators do reflect the *most* critical elements of success; practitioners should limit the number of indicators in order to ensure focus and avoid confusion.

Outcomes of Performance Improvement

Efforts to create a learning organization through performance improvement must, by their nature, be ongoing and intergenerational. Several years are often required before the full impact of human resource development interventions can be realized. In the time that performance improvement efforts related to student academic services have been conducted, certain trends and observations can be identified:

○ Staff cross-training and cross-functional teams have led to increased employee satisfaction (Foucar-Szocki and others, 2002).

○ Following performance improvement efforts, staff members are seen as being more courteous, responsive, and knowledgeable by both students and their parents, as measured by surveys (Dillon, 2002).

○ The use of campus curricula (such as human resource development, management, and communications) and the involvement of students as consultants in authentic learning environments augment student learning and staff development (Foucar-Szocki and others, 2001).

○ Following performance improvement initiatives, survey responses of student and staff satisfaction increased and staff turnover decreased (Black, 2002).

Outcomes of Place Improvement

Efforts to create positive change through place improvement are relatively new; the institutions referred to earlier are still collecting evidence. Although it may take a few more years to fully realize the impact of these efforts, certain trends and observations have become evident:

- Student satisfaction with the quality of student academic services is increasing, as measured by annual surveys (Foucar-Szocki and others, 2002).

- Staff satisfaction with their place of employment is increasing, as measured by surveys and decreased turnover (Black, 2002).

- One-stop service centers provide enhanced access to services and expanded choice for transactions between students and their institutions (Burnett, 2002).

- One-stop centers, supported by Web-based services, provide greater flexibility for changing student and institutional needs, as opposed to traditional, segregated service models (Burnett, 2002).

Outcomes of Process Improvement

Efforts to create efficient and effective systems through process improvement must be continual, collaborative, and comprehensive. Some measures of process improvement may be accomplished immediately; others may be more complex and require additional time. Examples of the impact of process improvement achieved by institutions referred to in this chapter include:

- Generalist approaches to services and closer placement of related services have resulted in less time being spent by students to resolve issues and complete tasks (Day and Pitts, 2002).

- Process mapping facilitates improved problem identification, diagnosis, and resolution (Lewis, 1999).

- Process improvement can reduce the number of steps in a process, the cost of the process, and the redundancies found in bureaucratic systems (Anderson and Elliot, 1999).

- Process improvement shifts the focus of the process from the institution to the student (Hayward, Pedersen, and Visser, 1999).

Application of the Continua

Like human fingerprints and DNA, no two higher education institutions are identical. The use of any model, instrument, or tool requires consideration of the distinguishing institutional factors if the model is to be relevant and valid. The following questions may be used to guide student academic services professionals in applying the LOOC and the SLOOC for the purpose of inspiring learning and collaboration for improvement.

How will our organizational mission be advanced through improved performance, places, and processes? How do elements of our institutional culture or subcultures support or oppose collaboration and change? What university characteristics (such as private or public status, residential or commuter nature, demographics, location, and history) must be considered as factors in performance, place, and process improvement? Are resources (human, fiscal, physical space, time, or materials) available, and can they be allocated to a project of this nature? Is expertise available on campus (for example, faculty consultants, undergraduate and graduate courses, and related university departments), or must it be solicited from beyond the campus? What climate factors might help or hinder a project of this nature (for example, economic cycles, funding sources, political issues, and faculty/staff morale)?

Two final, significant questions should be at the heart of any attempt to use the continua to improve performance, places, and processes. Is improvement likely to occur as a result of the organizational effort expended, and, if not, what else must be considered? Are students likely to be more successful as a result of their interaction with the organization, and how will we determine or measure their success?

Conclusion

This chapter began and ends with a question posed by Arthur Sandeen (2001, p. 204): "Does what we are doing and how we are organized help advance the mission of the institution?" Students attain higher levels of retention, graduation, development, and achievement when academic service providers are inspired and their work is collaborative and learning-oriented. Learning-oriented organizations encourage continuous individual and group improvement by enabling staff members and by encouraging students to take responsibility for their educational success. A learning-oriented organization addresses expectations for improvement, leadership for change, a systems approach, mechanisms for collaboration, and mechanisms to gather data in efforts to realize improvement in three domains: performance, places, and processes. *Performance improvement* expands the capacity of the student academic services staff to assist students in making educational progress. *Place improvement* makes facilities more accessible, flexible, and integrated in the delivery of student academic services. *Process improvement* makes student academic services more efficient for the institution and more effective for the student customer. Measurement ensures that student academic services will pursue continuous improvement. The LOOC and the SLOOC can be customized to provide a comprehensive framework for the creation of learning-oriented organizations in a variety of higher education settings.

References

Abbott, J. C. *Optimize Your Operation.* Greeneville, S.C.: Robert Houston Smith, 2000.

Anderson, L. M., and Elliot, W. F. "The Evolution of Enrollment Services." In D. Burnett and M. Beede (eds.), *Planning for Student Services: Best Practices for the 21st Century.* Ann Arbor, Mich.: Society for College and University Planning, 1999.

Baird, L. L. "The College Environment Revisited: A Review of Research and Theory." In J. C. Smart (ed.), *Higher Education: Vol. 4. Handbook of Theory and Research.* New York: Agathon Press, 1988.

Banning, J. H. "Creating a Climate for Successful Student Development: The Campus Ecology Manager Role." In U. Delworth, G. Hanson, and Associates (eds.), *Student Services: A Handbook for the Profession.* (2nd ed.) San Francisco: Jossey-Bass, 1989.

Beede, M. "Student Service Trends and Best Practices." In D. Burnett and M. Beede (eds.), *Planning for Student Services: Best Practices for the 21st Century.* Ann Arbor, Mich.: Society for College and University Planning, 1999.

Black, J. "Creating a Student-Centered Culture." In D. Burnett and D. Oblinger (eds.), *Innovation in Student Services: Planning for Models Blending High Touch/High Tech.* Ann Arbor, Mich.: Society for College and University Planning, 2002.

Blimling, G. S., and Whitt, E. J. *Good Practice in Student Affairs: Principles to Foster Student Learning.* San Francisco: Jossey-Bass, 1999.

Burnett, D. "Innovation in Student Services: Best Practices and Process Innovation Models and Trends." In D. Burnett and D. Oblinger (eds.), *Innovation in Student Services: Planning for Models Blending High Touch/High Tech.* Ann Arbor, Mich.: Society for College and University Planning, 2002.

Creamer, D. G., and Creamer, E. G. "Use of a Planned Change Model to Modify Student Affairs Programs." In D. G Creamer (ed.), *College Student Development*. American College Personnel Association Media Publication, no. 49. Alexandria, Va., 1990.

Damelio, R. *The Basics of Process Mapping*. Portland, Oreg.: Productivity, 1996.

Day, D. V., and Pitts, J. "Generalists in Cooperation with Specialists: A Working Model." In D. Burnett and D. Oblinger (eds.), *Innovation in Student Services: Planning for Models Blending High Touch/High Tech*. Ann Arbor, Mich.: Society for College and University Planning, 2002.

Dillon, K. E. "Student Service Standards: Valuing Contact." In D. Burnett and D. Oblinger (eds.), *Innovation in Student Services: Planning for Models Blending High Touch/High Tech*. Ann Arbor, Mich.: Society for College and University Planning, 2002.

Foucar-Szocki, D., and others. "Layers of Learning: Promoting Performance Improvement and Action Learning in Higher Education." *Proceedings: AHRD 2001 Conference*. (Vol. 2.) Baton Rouge, La.: Academy of Human Resource Development, 2001.

Foucar-Szocki, D., Harris, L., Larson, R. D., and Mitchell, R. L. "Layers of Learning: Planning and Promoting Performance Improvement and Action Learning." In D. Burnett and D. Oblinger (eds.), *Innovation in Student Services: Planning for Models Blending High Touch/High Tech*. Ann Arbor, Mich.: Society for College and University Planning, 2002.

Galloway, D. *Mapping Work Processes*. Milwaukee, Wisc.: ASQ Quality Press, 1994.

Hayward, K., Pedersen, K. A., and Visser, F. "Transforming with a Learner-Based Redesign." In M. Beede and D. Burnett (eds.), *Planning for Student Services: Best Practices for the 21st Century*. Ann Arbor, Mich.: Society for College and University Planning, 1999.

Hollowell, D. E. "Student Services: A Broad View." In M. Beede and D. Burnett (eds.), *Planning for Student Services: Best Practices for the 21st Century*. Ann Arbor, Mich.: Society for College and University Planning, 1999.

Huebner, L. A., and Lawson, J. M. "Understanding and Assessing College Environments." In D. G. Creamer (ed.), *College Student Development: Theory and Practice for the 1990s*. American College Personnel Association Media Publication, no. 49. Alexandria, Va.: American College Personnel Association, 1990.

Hunt, V. D. *Process Mapping: How to Reengineer Your Business Processes*. New York: Wiley, 1996.

Kleinman, R. "The Reengineering of Enrollment Services: Four Departments Become One." In M. Beede and D. Burnett (eds.), *Planning for Student*

Services: Best Practices for the 21st Century. Ann Arbor, Mich.: Society for College and University Planning, 1999.

Kotter, J. P. *Leading Change.* Boston: Harvard Business School Press, 1996.

Kramer, G. L., and Peterson, E. D. "Project 2000: A Web-Based Student Planning System." In M. Beede and D. Burnett (eds.), *Planning for Student Services: Best Practices for the 21st Century.* Ann Arbor, Mich.: Society for College and University Planning, 1999.

Kuh, G. "Understanding Campus Environments." In M. J. Barr and M. K. Dessler (eds.), *The Handbook of Student Affairs Administration.* (2nd ed.) San Francisco: Jossey-Bass, 2000.

Kuh, G., Siegel, M., and Auden, D. T. "Higher Education: Values and Cultures." In R. B. Winston Jr., D. G. Creamer, and T. K. Miller (eds.), *The Professional Student Affairs Administrator.* New York: Brunner-Routledge, 2001.

Lewin, K. *Principles of Topological Psychology.* New York: McGraw-Hill, 1936.

Lewis, M. "Reengineering Student Administrative Services." In M. Beede and D. Burnett (eds.), *Planning for Student Services: Best Practices for the 21st Century.* Ann Arbor, Mich.: Society for College and University Planning, 1999.

McMillan, J. H., and Donelson, R. F. "What Theories of Motivation Say About Why Learners Learn." In R. J. Menges and M. D. Svincki (ed.), *College Teaching: From Theory to Practice.* New Directions for Teaching and Learning, no. 45. San Francisco: Jossey-Bass, 1991.

Mitchell, R. L. "Collaboration." *Fables, Labels and Folding Tables: Reflections on the Student Affairs Profession.* Madison, Wisc.: Atwood, 1999.

Mitchell, R. L. "The Lexicon of Little Things." *Listen Very Loud: Paying Attention in the Student Affairs Profession.* Madison, Wisc.: Atwood, 2001.

Pascarella, E. T. "College Environmental Influences on Learning and Cognitive Development: A Critical Review and Synthesis." In J. C. Smart (ed.), *Higher Education: Vol. 1. Handbook of Theory and Research.* New York: Agathon Press, 1985.

Pascarella, E. T., and Whitt, E. J. "Using Systematic Inquiry to Improve Performance." In G. S. Blimling, E. J. Whitt, and Associates (eds.), *Good Practice in Student Affairs: Principles to Foster Learning.* San Francisco: Jossey-Bass, 1999.

Rothwell, W. J., and Kazanas, H. C. *Mastering the Instructional Design Process: A Systematic Approach.* San Francisco: Jossey-Bass, 1998.

Sandeen, A. "Organizing Student Affairs Divisions." In R. B. Winston Jr., D. G. Creamer, and T. K. Miller (eds.), *The Professional Student Affairs Administrator: Educator, Leader, and Manager.* New York: Brunner-Routledge, 2001.

Schroeder, C. C. "Student Development Through Environmental Management." In G. Blimling and J. Schuh (eds.), *Increasing the Educational Role of Residence Halls.* New Directions for Student Services, no. 13. San Francisco: Jossey-Bass, 1981.

Senge, P. M. *The Fifth Discipline: The Art and Practice of the Learning Organization.* New York: Doubleday/Currency, 1990.

Strange, C. C. "Managing College Environments: Theory and Practice." In T. K. Miller and R. B. Winston Jr. (eds.), *Administration and Leadership in Student Affairs: Actualizing Student Development in Higher Education.* Muncie, Ind.: Accelerated Development, 1991.

Strange, C. C. "Dynamics of Campus Environments." In S. R. Komives and D. B. Woodard (eds.), *Student Services: A Handbook for the Profession.* (3rd ed.) San Francisco: Jossey-Bass, 1996.

Swanson, R. A. *Analysis for Improving Performance.* San Francisco: Berrett-Koehler, 1996.

Wenger, E. C., and Snyder, W. M. "Communities of Practice: The Organizational Frontier." *Harvard Business Review.* 2000, *85*(1), 139.

Wingspread Group on Higher Education. *An American Imperative: Higher Expectations for Higher Education.* Racine, Wisc.: The Johnson Foundation, 1993.

Winston, R. B., Jr., Creamer, D. G., and Miller, T. K. *The Professional Student Affairs Administrator: Educator, Leader and Manager.* New York: Brunner-Routledge, 2001.

Yorks, L., O'Neil, J., and Marsick, V. J. "Action Learning: Theoretical Bases and Varieties of Practice." In L. Yorks, J. O'Neil, and V. J. Marsick (eds.). *Action Learning: Successful Strategies for Individual, Team and Organizational Development.* San Francisco: Berrett-Koehler, 1999.

20

LEADING STUDENT ACADEMIC SERVICES IN THE TWENTY-FIRST CENTURY

Gary L. Kramer

EDGERTON AND SCHULMAN (2000) compare the teaching, learning, and investigating roles of universities to a "small, lovely lake that occupies the center of Beijing University's campus. Irregular in shape, its rocky shores create an oasis of serenity at the heart of this bustling institution. The lake has a special characteristic: there is no point along the shore from which an observer can see the entire lake. To see all of it, one must move from one vantage point to another, looking carefully, taking note, and then moving on" (p. ii). They go on to say, "Those matters worth knowing well are rarely understandable from a single perspective, but finding a new vantage point can be remarkably illuminating" (p. ii).

It is hoped that the twofold and interconnected perspectives shared in this book—(1) organizing and managing student academic services from the student development point of view and (2) supporting and managing collaboration on the campus to systematically deliver academic services from preenrollment to graduation—have opened new "vantage points" and pathways for the reader to explore and have "illuminated" ideas to engage the university community in a conversation about student services on the campus. Moreover, upon reflection on the perspectives gained from a walk around the "student services lake," presented in this book, it is our hope that leaders and practitioners alike will be stirred to action or, as Senge (1990) puts it, to a state of "creative tension."

To both summarize the perspectives shared in this volume and help student services practitioners-leaders formulate the next steps, this chapter is organized around key resource information, tools, practices, and author recommendations. The first two sections recapture general concepts and tools essential to leading the campus conversation on connection and collaboration among student academic services departments; the final two sections provide a specific and comprehensive summary of best practices in student academic services from which institutional benchmarking can be drawn and a series of recommendations on how to apply principles to practice can be gleaned.

Creating a Vision for Student Academic Services

Senge's concepts of "creative tension" and the "organization as a generative learning community" (1990, p. 12) are useful frameworks for thinking about the student academic services organization as a learning community. Specifically, Senge challenges organizations to focus on where they currently are and what needs to be done to improve. For example, he describes creative tension as being resolved in two basic ways: (1) by raising reality toward the vision and (2) by lowering the vision toward the current reality. He explains that without vision there is no creative tension, but having vision without an understanding of current reality will more likely result in cynicism than creativity. The energy for change in creative tension, however, especially within the context of improving student academic services, comes from a clearly understood and balanced vision. This, coupled with the notions of a generative learning community—or, as Senge (1990) describes it, "a consummately adaptive enterprise" (p. 12)—implies a course of action that produces, creates, and looks at the world (organization) in new ways. In this type of environment, people are continually expanding their capabilities to shape not only their own future but the organization's as well. It fosters systemic, or cultural, thinking. Furthermore, as the concepts of creative tension and the generative learning community work hand in hand, everyone in the organization gains more insightful views on current reality as important issues are brought to the surface—governing ideas of purpose, vision, and core values by which people (providers) will live in the organization.

Student Academic Services as a Responsive and Generative Learning Community

Other facets of a generative learning community help campus leaders better organize, manage, and deliver today's student academic services.

Largely, these campus departments are effective because they are responsive and adaptive and they seek to understand the following issues.

First, departments must understand students' diversity and students' needs for access, accuracy, and timely and comprehensive information, especially students making up the growing nontraditional and distance learner populations. These student demographic changes on and off campus are discussed at length by Winston, in Chapter One, Carranza and Ender, in Chapter Fourteen, Johnstone and Shea, in Chapter Sixteen, and Torres, in Chapter Fifteen.

Second, departments should understand how current technology, unlike that which existed ten years ago, pervades higher education. In many instances, it has created new partnerships with student academic services providers and has added value in the delivery of these services (see Burnett and Oblinger, Chapter Two, Lonabocker and Wager, Chapter Seven, and Johnstone and Shea, Chapter Sixteen).

Third, whether educators agree about it or not, the public views higher education as a commodity or a service to be purchased. Its customers are students, governments, and businesses. However, it's nothing new for higher education to be held accountable to publics, governing boards, alumni, accrediting agencies, and, last but not least, the students it enrolls. As a learning organization, higher education— especially its student academic services departments—is—or should be—willing to adjust, adapt, and improve the institution to better serve its constituencies. Kuh, English, and Hinkle, in Chapter Eighteen, Schuh, in Chapter Three, and Foucar-Szocki, Larson, and Mitchell, in Chapter Nineteen, further expand on these points. And Potter's Chapter Seventeen is an excellent resource that sets forth the standards and criteria of excellence in student services. It helps student academic services providers focus and organize energies toward a common agenda by using such tools as the Academic Quality Improvement Project, Baldridge National Quality Program, and the Kaplan and Norton Balanced Scorecard, all of which enable providers to chart direction and effect improvement. Also, John Schuh, in Chapter Three, painstakingly tackles the importance of establishing strong and coherent interrelationships among student academic services programs and professionals. He also outlines valuable national reports to assist in the accomplishment of this aim, including (1) The Student Learning Imperative, (2) Principles of Good Practice for Student Affairs, and (3) Powerful Partnerships. As well, Creamer, Creamer, and Brown, in Chapter Ten, focus on applying quality educational principles in student academic services, and they propose a conceptual model of quality Principles of Good Practice, particularly for enhancing academic advising on the campus.

Above all, as Roger Winston notes in Chapter One, the primary reason why colleges and universities exist is to promote student learning and to advance knowledge through teaching, research, and service. He argues that as these characteristics of higher education are broadened to include student development, the roles of academic services and of the teaching faculty within the institution ought to become student-centric. Put another way, as Winston observes, students should not be viewed as being dependent on the faculty and staff; rather, the faculty and staff are dependent on students' presence for their jobs.

Best Practices in Student Academic Services

Earl Potter points out in Chapter Seventeen that the term *benchmarking* is often used as a synonym for best practice research and that it is the process of finding comparison data for a given set of measures. Drawing from two monographs published by the Society for College and University Planning (Beede and Burnett, 2000, and Burnett and Oblinger, 2002) and the proceedings from IBM's Innovation in Student Services Forum: Integration for the Future (2002), this section assimilates the research on best practices in student services. The institutions listed in Exhibit 20.1 have been recognized by the IBM Higher Education Group as employing best practices, and they have met the following criteria:

○ They are engaged in a process of redesign.

○ They have consolidated functions into one-stop centers.

○ They have evaluated organization models for appropriateness.

○ They have educated, trained, and cross-trained staff.

○ They have developed Web-based systems that allow for the integration of information and processes.

Conclusion: Applying Principles to Practice

Richard Light (2001), in *Making the Most of College,* quoted the following from Elie Wiesel: "Questions unite people, and answers divide them" (p. 83). Most projects are driven by good questions; oftentimes they result in new perspectives and information gained, but rarely is *the* answer readily available to fit every situation. In the case of this book, while several questions in the preface served as the heart, challenge, and overall guide for discussion and content, we claim no answers herein, only perhaps an enlightened perspective on improving student academic services on the campus.

Exhibit 20.1 IBM's Student Academic Services Best Practices

Model	Institution	Concept (Emphasis)
One-Stop Service Culture	Boston College	Student Services Center
	Carnegie Mellon	Enrollment Center (Hub)
	Fordham University	Enrollment Services
	James Madison University	Student Success Center
	Johnson County CC	Student Success Center
	Purdue University Calumet	Enrollment Services
	Seton Hall University	Call Center
	Tufts University	Student Services Bldg.
	University of Delaware	One-Stop Student Center
	University of Minnesota Twin Cities	One-Stop Student Center
	University of North Carolina at Greensboro	Student-Centered Culture
Web Student Planning (Integration)	Ball State University	Automated Course Transfer System (ACTS), Web Student Services
	Boston College	Self-Service Center (Agora)
	Brigham Young University	Academic Information Management (AIM)
	Indiana University	Indiana Student Information Transaction Environment (Insite)
	Kansas State University	Adviser Tools
	Kent State University	Career Portfolio
	Louisiana State University	Personal Access Web Services (PAWS)
	Regis University	Web Adviser
	University of British Columbia	eBusiness Service
	University of Buffalo	MyUB
	University of California	Academic Outreach Student Portfolio
	University of Delaware	One-Stop Shop
	University of Minnesota Twin Cities	One-Stop Shop
	University of North Carolina at Greensboro	Virtual Information Station
	University of Texas, Austin	Adviser Toolkit

Note: *Enrollment Centers generally include services for financial transaction, registration, records, and admissions.*

So, based on the questions raised in the Preface of this book and drawing from chapter content as well as from the perspective of expert authors in this book, I list the following recommendations, which are deemed essential to leading and making a qualitative difference in student services in the twenty-first century:

○ *Vision.* The vision of higher education should be a high-quality learning experience for students, and all aspects of the institution must respect and cooperate with one another. Otherwise, they will remain in "functional silos," and students' educational experiences will remain fragmented. Student services readers and providers, through the student-centric or development lens, should promote and affect horizontal versus vertical collaboration among services and thus enrich student learning and the educational experience (see Winston, Chapter One and Gordon and Kramer, Chapter Nine).

○ *Assessment of readiness.* Service providers should enhance student services through early identification of students' specific areas of growth that require immediate attention to foster successful academic performance and social adjustment (see Peterson, Lenz, and Sampson Jr., Chapter Five—in particular, their discussion of the two-factor readiness model and required levels of service). Put another way, services providers should know who is entering and proceeding in the system and how well they are progressing in it (see Carranza and Ender, Chapter Fourteen). Assessment is key to learning about students, their needs, the effectiveness and appropriate alignment of the services offered to them, and whether or not student services are cohesive, coherent, and, in general, positively influencing the lives of students.

○ *Applying quality educational principles.* On behalf of student growth and success, institutions should connect student academic services. In addition, institutions should carefully and thoughtfully review and apply various reports and standards that speak directly to student learning and academic and student affairs collaboration. Contemporary practice suggests that anything less than a collaborative approach can have deleterious effects on students (see Schuh, Chapter Three and Creamer, Creamer, and Brown, Chapter Ten).

○ *First-rate services.* Institutions should design or reengineer services physically and technologically from the student perspective and in a learner-centered environment. Burnett and Oblinger, in Chapter Two, describe how the way services are delivered oftentimes depends on the culture and values of the institution. First-rate student services, they claim and demonstrate through exemplary practices, can serve as a differentiator in attracting and retaining students and can enhance the institution's relationship with the student.

○ *Measure and increase staff performance.* Student academic service departments must be well oiled and connected to serve students well. From enrollment to graduation, authors in this book (see Chapters Four through Twelve) recommend creating convenient services, cross-training staff members, and consolidating services.

Put another way, the overriding recommendation that stems from these chapters is to unify the staff by combining quality principles of excellence, student development, ethical behavior, and organizational theory, and, where possible, to consolidate primary student academic services. This leads to greater collaboration among staff members, who constantly look for ways to simplify processes, enhance systems, and provide students with better service. Foucar-Szocki, Larson, and Mitchell echo this recommendation in Chapter Nineteen. Their chapter focuses on several recommendations to measure and increase staff performance.

○ *Technology as an enabler.* Institutions should integrate technology as they rethink the needs of the consumers of student academic services, reexamining the skills of the people involved and reengineering relationships throughout the organization. There is no question that technology, when carefully designed as a partner in delivering student services, can flatten organizational barriers and empower students (see Johnstone and Shea, Chapter Sixteen, and Lonabocker and Wager, Chapter Seven).

○ *Balancing the needs of all students.* Those who provide services to students need to clarify their own values toward diverse groups and retool their thinking to serve the success of diverse populations (see Torres, Chapter Fifteen), including distance learners (see Johnstone and Shea, Chapter Sixteen) and first-year students (see Cuseo, Chapter Thirteen, and Jacobs, Chapter Six).

○ *Graduation planning.* Institutions should organize student academic services with the goal of helping students understand that academic, career, and financial planning is critical to successful graduation planning (see Gordon and Kramer, Chapter Nine, Owens and Pekala, Chapter Twelve, Reardon and Lumsden, Chapter Eight, and Washburn and Priday, Chapter Eleven).

○ *Managing student academic services.* Looking outward from their own institutions, services providers will see a compelling case for change in the progress of our peers and competitors. Even ideas from very different industries can fuel the vision of service providers' imaginations. Furthermore, they should take care of their most precious assets—their personnel. Without employees, institutions cannot take care of students. By constantly improving and developing the staff, institutions can sustain a culture of growth, development, and shared responsibility (see Potter, Chapter Seventeen, and Foucar-Szocki, Larson, and Mitchell, Chapter Nineteen).

Like the Beijing University lake metaphor that began this chapter, the "student services lake" metaphor is complex, and students rarely understand it from a single perspective. In each, there is no single point from which observers, in this case our students, can understand the array of student services available to them. To understand the full array of services, they must move from one vantage point to another, looking carefully, taking note, and avoiding getting lost (or frustrated). Rather, as Kuh, English, and Hinkle state in Chapter Eighteen, if institutions of higher education are serious about promoting a culture that is sensitive to student needs and dedicated to the promotion of student success, they will strive to offer services that more closely approximate the students' many vantage points. Indeed, individual functional units must cultivate a systems perspective, allowing them to see how what they do contributes to the overriding goal of student success.

References

Beede, M., and Burnett, D. *Planning for Student Services.* Ann Arbor, Mich.: Society for College and University Planning, 2000.

Burnett, D., and Oblinger, D. *Innovation in Student Services: Planning Models and Blending High Touch/High Effect.* Ann Arbor, Mich.: Society for College and University Planning, 2002.

Edgerton, R., and Shulman, L. "Foreword: An Invitation for Reflection and Discussion." In G. Kuh (ed.), *National Survey of Student Engagement, The College Student Report.* Bloomington: Indiana University Press, 2000.

IBM Innovation in Student Services Forum: Integration for the Future. University of California, Berkeley. July 24–26, 2002.

Light, R. J. *Making the Most of College: Students Speak Their Minds.* Cambridge, Mass: Harvard University Press, 2001.

Senge, P. M. "The Leader's New Work: Building Learning Organizations." *Sloan Management Review,* 1990, (Fall), 9–17.

NAME INDEX

A

Abbott, J. C., 426
Abrams, H., 274
Agosto-Severa, A., 30
Aiken, M., 16
Ajzen, I., 103
Alberts, B., 206
Alexander, J. M., 275
Allen, W., 334, 336, 342
American Association for Higher Education, 56, 295
American Association of Collegiate Registrars and Admission Officers, 224, 226, 227, 229, 240
American Association of Higher Education, 178
American College Personnel Association, 55, 56, 207, 277, 286
American College Testing Program, 54
American Council on Education, 242
American Psychiatric Association, 112
Amit, K., 131
Anderson, L. M., 421, 432
Anton, W. D., 112
Arendale, D. R., 281–282, 322
Arendale, T., 323
Arnold, K., 13
Aslanian, C. B., 135
Assar, K. E., 396–397
Astin, A., 214, 219
Astin, A. W., 14, 18, 60, 61, 65, 273, 276, 298, 317, 337, 339, 375
Auden, D. T., 411
Austin, A. E., 300
Austin, D., 133
Axiotis, I. R., 132

B

Baird, L. L., 420
Baker, G. A., 274
Baker, R. W., 294
Baldrige National Quality Program, 207–208
Bandura, A., 103, 106, 107
Banning, J. H., 13–14, 424
Banta, T. W., 286, 394
Barefoot, B. O., 19–20, 283, 288–291, 293, 320, 323, 347
Bargh, J., 279
Barr, M. J., 286
Bartlett, T., 314
Bateman, M., 64
Baxter Magolda, M. B., 6, 17
Bean, J. G., 319
Bean, J. P., 61, 79, 103
Beede, M., 421, 423, 442
Bender, L. W., 277
Benware, C. A., 279
Berger, J. B., 54
Bergman, B., 128
Bernstein, B. L., 341
Bernstein, R., 38, 48–49
Betz, N. E., 112
Bingi, R., 340
Bishel, M. A., 30
Black, J., 38, 80, 94–95, 376, 431–432
Blackwell, J. M., 274
Blanc, R. A., 282
Blimling, G. S., 18–19, 56, 60, 429
Bliss, L., 277
Blowers, S. S., 135

447

SUBJECT INDEX

A

AACRAO SPEEDE Implementation Guide, 239

Academic achievement, predicting, 85–86, 337–338

Academic advising. *See* Advising

Academic affairs, 54–61, 277–278

Academic alliances, 296–297

Academic forgiveness, 239

Academic grievance policies, 240–242

Academic Information Management (AIM) System, 44, 45

Academic planning, definitions of, 188–189

Academic programs, marketing of, 91–92

Academic Quality Improvement Project (AQIP), 386–387

Academic records: history of, 223–226; policies regarding, 239–243; transcripts, 226–233; transfer credits, 237–239; twenty-first century methods for, 243–245

Academic services: to address readiness needs, 116–121; best practices in, 442; characteristics of student-centric units, 394–399; creating a vision for, 440; definition of, 9–10, xi; designing, 17–18; enrollment management and, 96–99; interaction of, 195–201; providing, 92; required levels of, 108–110; role of, 314–315; units, 394. *See also by type of service (e.g. career planning services)*; Good/best practices;

History of student services; Provider development; Services;

Academic skills, 111

Academic strategies, 320–323

Academic transfer issues, 237–239

Accessibility, 243–245, 405–406

Acculturation strategies, 87

Achievement, predicting academic, 337–338

Activities, selection of, 178. *See also* Experiences

Adaptive behaviors, 104

Adelphi University, 284

Adjustment issues, 273–274

Administration, 16, 23

Admissions, 42, 62, 85, 316

Admit level of enrollment management, 85–87

Adult students, 59–60, 135

Advising: academic planning, 188–189; application of quality principles to, 207–211; availability of advisers, 368; career, 183; at CCMU, 66; cooperation of, with career services, 196; delivery of, 218–219; developmental, 328, 343–344; during orientation of new students, 63–64, 129; for registration, 158–159; telecounseling, 86; training of advisers, 115; undergraduate students, framework for, 212; Web-based, 43–44, 363–364

Advisory boards, 199

Affective outcomes, predictors for, 342